Electrical Stimulation Research Techniques

METHODS IN PHYSIOLOGICAL PSYCHOLOGY

EDITOR: Richard F. Thompson
DEPARTMENT OF PSYCHOLOGY
STANFORD UNIVERSITY
STANFORD, CALIFORNIA

Vol. I. BIOELECTRIC RECORDING TECHNIQUES
Richard F. Thompson and Michael M. Patterson (Eds.)

Part A. Cellular Processes and Brain Potentials
Part B. Electroencephalography and Human Brain Potentials
Part C. Receptor and Effector Processes

Vol. II. NEUROANATOMICAL RESEARCH TECHNIQUES
Richard T. Robertson (Ed.)

Vol. III. ELECTRICAL STIMULATION RESEARCH TECHNIQUES
Michael M. Patterson and Raymond P. Kesner (Eds.)

Electrical Stimulation Research Techniques

Edited by

MICHAEL M. PATTERSON

College of Osteopathic Medicine
Ohio University
Athens, Ohio

RAYMOND P. KESNER

Department of Psychology
University of Utah
Salt Lake City, Utah

With a Foreword by Richard F. Thompson

ACADEMIC PRESS
A Subsidiary of Harcourt Brace Jovanovich, Publishers
New York London Toronto Sydney San Francisco 1981

ACADEMIC PRESS, INC.
111 Fifth Avenue, New York, New York 10003

United Kingdom Edition published by
ACADEMIC PRESS, INC. (LONDON) LTD.
24/28 Oval Road, London NW1 7DX

Library of Congress Cataloging in Publication Data
Main entry under title:

Electrical stimulation research techniques.

(Methods in physiological psychology; v. 3)
Includes bibliographical references and index.
Contents: Extracellular stimulation / James R. Ranck, Jr. -- Intracellular stimulation / John H. Byrne -- Microstimulation technique / Hiroshi Asanuma -- [etc.]
1. Brain stimulation. 2. Electric stimulation. 3. Brain--Localization of functions. 4. Neuropsychology--Technique. I. Patterson, Michael M. II. Kesner, Raymond P. III. Series.
QP388.E43 599.01'82 81-3657
ISBN 0-12-547440-7 AACR2

PRINTED IN THE UNITED STATES OF AMERICA

81 82 83 84 9 8 7 6 5 4 3 2 1

Contents

Chapter 4 **Stimulation of the Brain via Metallic Electrodes**

Robert W. Doty and John R. Bartlett

Chapter 5 **Depth Stimulation of the Brain**

José M. R. Delgado

Chapter 6 **Subcortical Stimulation for Motivation and Reinforcement**

C. R. Gallistel

Chapter 7 **Electrical Stimulation as a Tool in Memory Research**

Robert F. Berman and Raymond P. Kesner

Chapter 8 **Brain Stimulation Effects Related to Those of Lesions**

Robert L. Isaacson

Chapter 9 **Electroconvulsive Therapy—Who Needs It?**

Duane Denney

Chapter 10 **Electrical Stimulation of Peripheral Nerve**

John E. Swett and Charles M. Bourassa

Chapter 11 **Grid and Peripheral Shock Stimulation**

Fred A. Masterson

Contributors

Numbers in parentheses indicate the pages on which the authors' contributions begin.

HIROSHI ASANUMA (61), The Rockefeller University, New York, New York 10021

JOHN R. BARTLETT* (71), Center for Brain Research, University of Rochester Medical Center, Rochester, New York 14642

ROBERT F. BERMAN (173), Department of Psychology, Wayne State University, Detroit, Michigan 48202

CHARLES M. BOURASSA (243), Department of Psychology, University of Alberta, Edmonton, Alberta T6G-2E9, Canada

JOHN H. BYRNE (37), Department of Physiology, School of Medicine, University of Pittsburgh, Pittsburgh, Pennsylvania 15261

JOSÉ M. R. DELGADO (105), Departamento de Investigación, Centro Ramón y Cajal, Madrid, Spain

DUANE DENNEY (221), Department of Psychiatry, School of Medicine, University of Oregon Health Sciences Center, Portland, Oregon 97201

ROBERT W. DOTY (71), Center for Brain Research, University of Rochester Medical Center, Rochester, New York 14642

C. R. GALLISTEL (141), Department of Psychology, University of Pennsylvania, Philadelphia, Pennsylvania 19174

ROBERT L. ISAACSON (205), Department of Psychology, Center for Neurobehavioral Sciences, and Clinical Campus, State University of New York at Binghamton, Department of Psychology, Binghamton, New York 13901

RAYMOND P. KESNER (173), Department of Psychology, University of Utah, Salt Lake City, Utah 84112

*Deceased November 5, 1978.

Fred A. Masterson (297), Department of Psychology, University of Delaware, Newark, Delaware 19711

James B. Ranck, Jr. (1), Department of Physiology, Downstate Medical Center, Brooklyn, New York 11203

John E. Swett (243), Department of Anatomy, University of California, School of Medicine, Irvine, California 92717

Foreword

The major approaches that characterize the organization and functions of the brain can be grouped into four broad categories of techniques: electrophysiology, anatomy, chemistry, and behavior. All of these approaches to the study of the brain and its functions will be treated in this series, Methods in Physiological Psychology. The series began with a three-volume work "Bioelectric Recording Techniques" (Thompson and Patterson, 1973) and continued with the volume "Neuroanatomical Research Techniques" (Robertson, 1978). The current volume appropriately treats the other side of electrophysiology: electrical stimulation.

Electrical stimulation of the brain has been perhaps the most widely used and abused technique in the study of brain and behavior. Historically, the first application of direct electrical stimulation of the brain, by Fritsch and Hitzig in 1870, localized the motor area of the cerebral cortex and led ultimately to an understanding of its fine-grained organization. Over the years, the method has led to a number of major discoveries, perhaps the most important being electrical self-stimulation of the brain by Olds and Milner.

Electrical stimulation of nervous tissue is easy to do but difficult to do well. Problems include tissue damage, current spread, and interpretations of stimulation effects. In this volume Dr. Patterson and Dr. Kesner have done an admirable job of bringing together a group of leading experts who have in turn contributed superb chapters on topics ranging from intracellular stimulation to electroconvulsive therapy. As with the previous volume of this series, the chapters are not merely descriptions of techniques, although they are, of course, outstanding in this regard. The chapters emphasize conceptual issues and convey considerable knowledge and wisdom about the fascinating field of the brain and behavior.

Richard F. Thompson

Preface

As early as 1780, Galvin stimulated frog nerve and observed the resultant muscle twitch. Since that time, electrical stimulation of various types has been widely used in physiological and psychological research. Early in its history, electrical stimulation was used at a gross level to define brain areas receiving primary sensory inputs and as the motivational tool in psychological studies. As both the understanding of electrical potentials and techniques of stimulus delivery improved, stimulation in the periphery and in the central nervous system became more intensively utilized in mapping neural circuitry as well as in motivational research. More recently, the complexities involved in stimulating neural populations have been more fully recognized and have led to a more cautious use of electrical brain stimulation (EBS) for reasons of both theory and technology. These problems are now being overcome, and as a result, electrical stimulation is more frequently being used as a tool for elucidating the mechanics of brain function.

Techniques with such a long and rich history are often shrouded in mystique and at the same time are often used indiscriminately. In the case of electrical stimulation, probably the latter has been predominant. The delivery and parametric features of electrical stimulation are often cavalierly ignored by researchers as they use a technique that seems both simple and direct. Such indiscriminate application of electrical energy, whether in the periphery or in the brain can often have confounding effects on desired results through such mechanisms as spread of excitation, interference with recording devices, or alterations in the physiology of the organism. In addition, the complicated physics of electrical energy interacting with neural systems is not to be taken lightly. If used properly, however, electrical stimulation has been proven to provide an extraordinarily useful and powerful technique for the elucidation of behavioral and neurophysiological mechanisms underlying psychological processes.

A number of books and isolated chapters have appeared over the years emphasizing the application of electrical stimulation in elucidating physiological function and behavior with moderate emphasis on theory, methods, and varieties of use. However, since Sheer's 1961 book "Electrical Stimulation of the Brain," no comprehensive work emphasizing theory, techniques, and applications of electrical stimulation has appeared. Given new technological developments and further understanding of the mechanism of the action of electrical stimulation, it is an appropriate time for a work that emphasizes these aspects. Thus, the present book brings together experts in their respective fields who use electrical stimulation techniques at various levels of the organism to elucidate numerous physiological and psychological processes. The book is organized from molecular uses of electrical stimulation in the brain to global applications in peripheral shock. Some of the theoretical and technical issues that are addressed have received attention for many years but have never been brought together in the unique ways utilized by the authors of this book. Each chapter presents not only the technological details necessary to utilize the technique being discussed, but also theoretical background as well as insights from the user's own experience. The richness of experience that has gone into each chapter will provide the reader with insights not available in any other format and should allow an enlightened use of various techniques by either the novice or the more experienced researcher.

The first part of the book (Chapters 1, 2, and 3) deals with stimulation at a cellular level. In Chapter 1, Ranck discusses stimulation at an extracellular level with emphasis on both the principles involved and the practical use of extracellular stimulation for examining various brain functions. In Chapter 2, Byrne deals with the problems involved in stimulating within a single cell in the central nervous system and presents many useful circuits and monitoring techniques for this very complicated procedure. In the third chapter, Asanuma details his techniques for microstimulation of small groups of neurons and presents lucidly the applications as well as limitations of this relatively new procedure. In Chapter 4 by Doty and Bartlett and Chapter 5 by Delgado, the authors treat the use of electrical stimulation in larger brain areas, both in animals and humans, and present considerable detail on the problems associated with electrical charge transfer in the medium of the brain. The next two chapters (by Gallistel, and Berman and Kesner) contain excellent discussions on the use of electrical stimulation in psychological research as a tool in motivation, reinforcement, and memory processes. In these chapters is presented some of the complexities underlying the interpretation of psychological studies in which electrical stimulation has been employed. In Chapter 8, Isaacson considers one of the more complicated enigmas of electrical stimulation by contrasting it with the effects of lesion work in which it is clear that lesion and stimulation are not always equal and opposite in effect. In the next chapter, Denney gives an excellent review of electrical convulsive therapy in humans and provides a lucid argument for its continued careful use. In the tenth chapter, Swett and Bourassa provide one of the more complete and authoritative accounts of the techniques and theoretical complexities of electrical stimulation of peripheral nerves that has ever appeared. This seemingly simple technique is one that has often been misunderstood, and their chapter provides much-needed information. In the last chapter, Masterson gives an account of the application of electrical stimulation through grid and peripheral means. This technique, often used indiscriminately, is discussed here in great detail and should provide a wide range of researchers with a lucid description on this valuable research tool.

As is evident from this overview, the chapters provide a comprehensive review and synthesis of most of the electrical stimulation techniques used today. The rapid growth of methodology and technology in these areas has allowed many of these techniques to enjoy more use in recent years. The authors must be commended for their enlightened and updated descriptions of both the positive and negative aspects of their techniques.

The book is written and organized for use by both the experienced investigator and the novice—for those with a detailed knowledge of physics and electrical interactions as well as those who are approaching the area with a very limited knowledge of these interactions. We would like to take this opportunity to thank the College of Osteopathic Medicine at Ohio University and the Department of Psychology at the University of Utah for their support, the authors for their diligence, and the staff at Academic Press for their patience and assistance.

Chapter 1

Extracellular Stimulation

James B. Ranck, Jr.

Department of Physiology
Downstate Medical Center
Brooklyn, New York

ISBN 0-12-547440-7

I. Introduction

This chapter is intentionally pedagogic and simple. I have tried to discuss all of the known facts and principles of extracellular stimulation of the mammalian central nervous system, but I have tried to write it so that someone who is almost totally unfamiliar with the subject matter can follow it. Appendix I deals with current flow and should be read by those who do not know these physical principles as applied to excitable tissue. Appendix II is a simple statement of current flow in the brain. These facts and concepts are not widely known, and should be read by anyone unfamiliar with them. This chapter assumes the reader knows the facts and concepts in Appendixes I and II. Much of the research in this field involves mathematical or biophysical analysis; however, this chapter will not use mathematics, and the physical principles will be discussed in as simple terms as possible. The intent is *not* to instruct the reader on current research in the field, but rather to instruct the reader how to stimulate the brain with extracellular stimulation for uses in real experiments.

There is a major point that must always be remembered when talking about electrical stimulation of excitable tissue: *We stimulate cells*. It can be misleading to speak of stimulating a brain, a lateral hypothalamus, or a sciatic nerve. Whenever we have stimulating electrodes in a structure containing excitable cells and when enough current is passed, some cells that have parts in the vicinity of the stimulating electrode will be stimulated and others will not. Our ability to predict which cells will be stimulated is limited at present; however, we can predict it to some extent. The facts and the principles involved in this prediction will be developed in this chapter.

II. Basic Principles—The DC Case

An action potential is initiated by a depolarization of the transmembrane potential (V_m). The transmembrane potential (or voltage) is the difference between the voltage inside the cell (V_i) and the voltage outside the cell (V_o). Thus,

$$V_m = V_i - V_o.$$

Depolarization can thus occur by changing either V_i or V_o, or by changing both of them. When a microelectrode is put inside a cell and current is passed through the microelectrode, the cell will be depolarized by a current passing outward across the cell membranes. (In Appendix I the principles of current flow in tissue and across cell membranes is developed.) The greater the current crossing the cell membrane, the greater the depolarization. In this case, almost all the transmembrane voltage change is in the voltage inside the cell (V_i). The voltage outside the cell (V_o) changes very little, but this is not the case we are interested in.

When current is passed extracellularly, most of the voltage change is in the voltage outside the cell. We change transmembrane potential (V_m) *primarily by changing the voltage outside the cell* (V_o).

To explain what happens in real cases, it will be useful to first develop four extreme cases, all of which will involve stimulation by a monopolar cathode. The extracellular voltage due to this monopolar cathode will be most negative near the electrode tip and fall off with distance from the tip. Only the steady state (dc) case will be discussed initially.

CASE 1 (Fig. 1). The extracellular voltage (V_o) around a round small cell, say 20 μm in diameter, is made more negative by passing current. The ionic mechanisms working to maintain transmembrane potential (V_m) are unaffected, so the transmembrane voltage remains the same, and the voltage inside the cell (V_i) becomes more negative by the same amount as the extracellular voltage. The cell is *not* depolarized.

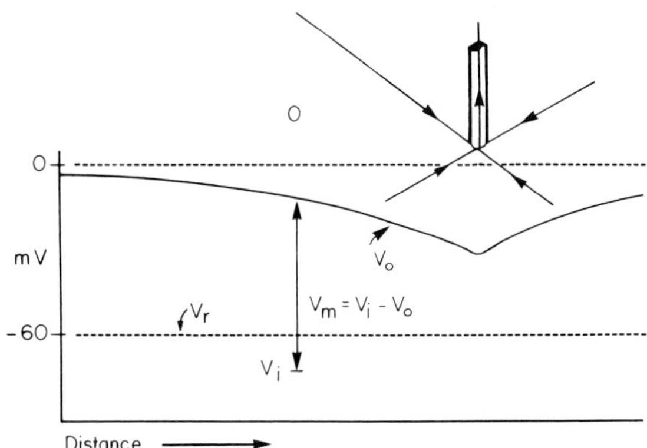

FIG. 1. A small diameter cell in an extracellular field (Case 1).

In Figs. 1–7, the abcissa is distance and the ordinate is voltage. V_o (extracellular potential), V_i (intracellular potential), V_m (transmembrane potential during current flow), and V_r (resting transmembrane potential, which is assumed to be −60 mV) are plotted as a function of distance. A stimulating monopolar cathode and lines of current flow (with arrows) are shown. The anode is a large distance away and is not shown.

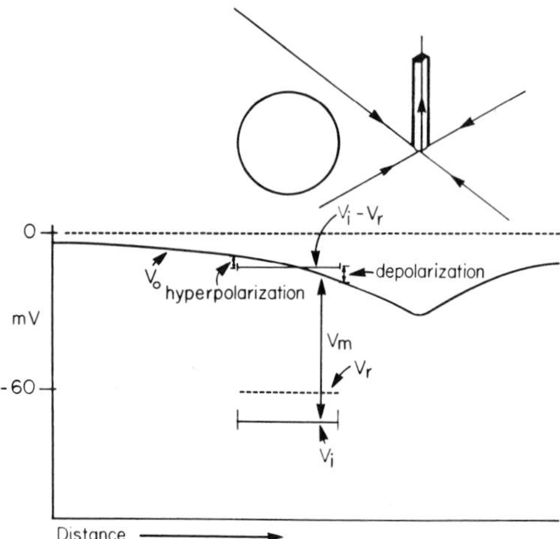

FIG. 2. A large-diameter cell in an extracellular field (Case 2).

CASE 2 (Fig. 2). A larger cell is in an extracellular potential field. Assume the membrane resistance of this cell is so great that no current effectively flows through the cell. Since there is no current flow in the cytoplasm, there can be no voltage difference in the cytoplasm, and V_i is the same throughout the cell. The ionic mechanisms maintaining V_m are the same, so the cell tries to maintain the same V_m. However, since the extracellular voltage (V_o) is not the same all around the cell, and V_i is the same everywhere, V_m cannot be the same everywhere. Roughly speaking, V_i will increase so that V_m is about the same on the average. This means that one side of the cell is depolarized, and the other hyperpolarized. Since we are interested in changes in V_m, it will be convenient to plot $V_i - V_r$, where V_r is the resting transmembrane potential.

CASE 3 (Fig. 3). This is the same as Case 2 except the cell is made to look more like a neuron. We are considering the extreme case of such a high membrane resistance that no current effectively flows through the cell. It also points out the fact that the larger the cell from end to end, the greater the maximum depolarization.

CASE 4 (Fig. 4a). Consider the case in which a neuronal membrane is of such low resistance that current flows freely across it. In this case, there will be current flowing in the cytoplasm of the neuron, and hence V_i will change with distance. For this very low resistance membrane,

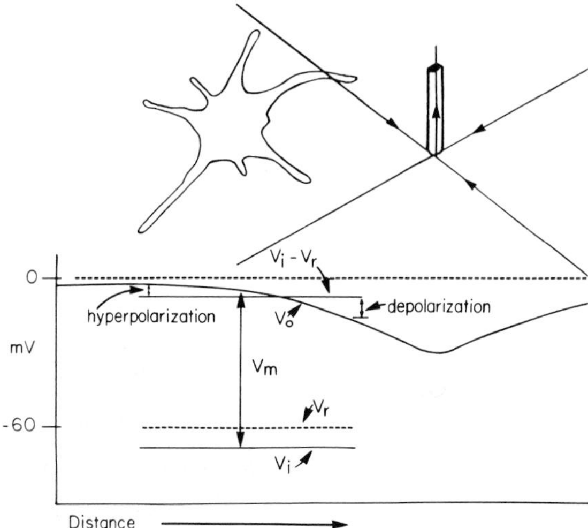

FIG. 3. Neuron with a very high membrane resistance in an extracellular field (Case 3).

changes in V_i will be the same as changes in V_o, and there will be no change in V_m anywhere and hence no depolarization. This never happens in the dc case but is approximately the case immediately after a pulse of current is turned on (see Section III-A).

CASE 5 (Fig. 4b) *The real case,* a cross between Cases 3 and 4. The membrane resistance of the neuron allows current to pass, but not freely. Current flows through the cytoplasm of the cell, so that there are changes in V_i with distance, but V_i does not change as much as V_o. One end of the cell is depolarized and the other hyperpolarized, but not as much as in Case 3. This leads to a result that may seem paradoxical to some. For the same sized cells in the *same extracellular* voltage field, the *more* current that flows through the cell, the less the depolarization. (If the current through the stimulating electrode increases, V_o will become more negative, more current will flow in the neuron, and it will be depolarized more. It is only in this sense that depolarization increases with increases in transmembrane current.)

Figure 5 gives the unrealistic case for a long fiber near a cathode, in which no current effectively flows through the cell. The depolarization is entirely due to V_o becoming more negative. This case is never true, but sometimes it is a fair approximation. Figure 6 gives the case where some current flows through the fiber, which is the real case.

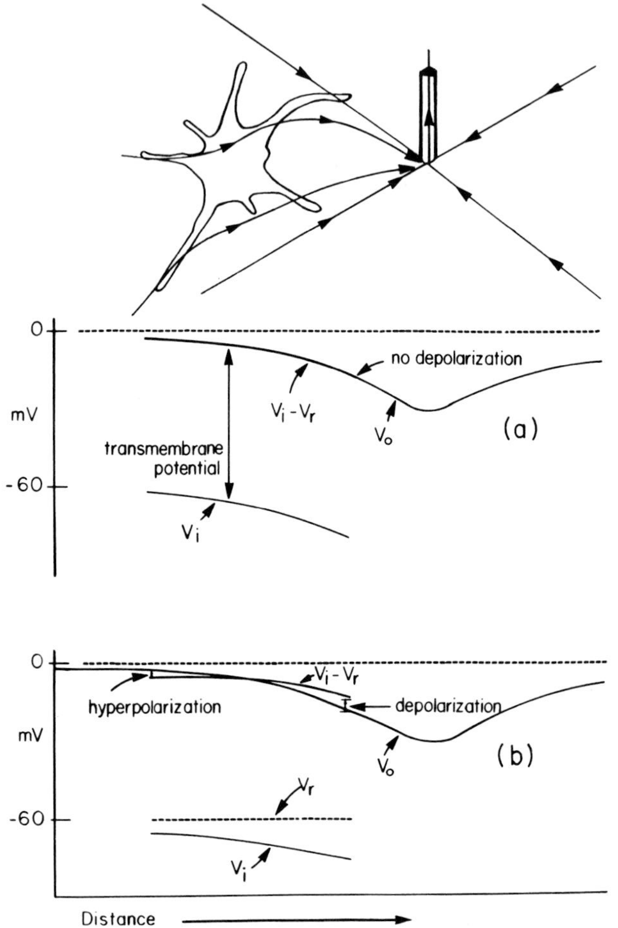

FIG. 4. A neuron in an extracellular field. (a) A very low membrane resistance (Case 4); (b) a normal membrane resistance (Case 5).

From these examples we can see that the most effective way to stimulate a cell is to have a highly localized change in extracellular voltage. If the extracellular voltage change is not localized, then the whole neuron, or a large part of the neuron, will change its intracellular voltage, and there will be little change in transmembrane potential. If the change in extracellular voltage is gradual over a long distance, then there is more opportunity for current to enter the neuron, because there is more surface area of neuron membrane for current to cross. As we have seen, the more current that flows in the neuron, the less the depolarization. But

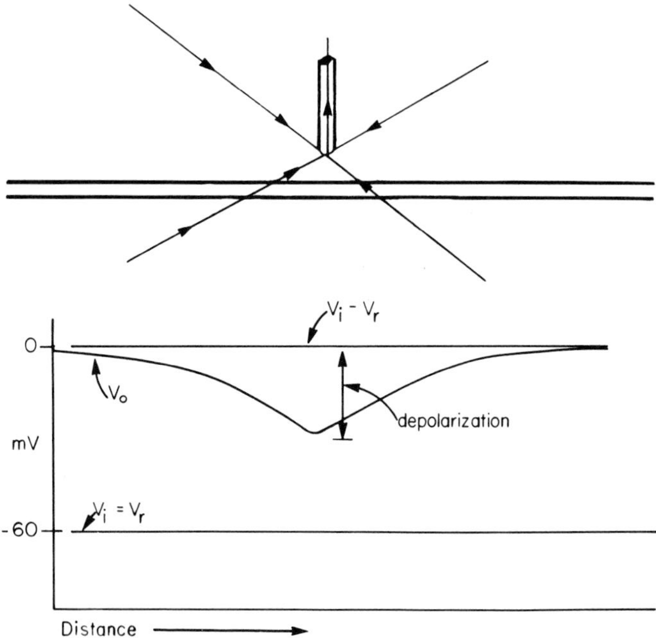

FIG. 5. An unmyelinated axon with a very high membrane resistance in an extracellular field.

let us try to be more quantitative and specific about what kind of distances are meant by the term "localized change in extracellular voltage." To do that, we must consider in more detail current flow in the neuron.

There are two kinds of voltage changes associated with dc current flow in the neuron that we must be concerned with: Voltage changes due to current flow through the resistance of the cytoplasm and voltage changes due to current flow across the membrane resistance. Since all neuronal cytoplasm seems to have about the same resistance per unit volume, this resistance will be just a function of the cross-sectional area of the cell. The bigger the area, the less the resistance per unit length. The resistance is proportional to 1 over the square of the radius of the fiber. The greater the voltage drop across the cell membrane due to current flow, the greater will be the depolarization of the cell when stimulated extracellularly. The greater the resistance of the cell membrane per unit length, the greater this voltage drop. The resistance of the cell membrane per unit length is decreased (by 1 over the radius of the fiber) as circumference of the cell increases, and increases as the resistance of the cell membrane per unit area increases.

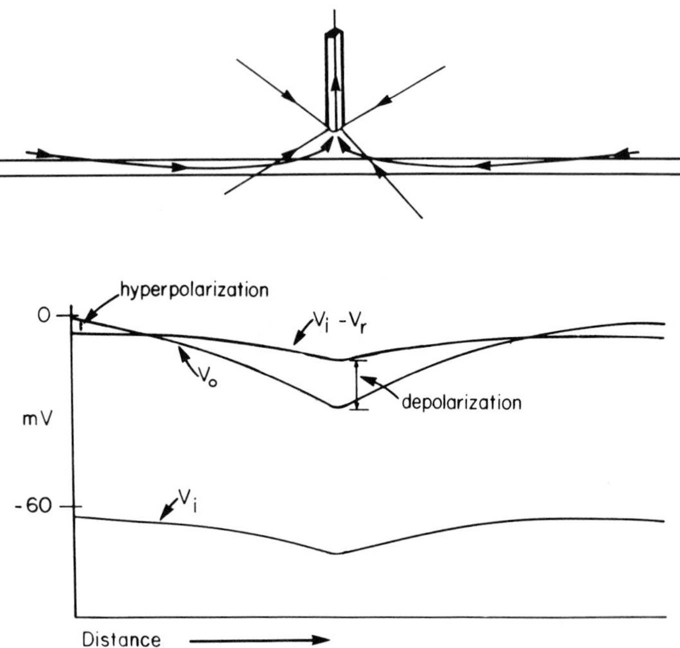

FIG. 6. An unmyelinated axon with normal membrane resistance in an extracellular field.

The greater the distance along a fiber, the greater the resistance to current flow in the cytoplasm. The greater the distance along a fiber, the *less* the resistance across the cell membrane (because the area of the membrane is greater). The length of fiber for which the resistance down the cytoplasm equals the resistance across the membrane is called the *length constant* of cell. (The length constant is also called "space constant" and "characteristic length.") The length constant is equal to $(R_m r / 2\,R_c)^{1/2}$, where R_m is the specific membrane resistance in Ω cm^2, R_c the cytoplasmic resistivity in Ω cm, and r the radius of the fiber in cm. If $R_m = 1000\ \Omega\ \text{cm}^2$, $R_c = 150\ \Omega$ cm, then for a 1 = μm radius fiber the length constant is 180 μm.

There are many implications of length constant, but for our purposes it leads to two general principles: *The longer the length constant of the cell, the more readily it will be stimulated,* i.e., the larger the radius of the fiber and/or the larger the membrane resistance, the more readily it will be stimulated. The other implication is that a length constant is the range of distance over which extracellular voltage differences will be important. *The greater the difference in extracellular voltage localized to distances of about one length constant, the more readily a fiber will be stimulated.* In fact, if there is about a 30 mV difference in extracellular voltage between two points one length constant apart on a long fiber (maintained for more than about two chronaxies; see Section III-A, then the neuron will probably be stimulated. The 30 mV was picked with the assumption that threshold was about a 20 mV depolarization, so for axons with lower threshold, even less voltage change is necessary. This is useful for quick calculations of what to expect from stimulation (see Section III-B).

In myelinated axons, current can flow across the node of Ranvier much more readily than across the internode. It will be convenient to approximate this by considering the case in which current can cross *only* the node, and no current flows across the cell membrane and myelin in the internode. The same considerations that were developed previously hold for myelinated axons (Fig. 7).

An important fact about myelinated axons is that internodal length is 200 times axis cylinder diameter (Bodian, 1951; Hess & Young, 1949). Internodal length is 120 times outside diameter, since the ratio of axis cylinder diameter to outside diameter is usually about 0.6 (Waxman &

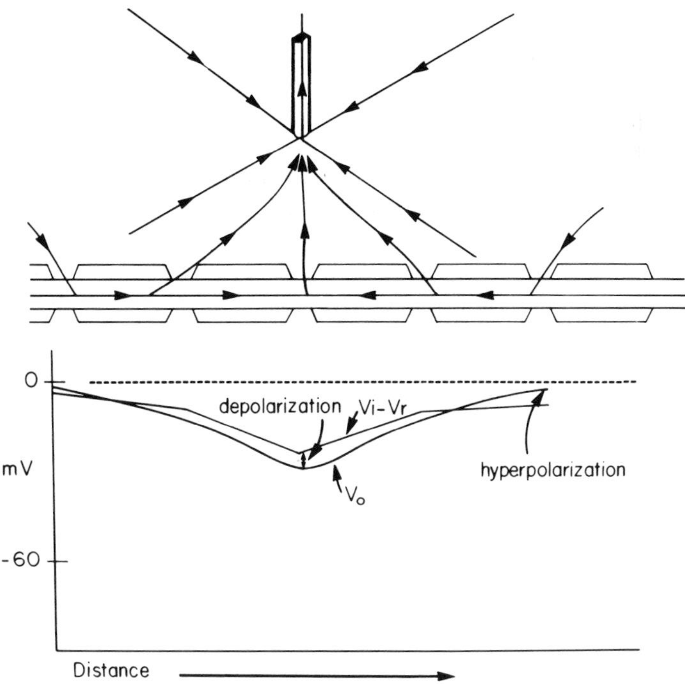

Fig. 7. A myelinated axon in an extracellular field.

Swadlow, 1977). (Almost all diagrams of myelinated axons, including Fig. 7 here, grossly distort the dimensions. The nodal width is about 2 μm in all axons. If the diameter is 5 μm, then the internodal length will be 600 μm. Clearly, Fig. 7 is not drawn proportionally.)

If one solves the equations for current flow in a myelinated fiber and compares it to the unmyelinated case, it turns out one can make a pretty good analogy between the line of reasoning used for unmyelinated fibers for the myelinated case and that one length constant is analogous to about two internodal lengths. The general principles stated for unmyelinated fibers can be restated for myelinated fibers by replacing the phrase "length constant" with "two internodal lengths."

III. Other Basic Principles

A. *Transients*

The previous discussion is all for the dc case. There is a capacity across the cell membrane that takes time to charge. A discussion of capacitative current and the way it introduces temporal delays is given in Appendix I. Anyone who stimulates nervous tissue should understand this and be facile with it.

The standard way of dealing with the transient effects in stimulation is with a strength–duration relation. In this case, one records the same response from some system and simultaneously varies the strength and the duration of constant current pulses. One can then plot the strength versus duration of the pulse to give a constant response (Fig. 8). Many strength–duration curves fit the empirical equation $I = I_r(1 + C/t)$, where I is the current, I_r is rheobase current, t is time, and C is chronaxie. Chronaxie is the time on a strength–duration curve for twice the rheobase current, which is the current required for a very long pulse. These same strength–duration curves also often can be fit with the equation $I = I_r/[1 - \exp(-t/\tau)]$, where τ is the time constant of the membrane. Chronaxie is about 0.7 of the membrane time constant. The relations given are approximate and adequate for most purposes.

There are substantial differences in chronaxie in different parts of the central nervous system. All central nervous system myelinated fibers that have been examined have chronaxies of 50–100 μsec. When gray matter is stimulated, the chronaxies are usually 200–700 μsec. In microstimulation studies, Asanuma, Arnold, and Zarzecki (1976) found cell

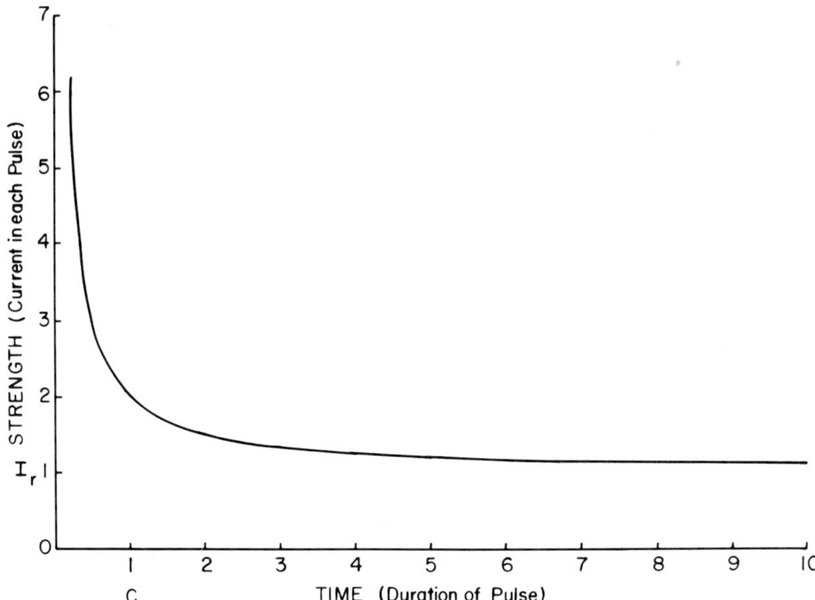

FIG. 8. A strength–duration curve, calculated from $I = I_r(1 + C/t)$. I_r (rheobasic current) is set equal to 1 on the ordinate; C (chronaxie) is set equal to 1 on the abscissa.

bodies to have a chronaxie of 140 μsec. There are some systems in which chronaxies of about 1.0 msec have been discovered, so there is a wide range of chronaxies seen (Ranck, 1975). If one wants to stimulate myelinated fibers, pulses of about 50 μsec should be used. If one does not want to stimulate myelinated fibers, then much longer pulses should be used. Perhaps the most important point is that an experimenter should construct a strength–duration curve for the system which he or she is stimulating, should know what the chronaxie is, and then should use an appropriate duration pulse.

In the peripheral nervous system, *C* fibers have a chronaxie of 1.5 msec, A-beta fibers (11.2 m/sec) 450 μsec, and A-alpha fibers 20 μsec (Li & Bak, 1976). Merrill, Wall, and Yaksh (1978) have shown that some central unmyelinated fibers have chronaxies of 156 to 380 μsec.

B. Axon Size

In the peripheral nervous system, one of the classical findings is that with extracellular stimulation of a nerve, the largest diameter axons are stimulated with the smallest amount of current, and the smaller axons require more current. This makes sense in terms of the principles developed in Section I-A, because the larger the diameter of a fiber, the longer its length constant; and for a myelinated fiber, the longer the fiber, the longer the internodal length. This holds just as well in the central nervous system as in the peripheral nerve. It is more difficult to demonstrate experimentally in the central nervous system but in the cases that have been examined, the larger fibers are stimulated with smaller currents. This relation of ease of extracellular stimulation to fiber diameter is the *opposite* of the "size principle" of Henneman, Somjen, and Carpender (1965). The size principle states that during recruitment of a group of neurons by increasing synaptic input, the smaller neurons will fire at the lowest intensity of input. It is not clear if this size principle is generally true for the central nervous system. However, it does make sense, and there are many suggestions that may be generally applicable, the best evidence for it coming from motoneurons. The reader should be aware of this so that he or she does not confuse the size principle with the relation of fiber diameter to extracellular stimulation. The reader should also be aware that this is a way in which extracellular stimulation may not mimic normal functioning, and be duly cautious of interpreting the effects of increasing stimulus strength.

C. *Electrode Tip Size*[1]

The voltage in the tissue r cm from a monopolar electrode with a spherical tip will be

$$V_o = \int_{\infty}^{r} I\,Res/(4\pi r^2)\,\mathrm{dr} = I\,Res/(4\,\pi\,r),$$

where Res is the resistivity of brain in Ω cm, r is radial distance from the center of the electrode tip in centimeters, and I is the current in amperes. The resistivity of gray matter is about 400 Ω cm (Havstad, 1976; Ranck, 1963a), so V_o in this case is about 30 I/r. From this relation, we can calculate how much current must be passed to cause a 30 mV

[1]Many of the ideas of the first paragraph of this section have not been previously published to my knowledge. They are the result of a correspondence with the late James Olds.

difference in extracellular voltage between a site just adjacent to the electrode and 600 μm away. (600 μm was picked as a value for a length constant.) For a 1-μm radius electrode tip, 3.3 μA will be necessary; for a 10-μm radius tip, more than 34 μA will be necessary. For a 100-μm radius electrode tip, more than 390 μA will be required. I do not know of any systematic studies in which current thresholds for some neural or behavioral events have been studied with different-sized electrodes in order to compare with these calculations. However, from unsystematic personal observation and comments in the literature, these values seem about three times larger than the minimum recorded. Perhaps these minimum values are due to fibers with long length constants and low thresholds (also, as pointed out in Appendix II, for distances less than 1 length constant, the resistivity is greater than the 400 Ω cm used in the calculation). The effect electrode size has deserves extensive study. Details of the size and shape of electrode tips should always be reported.

The use of small stimulating electrode tips thus can lead to much greater localization of the elements stimulated than with larger electrode tips. This use of small tips, called microstimulation, has been particularly effective in the study of spinal cord and motor systems (e.g., Abzug, Maeda, Peterson & Wilson, 1974; Asanuma & Arnold, 1975; Gustafsson & Jankowska, 1976).

However, small electrode tips present problems when used to stimulate large areas and when large currents are passed. When electrodes with small exposed tips are used, quite large current densities can occur at the electrode tip with repetitive stimulation. Asanuma and Arnold (1975) report getting bubbles from exposed tips of 15 μm to 30 μm with six pulses of 60 μA, each of 0.2 msec duration. The bubbles could be seen with a microscope when this current was passed while the electrode was in saline. It is a good idea to look for bubbles at the electrode tip with a microscope using the stimulus parameters actually used.

As can be seen from the sample calculation, the voltage one can get in tissue adjacent to an electrode with small electrode tips can be quite large even with small current values. Asanuma and Arnold (1975) have shown that stimulation under these circumstances can sometimes lead to a period of inexcitability, the excitability then recurring after a period of no stimulation. Presumably this is due to the very large extracellular voltage that can occur.

Note that all of these considerations of electrode size hold only for the tissue very close to the electrode. For stimulating elements that are more than about 50 μm from the electrode or more than several electrode tip radii away, there would be no effect of electrode size.

D. *Transverse and Longitudinal Current Flow*

Figure 9 defines the difference between transverse and longitudinal current flow in a cylindrical fiber. Transverse current flow is included in the situation of Case 1 (Fig. 1) and does not stimulate for the reasons given in the discussion of that case. Longitudinal current flow is the case of Figs. 4 through 7. This means that it is only the extracellular voltage gradient along the axis of a fiber that counts. A fiber lying normal to the voltage gradient (along an equipotential line) will not be stimulated.

It is only the voltage gradient in the direction of a fiber that stimulates. Therefore, with bipolar stimulating electrodes, fibers that run parallel to alignment of the tips will be more readily stimulated than fibers running perpendicular to the alignment of the electrode tips. Even if a fiber runs perfectly normal to a line between two bipolar electrodes it will still be stimulated, for there will be a voltage gradient in the direction of the fiber. However, this voltage gradient will not be as large as that running directly between the two electrodes.

E. *Effects of Inward Current and Anodal Surround Blocking*

If there is an outward current somewhere depolarizing a cell, there must be inward current somewhere else hyperpolarizing it (Fig. 10). As one depolarizes an axon more and more at one site, one is also hyperpolarizing it more and more at some other site. This can lead to a paradoxical result that we shall call "anodal surround blocking." Very large stimulating currents may cause this hyperpolarization to be large enough to block propagation of an action potential, which was not

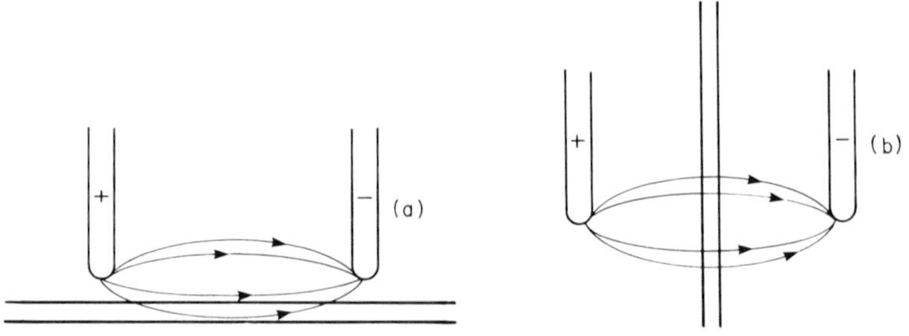

Fig. 9. Longitudinal (a) versus transverse (b) current flow in a fiber (from Ranck, 1975).

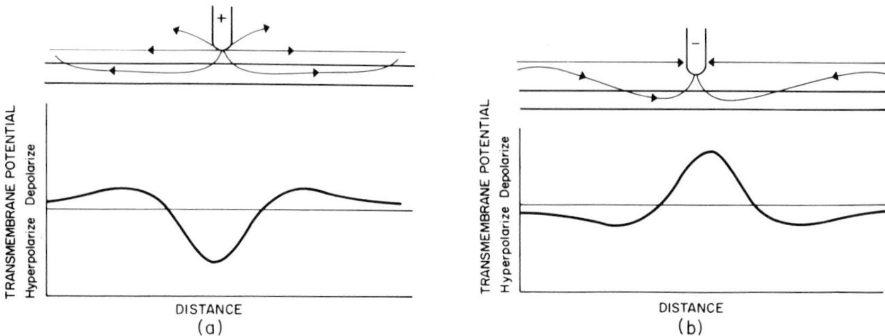

FIG. 10. The effects of inward (a) and outward (b) current flow of an unmyelinated fiber in an extracellular field (from Ranck, 1975).

blocked at smaller currents (Fig. 11). Thus, the fibers of a given diameter that are stimulated are those that pass through a *shell* around an electrode. Those that pass too close to the electrode and those too far away are not stimulated. A further paradoxical effect of this is that very close to the electrode a small-diameter axon may be stimulated and larger ones not stimulated. This effect is discussed in greater detail elsewhere (Ranck, 1975).

An axon is hyperpolarized underneath a monopolar anode. However, at some other site the axon must be depolarized, although the depolarization will be less than the hyperpolarization. Therefore, if enough anodal current is passed, it is possible to stimulate an axon. It usually

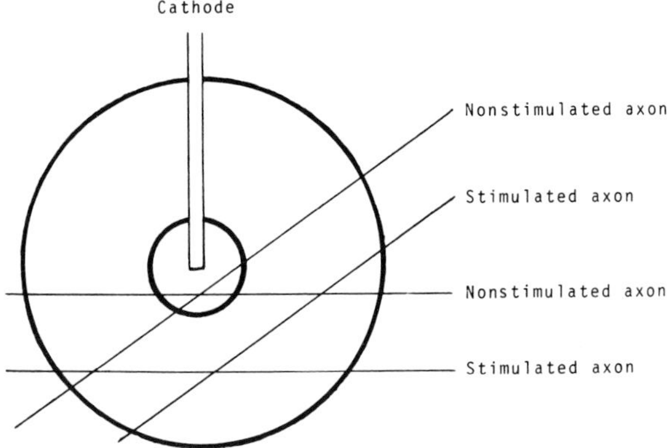

FIG. 11. The anodal surround effect (from Ranck, 1975).

takes three to seven times as much current to stimulate with anodal current as with cathodal.

IV. Other Facts

A. *Current–Distance Relations*

If two axons are identical, with the exception that one is closer to a stimulating electrode than another, the one which is closer will be stimulated by a smaller current. If one axon has a larger diameter than another, and the two are the same distance from a stimulating electrode, then the larger diameter axon will be stimulated with a smaller current. If the larger diameter axon is further away from a stimulating electrode than a smaller diameter one, then we will need to have more detailed information about diameter and distance from stimulating electrode to decide which will be stimulated with the smallest current.

The literature on current–distance relations in CNS stimulation has been reviewed (Ranck, 1975). Most of the data are consistent with each other (Fig. 12), and the data fit with theory. However, much more information is needed. The methods exist at present to work out current–distance relations for fibers of a wide range of conduction velocity. If this data were available, we would be able to know fairly well just which neurons we were stimulating. However, the data that is available now is not often used adequately. Ranck (1975) gives more detail on current–distance relations and instructions for using the data available.

B. *Stimulation near Cell Bodies; Polarity of Stimuli*

Most of what has been said so far relates only to stimulation of axons. However, if one puts a small stimulating electrode near a cell body, one can stimulate the neuron. Gustafsson and Jankowska (1976) have studied just which elements are stimulated in extracellular microstimulation of motoneurons. It seems very likely that often, if not always, local electrical stimulation near a cell body is stimulating the initial segment. Asanuma *et al.* (1976) have shown that with extracellular microstimulation the same small amounts of current may sometimes stimulate something in the vicinity of a cell body or an axon collateral of the cell, so that for a given electrode in gray matter, one might be stimulating the

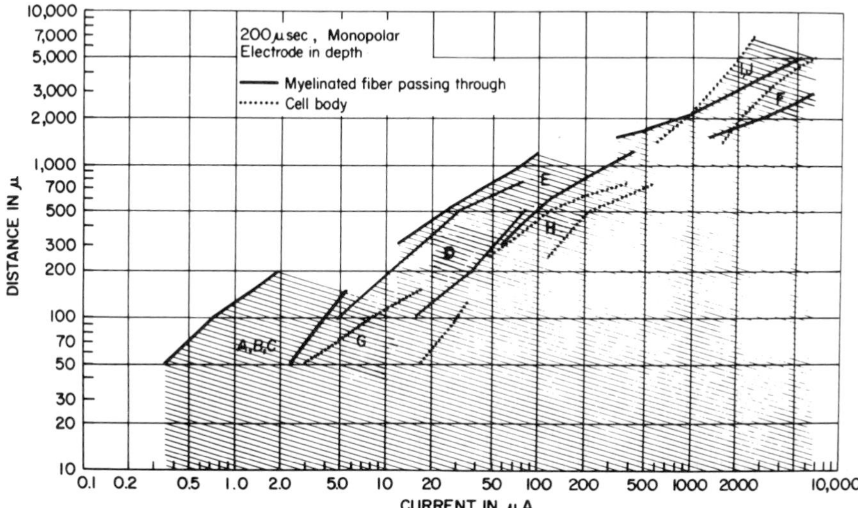

FIG. 12. Some current–distance relations normalized for a 200 μsec cathodal monopolar pulse in the depth of the brain from studies reported in the literature (from Ranck, 1975). [See Ranck, (1975) for explanations, references, and instructions on how to use this figure. For instance, the conduction velocities of these neurons probably are all greater than 10 m/sec. Neurons with slower conduction velocities would not be stimulated as far away from the electrode as those in the figure.]

cell bodies in the area, or axons of passage whose cell bodies are some distance away.

It has been known for over a hundred years that anodal stimulation of motor cortex often has a lower threshold for producing a movement than cathodal stimulation. There are studies done elsewhere in brain that sometimes show that when a stimulating electrode is on the opposite side of a cell body from the initial segment, anodal stimulation often has a lower threshold than cathodal. The basis for this is presumably that the neuron is stimulated at its initial segment, and that current from an anode on the other side of the cell body from the initial segment enters in the dendrite and leaves in the initial segment (Fig. 13). If the stimulating electrode is made negative, it may hyperpolarize the initial segment.

When one is stimulating in gray matter, it is not clear how often one is stimulating presynaptic endings. Presynaptic endings can certainly be stimulated (Wall, 1958), but I know of no quantitative data comparing this stimulation with that of axons. Clendenin, Ekerst, Oscarsson, and Rosen (1974) stimulated the surface of cerebellum with monopolar electrodes and recorded antidromic stimulation of mossy fibers in lateral

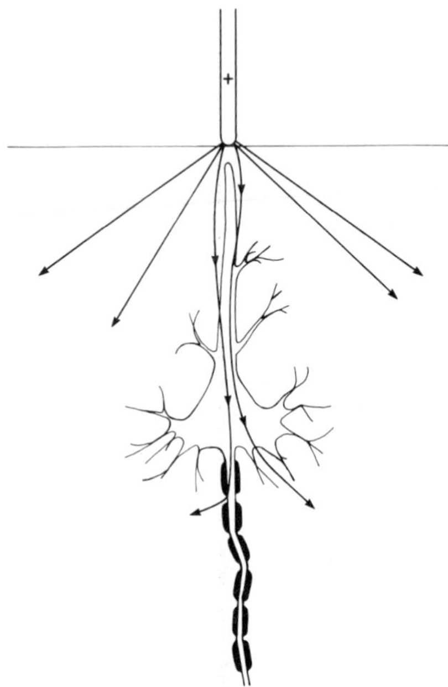

FIG. 13. Stimulation with an anode on the opposite side of the cell body from the axon. This is the basis for anodal stimuli having a lower threshold than cathodal stimuli (from Ranck, 1975). Current hyperpolarizes the apical dendrites but depolarizes the axon hillock. A cathodal pulse would therefore have a higher threshold than the anodal pulse.

reticular nucleus. They found that the threshold anodal stimuli was 36% of cathodal stimuli. Stimulation of presynaptic endings deserves extensive study.

C. *Refractory Periods, Supranormal Periods, and Subnormal Periods*

Waxman and Swadlow (1977) have reviewed their data on refractory periods of central nervous system axons, which vary from 0.6 to 2.0 msec. In general, the higher the conduction velocity, the shorter the refractory period. It would be useful to have data covering a greater range of conduction velocities than the 0.3 to 12.9 m/sec they studied. After the refractory period, there is a supranormal period in which the axons can be stimulated with less current, and there is an increase in conduction velocity. This may last for 18–170 msec. The effect is greatest in axons with low conduction velocities. After repetitive stimulation, there may also be a subnormal period. Similar results have been obtained in CNS unmyelinated fibers (Merrill *et al.*, 1978).

D. *Current as Strength Parameter*

As can be seen in all the discussions of factors which stimulate, it is extracellular voltage difference over the distance of one length constant that stimulates. In general, one cannot directly measure this, but one can calculate or estimate it if one knows the current passed, the resistivity of the tissue, and the electrode configuration. This calculation may be difficult when one is dealing with anisotropic tissue such as white matter and with tissue of different resistivities, but it still can be done. Therefore, one should report the current passed from the electrode. The voltage in the stimulating electrode will *not* be a good indicator of voltage in the tissue adjacent to the electrode or of the current flowing. This is because there is a large resistance at the electrode–tissue interface, and this resistance is not predictable between electrodes or with time in the same electrodes. Fortunately, there are many stimulating devices available that produce controlled amounts of current.

E. *Synchronous Firing*

When one electrically stimulates brain, there is synchronous firing of many neurons. This synchrony of firing is far greater than any synchrony that normally occurs, and it is not clear what the relation to this is to normal function. Lacking any other information, I would be equally willing to believe that electrical stimulation would (1) disrupt normal functioning of a system, (2) mimic normal functioning of a system, or (3) produce a result unrelated to normal functioning of the system. It is remarkable that result (2) seems to often be the case. Local chemical stimulation of an area presumably does *not* cause synchronous firing of neurons. This always must be kept in mind when comparing electrical and chemical stimulation.

One of the consequences of synchronous stimulation may be the accumulation in the extracellular space of substances released from neurons, or depletion of substances taken up by neurons. For instance, potassium is known to accumulate in some circumstances (Fertziger and Ranck, 1970). The rate of firing of the neurons involved will affect this accumulation or depletion, but synchrony will also be an important factor.

F. Repetitive Stimulation

Many effects of electrical stimulation can be seen only with repetitive stimulation. Most of the presumed reasons for this are outside the content of this chapter; however, some are relevant. A stimulus will always depolarize some neurons below threshold, and thus depolarization will then decrease with time as the membrane capacity discharges. This decrease of depolarization will be approximately, but not exactly, exponential with the time constant of the membrane. This means that if there is a second electrical stimulus within a few time constants of the membrane, there may be summation of subthreshold depolarization leading to stimulation of cells that would not be stimulated with a single pulse. It is remarkable that in central unmyelinated fibers there is increased excitability for 20 msec after subthreshold stimulation (Merrill *et al.*, 1978). Repetitive stimulation may also lead to local accumulation of potassium. Burke (1977) has discussed some of the synaptic factors of repetitive stimulation in an essay that is brief and worth reading.

G. Accommodation and Posthyperpolarization Excitation

When an axon is maintained at subthreshold depolarization, one often finds that the threshold for initiation of an action potential rises. This is called accommodation. When an axon is maintained at a hyperpolarized potential, the threshold for initiation of an action potential often falls. Sometimes it may fall so low that the threshold will be more hyperpolarized than the resting potential so that when the hyperpolarizing current is stopped and the axon returns to its resting potential, an action potential will be initiated. This is called "anodal break phenomena" or "posthyperpolarization excitation." In the central nervous system, these phenomena have been looked for only in intracellular recordings from cell bodies. Some cells show accommodation while others do not; some show posthyperpolarization excitation. I know of no studies on central nervous system axons. It is not clear how important these factors may be in electrical stimulation of brain.

H. Electrode Configuration

Most of what has been said in the foregoing relates to stimulation near a single electrode. Bipolar electrodes with two similar tips was discussed under the topic of electrode orientation in Section III-E. Perhaps the major reason for the use of various kinds of bipolar electrodes is to attenuate shock artifact (see Section IV-I). There is surprisingly little data or theoretical consideration of the effects of stimulation of the commonly used bipolar electrode configurations—side-by-side tips, staggered tips, and concentric electrodes. No doubt certain of these or other configurations could be used to advantage in certain cases, but it has just not been worked out.

All stimulation is bipolar in the sense that one needs two electrodes. The principles developed in this chapter show that we effectively stimulate monopolarity when the surface area of one electrode is much larger than the other, so that no stimulation occurs at the large electrode (see Section III-C). When the two electrode tips are separated by more than about two length constants of the fibers being stimulated, then we can consider the two electrodes to be independent. When they are closer than about two length constants, their effects interact.

I. Stimulus Artifacts and Stimulus Isolation

Frequently one wants to electrically stimulate the nervous system and then make an electrical recording immediately after. When this is done, there is often a problem with shock or stimulus artifact, which is an artifact in the recording due to the stimulating current which is passed. If one is not making an electrical recording, then there is no need to be concerned about it at all.

Shock artifact is due to three factors: (1) actual voltage in the tissue at the recording site, (2) capacity between stimulating and recording wires, and (3) overshoots due to the use of ac amplifiers. We shall discuss each of these in the following.

(1) Some sample calculations of actual voltages in the tissue at the stimulating site have been given in Section III-D, and these can sometimes be several volts. The magnitude of these voltages fall off with distance, but when one is recording events in the 100 μV range, as is often the case, the actual voltage at the recording site will often be very large. Since the stimulus duration is often short, one might think it would make little difference to lose, say, 0.1 msec of the record. However, often the recorded voltages are so large that the amplifier is saturated for a while afterward. Especially in those cases where rapid repetitive stimulation is used, one might want to record during the time of the actual stimulation. The major way to decrease the actual magnitude of the voltage due to stimulus current at the recording site is with stimulus isolation and symmetrical positioning of electrodes to manipulate zero potential surfaces. A stimulus isolation unit delivers a certain amount

of current (or a certain voltage difference) between two electrodes (S_1 and S_2 in Fig. 14). However, the absolute value of the voltage in the two electrodes is not fixed. If the two electrodes are identical and the tissue is grounded, then ground (or zero) voltage will be about halfway between the two electrodes, the dotted line in Fig. 14. If the stimulating electrodes are not isolated from ground, then one of the electrodes is usually at ground, and the other has a value which is larger than if the electrodes were isolated. The fact that the absolute value of the voltage at one of the electrodes is larger is not as important as the fact that with stimulus isolation there will be a zero potential *surface*. If one electrode is grounded, there will be zero voltage only at this electrode. If the stimulating electrodes are adjusted just right, in general symmetrical with respect to the recording electrodes (Fig. 14b), then the recording electrodes may be close to the zero potential during stimulation. For other electrode configurations, there will also be a zero potential surface, which in some cases can be adjusted so that it lies close to the recording electrodes. Even with "monopolar" stimulation the zero potential surface may be close to the recording electrode if the other electrode passing current is symmetrical with respect to the recording electrode (Fig. 14b). Concentric electrodes may sometimes give less artifact if they are not isolated and if the outer sleeve is grounded.

Sometimes it is useful to manipulate the zero potential surface by using stimulus isolation and connecting the two stimulating electrodes to the

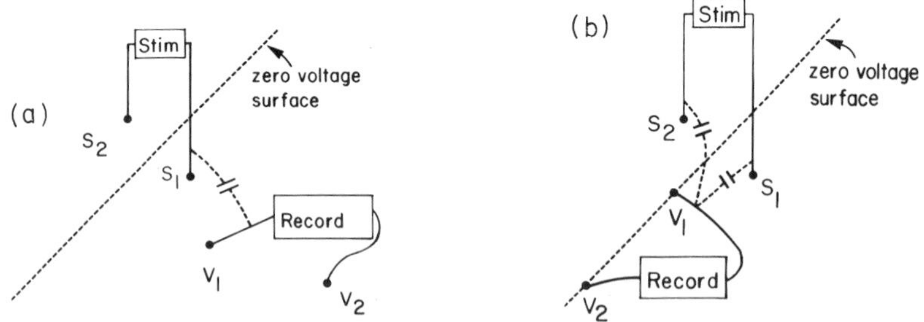

FIG. 14. Dealing with shock artifacts the wrong way (a) and the right way (b). In (a), V_1 and V_2 are recorded electrode tips, and S_1 and S_2 are stimulating electrode tips. V_1 records a larger stimulus voltage than V_2 because it is closer to the zero voltage surface. As drawn, the wires connected to V_1 have a capacity to wires connecting to one stimulating electrode, so there will be a voltage recorded from V_1 due to capacitative current flow. In (b), both V_1 and V_2 are on the zero potential surface and hence record no voltage change in the tissue directly due to stimulus current. As drawn, the wire connecting to V_1 has capacity to both stimulating electrodes. The stimulating electrodes have voltage changes in opposite directions, so if the capacities are exactly balanced, there will be no voltage in V_1 due to capacitative current picked up from capacity to stimulating electrodes.

ends of variable resistor (100 kΩ or more) and grounding the movable center contact (a Wagner ground). This allows one to move the zero potential surface between the two stimulating electrodes.

Isolation is also affected by the capacity between the stimulating electrodes and sites of fixed voltage, so in order to achieve good isolation, care should be taken to keep these capacities low.

(2) There is always a capacity between stimulating and recording electrodes (Fig. 14) that can cause substantial currents to flow in the recording electrode and, especially for high resistance electrodes, causes a voltage to be recorded. This can be reduced by keeping the wires to the stimulating and recording electrodes short and separated. When necessary, one can introduce a shield between stimulating and recording electrodes, but this may increase the capacity of the stimulating electrode to ground and decrease isolation unless care is taken. In severe cases where large capacitative interaction is unavoidable, one can sometimes intentionally introduce capacity between the stimulating and recording electrodes of opposite polarity to the one causing trouble.

(3) An ac-coupled amplifier can also introduce artifact, because after a pulse there will be an overshoot (V_b in Fig. 15). A numerical example will show the surprising magnitude of this effect. If there is 1 V in the recording electrode due to a pulse lasting 0.1 msec, this will cause an overshoot when the pulse is turned off, which will be 0.6 mV if the low frequency cutoff (down to 70% or 1.5 dB) is 1 Hz, 6.2 mV for 10-Hz cutoff, and 62 mV for a 100-Hz cutoff. These overshoots will decline

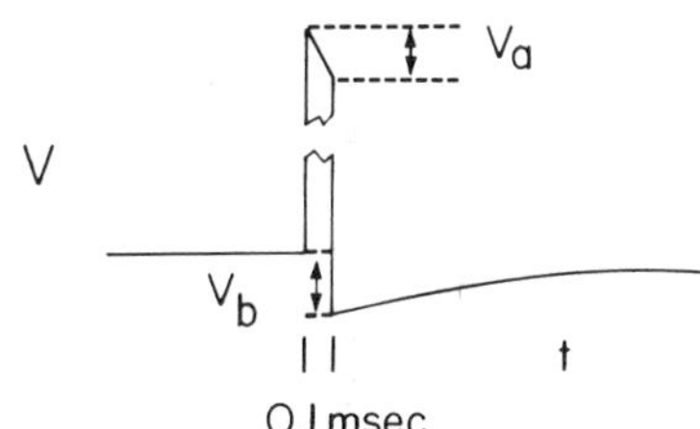

FIG. 15. The effect of the low cutoff frequency of an ac amplifier on shock artifact. This shows the voltage output of an ac amplifier versus time, recording the effect of a square pulse of current at a distance. A square pulse of current will produce a square pulse of voltage, but this will be recorded by an ac amplifier as a pulse that decreases with time by voltage V_a. V_a equals the initial voltage divided by the time constant of the amplifier times the duration of the pulse. When the current pulse is turned off, the voltage at the recording site will return to zero, but the output of the ac amplifier will show an overshoot V_b, which is equal to V_a. V_b will decay with the time constant of the amplifier. For short stimulus pulses, V_a will be a small proportion of the voltage at the recording site, but because this voltage at the recording site is often very large compared to the response, V_b may interfere with the recorded response.

with a time constant of 16 msec, 1.6 msec, and 0.16 msec, respectively. For low-level recording this can be a disaster. This may seem paradoxical at first, but the way to avoid this is to use as low a cutoff frequency as possible. The numerical example given should make the basis for this clear. Although the time constant of decay of the overshoot is longer for low cutoff frequencies, its size is substantially smaller and may be within tolerable limits.

Shock artifacts can also be eliminated by artifact suppressors in the input circuit (Freeman, 1971; Roby & Lettich, 1975). In most cases, shock artifacts can be eliminated by the means described here, but where this is not adequate, the additional complexity of artifact suppressors is warranted.

J. Antidromic Stimulation

When a fiber is electrically stimulated at a point, the action potential will propagate in any direction that the membrane is excitable, regardless of the normal (orthodromic) direction of propagation. When electrodes are in the central nervous system, in general they will stimulate some fibers orthodromically and others antidromically. If a fiber has two (or more) branches, an electrode may stimulate one branch antidromically, and then the action potential may propagate out the other branch orthodromically.

The strategy of recording from a cell body of a single neuron and mapping out the distribution of its axon by antidromic stimulation is an important method. The most important criteria of collision has been well-developed by Fuller and Schlag (1976).

It seems likely that at some branch points conduction failure may sometimes occur, presumably under normal conditions (Chung, Raymond, & Lettvin, 1970).

K. Stimulation to Measure Properties of Cells

Most of what has been said in this chapter involves situations in which one has been interested in stimulating cells in order to study some consequences of their activation. However, extracellular electrical stimulation can also be used to study some physiological properties of cells. Section III-A discussed the use of strength–duration measurements to estimate the time constant of membranes and to indicate when certain excited elements are likely to be myelinated axons (when chronaxie is less than 100 μsec). Extracellular stimulation has been used to measure internodal lengths of myelinated fibers (BeMent & Ranck, 1969b). The relative efficacy of anodal versus cathodal monopolar stimulation suggests what part of a neuron is being stimulated (see Sections III-E and IV-B). The Wall test (Wall, 1958) is widely used as an indication of presynaptic inhibition with afferent terminal depolarization. Woody's group of researchers in a series of papers (e.g., Woody, Knispel, Crow, & Black–Cleworth, 1976) have shown changes in excitability to extracellular microstimulation associated with conditioning, which has led to some interpretation at the level of cellular mechanisms. Gallistel, Stellar, and Bubis (1974), Edmonds, Stellar, and Gallistel (1974), and Edmonds and Gallistel (1974) have analyzed in detail some stimulation properties of self-stimulation and have tried to translate it into characteristics of the elements stimulated.

A knowledge of some physiological characteristics of elements stimulated in a given response can also be used to tag or identify the elements stimulated for comparison with the characteristics of elements producing other responses to stimulation in the same vicinity. This can help to answer the question if the stimulation of the same elements is involved in both responses. For example, some of the characteristics of stimulation in self-stimulation that have been determined are of interest both as physiological characteristics themselves and as a tag. The dual pulse measurement of refractory periods of elements involved in a response helps tag the elements. This can even be done in responses driven by repetitive stimulation (e.g., Coons, Schupf, & Ungerleider, 1976; Deutsch, 1964). Current duration relations and anodal versus cathodal stimulation properties have been determined by Matthews (1977). Strength and frequency of stimulation necessary for a given response in general are not very useful for determining physiological characteristics or for giving a physiological tag to the elements stimulated.

Each of these examples is important in its own right, but they all point up the importance of a concern with the cellular mechanisms involved in extracellular stimulation. Perhaps the moral of the whole chapter is "*Think cellular.*"

L. Practical Suggestions

(1) Use pulses of current, not voltage. The most interpretable data is for stimulation from a monopolar cathode. Use bipolar electrodes only when necessary to eliminate shock artifact.

(2) Do strength–duration curves routinely. Even a three-point curve (say, at 1 msec, 200 μsec, and 50 μsec) is useful. In many cases it is easy to do. Use 50 μsec pulses if you want to stimulate myelinated fibers.

(3) Use the current–distance relations that are known (see Section IV-A).

(4) Attend to other known facts such as anodal surround blocking, accommodation, orientation of effects of polarity, effects of electrode tip size, and the effects of pia mater.

(5) Use small electrode tips for localized stimulation.

(6) Report orientation of electrode tips when using bipolar electrodes, and also duration of any exposure of pial surface to air. Report in detail the size and shape of the electrode tips.

M. Annotated Suggestions for Further Reading

A review of extracellular stimulation that is less pedagogical than this chapter and that pays more attention to the experimental evidence for the assertions made in this chapter, is available (Ranck, 1975). Also, the properties of CNS axons have been reviewed by Waxman and Swadlow (1977). These two reviews are the next step beyond this chapter for anyone with interests in stimulating the mammalian CNS with extracellular electrodes.

Beyond this point, the field becomes biophysical and mathematical, and the serious stimulator should be aware of some of the literature in the field.

Cable theory from an intracellular point of view is well-covered by Rall (1977) and Jack, Noble, and Tsien (1975). Cable theory from an extracellular point of view is developed by Ranck (1963b).

Myelin theory from the point of view of extracellular stimulation in the peripheral nervous system is well-developed by McNeal (1976), who reviews much of the literature. Stimulation of central nervous system myelinated fibers over short distances is developed by Bean (1974). BeMent and Ranck (1969a, 1969b) have considered the problem over distances greater than 200 μm.

Current flow in brain has been reviewed by Nicholson and Freeman (1975) and by Havstad (1976).

Recent important papers on microstimulation are those of Gustafsson and Jankowska (1976), Abzug *et al.* (1974), and Asanuma *et al.* (1976).

Stimulation from neocortical surface has been analyzed by Marks (1977).

Acknowledgment

Dr. Steven E. Fox read an early version of this and made useful comments.

Appendix I: Current Flow

Current is (a), the motion of charged particles, or (b), the charging of a capacity. Net current is the sum of (a) and (b) in Fig. 16.

The motion of electrons is of negligible importance in biological current flow. All biological current flow is due to motion of ions. Thus, we will refer to this kind of current as *ionic current* or *resistive current*. In Fig. 16b, capacitative current (in amperes) is dq/dt, where q is charge (in coulombs), t is time in seconds, and d/dt is the time derivative. Since $q = CV$, where C is a capacity (in farads) and V is the voltage across the capacity, capacitative current is $CdV/dt + VdC/dt$. If nothing is moving in space, the capacity does not change, and the second term is zero. The direction of current flow is from the part becoming more positive to the part becoming more negative.

There is a capacity between any two points in the universe. Current cannot be created or destroyed; it always goes in circles. Therefore, across any closed surface at any instant, the net current flow is always zero. Examples follow:

1. If I hold some positive charge in my hand and walk across the room, there is a resistive current flow in the direction I am walking, since positive charge is moving in that direction. There is an exactly equal and opposite capacitative current, for the region into which the charge moves becomes more positive and the region from which it came becomes more negative. There is no net current.

2. If I suddenly switch a cell whose membrane is exclusively permeable to potassium (to use an unreal case for simplicity) from a solution of high potassium to one of low potassium, a very little amount of

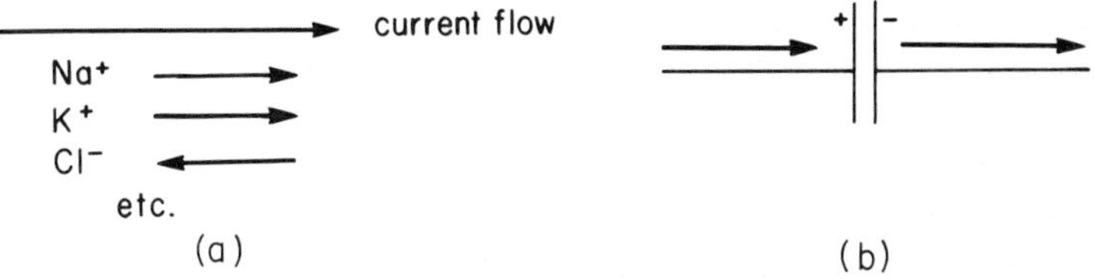

FIG. 16. Kinds of current flow: charged particle current (a) and capacitative current (b).

potassium diffuses out of the cell, and the inside of the cell becomes negative with respect to the outside. A transmembrane potential develops.

While the potassium is moving out, there is an outward ionic current, and an equal and opposite inward capacitative current (Fig. 17). All the ionic current is used to charge up the membrane capacity. There is no net current across the membrane. If the membrane is homogenous, there is no current in the cytoplasm and none in the interstitial space. If we use a model of the membrane as a capacitor in parallel with a resistor and battery, then it is as if we were only adding a battery, causing resistive current to flow out across the resistor and charge up the capacitor. When the potential across the capacitor is the same as in the battery, then there is no more current flow.

Therefore, *potential changes can occur without any net current flow.* Whenever there is a change in potential, there is always capacitative current flow, which, if the capacity remains constant, is CdV/dt. How much (if any) resistive current flows depends on the situation.

If there is a net current flow from point A to point B, then A is, or is becoming, relatively more positive with respect to B over what the potentials would be if there were no current flow at that instant. This is true whether the current is resistive, capacitative, or both. For the capacitative case, this is easy to see from Fig. 16b.

The case of resistive current is one where many students make mistakes. If the current flow is purely resistive, then for each charged particle that moves by a point, another comes to take its place. There is a net

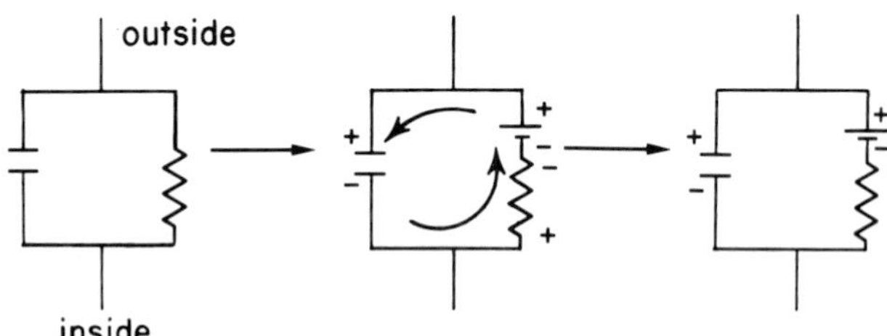

FIG. 17. Charging the membrane capacity with no net transmembrane current flow. In the circuit on the left, there is no "transmembrane battery," for there are no transmembrane concentrations gradients. The middle circuit illustrates the situation immediately after the extracellular potassium has been decreased, creating a "potassium gradient battery" across the membrane. A few potassium ions diffuse out of the membrane across the "membrane resistor" (an outward resistive current) and charge up the membrane capacity (an inward capacitative current). The resistive current is exactly equal and opposite to the capacitative current, so there is no *net* current flow. The circuit on the right shows the situation after the transmembrane current has become exactly the same as the "potassium gradient battery." There is no current flow.

movement of charge by a point, but not necessarily any change in charge concentration. The error that is commonly made is to say that if current is moving from A to B, we are taking positive charge away from A and adding it to B. But if this were true, then there would be no net current between A and B. If current is leaving A and only resistive current is flowing, then exactly that much must be coming up to A. Current can neither be created nor destroyed. Sometimes "current sources" and "sinks" are spoken of. This should not be taken to imply that current is being created at a "source," but rather that we are choosing to ignore how it gets there. I think the error may stem from thinking of only one charged particle at a time. A similar common error is made in the case when, say, a negative charge is added to the inside of a nerve fiber to hyperpolarize it. This hyperpolarization will propagate down the fiber with decrement, in this case without an action potential. The voltage change does *not* move down the fiber with the same speed that the charged particles move; the voltage change moves much faster. A few charged particles entering at one place in the fiber will influence the motion of other charged particles some distance away.

An analogy to water flow is useful here. If water in a water-filled pipe starts to flow from point A to point B, we are not emptying water at point A. For each molecule of water that moves by A, another comes up to take its place. Also, if we start the water moving at point A, by increasing the pressure, for example, the water will start moving at point B long before the molecules that had been at point A will reach point B. The pressure is transmitted much more rapidly than the individual particles move.

There will only be a net movement of ions (or any charged particles) from A to B if there is some driving force. In electrophysiology, the most common of these forces are active transport, concentration gradients, and voltage gradients. If there is ionic current flow in cytoplasm or in interstitial space where we know there will be no concentration gradients or active transport, then in order for ionic current to flow, there must be a voltage gradient. This voltage gradient must be such that if there is ionic current flow from A to B, A is relatively positive with respect to B. (Another way of saying the same thing is that if charge moves from A to B, then energy is dissipated, and the potential—which is energy—falls with distance.) Therefore, if in cytoplasm or interstitial fluid the potential at A is positive to that of B, current must be flowing from A to B. In order for A to be more positive than B, there must be more net positive charge at A than at B. This is because there is a capacity between any two points in space. Usually these capacities are so small we ignore them, but they are finite. If we start current flow through cytoplasm from A to B, we actually will have to add a very few more net positive charges to A or take them from B. The only capacities in animals that amount to enough to make a quantitative difference are across cell membranes.

Let us consider the case of net current flow across a cell membrane; we will speak of inward and outward current. If there is outward current somewhere, there must be just as much inward current somewhere else. But we can discuss each separately. The inward current can come in from an electrode placed in the cell or can cross the cell membrane at some other location. Most of the time a cell membrane has a potential across it but no current flow. This is why it is useful to think of a membrane battery. If we pass outward current, insofar as it is capacitative current, we are adding net positive charge to the inside of the membrane and taking it away on the outside, so we are depolarizing the cell. Insofar as this outward current is resistive current, we must have some force, which must be voltage, to drive the current, so we must be making the inside of the cell more positive. Therefore, *outward current* (whether resistive or capacitative) *depolarizes,* and *inward current hyperpolarizes*. The only qualification that must ever be added to these statements is the phrase, *compared to what the potential would be if there were no current flow*. This qualification enters in the case when the potential also changes due to some other cause, for instance, during an action potential. Any current that is passed during an action potential will have only a minor effect on the action potential unless that current is much larger than is ordinarily passed (except for voltage clamping). At each instance, outward current during an action potential will make the membrane more depolarized than if no current had been passed.

The model of the membrane as a capacitor in series with a battery and resistor is helpful for seeing these relations (Figs. 17 and 18). The transmembrane potential is the potential across the battery plus any potential across the resistor. If there is no transmembrane current, there is no potential across the resistor, so the transmembrane potential is the same as the battery. If there is, for instance, outward resistive current, it produces a potential across the resistor, the inside relatively positive to the outside, which subtracts from the potential of the battery. During a propagated action potential, the current flow across the resistor, the value of the resistor, and the membrane battery are all changing. The potential from the battery is by far the most important in this case. There is an inward current at the most depolarized (most inside positive) parts of the action potential that hyperpolarizes the membrane over what it would be if there were no current flow, but this is a minor effect.

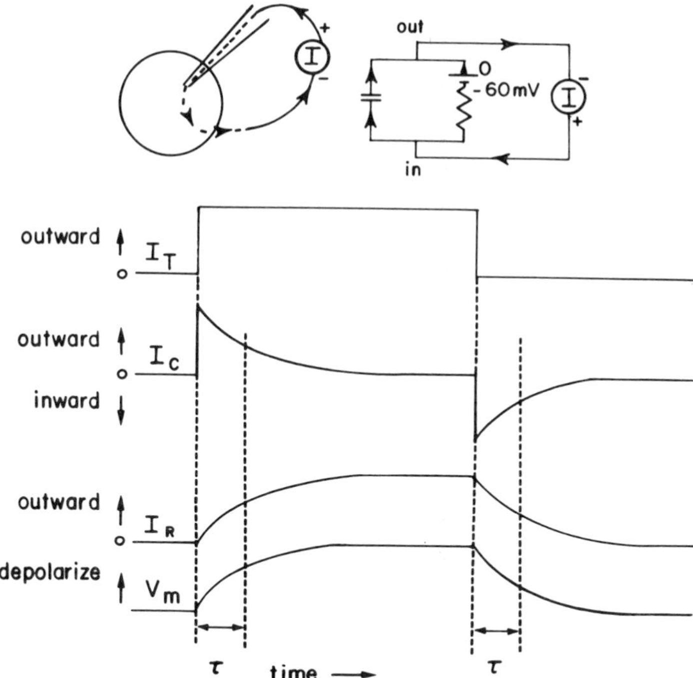

FIG. 18. Resistive and capacitative current flow across a cell while passing a pulse of current. τ is the time constant of the membrane; see text for details.

Consider the case of a microelectrode in a cell passing a pulse of constant outward current across the cell membrane for a short time. (Current, of course, is passing inward through the microelectrode, but we will consider only the current across the cell membrane; see Fig. 18.) Let us assume that there are no changes in the permeability of the membrane to any ions and that the membrane resistance can be considered constant, assumptions that will be true for small changes in potential. Before the current starts to flow, there is no resistive or capacitative current, and the transmembrane potential is at, say, -60 mV.

At the very first instant that the current starts to flow, all the current is capacitative current, for the transmembrane potential has not yet changed, so there is no potential to drive ions across the cell membrane. As the capacitative current charges up the membrane capacity, the transmembrane potential changes and some resistive current flows, so less of the net current is left to charge up the membrane capacity. Eventually all the current is resistive current, and the transmembrane potential does not change at all.

When the current is turned off, the extra charge on the membrane capacity flows through the membrane resistance until the potential returns to its resting potential.

The equation describing the potential when the current goes on is

$$\Delta V_{\mathrm{m}} = V_{\mathrm{m}} - V_{\mathrm{rest}} = I_T r_{\mathrm{m}} (1 - \exp(-t/r_{\mathrm{m}}c_{\mathrm{m}})),$$

where ΔV_{m} is the change from resting transmembrane potential in volts, V_{m} is transmembrane potential in volts, V_{rest} is the resting transmembrane potential in volts, I_T is the current passed in amperes, r_{m} is the total membrane resistance of the cell in ohms, c_{m} is the total membrane capacity of the cell in farads, and t is time in seconds.

The equation describing the potential when the current is turned off is

$$\Delta V_{\mathrm{m}} = V_{\mathrm{m}} - V_{\mathrm{rest}} = V_m^* \exp(-t/r_{\mathrm{m}}c_{\mathrm{m}}),$$

where V_m^* is the change from resting potential that existed at the instant that the current was turned off. The quantity $r_{\mathrm{m}}c_{\mathrm{m}}$ is called the *time constant,* and the units are in seconds. It takes one time constant to charge up the membrane to 63% of its steady-state value of V_{m} when a constant pulse of current is turned on, and one time constant for V_{m} to fall to 37% when the potential is turned off.

Appendix II: Current Flow in the Brain

When considering current flow through the brain, it is useful to think of the brain as packed cables, which run in different directions in different parts of the brain. The cables are cells, in particular, nerve fibers and glial processes. The current can flow in the interstitial space of the brain and also through cables (cells), the nerve fibers, and glial processes. The relative amounts of current that flow through cells vary in different parts of the brain, with different directions of current flow and with time.

When a pulse of current flows in the brain, at the very first instant in time, current will flow freely across the membrane capacity. It is impossible to get a perfect, instaneously discontinuous pulse of current, but for pulses that rise in times much shorter than the time constant of the cell membranes involved (50 μsec for myelinated fibers and a few msec for cell bodies and dendrites), this is not a bad approximation. For times much shorter than the time constant of the cell membrane, a lot of current will flow through the cell. At times longer than the time constant of the cell membrane, the dc case holds. However, even though a lot of current may flow through cells in the earliest stage of a pulse, this will not cause much change in the transmembrane potential of the cell (see Section II, Cases 4 and 5). Therefore, this early current is not of much interest to us if we are concerned with electrical stimulation that requires a change in transmembrane voltage.

At times of the order of a time constant of a membrane and longer, significant amounts of current flow only in the longitudinal direction of a fiber or process (Fig. 9). This means that the current will flow through a fiber only to the extent that it is oriented in the direction of the voltage gradient of the system. Ranck (1963b) has shown that if fibers are randomly oriented, one can consider current to be flowing through one-third of them (i.e., as if one-third were oriented in the direction of overall current flow and the other two-thirds normal to the direction of current flow and carry no current at all).

In cases where all the fibers run in the same direction, as in a tract of white matter, current will flow in fibers when current is flowing in the direction of the fibers. However, no current will flow through fibers when current is flowing perpendicular to the direction of the fibers. This means that the tissue has different resistivities in different directions; therefore, it is anisotropic (Ranck & BeMent, 1965). (A substance that has the same resistance in all directions, like most substances, is called isotropic.)

The proportion of current that flows inside cells and that which flows in the interstitial space vary depending on the orientation of fibers and direction of current flow. When all the fibers have the same orientation and current flows in the same direction as the fibers, perhaps as much as three-quarters of the current may flow inside the fibers. When current flows normal to fiber direction, no current will flow inside the cells. Where there are fibers and processes in all directions, as is the case in most gray matter, most of the current probably flows in the interstitial space, but perhaps one-fourth will flow through fibers and processes. (A lot of the uncertainty in these proportions is due to the uncertainties in the size of the interstitial space.)

The current that flows in fibers and processes is flowing in the cell as a cable. This means that the current enters over distances of the order of a length constant of the fiber. The length constant of most fibers is between 75 and 500 μm. When considering current flow over distances shorter than this, not much current flows in cells; therefore, over short distances the resistivity of brain is greater than over longer distances.

Both the interstitial space and the cytoplasm of cells is a purely resistive media (over the frequencies and current strengths of interest to us). However, the resistivity of cytoplasm is perhaps two to four times greater than that of interstitial fluid.

Bennett (1969) has shown that the pia mater has a resistance of 50–100 Ω cm^2 and a time constant of 3.0 msec. This resistance and capacitance is destroyed by a few minutes of exposure to air. I know of no cases of stimulation in which this has been taken into consideration.

The cerebrospinal fluid (CSF) has a much lower resistivity than the brain, about one-sixth that of gray matter at dc. This means that near ventricular or pial surfaces CSF will have a substantial effect on current flow. The exact patterns have not been experimentally or theoretically well-studied.

While white matter is anisotropic, gray matter is isotropic with a resistivity greater than white matter in the direction of the fibers and a resistivity less than white matter normal to the direction of fibers in white matter. Cerebrospinal fluid has a low resistivity. In a real case, this can lead to complicated patterns of current flow. Most real cases of interest have not been studied.

One must not forget that peripheral nerves run in the meninges. When stimulating electrodes are close to a meningeal surface, those peripheral nerves, which include fibers subserving pain, may be stimulated. This is probably unlikely in most cases, because the low resistance cerebrospinal fluid separates the brain from the arachnoid.

References

Abzug, C., Maeda, M., Peterson, B. W., & Wilson, V. J. Cervical branching of lumbar vestibulospinal axons. *Journal of Physiology (London),* 1974, **243,** 499–522.

Andersen, P., Silfvenius, H., Sundberg, S. H., Sveen, O., & Wigstrom, H. Functional characteristics of unmyelinated fibres in the hippocampal cortex. *Brain Research,* 1978, **144,** 11–18.

Asanuma, H., & Arnold, A. P. Noxious effects of excessive currents used for intracortical microstimulation. *Brain Research,* 1975, **96,** 103–107.

Asanuma, H., Arnold, A., & Zarzecki, P. Further study on the excitation of pyramidal tract cells by intracortical microstimulation. *Experimental Brain Research,* 1976, **26,** 443–461.

Bean, C. P. A theory of microstimulation of myelinated fibers. Appendix to C. Abzug, M. Maeda, P. W. Peterson, and V. J. Wilson. Cervical branching of lumbar vestibulospinal axons. *Journal of Physiology (London),* 1974, **243,** 499–522.

BeMent, S. L., & Ranck, J. B., Jr. A quantitative study of electrical stimulation of central myelinated fibers with monopolar electrodes. *Experimental Neurology,* 1969, **24,** 147–170. (a)

BeMent, S. L., and Ranck, J. B., Jr. A model for electrical stimulation of central myelinated fibers with monopolar electrodes. *Experimental Neurology,* 1969, **24,** 171–186. (b)

Bennett, M. V. L. Electrical impedance of brain surfaces. *Brain Research,* 1969, **15,** 584–590.

Bodian, D. A note on nodes of Ranvier in the central nervous system. *Journal of Comparative Neurology,* 1951, **94,** 475–483.

Burke, R. E. The effect of stimulation rate and pattern on synaptic transmission in the mammalian central nervous system. In F. T. Hambrecht & J. B. Reswick (Eds.), *Functional electrical stimulation.* New York: Dekker, 1977. Pp. 367–376.

Chung, S.-H., Raymond, S. A., & Lettvin, J. Y. Multiple meaning in single visual units. *Brain, Behavior and Evolution,* 1970, **3,** 72–101.

Clendenin, M., Ekerst, C.-F., Oscarsson, O., & Rosen, I. The lateral reticular nucleus in the cat. I. Mossy fibre distribution in cerebellar cortex. *Experimental Brain Research,* 1974, **21,** 473–486.

Coons, E. E., Schupf, N., & Ungerleider, L. G. Uses of double-pulse stimulation behaviorally to infer refractoriness, summation, convergence, and transmitter characteristics of hypothalamic reward systems. *Journal of Comparative and Physiological Psychology,* 1976, **90,** 317–342.

Deutsch, J. A. Behavioral measurement of the neural refractory period and its application to intracranial self-stimulation. *Journal of Comparative and Physiological Psychology,* 1964, **58,** 1–9.

Edmonds, D. E., Stellar, J. R., & Gallistel, C. R. Parametric analysis of brain stimulation reward in the rat. II. Temporal summation in the reward system. *Journal of Comparative and Physiological Psychology,* 1974, **87,** 860–869.

Fertziger, A. L., & Ranck, J. B., Jr. Potassium accumulation in interstitial space in epileptiform seizures. *Experimental Neurology,* 1970, **26,** 571–585.

Freeman, J. An electronic stimulus artifact suppressor. *Electroencephalography and Clinical Neurophysiology,* 1971, **31,** 170–172.

Fuller, J. H., & Schlag, J. D. Determination of antidromic excitation by the collision test: Problems of interpretation. *Brain Research,* 1976, **112,** 283–298.

Gallistel, C. R., Stellar, J. R., & Bubis, E. Parametric analysis of brain stimulation reward in the rat. I. The transient process and the memory-containing process. *Journal of Comparative and Physiological Psychology,* 1974, **87,** 848–859.

Gustafsson, B., & Jankowska, E. Direct and indirect activation of nerve cells by electrical pulses applied extracellularly. *Journal of Physiology (London),* 1976, **258,** 33–61.

Havstad, J. W. *Electrical impedance of cerebral cortex: An experimental and theoretical investigation.* Ph.D. thesis, Stanford University, 1976.

Henneman, E., Somjen, G., & Carpenter, D. O. Functional significance of cell size in spinal motoneurons. *Journal of Neurophysiology,* 1965, **28,** 560–580.

Hess, A., & Young, J. Z. Correlation of internodal length and fibre diameter in the central nervous system. *Nature (London),* 1949, **164,** 490–491.

Jack, J. J. B., Noble, D., & Tsien, R. W. *Electric current flow in excitable cells.* London & New York: Oxford University Press, 1975.

Li, C. L., & Bak, A. Excitability characteristics of the A- and C- fibers in a peripheral nerve. *Experimental Neurology,* 1976, **50,** 67–79.

Marks, W. B. Polarization changes of simulated cortical neurons caused by electrical stimulation at the cortical surface. In F. T. Hambrecht & J. B. Reswick (Eds.), *Functional electrical stimulation.* New York: Dekker, 1977. Pp. 413–430.

Matthews, G. Neural substrate for brain stimulation reward in the rat: Cathodal and anodal strength-duration properties. *Journal of Comparative and Physiological Psychology,* 1977, **91,** 858–874.

McNeal, D. R., Analysis of a model for excitation of myelinated nerve. *IEEE Transactions on Biomedical Engineering,* 1976, **BME-23,** 329–337.

Merrill, E. G., Wall, P. D., and Yaksh, T. Y. Properties of two unmyelinated fibre tracts of the central nervous system: lateral Lissauer tract and parallel fibers of the cerebellum. *Journal of Physiology* (London), 1978, **284,** 127–145.

Nicholson, C., & Freeman, J. A. Theory of current source-density analysis and determination of conductivity tensor for anuran cerebellum. *Journal of Neurophysiology,* 1975, **38,** 356–368.

Rall, W. Core conduction theory and cable properties of neurons. In J. M. Brookhart, V. B. Mountcastle, & E. R. Kandel (Eds.), *Handbook of physiology* (Sect. I, Vol. I, Pt. 1). Bethesda, Md: American Physiological Society, 1977. Pp. 39–98.

Ranck, J. B., Jr. Specific impedance of rabbit cerebral cortex. *Experimental Neurology,* 1963, **7,** 144–152. (a)

Ranck, J. B., Jr. Analysis of specific impedance of rabbit cerebral cortex. *Experimental Neurology,* 1963, **7,** 153–174. (b)

Ranck, J. B., Jr. Which elements are excited in electrical stimulation of mammalian central nervous system: A review. *Brain Research,* 1975, **98,** 417–440.

Ranck, J. B., Jr., & BeMent, S. L. The specific impedance of the dorsal columns of cat: An anisotropic medium. *Experimental Neurology,* 1965, **11,** 451–463.

Roby, R. J., & Lettich, E. A simplified circuit for stimulus artifact suppression. *Electroencephalography and Clinical Neurophysiology,* 1975, **39,** 85–87.

Wall, P. D. Excitability changes in afferent fibre terminations and their relation to slow potentials. *Journal of Physiology (London),* 1958, **142,** 1–21.

Waxman, S. G., & Swadlow, H. A. The conduction properties of axons in central white matter. *Progress in Neurobiology,* 1977, **8,** 297–324.

Woody, C. D., Knispel, J. D., Crow, T. J., & Black-Cleworth, P. A. Activity and excitability to electrical current of cortical auditory receptive neurons of awake cats as affected by stimulus association. *Journal of Neurophysiology,* 1976, **39,** 1045–1061.

Chapter 2

Intracellular Stimulation

John H. Byrne

Department of Physiology
School of Medicine
University of Pittsburgh
Pittsburgh, Pennsylvania

I. Introduction

Over the past 40 years, a tremendous increase in the understanding of the nervous system has occurred on two parallel levels. On one level there has been an increase in the understanding of the circuit properties of the nervous system—how individual neurons are interconnected to process information and generate various behaviors. On the second level,

ISBN 0-12-547440-7

there has been an increase in the understanding of the functions of the neuron itself—the biophysical mechanisms that underlie its electrical activity and integrative action. To a large extent, progress in these areas is due to the development of intracellular recording techniques, which in turn were made possible by the development of the glass capillary microelectrode by Graham and Gerard (1946). With these electrodes it became possible to monitor the intracellular potential of individual neurons and to record their response to natural sensory input and to electrical stimulation of afferent and efferent nerves (see Chapter 1). It soon became evident, however, that intracellular recordings gave only a limited view of the role individual neurons were playing in the concert of the nervous system. The activity of individual neurons could be correlated with various behaviors, but by recordings alone it was not possible to determine the quantitative contribution that each cell makes to the total behavior. Ideally, one would not only like to record the activity of individual neurons, but also systematically alter their activity to see how an individual cell contributes to any given behavior or information-processing step in the nervous system.

Parallel studies on the biophysical properties of neurons indicated the necessity of precisely controlling the membrane potential of individual neurons since most properties of nerve cells are dependent in some way on the membrane potential itself. For example, the initiation of an action potential is dependent upon the membrane potential reaching a critical level of depolarization (threshold), and the sign and effectiveness of synaptic potentials are dependent on the membrane potential. Thus, in order to study these biophysical phenomena in nerve cells, one must be able to systematically alter the membrane potential of the individual neuron under investigation. The development of intracellular stimulating techniques permitted an examination of the voltage-dependent biophysical properties of a neuron while at the same time providing a means of altering the ongoing activity of a neuron in order to assess its role in the generation of behavior. The purpose of this chapter is to give an introductory review of intracellular stimulation techniques for neurobiologists who have not had prior experience with electronic circuits and instrumentation. Previous reviews by Frank and Becker (1964), Dichter (1973), and Fein (1977) may also be useful.

II. Intracellular Stimulating and Recording with Separate Electrodes

As will be seen, there are a variety of methods available for intracellular stimulation, but in principle one of the simplest methods commonly utilized to alter the membrane potential of individual neurons is to impale the cell with two microelectrodes: one for recording the membrane potential and the other for stimulation. This arrangement is illustrated in Fig. 1a. The intracellular electrode on the right is connected to an appropriate high-input resistance amplifier system that records the membrane potential. The second electrode on the left is then connected to a suitable current source. The details of the biophysical events underlying a cell's response to an applied current are rather complex and will not be described here (for review, see Katz, 1966). As a first approximation, however, an unexcited neuron can be considered to act as a simple resistor in series with a battery. The battery represents the potential difference between the inside and outside of the neuron, which is primarily due to a concentration difference of potassium between the inside and outside of the cell and a high resting permeability to potassium ions (for details, see Katz, 1966). The resistor represents the membrane resistance, which is due to the cell's resting permeability to ions, that is, the ability of ions to move across the cell membrane. Using this simple neuron model and the diagram of Fig. 1a, the complete equivalent electrical circuit for the experimental preparation of Fig. 1a can be redrawn as illustrated in Fig. 1b. The membrane resistance is R_m, and the resting potential (E_m) is represented by the 60 mV battery in series with R_m. R_{re} is the resistance of the recording electrode, which is connected to the input amplifier, and R_{se} is the resistance of the stimulating electrode, which is connected to the current source. Throughout this chapter, it will be assumed that the input resistance of the recording amplifier is much higher than the electrode and membrane resistance. As a result, no current flows through the recording amplifier (see Brown, Maxfield, & Moraff, 1973, for recording techniques) and the right-hand side of the circuit can be neglected. There is a simple series circuit to the left consisting of the current source, the stimulating electrode resistance, the membrane resistance, and the membrane battery. Thus, by a suitable setting of the current generator, current can be passed across the cell membrane resistance creating a potential difference across that resistance given by Ohm's law ($\Delta V_{R_m} = I \times R_m$, assuming the membrane resistance is constant). This potential difference will be equal to the change in the membrane potential as seen via the recording electrode.

The major practical consideration with this circuit is that the resistance of the current source (an ideal current source has infinite resistance) must be much greater than the membrane resistance. Otherwise, the current source will load down the cell and cause the membrane potential and changes in the membrane potential recorded to be attenuated. To examine these loading or attenuating effects of a nonideal current source, consider Fig. 1c. In this circuit the current source has a finite resistance

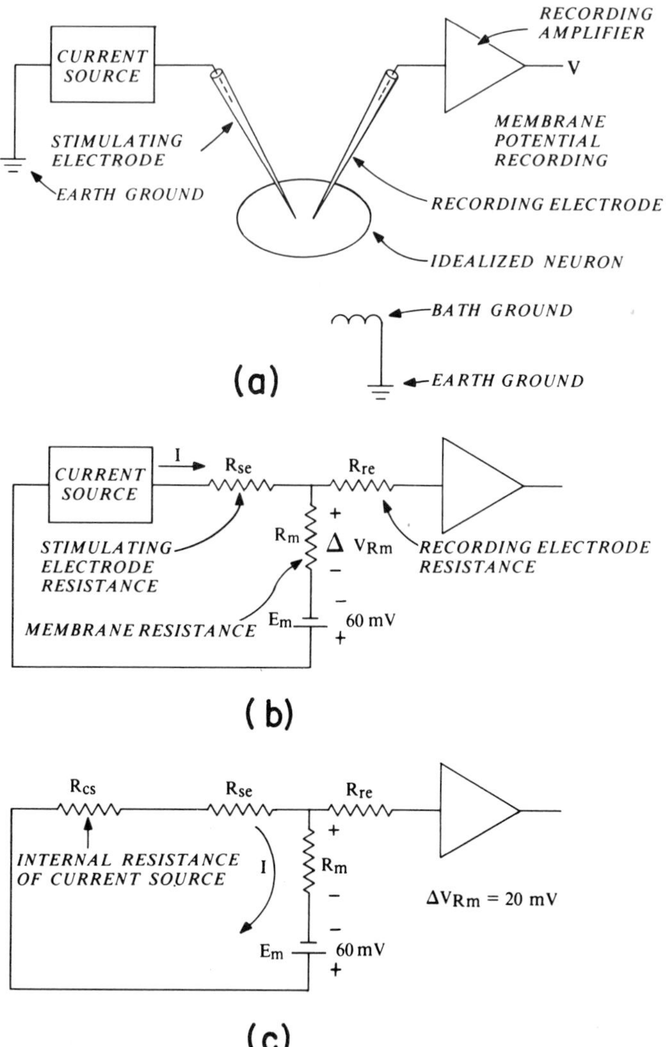

FIG. 1. Intracellular stimulation and recording with separate electrodes. (a) A schematic diagram of a typical experimental arrangement is illustrated here. A neuron is impaled with two microelectrodes; one for recording the intracellular potential and the other for passing current. The stimulating electrode is connected to a constant current generator while the recording electrode is connected to a high-input resistance recording amplifier. (b) An equivalent electrical circuit diagram of the experimental arrangement in part (a) is shown here. As a first approximation, an excitable membrane can be considered as a membrane resistance (R_m) in series with a potential (E_m), which represents the potential generated by the concentration difference of potassium ions across the cell. The circuit also includes equivalent resistances for the stimulating (R_{se}) and recording (R_{re}) electrodes. (c) An equivalent circuit diagram illustrating loading effects of a current source with finite internal resistance. The current source internal resistance is represented by R_{cs}. Even though the current source is unenergized, its internal resistance offers a path for current flow from the cell to ground.

(R_{cs}). For the sake of the analysis, assume the current source internal resistance is 1 megohm (1 MΩ = 10^6 ohm), the stimulating electrode resistance 1 MΩ, and the membrane resistance also 1 MΩ. Even though the current source is unenergized, its internal resistance forms a pathway for current from the cell to ground. For any loop circuit of the type illustrated in Fig. 1c, the sum of the voltage drops around the loop produced by the current must equal zero. Using this conservation law and Ohm's law:

$$0 = I \times R_{cs} + I \times R_{se} + I \times R_m - 60. \tag{1}$$

Solving for I,

$$I = 60/(R_{cs} + R_{se} + R_m). \tag{2}$$

There will be a current flowing in the loop as long as the resistance of the current source is finite. For the values given,

$$I = 60 \text{ mV}/3 \text{ M}\Omega \doteq 20 \text{ nA}, \tag{3}$$

where

$$1 \text{ nA} = 10^{-9}\text{A} \qquad 1 \text{ mV} = 10^{-3}\text{V}.$$

The voltage drop across the membrane resistance as a result of the loading of the current source will be

$$\begin{aligned} \Delta V_{R_m} &= \text{I} \times R_m \\ &= (20 \text{ nA}) \times (1 \text{ M}\Omega) \\ &= 20 \text{ mV}. \end{aligned} \tag{4}$$

Thus, the recording circuit will record a voltage across the cell of $-60 + 20$ mV, or -40 mV. The current source has led to an attenuation of the membrane potential by 20 mV.

By combining Eqs. 2 and 4, a more general form of the attenuation produced by a current source of finite resistance can be obtained. From Eq. 4,

$$\Delta V_{R_m} = I \times R_m,$$

but from Eq. 2,

$$\text{I} = Em/(R_{cs} + R_{se} + R_m).$$

Thus,

$$\Delta V_{R_m} = [Em/(R_{cs} + R_{se} + R_m)] \times R_m. \tag{5}$$

By rearranging,

$$\Delta V_{R_m} = \frac{Em}{(R_{cs}/R_m) + (R_{se}/R_m) + 1}. \quad (6)$$

Ideally, the voltage drop produced by the internal resistance of a current source should be negligible. As seen in Eq. 6, this can be accomplished by making the resistance of the current source much larger than the resistance of the membrane to be stimulated. When R_{cs} is large in Eq. 6, the voltage attenuation will be small. Note that the electrode resistance could also be made a high value, but this has the unsatisfactory side effect of poor current-passing capability and unstable electrode resistance. For most practical considerations, the internal resistance of the current source should be greater than $10^9\ \Omega$.

III. A Simple Circuit for Intracellular Stimulation with Two Electrodes

The current source illustrated in Fig. 1a can be replaced by a battery or other voltage source in series with a high value resistor. Figure 2 illustrates the equivalent circuit for this simple scheme for passing constant current into a cell. The membrane potential battery has been eliminated to simplify the analysis. The current source is simply a battery (V_{bat}) with a high resistance (R_{cs}) in series with it. As long as the value of R_{cs} is larger (by a factor of 100 to 1000) than the membrane resistance, no significant attenuation of the membrane potential occurs (see Eq. 6). In Fig. 2, the current supplied by the stimulating circuit will simply equal

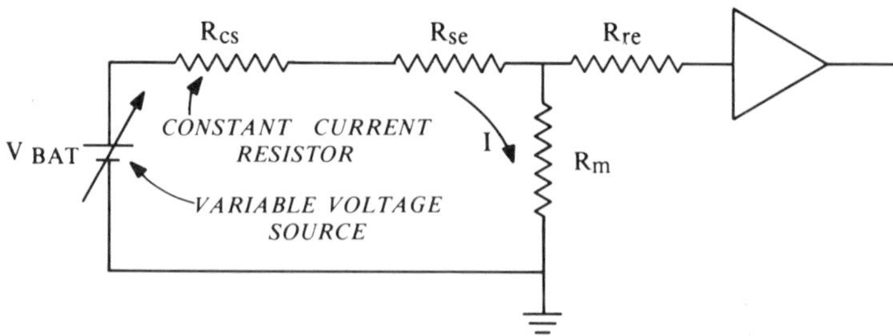

FIG. 2. A simple constant current generator circuit. A constant current can be generated by placing a high-value resistor (R_{cs}) in series with a battery. As long as the membrane (R_m) and stimulating electrode resistance (R_{se}) are much less than the constant current resistor (R_{cs}), the current into the cell will simply be determined by the value of the stimulating battery divided by the value of the constant current resistor.

$$I = V_{bat}/(R_{cs} + R_{se} + R_m). \quad (7)$$

Note that as long as the series resistor (R_{cs}) is large compared to the electrode and membrane resistance, the current is simply a function of the stimulating battery and series current resistor. The electrode and membrane resistances can vary, but the stimulating current will be constant as long as the variations do not approach the value of the series resistor (R_{cs}). In essence, the circuit is a constant current generator, and for this reason the large series resistor (R_{cs}) is sometimes referred to as a constant current resistor.

Because of the small size of many neurons and the inability to visualize their location, it is often impossible to impale a single cell with two electrodes as illustrated in Fig. 1. A convenient compromise is to use a double-barreled microelectrode (Mendelson, 1967). Such an electrode consists of two single electrodes fused together, so that both tips are in close apposition to each other. The double electrode can then be used to impale a cell as if it were a single barrel, but now one barrel can be connected to the recording amplifier and the second connected to the current source. One disadvantage, however, is that there is often some coupling between barrels so some artifacts are produced in the recording electrode when current flows through the stimulating barrel (Tomita, 1962).

IV. Intracellular Stimulation and Recording with a Single Electrode

A. *The Passive Circuit*

1. Equivalent Circuit

In many instances the small size of individual neurons prevents even the use of double-barreled microelectrodes for stimulation and recordings. In such situations, stimulation and recording can be accomplished by using only a single electrode. This basic scheme originally developed by Araki and Otani (1955) is now widely utilized for intracellular stimulation and recording from small neurons. A circuit that permits simultaneous recordings and stimulation through a single electrode is illustrated in Fig. 3a. The idealized nerve cell is impaled with a single electrode, which is in turn connected on the right side to a recording amplifier and on the left to a constant current generator consisting of a voltage source (V_{bat}) and a constant current resistor (R_{cs}). The circuit at first glance seems like a simple and straightforward way of intracellular

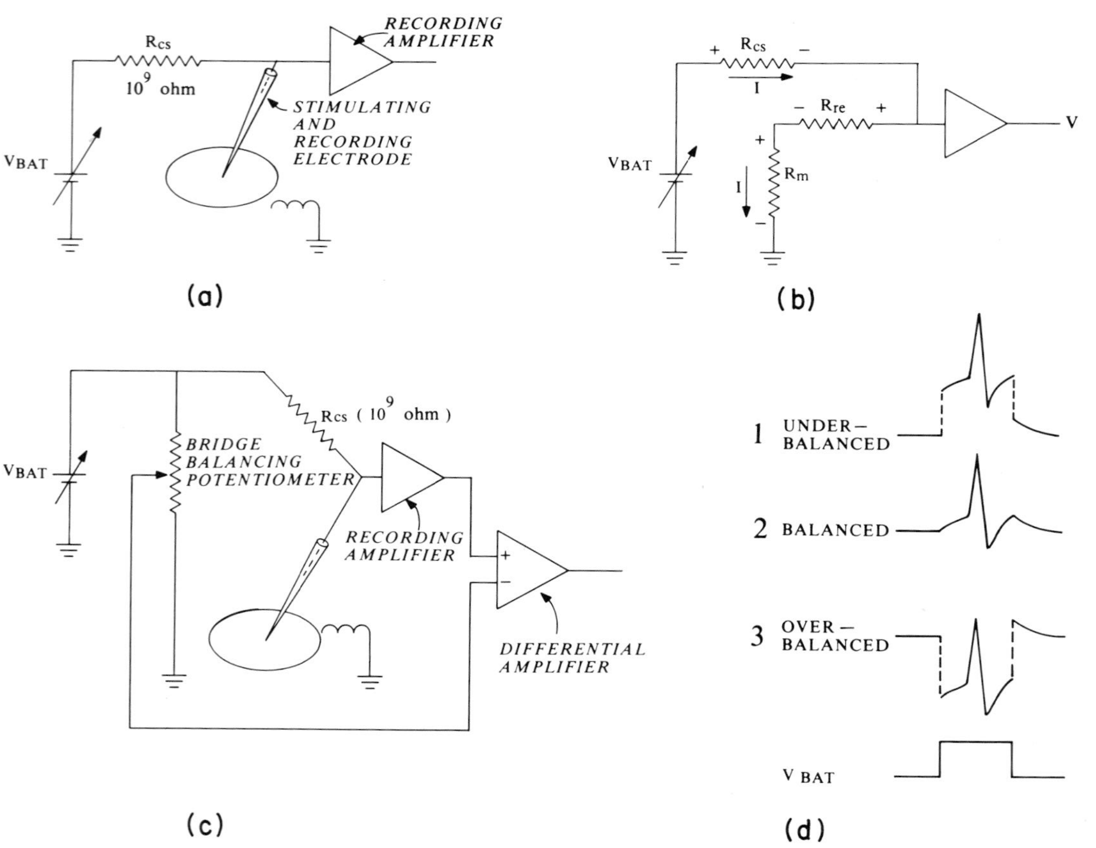
RECORDING AMPLIFIER
Rcs
10^9 ohm
STIMULATING AND RECORDING ELECTRODE
VBAT
(a)
Rcs
I
Rre
Rm
VBAT
V
(b)
Rcs (10^9 ohm)
BRIDGE BALANCING POTENTIOMETER
VBAT
RECORDING AMPLIFIER
DIFFERENTIAL AMPLIFIER
(c)
1 UNDER-BALANCED
2 BALANCED
3 OVER-BALANCED
V BAT
(d)

recording and stimulation. The equivalent circuit of Fig. 3b seems similar to that of the circuit for the two-electrode configuration (Fig. 2), but there is one critical and important difference. The highmegohm constant current resistor (R_{cs}) is connected to the amplifier side of the recording electrode (R_{re}), not to the cell side as previously illustrated in Fig. 2. What this means is that current flowing out of the stimulating pathway will cause a voltage drop across the recording electrode resistance given by $\Delta V_{R_{re}} = I \times R_{re}$. Thus, in addition to the voltage drop across the membrane (which we want to record), one also records an undesirable voltage drop across the electrode resistance. For example, let the recording electrode resistance and membrane resistance equal 1 MΩ. If a 10 nA current is passed, 10 mV will be produced across the cell, and an additional 10 mV drop will be produced across the electrode resistance. The recording amplifier records a net drop of 20 mV, but the membrane potential has actually changed only by 10 mV.

2. Balancing the Bridge

In principle, a rather simple means of eliminating the artifact induced in the recording system by the voltage drop across the electrode resistance is to subtract a potential from the recorded signal, which is equal

---

Fig. 3. Intracellular stimulating and recording with a single microelectrode: Passive method. (a) This is a simplified schematic diagram of the experimental preparation. A single microelectrode is connected to the recording amplifier and also to one side of a high-value constant current resistor. The other side of the resistor is connected to a suitable voltage source (V_{bat}). (b) An equivalent electrical circuit for the experiment configuration illustrated in part (a) is shown here. There is a series pathway from the stimulating battery to the constant current resistor (R_{cs}), the recording electrode resistance (R_{re}), and the membrane resistance (R_m). Note that the current generated produces a voltage drop across the membrane resistance as well as an undesirable voltage drop across the recording electrode resistance. (c) Shown here is a typical bridge circuit for balancing out the undesirable potential drop across the recording electrode resistance. The voltage source (V_{bat}) is not only connected to the constant current resistor (R_{cs}) as in part (a), but also to the upper arm of a bridge balancing potentiometer. The wiper of the potentiometer is adjusted so that the voltage drop across the lower portion of the potentiometer is equal to the voltage drop across the electrode resistance. (d) Typical waveforms produced by the circuit of part (c) are illustrated here. A sufficient current was generated by V_{bat} (lower trace) to fire an action potential. In the uppermost trace (d-1), there is a large step deflection that precedes the slow membrane potential changes. This deflection is due to the voltage drop across the recording electrode resistance. In the second trace (d-2), the wiper of the bridge balance potentiometer is adjusted to balance out the voltage drop across the electrode resistance. The membrane potential does not charge instantaneously with the application and removal of the stimulus due the membrane capacitance, which is not illustrated in the equivalent circuit of part (B). The third trace (d-3) illustrates the case where more voltage is dropped across the lower arm of the bridge balance potentiometer than is dropped across the electrode resistance.

to the voltage drop across the recording electrode. A simple circuit utilized for this function is illustrated in Fig. 3c. Here, the stimulating voltage pulse is fed not only to the constant current resistor, but also to one side of a bridge balancing potentiometer. The slider of the potentiometer in turn is fed to the negative input of a differential amplifier while the output of the recording amplifier is fed to the positive input of the differential amplifier. The wiper of the potentiometer is then adjusted so that the voltage drop across the potentiometer is equal to the voltage drop across the recording electrode. Typical waveforms produced with this circuit are illustrated in Fig. 3d. Here, the stimulus intensity is adjusted to generate an action potential. When the bridge potentiometer is unbalanced, there is a large positive potential superimposed on the action potential waveform that represents the voltage drop across the electrode. As the wiper arm is adjusted, the voltage drop across the electrode is counterbalanced by the voltage drop across the potentiometer. Proper balance is obtained when there is a smooth transition from the baseline to the membrane potential changes produced by the current pulse (Fig. 3d-2). Overbalance occurs when more voltage is dropped across the balance potentiometer than is dropped across the electrode (Fig. 3d-3). In this case there is actually a negative going-step deflection.

B. The Active Circuit

While the passive bridge method of recording and stimulating through a single electrode is widely utilized and extremely simple, it has two disadvantages. In cases where very high-resistance microelectrodes are utilized, the constant current resistor can attenuate the membrane potential changes (the constant current resistor must always be at least 100 to 1000 times the recording electrode resistance). In addition, in order to pass suitable current into a cell, a relatively high voltage must be utilized. To overcome these difficulties, an active circuit developed by Fein (1966) can be utilized. A simplified version is illustrated in Fig. 4a. In this circuit a current passing resistor (R_s) connected to the microelectrode is also connected to a voltage source, but the return side of the voltage source is connected to the output of the recording amplifier and not to earth ground as previously (*e.g.*, Fig. 3a). In principle, this circuit has an infinite input resistance and enables the use of smaller stimulating voltages to achieve comparable stimulating currents as for the passive circuit. To examine the operation of this circuit, consider Fig. 4b.

From a simple conservation of current, the sum of the currents at node A must balance. Thus,

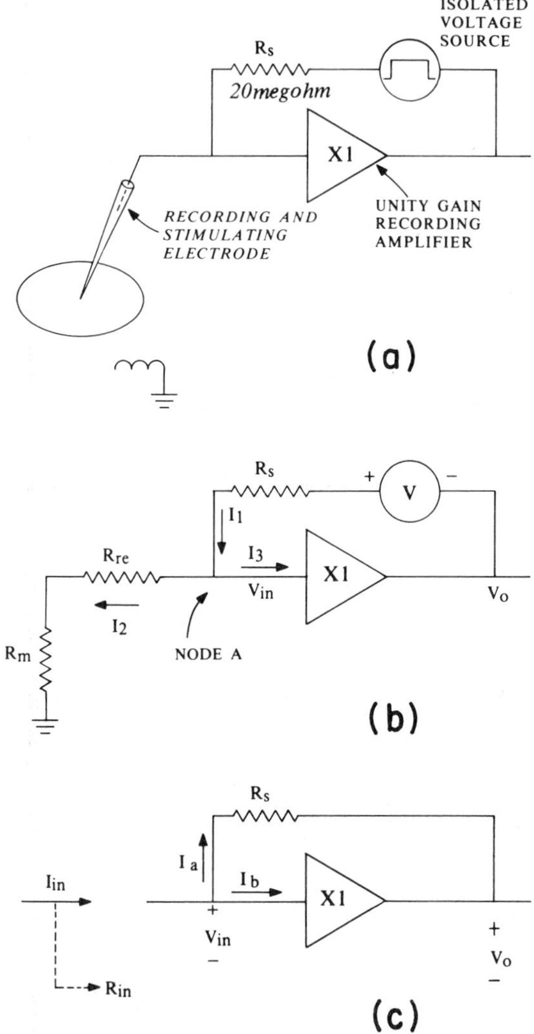

FIG. 4. Intracellular stimulating and recording with a single electrode: Active method. (a) In this schematic diagram of experimental preparation, a single microelectrode utilized for stimulation and recording is connected to a unity gain high-input resistance recording amplifier and also to a relatively low-value stimulating resistor (R_s). The other side of R_s is connected to an isolated voltage source, which is in turn connected to the output side of the unity gain recording amplifier. (b) An equivalent electrical circuit of the preparation illustrated in part (a); see text for details. (c) A method for measuring the equivalent input resistance of the recording circuit; see text for details.

$$I_1 = I_2 + I_3, \tag{8}$$

but since the recording amplifier has essentially infinite input resistance, I_3 will be negligibly small in the limit zero. Thus,

$$I_2 = I_1. \tag{9}$$

The current I_1 in the upper branch of the circuit is determined by the difference in potential across the branch divided by the resistance of the branch:

$$I_2 = (V + V_o - V_{in})/R_s. \tag{10}$$

But since the amplifier is unity-gain $V_o = V_{in}$, and

$$I_2 = V/R_s. \tag{11}$$

Thus, the current flowing into the microelectrode simply will be determined by the value of R_s and the voltage source V, and the current will be independent of the microelectrode resistance. The circuit is a constant current generator. In practice, a value of R_s of about 10 to 20 MΩ is commonly used (Fein, 1966), whereas values of the constant current resistor for the passive bridge circuits are typically 100 to 1000 MΩ. Thus, the active bridge circuits can generate currents with voltage sources 1/10 to 1/100 of those needed for comparable currents generated with the passive circuits.

As indicated earlier, one disadvantage of the passive bridge circuit was a possible attenuation introduced by the constant current resistor. The active bridge circuit essentially offers no attenuation of the neural signal or resting potential because in principle it has an infinite resistance. To examine the input resistance, a small current is applied to the input side of the circuit as illustrated in Fig. 4c (the voltage source, V, has been set equal to zero to simplify the analysis). This input test current would lead to a voltage drop V_{in}. From Ohm's law, the equivalent input resistance of the circuit or the resistance the neuron will "see" will be

$$R_{in} = V_{in}/I_{in}. \tag{12}$$

Some of the test current (I_{in}) will branch into the feedback resistor R_s, and the remainder will flow into the input amplifier. But since the amplifier has essentially an infinite input resistance, I_b will equal zero and I_{in} will equal I_a. Thus,

$$R_{in} = V_{in}/I_{in} = V_{in}/I_a, \tag{13}$$

but

$$I_a = (V_{in} - V_0)/R_s \tag{14}$$

since the input amplifier is unity-gain $V_{in} = V_o$, and $I_a = 0$. Thus,

$$R_{in} = V_{in}/0 = \infty. \tag{15}$$

Thus an important feature of the active bridge circuit is that its equivalent input resistance is infinite.

While the active bridge circuit has a number of advantages over the passive bridge circuit, it is of critical importance for its proper operation that the gain of the input amplifier be unity. Like the passive circuit, the active circuit utilizes a single electrode for stimulating and recording. Thus, as with the passive circuit, an undesirable voltage is dropped across the recording electrode by the stimulating current. This voltage must be removed by a balancing circuit similar to that used for the passive circuit in Fig. 3c (See also Fein, 1966.)

C. *The Chopped Current Clamp*

The two previous methods of stimulating and recording with a single electrode have the disadvantage of an undesirable voltage drop produced across the recording electrode that must be balanced out with a suitable bridge circuit. While in principle it is easy to remove this artifact (Fig. 3c, d), in practice it is considerably more difficult since the electrode resistance frequently changes during the experiment and in most cases the resistance changes as current is passed through it. With the chopped current method developed by Brennecke and Lindemann (1971) the necessity of a bridge circuit to balance the voltage drop across the electrode is eliminated. Figure 5 is a simplified diagram of this mode of intracellular stimulating and recording. The essential idea behind this circuit is to use a single electrode for recording and stimulating but not simultaneously. The electrode is switched rapidly between a recording mode and a stimulating mode with a chopper circuit. This type of operation is possible since in addition to the membrane resistance, there is an inherent membrane capacitance to charge or discharge. For a step current pulse, the time required for the membrane potential to change by 63% of its total change is known as the time constant (τ) and is equal to the product of the membrane resistance and membrane capacitance.

$$\tau = R_m \times C_m. \tag{16}$$

The electrode resistance, on the other hand, essentially has no parallel capacitance. Thus, the voltage drop across it, produced by the current pulse, changes instantaneously with the stimulating pulse onset or removal. To exploit these differences, one can polarize the membrane not with a single square pulse but with a train of brief pulses (Fig. 5b).

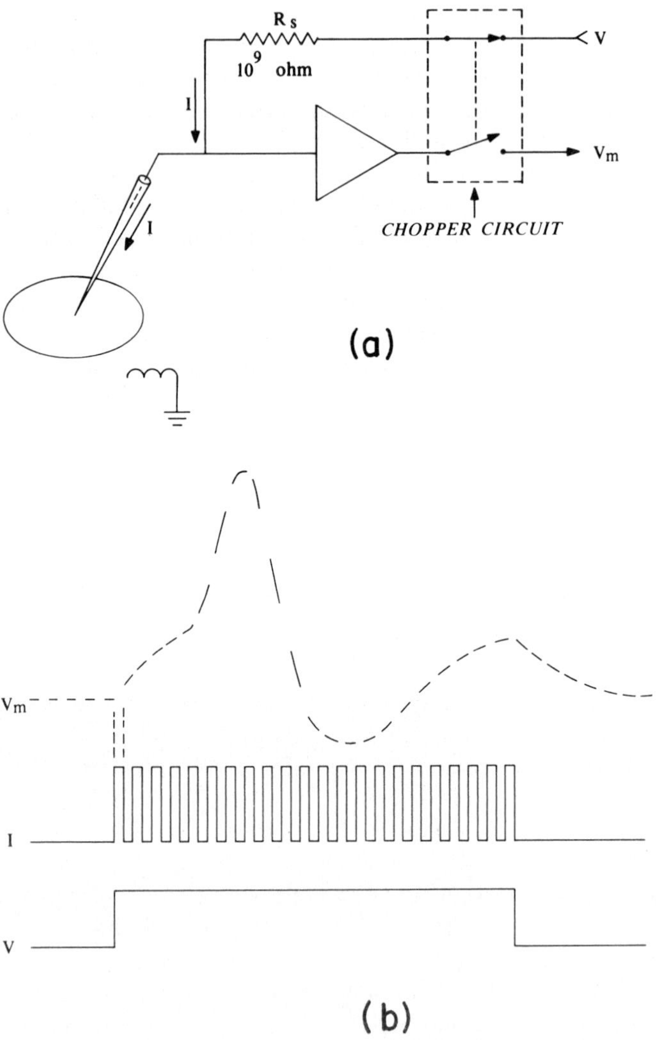

FIG. 5. The chopped current clamp method of stimulating and recording from a single microelectrode. (a) This schematic diagram of the experimental preparation shows that the current to polarize the cell is generated by voltage source V in conjunction with the constant current resistor R_s. A chopper circuit rapidly switches the circuit between a recording and stimulating mode. (b) Typical waveforms are produced when a neuron is stimulated with sufficient current to generate an action potential. Note that when the stimulating pulse is delivered, the recording circuit is disabled. In this way, the voltage drop produced by the current flowing across the electrode resistance is not recorded.

Membrane potential is measured during the interval between the pulses when the voltage drop across the electrode resistance is zero but while the membrane capacitance is only partially discharged. The major requirement of this technique is that the pulse interval be short compared to the membrane time constant. For additional details, see Brennecke and Lindemann (1971) and Wilson and Goldner (1975).

V. Current-Monitoring Techniques

Thus far I have focused on the techniques utilized for intracellular stimulation. But it is also of critical importance to know precisely the magnitude and waveshape of the current passed into the cell. The following is a review of several current monitoring techniques that are frequently utilized in conjunction with the stimulating techniques illustrated in Sections II-IV.

A. *Monitoring the Current on the Electrode Side of the Preparation*

One method of monitoring the current is to measure the voltage drop across the constant current resistor. Figure 6 illustrates one simple circuit. Each side of the constant current resistor is connected to the input of a differential amplifier. The output of the amplifier(V_c) measures the voltage drop across the resistor and if the value of the constant current resistor is known (here it is 10^9 Ω), the stimulating current simply can be calculated by Ohm's law:

$$I = V_c/R_{cs} = V_c/10^9. \tag{17}$$

The primary requirement of this configuration is that the input resistance of the differential amplifier be high compared to the resistance of the constant current resistor and the resistance of the stimulating electrode. If the input resistance of the differential amplifier is low, current will flow into the amplifier rather than into the stimulating electrode, and a false measurement of the actual current stimulating the cell will be obtained.

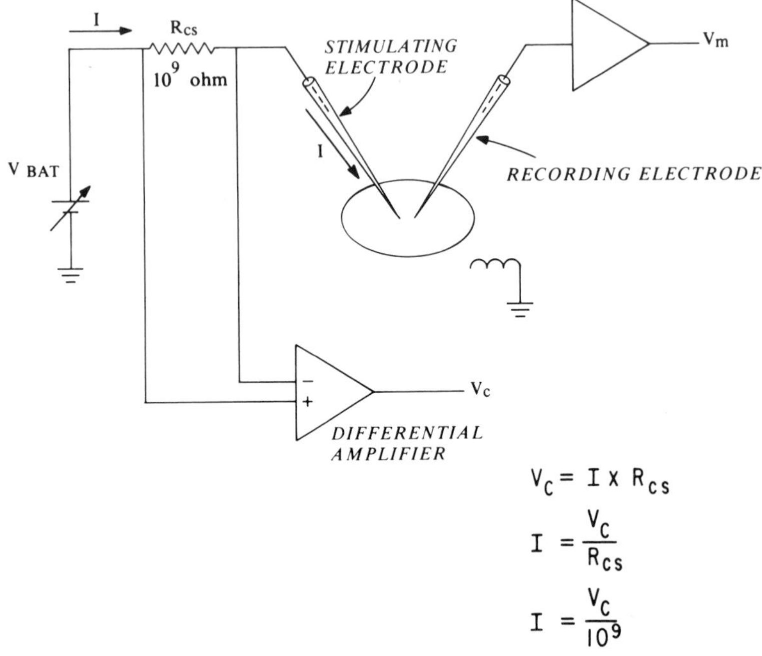

FIG. 6. Current monitoring on the electrode side of the preparation. The voltage drop across the constant current resistor can be used as a monitor of the current flowing into the stimulating electrode. The input resistance of the differential amplifier recording this voltage drop must be significantly greater than the value of R_{cs} so as not to provide an alternative pathway for current flow to ground.

B. *Monitoring the Current on the Ground Side of the Preparation*

1. Passive Method

As illustrated in Fig. 7, an alternative way of monitoring the current and avoiding the use of a high input resistance differential amplifier, is to measure the voltage drop across a resistor in the ground side of the preparation. The return path for current from the stimulating electrode is the bath or preparation ground. Therefore, the current flowing through the ground side of the preparation will be exactly equal to the current flowing through the stimulating electrode. To monitor this current on the ground side of the preparation, the connection between preparation ground and earth ground is broken and a low-value resistor (R_{cm}) is inserted. The stimulating current will produce a voltage drop across that

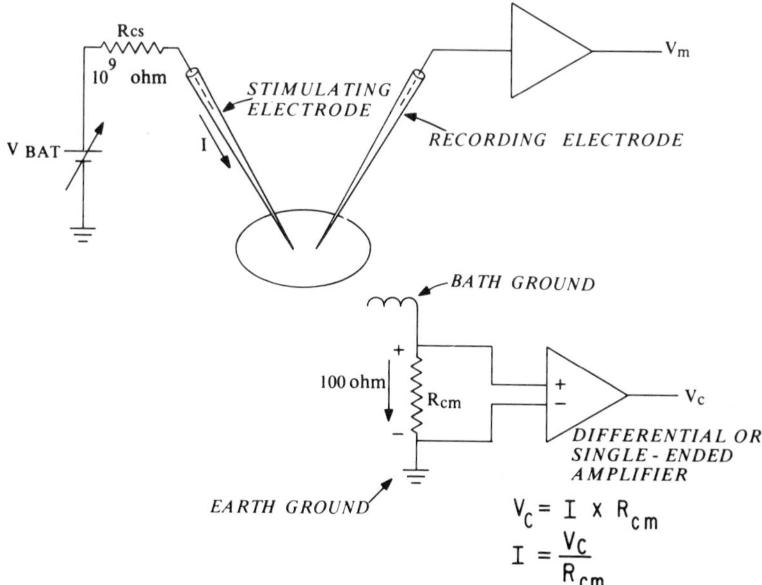

FIG. 7. Monitoring current on the ground side of the preparation: Passive method. The normal connection between bath ground and earth ground is broken, and a low-value resistor (R_{cm}) is inserted. The voltage drop across this resistor will be proportional to the current flowing from the stimulating electrode into the cell.

resistor which can then be measured by an appropriate voltmeter. In the circuit of Fig. 7, a resistor (R_{cm}) is placed in series with the preparation and earth ground. By measuring the voltage drop (V_c) across R_{cm}, the stimulating current is readily calculated.:

$$I = V_c/R_{cm}. \tag{18}$$

Note that in this configuration a differential amplifier is actually not necessary since one side of the resistor is at ground (zero potential). The major disadvantage with this scheme is that a resistance is introduced in series with the preparation. Thus, the potential (V_m) recorded as a result of stimulating the cell not only will represent the voltage across the membrane resistance, but also the voltage drop across the current monitoring resistance.

$$V_m = I \times R_m + I \times R_{cm} \tag{19}$$

$$= I \times (R_m + R_{cm}) \tag{20}$$

Thus in order that this technique not introduce an error in the membrane potential recording circuit, R_{cm} must be kept small with respect to the membrane resistance; a value as small as possible should be utilized. The limitation is that the smaller R_{cm} is made, the smaller the resultant voltage drop across it. With small voltage drops, a high-gain amplifier must be utilized to monitor the voltage drop across drop across R_{cm}. An additional complication with measuring current on the ground side of the preparation is that this method measures the total current through the preparation. If two cells are stimulated, the circuit measures the total current through both cells; it is impossible to distinguish how much current goes through each cell. In addition with this method of monitoring current, it is essential that the current monitor resistor is the only pathway from the bath or preparation ground to each ground. Frequently saline can drip from the preparation and form an alternative pathway to ground. Thus current flowing through the current monitoring resistor will not accurately reflect the total current flowing through the cell(s) stimulated.

2. Active or Virtual Ground

As mentioned above, one disadvantage with measuring the current on the ground side of the preparation is the introduction of a series resistance on the ground side. An alternative technique that partially circumvents this problem is known as a virtual ground. Figure 8 illustrates the basic scheme. The preparation ground is connected to the negative input of a operational amplifier (opamp), and the positive side of the opamp is connected to earth ground. [Operational amplifiers are used extensively in current neurophysiological instrumentation. A detailed description of their operation is beyond the scope of this paper, but the reader may find introductory accounts in Malmstadt, Enke, and Toren (1962) and Tobey, Graeme, and Husleman (1971).] Essentially, an operational amplifier is a differential amplifier with infinite gain. By the proper use of feedback circuits, one not only can constrain the gain of the circuit, but also generate circuits that perform specific signal processing functions. One such specialized circuit is known as a current-to-voltage converter (Fig. 8). To consider the operation of this circuit, it is necessary to examine the currents flowing in each of the various branches of the opamp's external circuit. Consider the currents at node A. By conservation of current,

$$I = I_1 + I_2. \tag{21}$$

But the input resistance of an ideal opamp is infinite, so no current will flow into the negative input terminal and $I_2 = 0$. Thus, $I = I_1$. Now I_1 will simply be equal to the current flowing through the feedback resistor

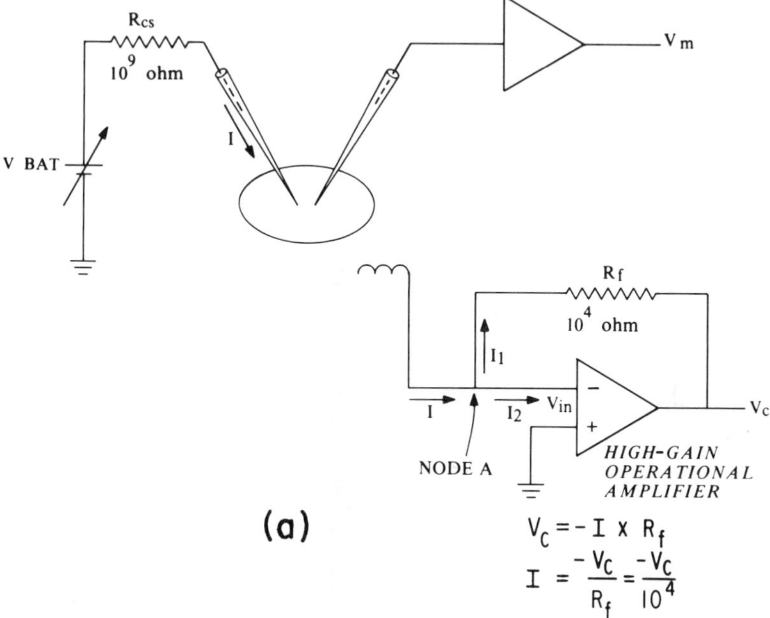

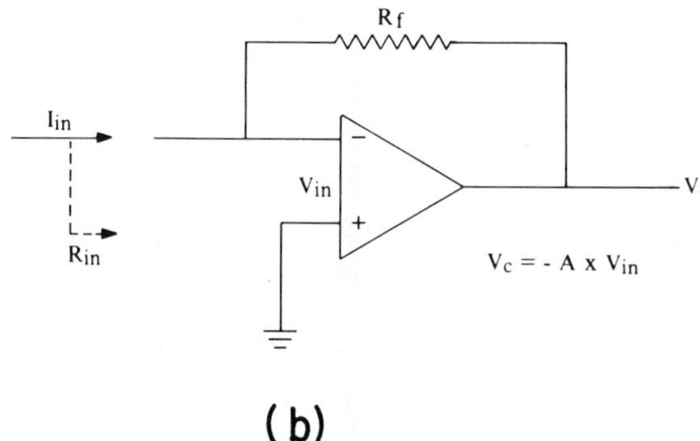

FIG. 8. Monitoring current on the ground side of the preparation: Active or virtual ground. (a) The normal connection between ground electrode in the bath and earth ground is broken, and the bath electrode is connected to the negative (inverting) input of a high-gain operational amplifier. The positive (noninverting) input of the opamp is connected to earth ground. The output voltage of the operational amplifier will be proportional to the current flowing from the stimulating electrode into the cell. This circuit accomplishes the current-to-voltage conversion with little introduction of a series resistance on the ground side of the preparation. (b) A method for measuring the equivalent input resistance of the circuit of part (a) is shown here; see text for details.

R_f, which in turn will equal the voltage drop across the resistor divided by the value of the feedback resistor.

$$I_1 = I = (V_{in} - V_c)/R_f. \tag{22}$$

But V_c and V_{in} are related by the internal amplification (A) of the opamp

$$V_c = -A \times V_{in}, \tag{23}$$

or

$$V_{in} = -V_c/A. \tag{24}$$

Thus,

$$I = \frac{(-V_c/A) - V_c}{R_f} \tag{25}$$

$$= \frac{-V_c \times (1 + 1/A)}{R_f}. \tag{26}$$

The internal amplification (A) of most opamps is greater than 100,000; therefore, for most practical purposes,

$$I = -V_c/R_f. \tag{27}$$

Thus, the stimulating current flowing through the preparation simply will be proportional to the output voltage of the opamp. The utility of the current-to-voltage converter circuit is that it provides a monitor of current without introducing significant series resistance in the ground side of the preparation. To see how this works, examine the isolated opamp circuit in Fig. 8b. To test the input resistance of this or any device, one can introduce a current to the device and measure the resultant potential change. Suppose we introduce a certain current I_{in} into the input which produces a certain voltage (V_{in}) at that input. Thus, the input resistance R_{in} will equal

$$R_{in} = V_{in}/I_{in}. \tag{28}$$

Due to the feedback configuration,

$$V_{in} = -V_c/A \tag{29}$$

$$R_{in} = \frac{-(V_c/A)}{I_{in}}, \tag{30}$$

but from Eq. 27

$$V_c = -R_f \times I_{in}. \tag{31}$$

Thus,

$$R_{in} = \frac{(R_f \times I_{in})/A}{I_{in}} = \frac{R_f}{A}. \tag{32}$$

So for a feedback resistance of 10^4 Ω and an internal opamp gain (A) of 10^4, the resistance that the current monitor circuit introduces is only 1 Ω. For the reason of its low resistance, the current-to-voltage circuit when utilized to monitor current on the ground side of the preparation is known as a virtual ground.

It should be pointed out that while the virtual ground circuit reduces the series resistance problems associated with placing a resistor in series with the preparation and earth ground, the virtual ground nevertheless still can measure only total current through the bath, and one must take care to avoid alternative current paths from preparation to earth ground.

VI. Summary

This chapter summarizes some of the various techniques utilized for intracellular stimulation. Of the various techniques given, no single technique is optimal for every situation. The simplest technique is the use of two separate electrodes, one for stimulation and the other for recording the resultant potential changes produced by the polarizing current. This technique avoids the sometimes serious problems of properly balancing the bridge circuit. However, with this technique, the cell impaled must be large and sufficiently visible to be impaled with the two electrodes. While this situation is in many cases available in invertebrate ganglia in which the individual neurons are large and on the surface (e.g., Kandel, 1976), it can rarely be achieved in vertebrate preparations. A convenient compromise is to use a double-barreled microelectrode in which the two barrels are fused so that a cell can be impaled simultaneously with the stimulating and recording electrodes. These electrodes are usually large, however, and could cause damage to small neurons.

As a result of the limitations of the use of two single electrodes or a single double-barreled electrode, one is frequently forced to turn to the use of a single microelectrode for stimulating and recording. The primary disadvantage with this technique is that the stimulating current produces a voltage drop across the electrode that in turn must be balanced out by a suitable bridge circuit. Unfortunately, the electrode resistance drifts with time and also changes as a function of the current passed through it. As a result in practice, it is extremely difficult to maintain proper bridge balance.

The chopped current clamp mode eliminates the problems with balancing the bridge, but in practice this method is best utilized for slow potential changes. As a result, the optimal intracellular stimulation technique must be decided on an individual basis depending on cell size, accessibility, and time course of the potential changes one wishes to record.

Just as there is no optimal intracellular stimulation technique, there is also no single optimal way of monitoring the resultant currents produced. In principle, the simplest method is to monitor the current on the stimulating electrode side of the preparation. The problem here is that fairly specialized circuitry must be utilized to avoid the monitoring circuit influencing the actual current delivered to the electrode. This method does have the advantage of not introducing any series resistance on the ground side of the preparation.

The most popular method used to measure the stimulating current is perhaps the virtual ground. Some series resistance is introduced, but this is generally quite small compared to the membrane resistance and resistance of the extracellular fluid. One disadvantage with this method is that it measures the total current through the preparation. Thus, if one wishes to stimulate two cells simultaneously, it is not possible with the virtual ground to determine the current passed through each cell. One means of avoiding this problem would be to utilize a virtual ground circuit to measure the total current and a current monitor on the stimulating electrode side of one of the cells. The current passed into the second cell could then be obtained by electronically subtracting the single-cell current monitor signal from the virtual-ground current monitor signal.

Acknowledgment

I would like to thank John Koester, Steve Thompson, and Susan Tritt for reviewing an earlier draft of this manuscript. This work was partially supported by NIH grants NS13511 and NS00200.

References

Araki, T., & Otani, T. Response of single motoneurons to direct stimulation in toad's spinal cord. *Journal of Neurophysiology*, 1955, **18**, 472–485.

Brennecke, R., & Lindemann, B. A chopped-current clamp for current injection and recording of membrane polarization with single electrodes of changing resistance. *TIT Journal of Life Sciences*, 1971, **1**, 53–58.

Brown, P. B., Maxfield, B. W., & Moraff, H. *Electronics for neurobiologists*. Cambridge, Mass.: MIT Press, 1973.

Dichter, M. A. Intracellular single unit recording. In R. F. Thompson & M. M. Patterson (Eds.), *Bioelectric recording techniques* (Pt. A). New York: Academic Press, 1973. Pp. 3–21.

Fein, H. Passing current through recording glass micro-pipette electrodes. *IEEE Transactions on Biomedical Engineering,* 1966, **BME-13,** 211–212.

Fein, H. *An introduction to microelectrode technique and instrumentation.* New Haven: W-P Instruments, 1977.

Frank, K., & Becker, M. Microelectrodes for recording and stimulation. In W. Nastuk (Ed.), *Physiological techniques in biological research* (Vol. 5, Pt. A). New York: Academic Press, 1964. Pp. 22–87.

Graham, J., & Gerard, R. W. Membrane potentials and excitation of impaled single muscle fibers. *Journal of Cellular and Comparative Physiology,* 1946, **28,** 99–117.

Kandel, E. R. *Cellular basis of behavior.* San Francisco: Freeman, 1976.

Katz, B. *Nerve, muscle, and synapse.* New York: McGraw-Hill, 1966.

Malmstadt, H. V., Enke, C. G., & Toren, E. C., Jr. *Electronics for scientists.* New York: Benjamin, 1962.

Mendelson, M. A simple method of fabricating double-barreled micropipette electrodes. *Journal of Scientific Instruments,* 1967, **44,** 549–550.

Tobey, G. E., Graeme, J. D., & Husleman, L. P. (Eds.). *Operational amplifiers design and applications.* New York: McGraw-Hill, 1971.

Tomita, T. A compensation circuit for coaxial and double-barreled microelectrodes. *IRE Transactions on Bio-Medical Electronics,* 1962, **BME-9,** 138–141.

Wilson, W. A., & Goldner, M. Voltage clamping with a single microelectrode. *Journal of Neurobiology,* 1975, **6,** 411–422.

Chapter 3

Microstimulation Technique

Hiroshi Asanuma

Rockefeller University
New York, New York

I. Introduction

Microstimulation technique is designed to stimulate a known group of neurons located in a small area near the electrode. The advantage of this technique is that one can stimulate and record from the same group of neurons with the same electrode. Both pipette and metal electrodes can be used for this purpose, but a metal electrode has several advantages. (*a*) The impedance is lower than pipettes, ranging from several hundred

ISBN 0-12-547440-7

kilohms to a megohm which stabilizes both stimulation and recording; (*b*) since the shaft is filled with metal wire, the electrode is free from troubles caused by tissue plug during insertion; (*c*) the shaft, especially near the tip, is harder than pipettes, and the electrode advances straightforward toward the target; (*d*) it is easier to make lesions for reconstruction of electrode tracks with the metal electrode. For these reasons, we use mainly metal electrodes for microstimulation. However, since the tip of a pipette electrode is smaller than a metal electrode, the pipette electrode is better suited for finer mapping of threshold changes along the penetration such as for revealing the fine structure of terminal axon branches (Jankowska & Roberts, 1972).

II. Electrode

The electrode must be small in diameter to avoid tissue damage while the shaft must be securely insulated from the medium to prevent the leakage of the stimulating current. For this purpose, we use a glass pipette with the tip tapered by an electrode puller and then broken to form a tip of about 10 μm outside diameter. Then, electrolytically tapered tungsten wire is inserted through the pipette until the tapered wire fits snugly into the pipette tip. The protruding tungsten wire is shortened by electrolytic etching under direct microscopic observation to form an exposed tip of the required length, usually 10–15 μm (Stoney, Thompson, & Asanuma, 1968).

a. Etching. For etching the tungsten wire tip, we use a mixed solution of 50% KCN and 30% NaOH and apply alternating current of 2–6V. To obtain smooth etching, we gently stir the solution during the process. Tungsten wire of any diameter can be used, but thicker wire of 100 μm diameter is used for ease of manipulation. To obtain a fine-tip taper, the wire should be etched by making a loop and dipping the center of the loop into the solution (Fig. 1). By moving the loop in and out of the solution, a tip of smooth taper can be obtained. If the wire is etched by dipping the cut end into the solution, the grade of the tapering is often so steep that the tip of the wire will not reach the tip of the pipette.

b. Glass tubing. Any tubing can be used, but we prefer standard tubing of 2.0 mm outside diameter (Corning glass) because of the ease of inserting and sealing the tungsten wire. For sealing the wire, we use

FIG. 1. A looped tungsten wire is dipped in the etching solution (KCN + NaOH) placed on a stirrer. The loop is moved in and out of the solution by the manipulator during the etching to obtain gentle tapering of the wire.

Wood's metal[1] with a melting point of 70°C. Pieces of small rod are made by sucking melted Wood's metal into a plastic tubing. After inserting a tapered tungsten wire almost to the broken tip of a pipette under the microscope, insert the rod and a piece of copper wire into the other end of the pipette (Fig. 2). The rod can then be heated with a small flame, and while the rod melts, push the tungsten wire until the tapered wire fits snugly into the pipette tip. The excess tungsten wire extending from the back of the electrode is then cut off, and the copper wire is used

[1]Mallinckrodt Inc., P.O. Box 5840, St. Louis, Mo. 063134.

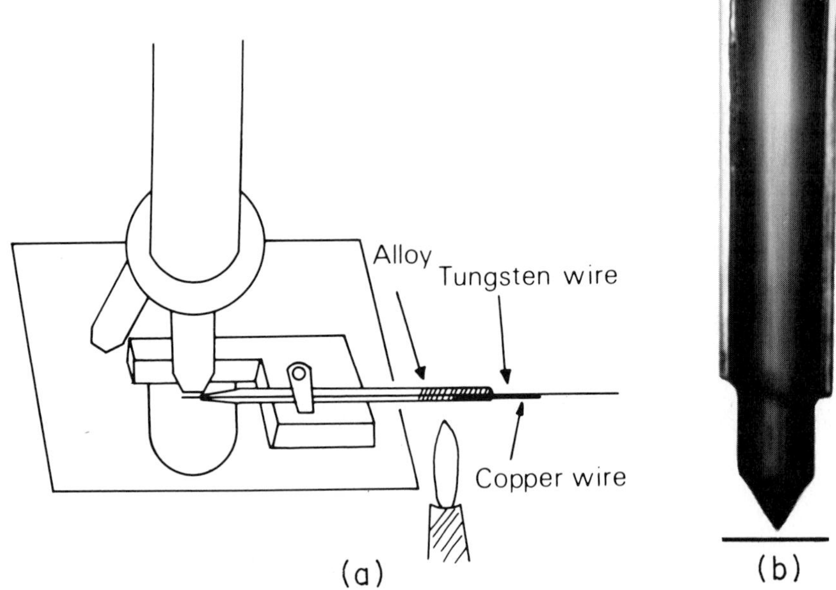

FIG. 2. (a) Diagram shows sealing of the electrode shaft. The tip of the tungsten wire is fitted snugly to the pipette tip by tapping the other end of the wire while the alloy is still melted. For further details, see text. (b) An example of a typical tungsten-in-glass electrode. Calibration: 10 μm.

as a lead to the amplifer. The tungsten wire protruding from the tip is shortened by electrolytic etching under direct microscopic observation to form an exposed tip of 10–15 μm in length. This is done by forming a small loop with a platinum wire and making a small meniscus with the electrolytic fluid. This small meniscus can be brought into microscopic field, and by passing a current through the electrode, a desired length of exposed tip can be made. A platinum electrode can be made exactly the same way although it takes longer for etching.

A metal electrode insulated with lacquer can also be used for microstimulation. However, if excessive current is passed inadvertently, the insulation tends to crack or peel off, and the stimulating current leaks diffusely from the shaft of the electrode. Such damaged electrodes frequently can still pick up unitary spikes, but the microstimulation is ineffective.

III. Stimulating Current

The type of electrode described in Section II can pass current pulses of more than 100 μA, but there is an upper limit for the current because of noxious effects produced by excessive current (Asanuma & Arnold, 1975). When a train of pulses is used, current of about 40 μA starts producing noxious effects. With stronger currents (60 μA or more), the electrode tip starts bubbling and destroys the tissue. To avoid this damage, compensation current (see Section V) can be used, but this is effective only within a limited range, and the only secure way for passing larger currents is to increase the size of the electrode, thus sacrificing the capacity to isolate unitary spikes when used as a recording electrode. The simplest way of testing for tissue damage is to record the same unitary spikes before and after microstimulation.

A. *Effective Current Spread*

There are many theories concerning the spread of the current. A basic question is whether the effective stimulating distance is linearly proportional to the threshold current (Bean, 1974; BeMent & Ranck, 1969) or proportional to the square of the current (Asanuma & Sakata, 1967; Bagshaw & Evans, 1976; Marcus, Zarzecki, & Asanuma, 1979; Roberts & Smith, 1973). We have studied this relationship for pyramidal tract (PT) cell bodies (Stoney *et al.*, 1968), PT axon collaterals (Asanuma, Arnold, & Zarzecki, 1976), and PT axon branches in the spinal cord (Marcus *et al.*, 1979). It seems that the relationship is the same for all three PT elements. Our analysis has shown that the quadratic relationship approximates the results better than the linear relationship (Marcus *et al.*, 1979), but it should be noted that in the low threshold range ($\leqslant 20$ μA), the difference is very small between the two equations. We use the equation, $i = kr^2$, where r is the distance from the electrode to the target neuron (Asanuma and Sakata, 1967). The r value can be estimated by application of the Pythagorean theorem as shown in Fig. 3a, and the equation becomes $i = k\,(r\,min^2 + d^2)$. This threshold (i)–distance (d) relationship can be plotted on a graph (Fig. 3b) and by using the least square method, the k value can be calculated. The k value depends on the excitability of the target tissue and ranges from 450 (Marcus *et al.*, 1979) to 1000 (Stoney *et al.*, 1968).

IV. Single versus Repetitive Stimulation

The effect of microstimulation depends on the intensity of stimuli as well as on the number of pulses. It is generally preferable to use as weak current as possible because the weaker the current, the smaller the area effected, and hence it is easier to analyze the results. Therefore, the

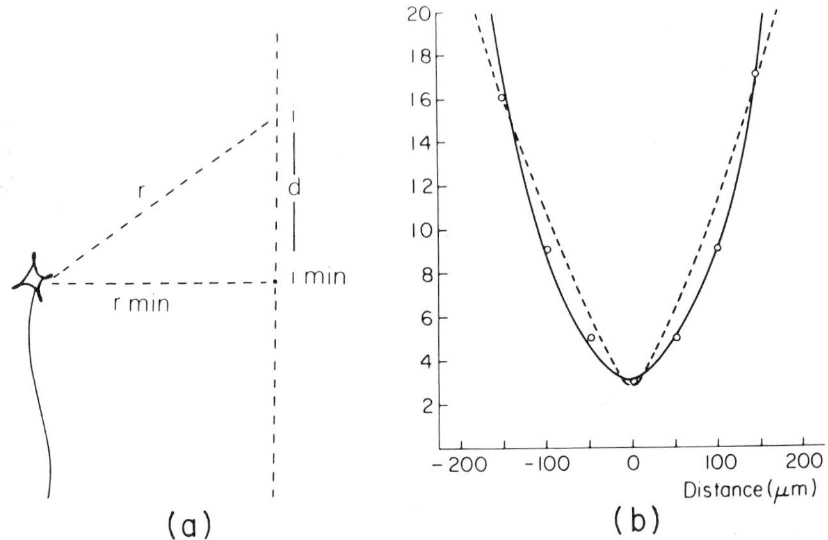

FIG. 3. (a) Relationship between the electrode track and a target neuron. Threshold current for a given neuron can be measured along the electrode insertion. Assuming the site of minimum threshold current (*i min*) to be closest to the target neuron, the distance from a given site (r) can be expressed by $r = (r\ min^2 + d^2)^{1/2}$. The distance along the electrode track is denoted by d. (b) An example of threshold (ordinate)–distance (abscissa) relationships for a pyramidal tract-neuron during electrode insertion. Zero denotes the site of minimum threshold. Circles were obtained from actual experiments. Theoretical threshold–distance curves are shown for linear (broken line) and quadratic (solid line) relationships computed using the least square method. For further details, see text.

determination of frequency of pulses and duration of the train becomes important in planning the experiment.

It is known that single-pulse microstimulation produces direct and synaptic activation of neurons (Stoney *et al.*, 1968). When repetitive pulses are used, the synaptic activation becomes greater after several stimuli (Jankowska, Padel, & Tankaya, 1975). The synaptic activation occurs not only at the site of stimulation, but also at the site of neural destination. However, no matter how great the synaptic activation is, it originates from the site of stimulation. Hence, the general principle that "the weaker the current, the better" still holds.

The determination of stimulus parameters must be made depending on the purpose of the experiment. Generally speaking, a longer train (30–40 msec) of high frequency (300–400 Hz) pulses is more effective than a shorter train of low frequency pulses. However, since excessive current produces noxious effects, the total amount of current should be kept minimal.

V. Stimulus Artifact

Whenever nearby tissue is electrically stimulated, it inevitably produces huge artifacts which obscure observation of electrical events immediately following the stimulation. One way of canceling the artifact is to use the Wheatstone Bridge method, but practical usage of this method is limited to the intracellular recordings in which applied current is weak (on the order of nanoamperes). When a current of the order of micro- or milli-amperes is used, it inevitably polarizes the electrode tip which, by nature, cannot be compensated by the bridge method. One way of reducing the artifact is to cancel the polarization by applying a short current pulse of opposite direction immediately following the stimulating current (Asanuma and Rosén, 1973). We routinely use a negative stimulating pulse of 0.2-msec duration, which is followed by a positive pulse of 0.1-msec duration. This negative–positive pulse is composed by combining two pulse generators and two isolators as shown in Fig. 4. By controlling the height of the second pulse, the artifact is nearly completely suppressed immediately after the stimulus. If the output of the power amplifiers is made in such a way that the magnitude of the second pulse is proportional to that of the first pulse, then the artifact is automatically canceled, irrespective of the stimulus intensity.

Since the total duration of stimulating pulses is 0.3 msec, the baseline comes back to the original level 0.4–0.5 msec after the start of a stimulus. This is a sufficiently short time because at threshold stimulus, the minimum latency for a transynaptically evoked postsynaptic potential (psp)

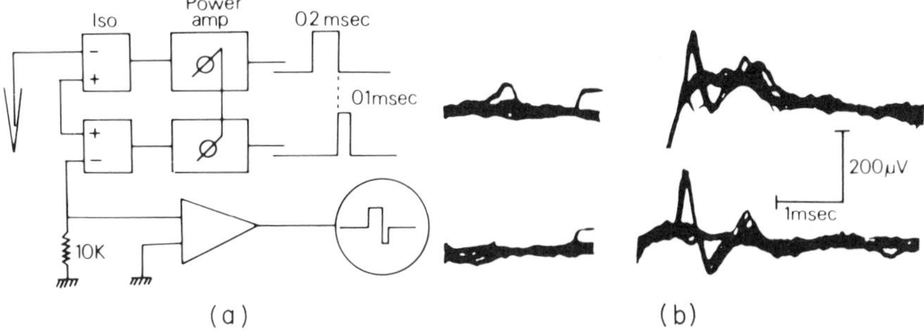

FIG. 4. (a) Schematic diagram of delivering cancellation current using conventional isolation units. The falling phase of stimulating pulse (0.2 msec) triggers other pulse (0.1 msec) and they are fed into power amplifiers and then isolators that are connected in series. (b) An example of artifact cancellation. Upper line: superimposed sweeps in which a neuron was stimulated at threshold currents. Note 50% appearance of the spikes. Lower line: cancellation currents greatly reduced the artifact, but did not change the threshold. For further details, see text.

elicited by stimulation of nearby tissue is 0.8 msec (Asanuma & Rosén, 1973). By carefully adjusting the second pulse, even a part of an action potential elicited directly by the stimulus can be observed through the recording electrode placed near the stimulating electrode.

A question arises as to whether the cancellation current changes the threshold for activation of the target cell. This has been examined on several occasions, and it has been concluded that the cancellation current practically does not change the efficiency of the negative stimulating pulse (Asanuma *et al.*, 1976). This has been explained in the following way: The stimulus current first produces a local response and then initiates a spike discharge. Even with the intensity just above the threshold, the local response developed during the period of stimulation (0.2 msec) is already powerful enough to withstand the anodal blocking effect produced by the cancellation current, hence the threshold value is not changed significantly.

A. *Lateral Effects of Cancellation Current*

One of the problems encountered when using a train of stimulating pulses is that the amount of current frequently fluctuates during the course of a train, especially when a long train is used. The cancellation current markedly eliminates the fluctuation most probably by the elimination of polarization at the electrode tip which would otherwise accumulate and change the impedance of the electrode. The disadvantage of using cancellation current is that since tungsten is positively charged, the positive current etches the exposed tip rapidly, and the electrode becomes incapable of passing the current. This can partially be prevented by using platinum wire or by plating the exposed tip with gold. We use gold plating solution sold for jewelers, and the result is satisfactory.[2]

VI. Identification of Electrode Tracks

Because the diameter of a tungsten in glass electrode is only 20–30 μm at the distance of 1–2 mm from the tip, the track cannot be identified unless lesions are made. The beauty of the glass-coated tungsten electrode is the ease and security of making lesions. We used a negative current of 5, 10, or 20 μA for 10 sec, and the size of the lesion is

[2]Borel Group, 15 W. 47th St., New York, N.Y. 10036.

approximately 100, 200 or 300 μm, respectively. Since the current will never leak from the shaft of the electrode, we never experienced problems in reconstructing the tracks. When a fluid-filled pipette is used, we use fast green FCF method to mark the tip location (Thomas & Wilson, 1965).

VII. Electrode Insertion

The glass-coated tungsten pipette electrode is excellent for not damaging the tissue because of the small diameter of the shaft and its low impedance. However, a disadvantage is that the shaft is not strong enough to penetrate the dural membrane. It is possible to make a slit in the dura and penetrate through the slit, but this is not practical in chronic experiments. We use this electrode primarily in acute experiments with the dura opened and the cortex exposed. Readers who are interested in chronic microelectrode experiments should use other types of electrodes.

Acknowledgment

The author would like to express his thanks to Ms. K. Arissian for her help while developing this electrode and also in preparing the illustrations.

References

Asanuma, H., & Arnold, A. P. Noxious effects of excessive currents used for intracortical microstimulation. *Brain Research*, 1975, **96**, 103–107.

Asanuma, H., Arnold, A., & Zarzecki, P. Further study on the excitation of pyramidal tract cells by intracortical microstimulation. *Experimental Brain Research*, 1976, **26**, 443–461.

Asanuma, H., & Rosén, I. Spread of mono- and polysynaptic connections within cat's motor cortex. *Experimental Brain Research*, 1973, **16**, 507–520.

Asanuma, H., & Sakata, H. Functional organization of a cortical efferent system examined with focal depth stimulation in cats. *Journal of Neurophysiology*, 1967, **30**, 35–54.

Bagshaw, E. V., & Evans, M. H. Measurement of current spread from microelectrodes when stimulating within the nervous system. *Experimental Brain Research*, 1976, **25**, 391–400.

Bean, C. P. A theory of microstimulation of myelineated fibers. *Journal of Physiology (London)*, 1974, **243**, 514–522.

BeMent, S. L., & Ranck, J. B., Jr. A quantitative study of electrical stimulation of central myelinated fibers. *Experimental Neurology*, 1969, **24**, 147–170.

Jankowska, E., Padel, Y., & Tankaya, Y. The mode of activation of pyramidal cell by intracortical stimuli. *Journal of Physiology (London)*, 1975, **249**, 617–636.

Jankowska, E., & Roberts, W. J. Synaptic actions of single interneurones mediating reciprocal Ia inhibition of motoneurones. *Journal of Physiology (London)*, 1972, **222,** 623–642.

Marcus, S., Zarzecki, P., & Asanuma, H. An estimate of effective spread of stimulating current. *Experimental Brain Research*, 1979, **34,** 68–72.

Roberts, W. J., & Smith, D. O. Analysis of threshold currents during microstimulation of fibres in the spinal cored. *Acta Physiologica Scandinavica* 1973, **89,** 384–394.

Stoney, S. D., Jr., Thompson, W. D., & Asanuma, H. Excitation of pyramidal tract cells by intracortical microstimulation: Effective extent of stimulating current. *Journal of Neurophysiology*, 1968, **31,** 659–669.

Thomas, R. C., & Wilson, V. J. Precise localization of renshaw cells with a new marking technique. *Nature (London)*, 1965, **206,** 211–213.

Chapter 4

Stimulation of the Brain Via Metallic Electrodes

*Robert W. Doty and John R. Bartlett**

Center for Brain Research
University of Rochester Medical Center
Rochester, New York

*Deceased, November 5, 1978.

ISBN 0-12-547440-7

I. Introduction

The transfer of electrical charge from a metallic conductor of electrons to the ions of an aqueous medium is a process of considerable complexity. Its nature varies with the voltage, the metal, the direction and density of the current, the type and concentration of the solutes in which the metal is immersed, and even the past history of the electrode. Despite concern over these processes for more than 100 years of electrophysiology, there is still much to be learned about them and how best to effect charge transfer into neural tissue for protracted periods over permanently implanted electrodes. In those instances where single, brief stimulus pulses, or trains of stimuli at moderate intensity and duration (e.g., 0.2-msec rectangular, 200-μA monophasic pulses at 50 Hz for 2 sec), are delivered via conically tipped electrodes of 100- to 200-μm diameter platinum wire at infrequent intervals, the consequences of such stimulation are usually innocuous, and thresholds for behavioral or physiological effects may remain constant over many weeks or months (Bartlett, Doty, Lee, Negrão, & Overman, 1977; Delgado, 1959; Doty, 1965; Doty, Rutledge, & Larsen, 1956; Gerken & Judy, 1977). However, even in such cases the idiosyncracies of each electrode–tissue interface are undoubtedly critical in determining the threshold for effective stimulation. If stimulus trains endure for more than a few seconds, elevations of threshold are inevitably produced by electrolysis, unless certain precautions are taken.

II. The Metal–Tissue Interface

A. *Electrochemistry of Platinum Surface*

Extensive experience and experimentation (Bollinger & Gerall, 1971; Dymond, Kaechele, Jurist & Crandall, 1970; Loucks, Weinberg, & Smith, 1959; McFadden, 1969; Wetzel, Howell, & Bearie, 1970) have consistently shown platinum or platinum alloys to be much superior to various stainless steels in electrical behavior and resistance to corrosion, and it is presently the metal of choice for chronic implantation. Silver is clearly to be avoided.

For a platinum electrode in a 0.154 *M* (0.9%) solution of NaCl, the following reactions occur as voltage is increased (Brummer & Turner, 1975; see also Dymond, 1976);

From 0–0.35 V, *hydrogen atom plating:* (1)

$$\mathrm{Pt-H} \rightleftarrows \mathrm{Pt} + \mathrm{H}^+ + e^-.$$

This reaction involves a charge of 0.25 mC/real cm^2, but if organic compounds are present, this charge acceptance is reduced, probably because of restriction of the metallic surface available to hydrogen adsorption. The latter circumstance would hasten the progress toward hydrolysis of water with continued passage of current.

From 0.35–0.85 V, *double layer charging:* (2)

$$\mathrm{Pt}\,(-)\ \text{repels}\ \mathrm{Cl}^- \rightleftarrows \mathrm{Pt}\,(+)\ \text{attracts}\ \mathrm{Cl}^-.$$

This reaction makes a relatively small contribution to charge transfer (0.025 mC/real cm^2); but being nonchemical in nature it confers on the electrode the properties of a capacitor.

From 0.85 V, *surface oxidation:* (3)

$$\mathrm{Pt} + \mathrm{H_2O} \rightleftarrows 2\mathrm{H} + 2e^-.$$

This reaction can contribute about 0.5 mC/real cm^2, but it is diminished by adsorption of Cl^-.

All of the foregoing reactions are fully reversible and do not involve toxic products. Thus, if charge transfer could be restricted to these reactions, electrical stimulation of neural tissue would be physically innocuous. There are, however, several uncertainties that make these theoretical predictions somewhat unsatisfactory empirically. The kinetics of these three reactions have not been delineated, and their time course may actually be of significance when electrical pulses of only a few 100 μsec are employed. As already noted, the presence of organic compounds can perturb or modulate these processes.

It is the fourth reaction (among others that will not be discussed; see Brummer & Turner, 1975) that will rapidly produce irreversible damage to neural tissue if allowed to occur to any great degree.

For 1.8 V, *hydrolysis:* (4)

$$2\,\mathrm{H_2O} \rightarrow \mathrm{O_2} + 4\mathrm{H}^+ + 4e^-$$

In this reaction, oxygen gas is evolved at the anode, and hydrogen gas is evolved at the cathode. Since these gases leave the solution, the reaction is irreversible. It will carry charge continuously so long as adequate voltage is applied. The generation of hydrogen ions also changes the pH. This and the disruption of tissue structure by gas pressure make predictably deleterious stimuli which exceed 1.8 V (or lower under certain circumstances; see Fig. 1). Again, however, there is some uncertainty about the kinetics of the reaction, and it is not known whether in the first 100 μsec or so the oxygen and hydrogen might still be available for recombination to water were the applied potential to be reversed.

B. Attempts to Control Adverse Effects of Charge Transfer

It is this idea, in essence, that underlies the "Lilly" waveform (Lilly, Hughes, Alvord, & Galkin, 1955), originated and still often used with the intent of producing noninjurious electrical stimulation. The hope was that the deleterious reactions set in motion by an initial stimulating current pulse lasting about 30 μsec could be effectively reversed and thus canceled by a second 30-μsec pulse of opposite polarity and equal charge occuring within 200 μsec of the first. The net charge transfer thus being zero for each pulse pair, it was reasoned that the net electrochemical effect might also be nil. To a first approximation this appears to be true, although no rigorous studies of the electrochemical effects have been performed. There are, however, two serious difficulties associated with the use of the "Lilly" pulse pairs. The first is that with brief intervals between the pair of pulses, extraordinarily high levels of current are required for effective stimulation. This is attributable to the same effect which conveys upon the Lilly waveform its singular advantage. The second pulse of the pair tends to erase or reverse not only the electrochemical reaction to the first pulse, but also much of the physiological excitatory effect it has produced. Using stimulation of the optic tract of the cat, and recording the presynaptic potential evoked in the lateral geniculate body, it is easily demonstrated that an anodal pulse following immediately after presentation of a cathodal pulse greatly diminishes the effectiveness of the latter, e.g., for 20-μsec pulses at a 20-μsec interval the threshold is doubled (as compared to a single pulse—Bartlett and Doty, unpublished).

More subtle, but even more likely to produce deleterious effects, is the fact that the anodal versus cathodal processes are asymmetrical (Weinman & Mahler, 1964; and Fig. 1). This is as true for sinusoidal, oscillatory waveforms, e.g., the commonly used 50- or 60-Hz alternating current or the modulated 5 kHz form of stimulation devised by Wyss (see Hunsperger, 1969), as it is for the Lilly pulse pairs. As a consequence of this asymmetry, what amounts to rectification can occur, so that a dc voltage can accumulate, depending upon various characteristics of the metal–tissue interface and the stimulus generator, despite the equality of injected charge in the cathodal versus anodal phases.

Figure 1 illustrates this asymmetry for the dc mode (with charge trans-

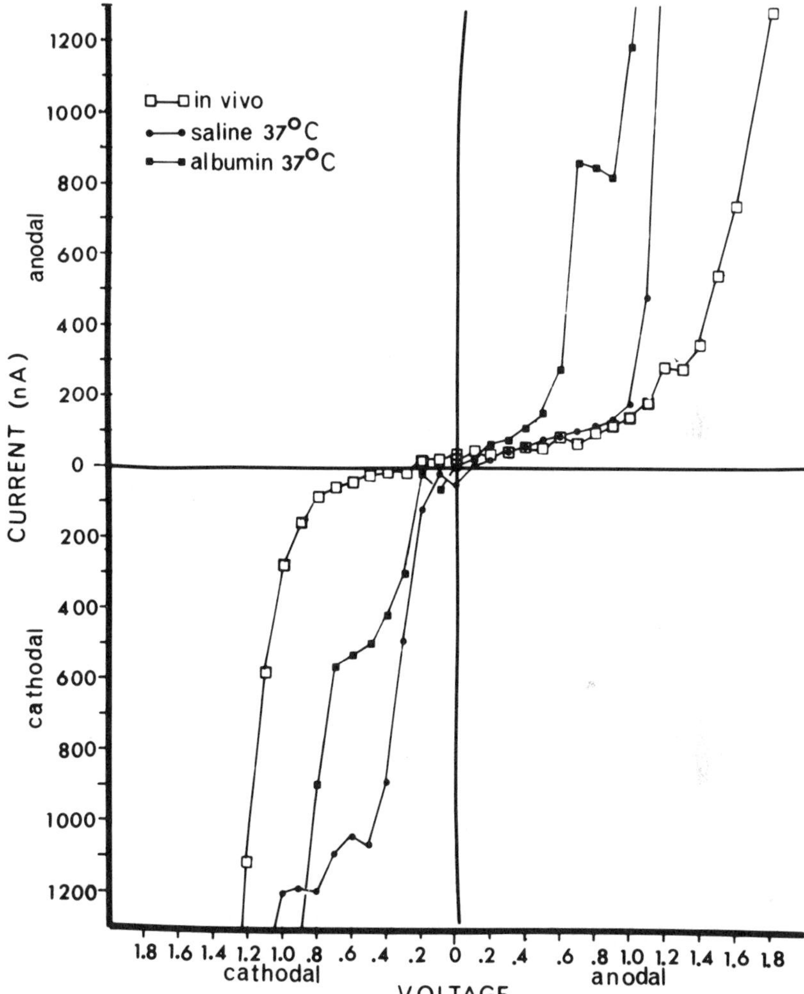

FIG. 1. Equilibrium current for 200-μm diameter Pt–Ir electrodes with conically shaped, uninsulated tips, measured 5 sec after imposition of a gradual (5 sec) shift in level of voltage clamp. "*In vivo*" is average of observations on six electrodes in striate cortex of three macaques. Note that the resistance for these chronically implanted electrodes is >1 mΩ (current $\leqq 100$ nA) between $+0.8$ and -0.8 V, but then falls abruptly to 60 kΩ as the voltage exceeds these levels. In the latter instance, the current is presumably being carried by hydrolysis, which occurs much more readily in unbuffered or "open" solutions. The "albumin" was sterile human albumin normally used for transfusions; the "saline" was 0.154 *M* NaCl. Applying the dc voltages for 1 hr within the range ± 0.8 V to the chronically implanted electrodes had no effect upon the monkeys' threshold for subsequent detection of 0.2-msec cathodal pulses at these loci, whereas higher dc voltages (and current) produced elevation in such thresholds.

fer controlled simply by electrode–tissue impedance). Here, voltage was applied between a platinum–iridium "stimulating" electrode (of small surface area) and a large "indifferent" platinum electrode, and the resulting current was measured after several seconds, when the system had reached a steady state. (Even so, some hysteresis is apparent at "zero" volts.) In Fig. 1 it can be seen that the current induced to flow in the anodal direction between 0.1 to 1.0 V differs greatly from that in the cathodal direction in this voltage range. For instance, at 1.0 V *in vivo* the cathodal current was 300 nA versus 100 nA for anodal current. An encouraging feature of the situation depicted in Fig. 1 should also be noted: the range of voltage over which current flow remains minimal is much greater for the permanently implanted electrodes (*in vivo*) than for the *in vitro* tests. It can be inferred that at the point where the current steeply increases upon slight increase in voltage, the primary reaction carrying the current is hydrolysis. Indeed, the pecular discontinuities on the *in vitro* (saline and albumin) curves probably arise from erratic alteration of electrode surface area, and hence impedance, consequent to formation of gas bubbles. In summary, Fig. 1 shows that the characteristics of an electrode are greatly different when it serves as anode versus cathode; and that, fortunately, the range of voltages available without hydrolysis is greater *in vivo* than *in vitro.* As will be described below, this property can be advantageously employed to reduce or eliminate tissue damage by effective stimulating currents.

Presently used generators of electrophysiological stimuli operate either as constant voltage or constant current devices. Constant voltage pulses have two advantages: (1) the voltage can be set for a level below that which would produce hydrolysis; and (2) the output impedance of the circuit usually being low, any charge remaining on the electrodes after the stimulus pulse will dissipate through this relatively low impedance during the interpulse interval. However, there are serious disadvantages in that the impedance of the electrode–tissue interface will determine the stimulating current applied. Since this impedance changes greatly during each stimulus pulse and varies from one electrode to another or even from moment to moment with the same electrode, the physiological effectiveness of the stimulus cannot be adequately controlled and may thus have a large element of uncertainty (see Dymond, 1976; Weinman & Mahler, 1964).

Constant current stimulation, on the other hand, offers much more satisfactory control of the stimulus. It does so at the cost of having a very high output impedance for the stimulus generator, and dissipation of the charge built up on the electrodes by each constant current pulse will thus be relatively slow. Of course, depending upon the exact value of this output impedance of the stimulator, as well as the properties of the electrode and the current required, stimulus repetition rates as low as 1 Hz may quickly build up residual charge that forces the voltage into the hydrolytic range in order to maintain the current at a constant level. The reader should be aware of this characteristic of constant current stimulators, for it can very rapidly produce irreversible tissue damage by hydrolysis. Figure 2 diagrams the voltage developed across a Pt electrode during application of a constant current pulse. It rises abruptly because of the resistance of the electrode–tissue interface, the "access resistance," which is determined by the effective surface area of the electrode and the conductance of the aqueous medium (Svaetichin, 1951). The electrode then starts to undergo reactions (1–3), as noted earlier, gradually accepting more and more charge, which produces a back electromotive force (emf), and hence resistance, termed "polarization." Once the available reversible reactions have saturated, the current must be carried by hydrolysis, a process which proceeds readily, thus offering little or no increased resistance, and the voltage thereafter remains essentially constant (Fig. 2). As can be seen from Fig. 2, the occurrence of hydrolysis consequent to constant current pulses is thus easily determined by monitoring the stimulus voltage; if it "flattens" prior to termination of the pulse, reaching 1.5–2.0 V, hydrolysis is almost certaily occurring.

If the electrode has been polarized to only a few tenths of a volt by the first pulse, it may not fully discharge before the next pulse is applied after an interval, e.g., of 10 to 100 msec. Thus, succeeding pulses may sum with this residual polarization of preceding pulses until the hydrolytic voltage is attained. The number of pulses, pulse frequency, and so on, at which hydrolysis will occur will, of course, depend upon the characteristics (capacitance) of the electrodes and the output impedance of

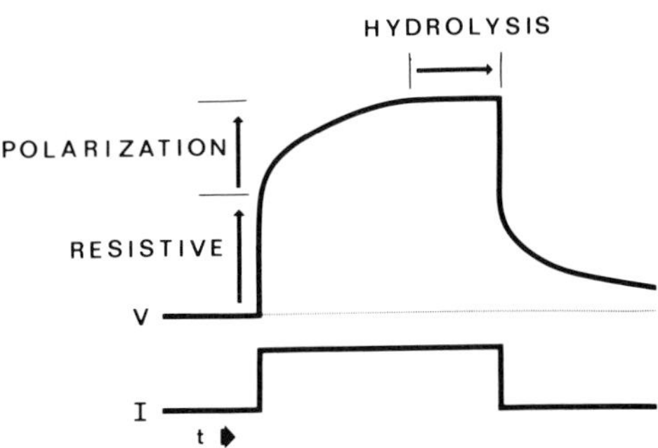

FIG. 2. Voltage recorded at a 200-μm diameter Pt–Ir electrode in the brain when a 0.2-msec pulse of constant current is applied at typical levels of 1–2 mA.

the stimulator, but it is a very common problem in the range of most physiological tetanization with constant current generators. Fortunately, this serious drawback of constant current stimulators is rather easily avoided. The stimulating circuit can be so designed that the termination of the stimulus pulse activates a transistor which effectively short-circuits the electrodes through a low-resistance path throughout the interpulse interval. It thereby discharges the residual polarization and prevents the accumulation of charge from one pulse to the next. We have termed this transistor short-circuiting arrangement an "exhauster" (Bartlett *et al.*, 1977; Appendix, this chapter) since it "exhausts" the accumulating charge from the electrode. Others have termed this circuitry an "inter-stimulus shorting control" (Silverman, Ball, & Cohn, 1975) or a "hybrid" stimulator (del Pozo & Delgado, 1978).

The exhauster, of course, provides no protection against producing hydrolysis should sufficiently high voltage develop during each stimulus pulse. There are presently two schemes by which such occurrence of hydrolysis can be reduced or eliminated. Neither is ideal, but they can achieve protracted effective application of electrical stimuli to the central nervous system without initiating toxic electrochemical reactions.

The first of these, the tantalum pentoxide (Ta_2O_5) capacitor electrode (Guyton & Hambrecht, 1973, 1974) by its nature produces no faradaic flow of current when it is operated as an anode, and thus cannot produce hydrolytic or pH changes. It is formed of sintered tantalum, which has a porous, and hence extensive, surface. By anodizing this surface, a very thin, nonconductive layer of Ta_2O_5 is formed ($\sim$ 2-nm thickness per volt), creating a capacitor, which for 5 V anodization can have a capacitance as high as 175 $\mu F/cm^2$).

This is more than sufficient to produce effective anodal-stimulating pulses applied to the pial surface of the neocortex (Bartlett *et al.*, 1977; Guyton & Hambrecht, 1973). To apply repetitive pulses in the anodal capacitative mode, the charge from each pulse must be removed before delivering the next, thus necessitating an "exhauster" type of circuit to provide a low-resistance path between the "active" and "indifferent" electrodes in the interpulse interval.

With present techniques, it has not yet been practical to fabricate Ta_2O_5 electrodes to penetrate into neural tissue. Operating the electrode as an anode is, of course, advantageous for applying stimuli to the surface of the neocortex (Phillips & Porter, 1977), but cathodal stimuli are usually more effective when the electrode more closely approximates the neural elements to be stimulated. If cathodal pulses are applied to the tantalum capacitor electrode, the Ta_2O_5 coating is destroyed and the electrode loses its major capacitative properties.

The other method for producing effective stimulation with reduced risk of hydrolysis is considerably more cumbersome, in that it requires three rather than two electrodes and some moderately complicated circuitry (Fig. 3). However, it has the added advantage of yielding significant information about the characteristics of the stimulating electrode (Figs. 4 and 5). The basic idea is to utilize the full anodal–cathodal range of voltages short of those that produce hydrolysis. To this end, the stimulating electrode ("test" electrode in Fig. 3) is held at a predetermined level of anodal polarization (hence the term "Anapol" for the device) relative to a passive "reference" electrode. This is usually +0.2 to +0.7 V and is achieved by briefly passing a 20–50 μA current between the stimulating electrode and a "counter" electrode to anodize the stimulating electrode after each cathodal-stimulating pulse. As can be seen from Fig. 1, if this anodal polarization (*in vivo*) does not exceed about 0.8 V, the continuing flow of current is <0.1 μA, which in use with 127–200-μm diameter Pt–Ir electrodes has produced no detectable effects. The cathodal stimulus pulse starts from this anodal level (Fig. 4) and thus has much greater leeway before attaining the cathodal voltage necessary for hydrolysis. For example, if a 1.4 V cathodal pulse were to be applied to an electrode held in the usual manner at 0 V, the hydrolytic range might be reached; but if the pulse starts at +0.7 V, the 1.4 V cathodal pulse will carry only to −0.7 V, still well within the range of reversible, noninjurious reactions. While the pulse delivered has constant current, and hence the voltage levels attained are uncontrolled (up to the compliance voltage of the constant current circuit), the current required for effective stimulation is commonly only one-third to one-tenth that which would demand voltages approaching the hydrolytic range. Thus, stimuli several times the threshold can usually be utilized without danger of hydrolysis.

Both the Ta_2O_5 capacitor electrodes and the Anapol system have been used to apply stimuli to striate cortex of macaques continuously for 1 to 8 hr at 50 Hz (Bartlett *et al.*, 1977; Bartlett & Doty, unpublished) at certain loci without evidence of any deleterious effect. However, other loci subjected to what physically appears to be the same treatment may suffer a temporary (1–5-day) elevation of threshold by 50–100% (e.g., from 0.15 to 0.3 mA for the monkey to detect and respond to 0.2-msec pulses at 50 Hz). The reason why the threshold for detection of the stimulation is elevated at some loci while others remain immune to the effects of protracted stimulation is presently obscure. Among the more likely possibilities are (1) some induced change in characteristics of the connective tissue sheath, which encapsulates all electrodes implanted for more than a few days (although it is difficult to imagine how one sheath

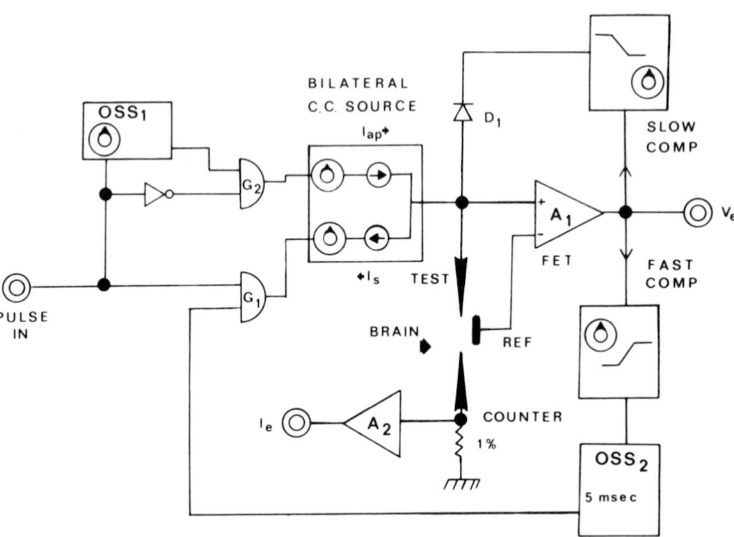

FIG. 3. Principal components of the Anapol stimulating system. (1) Via G_1 an external input pulse at "pulse in" enables the "bilateral constant current source" to produce a preselected negative going pulse of current (I_s) through the "test" and "counter" electrodes; (2) via G_2 disables the normally "on" anodal constant current supplied to these electrodes; and (3) triggers, on its falling edge, the "anodal polarization delay" single-shot OSS_1. The voltage between the "test" electrode and the passive "reference" electrode is measured by the high-input impedance instrumentation amplifier A_1, which provides the input to a "slow voltage-comparator," a "fast voltage-comparator," and a monitoring oscilloscope (V_e). The faster comparator (a normal op amp comparator) switches if a preselected cathodal voltage, i.e., a voltage chosen to avoid hydrolysis, is present between the "test" and "reference" electrodes. This switching triggers the single-shot "OSS_2," which disables cathodal current flow via G_1. Otherwise, at the falling edge of the input pulse at "pulse in," the cathodal constant current is disabled and, after the delay provided by OSS_1, a preselected anodal current (I_{ap}) is applied between the "test" and "counter" electrodes. This slowly anodizes (normally 20–50 μA) the test electrode until the voltage between it and the "reference" electrode causes the output of the slow voltage-comparator to be about 0.7 V more negative than the potential of the "test" electrode. At this point, diode D_1 begins to conduct, and the anodal current supplied by the "bilateral constant current source" is shunted into the output of the "slow comparator." (The "Slow Comparator" is simply a low-gain op amp operated as a comparator. This avoids the oscillation that would occur as the current to the "test" electrode is shunted and then reapplied when the polarization level falls a few millivolts.) The test electrode is thus held at a preselected anodal potential until the next pulse is applied to the "pulse in" input; a level that is determined by the reference setting of the "slow comparator." The anodal and cathodal current (I_s and I_{ap}) passing through the "test" and "counter" electrodes is measured via A_2 (I_e). See text and also Fig. 4.

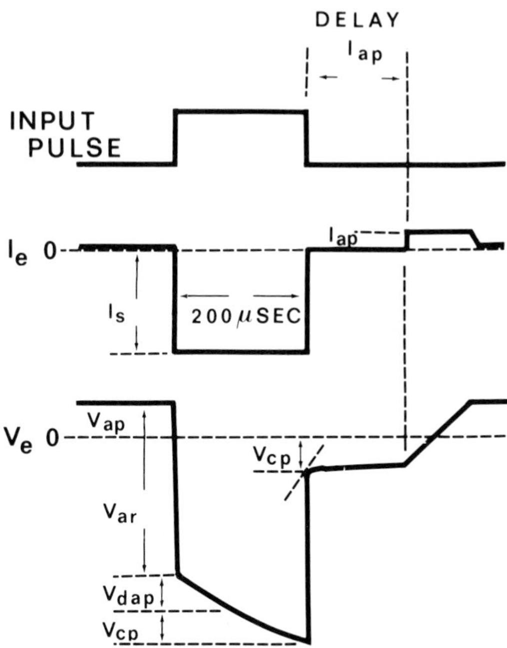

FIG. 4. Typical waveforms for Anapol stimulation. At the onset of cathodal current (I_s), the potential (V_e) of the "test" electrode is more positive than zero. The rapid fall in electrode potential at the onset of current flow (V_{ar}) is due to the electrode's access resistance, while the first portion of the subsequent slow fall in potential (V_{dap}) represents the depolarization of preexisting anodal processes. This is followed by a further fall in potential (V_{cp}), which is due to cathodization of the "test" electrode, the total representing the charge acceptance of the electrode for this level of current. At the end of the cathodal current pulse, I_e goes to zero and so does V_{ar}. This leaves the electrode at a potential, which depends on its cathodal polarization or, in other words, V_{cp}. There is a slow depolarization of the cathodal process during the period of no applied current probably because of some small leakage of current from the constant current source. The level of cathodal polarization is thus measured, as shown, from a tangent at 45° to V_{ar}. At the end of the anodal polarization delay (Delay I_{ap}), anodal constant current (I_{ap}) is applied to the "test" electrode in order to return it to its initial anodization level where it is held until the next cathodal pulse.

might so differ from another); (2) an alteration of the vascular supply, either by direct electrical stimulation of blood vessels (a feature perhaps more likely for the capacitor electrodes that must rest upon the pia mater) or by metabolic products from the neural excitation; (3) mechanical damage of neurons by the abrupt movement of their charged membranes in the applied electrical field (electrokinesis—see Elul, 1967); or (4) a physiological effect, such as "fatigue," i.e., alteration of transmembrane ionic concentrations or depletion of synaptic transmitter, and so on,

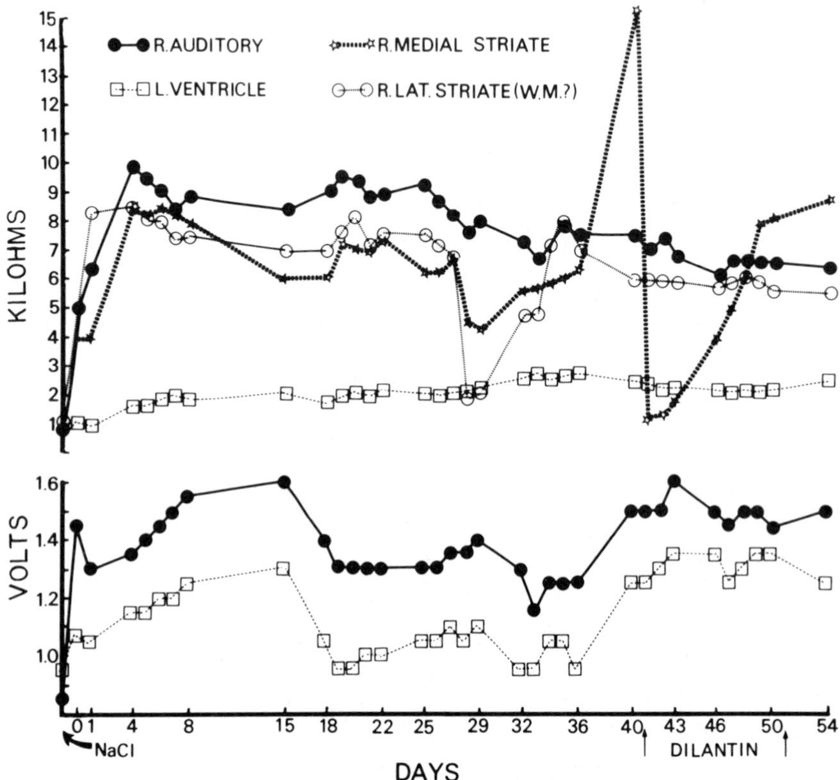

FIG. 5. Access resistance (in kilohms) and charge acceptance (in volts, V_{dap} and V_{cp} in Fig. 4) for 200-μm diameter Pt–Ir electrodes with estimated geometric surface area of 1.6 × 10^{-3} cm^2, implanted in brain of a rabbit for 54 days as indicated. Initial values are for these electrodes in 0.154 *M* NaCl. Note general congruence of the fluctuations in values at different electrodes in gray or white matter, but (1) low and relatively invariant access resistance of electrode in ventricle and (2) large, unexplained variation in access resistance independently of charge acceptance. Values of charge acceptance were not plotted for two electrodes as they were bracketed by the two shown.

although here, too, the vagaries in presence or absence of the effect are difficult to explain. Delgado and Mir (1966) were able to stimulate the pupillomotor system in macaques continuously for 21 days without sign of "fatigue," but other loci do show "fatigue" at various rates (Delgado, 1959).

With the Anapol system it is relatively easy to measure, by electronic integration, the net charge in coulombs applied to the electrode–tissue interface in the anodal versus cathodal phases of each cycle, and to arrange the stimulus parameters so that the net charge transfer is nil. That this "zero charge loss" procedure for applying electrical stimulus pulses is actually effective in limiting ionic loss from the electrode was demonstrated directly by experiment (Bartlett & Doty, unpublished). Anapol pulses of 0.2 msec were applied to a series of nichrome electrodes for 15 min at 50 Hz, using "zero charge loss" for one set of electrodes and a loss of 100 nC/cycle (totaling 4.5 mC) for the other. In each case the stimulus pulses were 1.0 mA. Those sites at which the charge loss had occurred were surrounded by a halo of iron, as revealed by the ferrocyanide reaction, for a radius of about 0.5 mm, whereas no evidence of metal loss was apparent in the cases of "zero charge loss." It would thus seem that, at least for the case of iron, ions that might start to leave the electrode during a stimulus pulse can be recaptured if the direction of current flow is reversed and balanced, validating Lilly's idea of reversibility of the electrochemical change, but also demonstrating that some precision of measurement may be required to be certain that "zero charge loss" is actually achieved. Obviously, when such is the case, the Anapol stimulus electrode is operating rather similarly to the Ta_2O_5 capacitor electrode in that there is no (net) flow of ionic current. However, it can be calculated that even a minor imbalance might produce very significant effects over an extended period of time; for example, at 50 Hz if the imbalance were only 1 nC/cycle, almost 2×10^{-9} moles H^+/h would be produced, which, in a volume of 3×10^{-8} liters surrounding the electrode tip out to 100 μm, would bring the pH to 1.2 in an unbuffered solution.

C. *Other Characteristics*

Another aspect of the measurements readily available with the Anapol circuitry is presented in Fig. 5, which is typical of an extensive series of observations in striate cortex both of rabbits and of macaques. First, it can be seen that both the access resistance of the electrodes, and the degree of additional polarization they undergo for application of a given pulse–charge (100 nC, i.e., 500 μA for 200 μsec) while being held at an anodal polarization of 0.4 V, was much greater after implantation in the brain than when the electrodes were initially tested in physiological saline or Ringer's solution. These increases often took several days to develop fully, and thus to some degree may reflect the gradual investiture of the electrodes with a connective tissue sheath. On the other hand, since the electrode believed to be in the ventricle displayed little change in access resistance (Fig. 5), and a substantially smaller charge acceptance than electrodes in brain, the effects observed cannot all be ascribed to this encapsulation.

The vagaries of the daily fluctuation in access resistance and charge acceptance (Fig. 5) are, at present, essentially mysterious. While each of these measures tends to vary *pari passu* for different electrode loci, thus probably reflecting some overall change in the state of the animal or of the brain, there are also substantial changes that can occur independently at single loci. No correlation has been found between access resistance and charge acceptance, a fact inherently surprising, since both would be expected, *a priori,* to be related to surface area of the electrode. However, the "effective" surface area of an electrode implanted in the brain seems to bear only minimal relation to actual "geometrical" surface area. The access resistance will also be influenced by the overall charge-carrying capacity of the electrolyte solution, whereas the charge acceptance is determined by the surface chemistry of the electrode in relation to the concentration of available ionic species and the voltage applied.

In one experiment, where 12 implanted electrodes were available in striate cortex of a macaque, the access resistance could be shown to vary significantly in relation to the visual environment, i.e., darkness or general illumination enhanced by stroboscopic flashing (Bartlett & Doty, unpublished). The access resistance was decreased by illumination as much as 1.0 kΩ (about 20%) at some electrodes, but others showed little or opposite change, the average being only 4.7% ($P < 0.01$). For the data in Fig. 5, however, the rabbit was always in a normally lit chamber. Thus, the day-to-day fluctuations are unlikely to be attributable to changes in the external environment or the rabbit's responses thereto.

In macaques, using 127-μm diameter Pt–W electrodes, there was a significant correlation ($p < 0.05$, $r' = -0.64$) between access resistance and the threshold for the monkey to detect stimulation with 200-μsec pulses at 50 Hz. The higher the access resistance, the lower the threshold, suggesting that current density is probably the critical factor since, other things being equal, access resistance is inversely proportional to the surface area of the electrode. With microelectrodes (70–30% Pt–Ir, glass-insulated, impedance 0.2–5.0 MΩ at 1 kHz), thresholds for macaques to detect such excitation of striate cortex is substantially lower than with macroelectrodes, but it is also critically dependent upon location of the electrode within the laminar organization of the striate cortex (Bartlett & Doty, 1980). For the macroelectrodes, the threshold ranges between 50 and 350 μA, averaging about 100 μA. For microelectrodes, the threshold commonly lies between 15 and 25 μA, but in certain areas still being determined, as little as 2.0 μA can be consistently effective. It should be noted, of course, that the Anapol system is impractical with microelectrodes because of difficulty in controlling the nanoampere-charging current that their high impedance would require.

III. Preparatory Techniques

A variety of techniques have been developed over the years in this laboratory for chronic electrical stimulation and recording from the brain in alert, behaving animals. Four of these are perhaps sufficiently unique as to deserve general description.

A. A Transdural Intracortical Electrode

For many years we placed electrodes within the neocortex under direct vision after opening the dura mater. While this had the advantage of allowing placement in relation to vascular patterns and sulcal landmarks, there were two serious disadvantages. First, because of reduced intracranial pressure in the anesthetized state, a considerable space develops between the brain and the skull, particularly after opening the dura mater. While such abnormal relations can to some degree be alleviated by elevation of the hindquarters and other manipulations, the problem still often remains that while the electrodes are fixed to the skull, their ultimate relation to the brain is unsatisfactorily indeterminate. In other words, electrodes affixed to the skull and, at time of implantation, barely penetrating the neocortex, ultimately find emplacement within the adjacent white matter when the brain returns to its normal volume in the alert state and impales itself upon the electrodes fixed to the skull. The second difficulty is that exposure of the pia arachnoid to foreign agents, necessary to hold the electrodes in place, in some instances precipitates the slow development of a tumor-like fibrous mass that grossly deforms the brain.

Both of these difficulties seem to be avoided by the present technique that leaves the dura mater intact. Electrodes (Fig. 6) are constructed of wire that is sufficiently stiff and sharp that it can readily penetrate the dura mater, yet does so only to a predetermined depth because of a Teflon cuff glued around the electrode.

The electrodes are manufactured from insulated 92% Pt–8% W 127-μm (36 gauge) diameter wire. The wire is cut against a metal surface

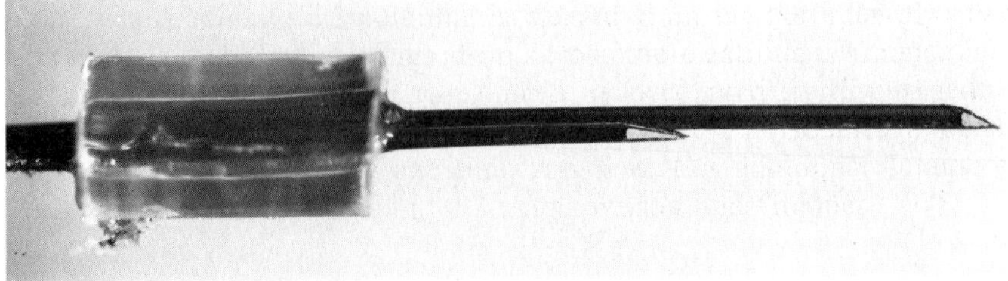

FIG. 6. "Bipolar" electrodes for transdural implantation, cut from insulated 0.127-mm diameter wire of 92% Pt–8% W. These electrodes are sufficiently stiff and sharp to penetrate the dura mater of a mature macaque, and when placed so that the Teflon cuff rests on the dural surface, the deep electrode will lie approximately at the boundary between white and gray matter. Tip-to-tip separation, 1.6 mm; Teflon cuff, 0.8-mm outside diameter, and 1.5 mm long. See text for further details.

using a carbide steel scalpel blade at an angle of about 60° to make a chisel-shaped smooth uninsulated point. The wire or wires are then threaded through a small piece of Teflon tubing, which is glued at the desired location by allowing a small quantity of cyanoacrylate cement to flow into the tubing by capillary action. The surface of the Teflon is previously treated to ensure better bonding with the cyanoacrylate.

For implantation, the electrodes are sterilized in benzalkonium chloride and inserted into a piece of plastic tubing, which in turn is held in a stereotaxic carrier. The electrode is then positioned over a previously drilled 1-mm diameter hole in the skull, grasped with microforceps, and inserted through the dura mater. It is then cemented in place with methyl methacrylate in the usual manner.

The wire for these electrodes is very stiff and thus somewhat refractory for positioning because of the curvature imparting to it by spooling. For precise control, it would probably be advisable to start with pieces of straightened wire, which would then have to be individually insulated. Somewhat surprisingly, perhaps because of the small diameter of the wires, there has been essentially no problem with hemorrhage in inserting over 100 of these electrodes in the highly vascular striate cortex of macaques. There are occasional problems from failure to visualize cortical landmarks. However, the very small opening in the skull, and the preservation of the dura mater has kept the pia arachnoid in a pristine condition, and the depth of penetration of the electrodes has been largely as intended.

B. A Multichannel Connector

After a large number of electrodes have been implanted in the brain, the surgeon then commonly faces the prospect of a protracted effort in soldering the lead wires to a connector in proper order and without producing any short circuits. The arrangement shown in Fig. 7 removes much of the frustration from this experience. Rather than having to solder wires to the underside of a connector, it merely is necessary to place the wire within a piece of brass tubing and crimp the tubing to make the connection. The connecting device has already been affixed to the skull before this procedure begins. (The preparation for the fixation of the connector to the skull is the first thing done after incising the scalp. The periosteum is removed from the skull, and 000-120 stainless steel bolts are then placed in clean dry bone and embedded in methacrylate. At the termination of the implantation procedure, the connecting device is then affixed to this previously prepared base.) After all of the wires have been connected, they are covered with methacrylate in the usual manner (Fig. 8).

C. *Head Restraint*

In many situations, particularly with microelectrode recording in the alert monkey, it is necessary to hold the head in such a way that gross movement is precluded. This has customarily been accomplished by

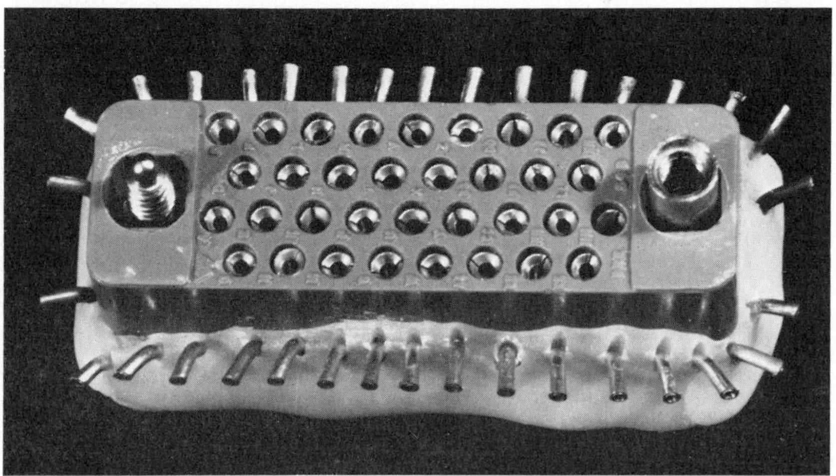

FIG. 7. Connector with 34 channels, prepared for implantation. Soft brass tubing has been soldered to the pins on the underside of the connector, fixed and insulated by methacrylate, and brought to the side for easy access after the device has been cemented to the skull. Connections are made simply by crimping the brass tubing after insertion of the lead wire. It is, of course, necessary to code which tube is connected to which receptacle. Note the arrangement of male and female jackscrew guides that ensure proper orientation of the connecting plug, and also serve to fix it securely in place.

FIG. 8. Macaque several months after implantation of device shown in Fig. 7. The wires from brain to the connector have been covered with methacrylate.

implanting various arrangements of bolts in the skull and affixing them to some framework during the time of daily experimentation. However, despite all precautions and ingenious techniques of implantation, a discouragingly large proportion of the implanted bolts come loose in the skull over a period of months, particularly in juvenile animals. Further-

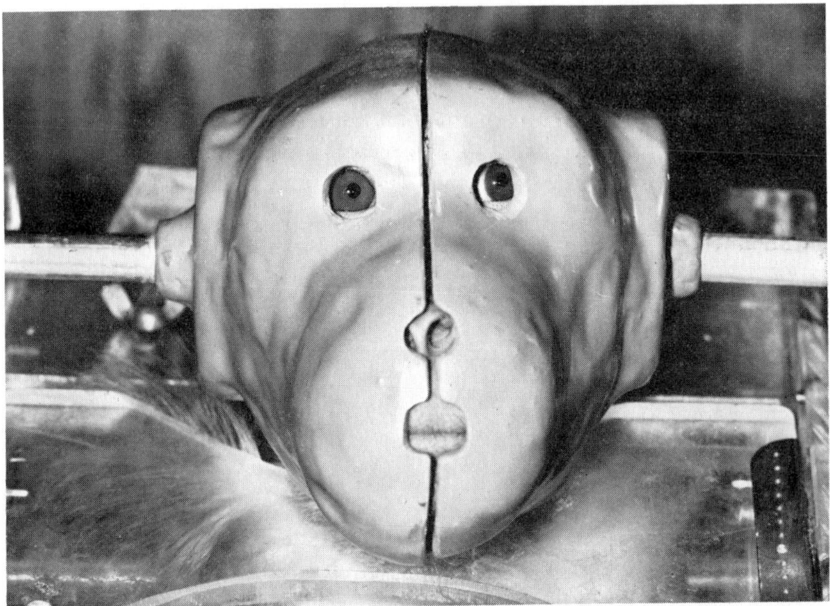

FIG. 9. Individually fitted fiberglass–resin helmet for head restraint. Note in this animal, deviation of gaze is consequent to transphenoidal section of the optic chiasm.

more, because of the flexibility of the skull and its gradual growth, this procedure of restraint is impractical for infants or very young animals. Thus, we have developed the device shown in Fig. 9. Because of the wide variation in shape of each monkey's head, it has so far been desirable to tailor each such restraining helmet to the individual animal, although it seems likely that once a sufficient inventory of helmets has been manufactured, certain of them will be transferable from one animal to another. The animal does have some freedom of movement within the helmet and tolerates the device for several hours. Experience has shown that for the recording of single unit activity from the alert animal, this type of restraint is equally as satisfactory as that using bolts implanted in the skull.

The general procedure is to obtain a plaster of Paris[1] model of the monkey's head and build the helmet around it using fiberglass and resin.[2]

To obtain the casting of the monkey's head, a mold first must be made. This is done by preparing a liter or so of "artists' moulage."[3] This is a mixture of gelatin, clay, and hair, normally used by artists and an-

[1]Penfield Chemical Products, 64 Whitney Road, Penfield, N.Y. 145266.

[2]Bondex International, Inc., Toms River, N. J. 08753.

[3]Plastico Moulage, Sculpture House, 38 East 30th Street, New York, N.Y. 10016.

thropologists for obtaining life or death masks, models of hands, and so forth. The material flows well at body temperature but congeals into a flexible, soft mold at room temperature. It must be prepared, however, by cooking in a double boiler and heating to about 70+°C to dissolve it thoroughly. This will take 1–1.5 hours and must thus be started some time before the monkey is prepared. The same material can be used repeatedly, i.e., previous molds are redissolved by heating in the double boiler. (This material, incidentally, is also useful for making models of a brain, prior to histological processing, to show location of electrodes or extent of cortical ablation.)

The food-deprived monkey is anesthetized with intravenous or intrapleural secobarbital, and is given a small dose of atropine to curtail salivation. The head and neck are shaved, and the vibrissae or guard hairs removed. Using a laryngoscope, the trachea is then intubated, and the tube taped in place so that it will not slip out during subsequent manipulation. It is helpful to use a spray of topical anesthesia in the laryngeal area to cut down the amount of gagging during the intubation.

The monkey's jaw is taped closed, and the nostrils occluded to prevent material from running into them. The animal is then draped supine on a V-shaped animal board with its head suspended down over one end into a large bowl that will accommodate a liter of molding moulage. The ears are taped to the side of the head so as to simplify the interior contours of the ultimate helmet. The moulage is cooled to about 45° to 48°C and then poured over the monkey's head within the retaining bowl, being careful, of course, that the material does not occlude the tracheal cannula yet covers the underside of the jaw.

It is essential that the moulage cool thoroughly before starting to remove the monkey's head from it. To this end, the retaining bowl is made of metal, and is placed in a second pan of ice water to hasten the cooling.

To remove the head from the moulage, the mold is cut longitudinally on the underside of the jaw with a blunt, thin spatula. If the positive plaster of Paris cast is not to be made until the following day, the mold should be protected from drying by keeping it in a plastic bag in the refrigerator. For reuse, the moulage material is also always kept in a sealed, moisture-proof container to prevent its dessication.

In making the positive cast of the head, it is useful to embed it upon a metal rod for subsequent ease in handling. The rod, deeply scored so that it will be retained within the plaster, is thus inserted into the cavity of the mold as the plaster is being poured in. The mixture of plaster and water should be sufficiently thin so that it can be stirred into all crevices of the mold without entrapping air. The positive plaster casting is removed from the moulage mold just as the monkey's head was removed. This is done carefully to preserve the mold in the event that the casting is defective. Minor defects in the casting can be built up with more plaster, clay, or wax, which is often necessary around the ears.

The finished product is an exact duplicate of the entire head of the monkey. This casting, now held by the supporting rod, provides the basis for the construction of the plastic helmet. To prevent adherence between the plaster and the resin from which the helmet is made, the casting must be thoroughly coated with petroleum jelly, grease, or a thin layer of wax. Since the fumes from the resin are moderately toxic, it is best to perform all of the subsequent operations in a ventilating hood, or at least in a well-ventilated room. The resin is catalytically activated and, of course, it is essential that none of the resin inadvertently contact the catalyst; proper precautions thus must be followed in this regard. The catalytic processing of the resin generates heat, and the larger the mass of resin the greater the rise in temperature and therefore the greater the rapidity of curing. The curing of the rather thin coats applied to the casting to make the helmet can be accelerated by use of a heat lamp, but care must be taken not to cure too large a mass too rapidly or the material may crack.

Mix only enough resin to be used in a 15-minute session, adding catalyst according to directions on the package, about 15 drops per 30 ml of resin; more catalyst will produce more rapid setting, and so on.

Disposable latex examination gloves are used in handling the material, and a disposable drop cloth should be placed beneath the casting, since the process from here on is somewhat messy. The resin can be dissolved in acetone, if necessary.

The first step is to coat the casting with a relatively thin layer only of the resin, a step that is best done after the resin has become slightly viscous so that it does not all run off. As this coating of resin begins to harden and becomes tacky, previously prepared strips of fiberglass cloth, 1–2 cm wide and 4–12 cm long, are applied to the surface. The fiberglass is either applied directly to the casting and then coated with resin, or first dipped in the resin and then applied. Whichever method is employed, care should be taken that no air bubbles are trapped in the process. Should one coat of resin become completely hard and cured prior to the application of another, it is advisable to roughen the surface to assure proper adhesion of the second coat to the first. The thickness of the resin–fiberglass helmet is gradually built up by applying the cloth strips at right angles to the previous layer until a thickness of 3–5 mm has been obtained.

The next step is to provide some means of securing the helmet to a rigid framework. This can be done by embedding the connections within the resinous matrix of the helmet itself. To that end, a "flexaframe foot" (Fisher Scientific Company,[4] #14-677), which accommodates $\frac{1}{2}$-inch round stock, is placed roughly over the area above the ear on each side; but, of course, other points of attachment can be employed depending upon the uses to which the helmet will ultimately be put. In our instance where we are working on the occipital area and in the midline, the helmet will be cut sagittally down the midline into two equal halves, and the helmet is placed upon the animal by bringing these two halves together while centered upon the head (Fig. 9). Thus, the two halves will be held together by pressure exerted onto the flexaframe feet by the metal rods and will be secured to an appropriate framework. In placing the flexaframe feet it is helpful to make them parallel to each other. Thus, the helmet is tipped on its side, and a flat surface filed at the point where the foot will be placed. A well is then formed with masking tape surrounding this area, and this serves to retain the mixture of resin and cloth fibers into which the flexaframe foot is set, with its orientation parallel to the sagittal plane being assured by the filed, flattened surface.

When the helmet is complete, it is given a final coat of resin alone, which will produce a smooth, hard surface. The two halves of the mask are then separated by cutting down the sagittal plane with a hacksaw or thin dental bur until the plaster is encountered. Various holes for the nostrils, mouth, and eyes, and access to implanted electrical connections can then be drilled and filed in the helmet as necessary. One should be certain, of course, that the interior of the helmet is smooth and free of any sharp protuberances that might produce discomfort to the wearer. In use, it is helpful to file flats on the round metal stock used to immobilize the helmet, otherwise the animal is able to rotate the helmet about the vertical axis.

D. *Insertion of Microelectrodes*

We have developed a means of inserting microelectrodes through a 1-mm hole drilled in the skull of monkeys, cats, or rabbits. This procedure seems to have some advantage for chronic recordings over that commonly employed in which a much larger opening is made in the skull. The advantage of the very small skull opening is that, theoretically, a rather large number of them can be made over a period of months with only minimal exposure of the dura mater at any one time. However,

[4]Fischer Scientific Company, 711 Forbes Avenue, Pittsburgh, Pa. 15219.

there may be some problem with bone erosion in placing substantial numbers of these holes and affixed guides to the exposed skull over a period of weeks or months.

The basic idea involves utilization of fittings from hypodermic syringes. The plastic hub of a hypodermic syringe needle is prepared for fixation to the skull. The needle is placed in a lathe and a groove cut in the hub so that methacrylate cement will be bound in this groove. The hub is then cut off, providing a fitting with a length of 4–6 mm. Using aseptic precautions on the anesthetized animal, a 1-mm diameter hole is drilled very carefully through the skull using a stereoscopic microscope with axial illumination. The dura mater is then exposed and bone chips carefully removed using sterile dental absorbent points, without applying pressure on the underlying brain. The hypodermic needle hub is cemented to clean, dry bone concentric with this prepared hole in the skull. The skin is stitched around the hub in such a way that the top of the hub is essentially flush with the surface of the scalp. The orifice of the hub is closed with sterile bone wax and sealed in place with a heated bolt of appropriate diameter.

The hypodermic needle hub has been employed since it accepts, with a perfectly snug fit, the tapered male end of a hypodermic syringe. It is from a glass tuberculin syringe that a lightweight hydraulic (oil, brake fluid, or silicone) microdrive can be manufactured (Fig. 10; see Bartlett & Doty, 1980). The glass syringe and piston are scored and broken to suitable length. A piece of hypodermic needle tubing is cemented to the end of the piston concentric with the opening in the barrel of the syringe (Fig. 10a). This will accommodate the microelectrode by a pressure fit, and when the syringe barrel has been secured into the hypodermic needle hub implanted over the hole in skull, the microelectrode will be driven out the end of the barrel, through the dura mater, and into the brain. Connection to the microelectrode is made via a coiled wire passing from the hypodermic needle tubing and out a hole in the bottom of the syringe barrel to a connector glued to its side (Fig. 10b). The hydraulic connection is made via a Luer-Lok fitting glued to the other end of the syringe barrel and passing via Teflon tubing to a second tuberculin syringe driven by a micrometer. With this simple arrangement, there is some possibility that the advance of the micrometer will not accurately reflect advance of the microelectrode because of leakage of the fluid along the piston in the microdrive. This problem can be somewhat reduced by using a longer piston (which adds to the mass of the microdrive and diminishes the total excursion obtainable) and a higher viscosity silicone fluid. In any event, single units are readily obtained and held for minutes or hours using this microdrive in conjunction with the head restraint system shown

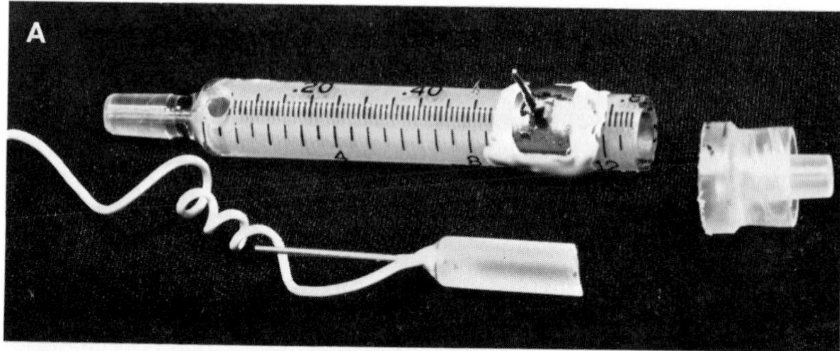

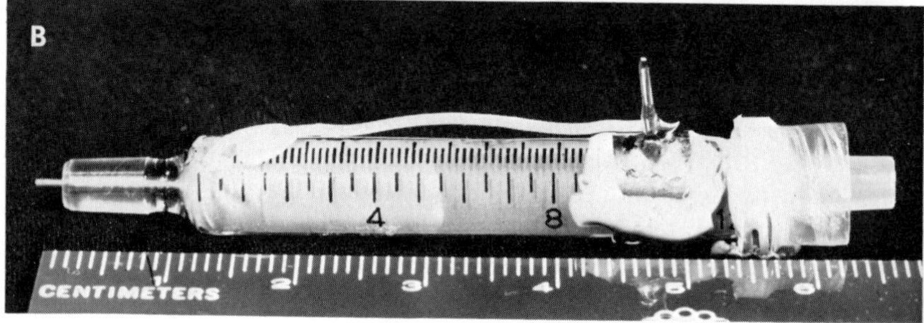

FIG. 10. Microdrive constructed from glass tuberculin syringe (a) before assembly and (b) after assembly. Microelectrode is inserted into tubing at end of piston; lead wire to electrode is spiraled about the tubing, exits through the hole, and is soldered to connecting pin cemented to barrel. See text for further details.

in Fig. 7 for macaques (Bartlett & Doty, 1980) or with no head restraint whatever for rabbits (Kahrilas, Doty, & Bartlett 1980).

Summary

When the voltage imposed upon a metallic electrode is increased while the electrode is in a conducting aqueous medium, the current is carried by various chemical reactions until, at a level of about 1.8 V, electrolysis of the water occurs. Because of changes in pH and the development of gas pressure, this reaction is highly deleterious to living tissue. Three procedures have been developed to pass effective stimulating currents without producing hydrolysis: balanced biphasic pulse pairs; the tantalum pentoxide capacitor electrode; and the Anapol system, which, in producing cathodal pulses from an anodally charged electrode, effectively doubles the "safe" working voltage. Some of the practical problems associated with these and other stimulating procedures are discussed. In addition, techniques are outlined for implanting and connecting arrays of intracerebral electrodes, for passing microelectrodes into the brain through 1-mm holes in the skull, and for restraining the head within a close-fitting plastic helmet.

Appendix: A Simple, Accurate, and Optoelectrically Isolated Constant Current Stimulator *

The device to be described provides rectangular, monophasic constant current pulses from 1 μA to 9.999 mA intensity with 1-lgmA increments. The circuitry is battery operated and isolated from control-circuit ground by a high-speed optoelectric isolator. An optional circuit provides for short-circuiting, i.e., "exhausting," the charge that develops on the stimulating electrodes during passage of stimulating currents (see this chapter). In addition, a radio frequency relaxation oscillator circuit provides an 80 V "compliance-voltage" for the constant current source, thus eliminating the need for a separate high-voltage battery supply.

The stimulator's circuitry was developed in response to the need for a compact, highly accurate constant current stimulator for routine electrophysiological stimulation. The problem of accuracy has, of course, a number of different aspects. For example, the absolute accuracy of the device, the repeatability of current settings, and the human error factor in dial readings. Although reasonably accurate, the use of potentiometers as current selection devices is beset with problems of repeatability, and their circular dials are notoriously difficult to read. Even with "digital" type multiple-turn potentiometers, high accuracy is difficult to obtain because their mechanical linkage introduces considerable error in repeatability. In the present device these problems are overcome for the most part by the use of a truly "digital" voltage divider (Digivider–Digitran Corp.[1]) in which four clearly labeled thumb-wheel switches select an appropriate set of fixed resistors. In essence, repeatability is limited only by the variability in switch contact resistance, which, in the present case, is less than .001%. The "Digivider's" linearity, the factor that largely determines the absolute accuracy of the

*Prepared by John R. Bartlett, for Progress Report #29, Contract NIH 70-2279, September 30, 1977.

[1]Digitran Co., Division of Becton, Dickinson and Co., 855 S. Arroyo Parkway, Pasadena, Ca. 91105.

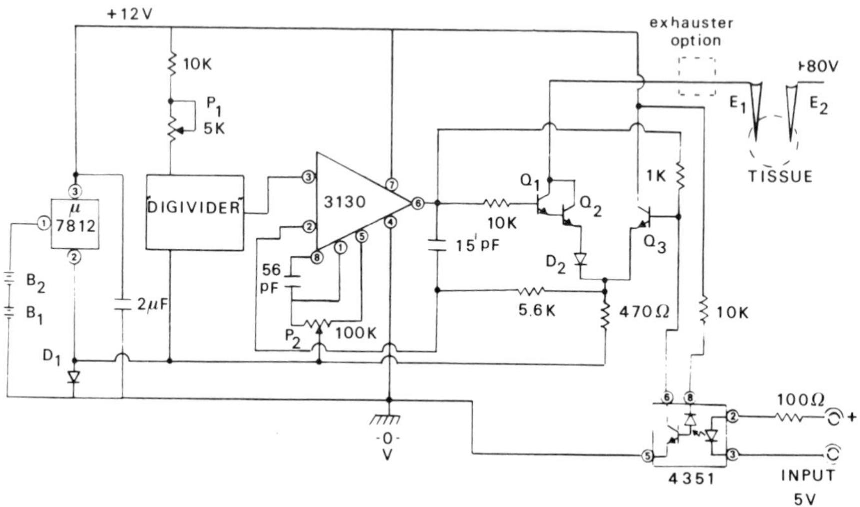

FIG. 11. Constant current source. See text for details.

stimulator, is 0.1% while the large, easily read switch markings not only eliminate the parallactic errors encountered in dial reading, but also greatly reduce the likelihood of simply misreading the current setting.

For high-intensity stimulation (e.g., 10 mA), constant current stimulators must have a "compliance-voltage" in the neighborhood of 80–100 V, since the access resistance of even fairly large-tipped electrodes can be on the order of 6–7 kΩ. Traditionally, a radio "B" battery has been used for the compliance-voltage source. These batteries are rather bulky and increasingly expensive as low-voltage solid-state circuitry makes their use unnecessary. To eliminate the need for such batteries, a small radio frequency (~250 kHz) relaxation oscillator circuit was designed to provide an unloaded output voltage of about 80 V. This circuit is powered from the same rechargeable battery circuit required for the constant current source, and when unloaded draws only about 10 to 14 mA of current at 12 V (120–144 mW). It is capable of providing no more than 2 mA of continuous current at an output voltage of 40 V (80 mW), but this is of little consequence since electrophysiological stimulation normally consists of low duty-cycle pulses, e.g., 1 msec, 1 mA, 50 Hz (4 mW/sec at 80 V). Consequently, the only limitation is that the stimulator cannot be used to produce "dc" lesions. Elimination of the compliance voltage "B" battery allows the entire stimulator to be housed in a 3 × 8 × 5-inch cowl type "Mini Box."[2]

To simplify presentation, the constant current, the optional exhauster circuit, and the high-voltage source are shown separately in Figs. 11,

[2]Bud Industries, Inc., 4605 E. 355th St., Willoughby, Ohio 44094.

12, and 13, and in their most basic form, namely, with neither a peripheral circuit for recharging the Ni–Cd battery supply, an on–off power switch, a circuit for reversing the "polarity" of stimulation nor, and perhaps most important, a meter circuit for monitoring battery status. These are all relatively simple circuits and may be found in most electronic circuit handbooks or, in the case of battery charging, in the handbooks provided by various battery manufacturers. A listing of components for the various circuits is given in Table 1.

Constant current source Power for both this circuit and the high-voltage source is derived from two 9.6, 150 mAh rechargeable Ni–Cd batteries (B_1 and B_2); see Fig. 11. The output of the battery supply is stabilized at 12 V by the μ7812 active voltage regulator. The active constant current circuit centers around the 3130 operational amplifier (RCA—CD3130) that is operated in the classical "noninverting" mode; the input at pin 3 is taken from the "Digivider" and the negative feedback at pin 2 from the 470-Ω "current-sensing" resistor. The 3130 is a FET-input and FET-output amplifier and is critical to this particular circuit in that (*a*) it can operate from a single-sided power supply (+12 V versus

TABLE I

ELECTRONIC COMPONENTS

Constant Current Source	
B_1 and B_2	Burgess, CD24, 9.6 V, Ni–Cd battery
"Digivider"	Digitran Corp., K094-0013, 10 Ω
3130	RCA, CD 3130 operational amplifier
Q_1 and Q_2	2N5551 150-V NPN transistor
Q_3	2N3904 NPN transistor
D_1 and D_2	1N914 Diode, 100 V_R
4351	Hewlett–Packard 4351, high-speed, optoelectric isolator
μ7812	Fairchild μ7812, 12-V voltage regulator
P_1 and P_2	10-turn, carbon, potentiometers
Exhauster Option	
(As shown)	
High Voltage Source	
Q_1	2N5551, 150-V NPN transistor
Q_2	2N3906, PNP transistor
Q_3	2N3904, NPN transistor
Q_4	2N6027 Programmable-Unijunction Transistor (PUT)
D_1 and D_2	1N914 diode, 100 V_R
D_3–D_5	1N4004 diode, 400 V_R
L_1	Miller type 4662, 1 mH R.F. choke coil
L_2	Miller type 70F-252AF R.F. choke coil
C_1 and C_2	10 μF, 15 WVDC and 2 nF, 15 WVDC, respectively
C_3 and C_4	0.1 μF, 150 WVDC and 2 μF, 150 WVDC, respectively
P_1 and P_2	10-turn carbon "trim" potentiometer
P_3	single turn; carbon, "trim" potentiometer

±12 V); (*b*) its output can approach within about 100 mV of the –0– voltage rail; and (*c*) its high input resistance (1000 MΩ) by "loading" does not degrade the inherent accuracy of the "Digivider."

In operation, the 3130 attempts to maintain the voltage across the 470-Ω current-sensing resistor at the same value as the voltage provided by the "Digivider" at pin 3. Thus the current through the 470-Ω resistor is simply the Digivider output voltage divided by 470 Ω. When transistor Q_3 is cut off by applying a 5-V pulse to the input of the 4351 optoelectric isolator, the current necessary to generate the appropriate voltage across the 470-Ω resistor passes through the high-voltage transistors Q_1 and Q_2 and the diode D_2, and consequently through the stimulating electrodes E_1 and E_2. Since Q_1 and Q_2 form a "Darlington" pair, the error current due to Q_1's base current is very small. (The error current is the difference between the current passing through the 470-Ω resistor and that passing through the electrodes.) Because of the base-to-emitter "turn-on" voltages (~0.7 V) of Q_1 and Q_2 and the forward "turn-on" voltage of D_2 (~0.7V), the output voltage of the 3130 will always be about 2.1 V more positive than the voltage across the 470-Ω resistor when Q_1, Q_2, and D_2 are conducting. When the 5-V input voltage is removed from the optoelectric isolator, the base of Q_3 rises toward the output voltage of the 3130. However, since Q_3 will conduct as soon as its base-to-emitter "turn-on" voltage is exceeded, the output of the 3130 actually falls because Q_3 is capable of passing sufficient current to maintain the appropriate voltage across the 470-Ω resistor in the absence of Q_1 and Q_2 conduction. Thus the voltage difference between the output of the 3130 and the 470-Ω resistor falls to about 0.7 V, and this in turn is not sufficient to keep Q_1, Q_2, and D_2 turned on. The result is that the current passing through E_1 and E_2 is shut off. The advantage of this "push–pull" arrangement is that when any intensity of current pulse is to be delivered, the output of the 3130 must rise only about 1.4 V. In similar circuits the rise time of the output current pulses depends on how fast the current can reach its final value, which generally means how fast the amplifier can "slew," i.e., reach a given voltage when presented with a large signal input. Also, the "squareness" of the pulse "corners" depends on the slewing and the "settling time" of the amplifier, both of which suffer when the amplifier output must make large voltage excursions. In the present circuit the maximum voltage change at the amplifier output is about 1.4 V and constant for all output currents. At a "slewing" rate of 10 V/μsec, this 1.4 V is reached in less than 1 μsec, and the result is stimulation pulses having a very rapid onset and offset, i.e., sharp corners. While probably not critical to electrophysiological stimulation *per se*, this feature is important when attempting to measure access resistance, electrode polarization, and so on. It should be noted that this advantage is maintained by the use of the high-speed diode-to-diode 4351 optoelectric isolator. The 15 pF capacitor is just sufficient to compensate for the stray capacitative losses in the Q_1, Q_2, Q_3, and D_2 complex and keeps the 3130 from breaking into oscillation. Diode D_1 provides a pseudoreference buss about 0.7 V greater than the –0– voltage rail, thus the ability of the 3130's output to reach zero is never tested, and there is added assurance that Q_1, Q_2, and D_2 will be shut off when the Digivider output voltage is "zero."

Calibration of the circuit is via the trim potentiometers P_1 and P_2. The input circuit is activated with the "Digivider" set at 0000. P_2 is then adjusted until output current is just zero. Then, with the Digivider set at 9.999, P_1 is set for current output of 9.999 mA.

A. *Optional "Exhauster" Circuit.*

As such, the optional "exhauster" circuit shown in Fig. 12 requires no power of its own, its activation being entirely due to "stealing" and a small current (~1 μA per volt developed across the stimulating electrodes) from the constant current source when an output to the stimulating electrodes is present. Its purpose is to provide a pathway by which the charge that accumulates on metal electrodes (see pp. 76–78) during current flow can be dissipated between current pulses. Without such a pathway, the electrode can charge to the level of hydrolysis even during low-frequency pulsing. With no current flow to the collectors of Q_1 and Q_2 of the constant current circuit, the gate (g) of the 2N6450, depletion type FET, is at its drain potential (d) and the source (s) to drain resistance is of the order of a few hundred ohms. Consequently, electrodes E_1 and E_2 are connected together via both the 2N6450 transistor and the 15-kΩ resistor, which acts to limit the peak discharge current flowing from the electrodes. Following a current pulse, electrode E_1 will be negative relative to E_2 and will discharge through this transistor–resistor circuit until

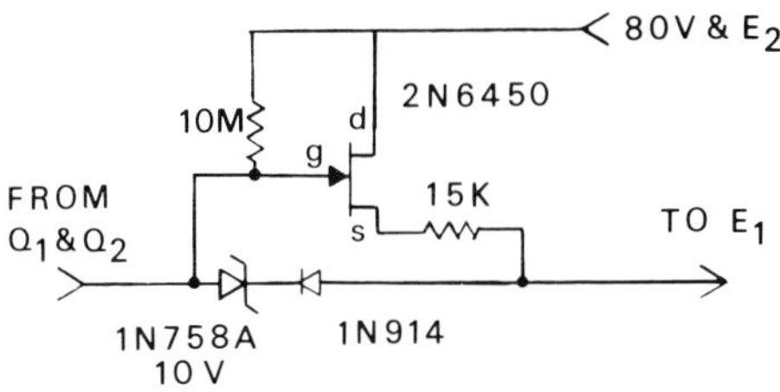

FIG. 12. Optional "exhauster" circuit. See text for details.

the potential between E_1 and E_2 is zero. The 1N914 diode ensures that the negative potential at E_1 cannot make the transistor gate voltage equal to the source voltage and in turn ensures full "turn-on" of the transistor.

During a stimulation pulse, when current flows to the collectors of Q_1 and Q_2, a 10-V potential drop develops across the 1N758A Zener diode. This potential is constant regardless of the voltage between E_1 and E_2 and is sufficient to "pinch-off" the 2N6450 transistor. Pinched-off, the source to drain resistance of the transistor rises to several hundred million ohms and thus the current bypass around E_1 and E_2 is all but eliminated. The result is that virtually all the current to Q_1 and Q_2 must pass through the stimulating electrode; the only exception being the current flowing in the 10-mΩ resistor, which, again, is about 1 μA + 0.1 μA per volt developed across the electrodes E_1 and E_2. For an 80-V drop across E_1 and E_2, this "error" current would be about 9 μA.

B. Compliance-Voltage Source

The basic part of this circuit is a "flip-flop" type relaxation oscillator formed by the transistors Q_1 and Q_2 and coil L_1, and operating at a frequency of about 250 kHz (Fig. 13). Starting at the point when Q_1 first turns on, L_1 is unsaturated and the collector of Q_1 is low because of the high impedance of L_1. This in turn ensures the turn-on of Q_2 whose collector feeds back to Q_1 to keep Q_1 and itself turned-on. As current continues to flow, L_1 begins to saturate and its impedance drops toward zero. This forces the collector of Q_1 to move toward the +12V rail and eventually to shut off Q_2, which, by feedback to Q_1's base, shuts off Q_1

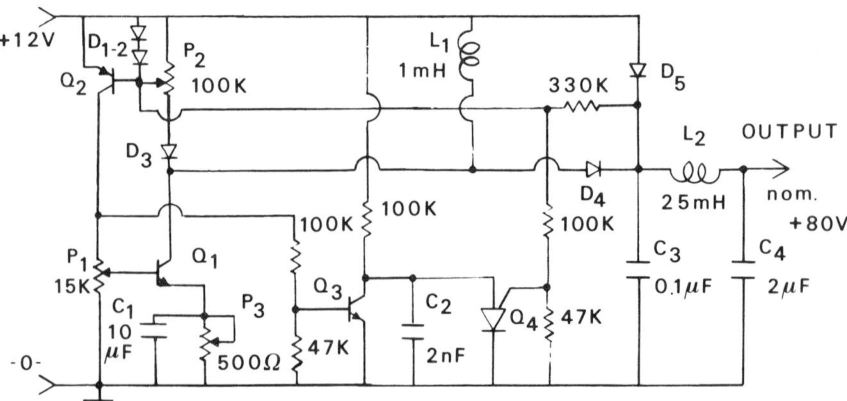

FIG. 13. Compliance voltage source. See text for details.

and thus rapidly terminates the current flow to L_1. The magnetic field of L_1 thus collapses, generating a high-voltage "back emf" at the collector of Q_1. This voltage is positive to both the –0– voltage and +12V rails and ensures that Q_2 and thus Q_1 remain off. At the same time the diode D_4 conducts and the "back emf" charges C_3 and eventually C_4 (C_3 and C_4 are always charged to about 12 V due to D_5). The "back emf" eventually falls toward zero, Q_2 is turned on again and, in turn, causes Q_1 conduct, thus beginning a second saturation of L_1.

The capacitors C_3 and C_4 and the coil L_2 form a storage and filter network for the output voltage, while the 330 kΩ resistor provides a negative feedback pathway from C_3 to Q_2. As the voltage of C_3 rises, this feedback causes Q_2 to cut off earlier and earlier in the saturation cycle of L_1, and thus less and less energy is available to charge C_3 and C_4. In turn, this stabilizes the unloaded output voltage at about 80 V and decreases the circuit's unloaded energy requirements.

When "tuned" for maximum efficiency, the oscillator is very near a "stall condition" and to ensure that it will always start, the circuit composed mainly of Q_3, Q_4, and C_2 is added to the high-voltage (Q_1, Q_2, and L_1) oscillator circuit. This "start-up" circuit is another relaxation oscillator centered around the "Programmable-Unijunction Transistor" (PUT), Q_4. When the high-voltage oscillator is running, the voltage across C_2 fails to reach a level sufficient to trigger the PUT because Q_3 is alternately turned on and off at a frequency whose period is much less than that needed to charge C_2 through the 100 kΩ resistor of Q_3's collector circuit. However, should its high-voltage oscillator fail to start (Q_2 locked in the off-state), the PUT circuit will "fire" within a few milliseconds and, by forcing Q_2 to turn on, start the high voltage oscillator.

To achieve maximum efficiency the high-voltage oscillator must be tuned by potentiometers P_1, P_2, and P_3. As all adjustments are interactive, this is somewhat tedious and requires the current flow to the circuit to be measured at the same time the circuit's output is continuously driving a load of about 20 kΩ. The voltage across this load should be about 40 V, and the current to the circuit via the +12 V power rail about 10–6 mA when a peak efficiency of about 66–48% is obtained. Initially, in starting the high-voltage oscillator, P_1, P_2, and P_3 should be about midrange.

The prototype stimulator has now been in service for about 18 months, and a second unit is just entering service. The first unit has been used in conjunction with standard electrophysiological recording, and no interference from the compliance-voltage oscillator circuit has been seen. For routine threshold determinations in behavioral experiments, the stimulator has rapidly become the favorite of the technical staff, mainly because of its size and easy-to-read dial. Repeated checks for accuracy have shown the circuitry to be so stable that, except for particularly critical measurements, the use of auxiliary current-measuring apparatus has been abandoned. At average currents and frequencies of stimulation, about 4 to 6 hr of continuous usage may be expected per battery charge.

Acknowledgments

Original observations described herein, as well as the preparation of this chapter, have been made under NIH Contract 70-2279 from the National Institute of Neurological and Communicative Disorders and Stroke, National Institutes of Health.

References

Bartlett, J. R., & Doty, R. W. An exploration of the ability of macaques to detect microstimulation of striate cortex. *Acta Neurobiologiae Experimentalis 40*, 1980, **40,** 713–728.

Bartlett, J. R., Doty, R. W., Lee, B. B., Negrão, N., & Overman, W. H., Jr. Deleterious effects of prolonged electrical excitation of striate cortex in macaques. *Brain, Behavior and Evolution*, 1977, **14,** 46–66.

Bollinger, S. F., & Gerall, A. A. Intracranial self-stimulation and impedance as functions of electrode and stimulus source. *American Journal of Physiology*, 1971, **220,** 264–269.

Brummer, S. B., & Turner, M. J. Electrical stimulation of the nervous system: The principle of safe charge injection with noble metal electrodes. *Bioelectrochemistry and Bioenergetics*, 1975, **2,** 13–25.

Delgado, J. M. R. Prolonged stimulation of brain in awake monkeys. *Journal of Neurophysiology*, 1959, **22,** 458–475.

Delgado, J. M. R., & Mir, D. Infatigability of pupillary constriction evoked by hypothalamic stimulation in monkeys. *Neurology*, 1966, **16,** 939–950.

Del Pozo, F., & Delgado, J. M. R. Hybrid stimulator for chronic experiments. *IEEE Transactions on Biomedical Engineering*, 1978, **BME-25,** 92–94.

Doty, R. W. Conditioned reflexes elicited by electrical stimulation of the brain in macaques. *Journal of Neurophysiology*, 1965, **28,** 623–640.

Doty, R. W., Rutledge, L. T., Jr., & Larsen, R. M. Conditioned reflexes established to electrical stimulation of cat cerebral cortex. *Journal of Neurophysiology*, 1956, **19,** 401–415.

Dymond, A. M. Characteristics of the metal-tissue interface of stimulation electrodes. *IEEE Transactions on Biomedical Engineering*, 1976, **BME-23,** 274–280.

Dymond, A. M., Kaechele, L. E., Jurist, J. M., & Crandall, P. H. Brain tissue reaction to some chronically implanted metals. *Journal of Neurosurgery*, 1970, **5,** 574–580.

Elul, R. Fixed charge in the cell membrane. *Journal of Physiology (London)*, 1967, **189,** 351–365.

Gerken, G. M., & Judy, M. M. Electrode polarization and the detection of electrical stimulation of the brain. *Physiology and Behavior*, 1977, **18,** 825–832.

Guyton, D. L., & Hambrecht, F. T. Capacitor electrode stimulates nerve or muscle without oxidation-reduction reactions. *Science*, 1973, **181,** 74–76.

Guyton, D. L., & Hambrecht, F. T. Theory and design of capacitor electrodes for chronic stimulation. *Medical and Biological Engineering*, 1974, **12,** 613–620.

Hunsperger, R. W. Die asynchrone und lokal umschriebene Riezwirkung von Mittelfrequenz-Dauerströmen im Hypothalamus der Katze. *Experimental Brain Research,* 1969, **9,** 164–182.

Kahrilas, P. J., Doty, R. W., & Bartlett, J. R. Failure to find luxotonic responses for single units in visual cortex of the rabbit. *Experimental Brain Research,* 1980, **39,** 11–16.

Lilly, J. C., Hughes, J. R., Alvord, E. C., Jr., & Galkin, T. W. Brief, noninjurious electric waveform for stimulation of the brain. *Science,* 1955, **121,** 468–469.

Loucks, R. B., Weinberg, H., & Smith, M. The erosion of electrodes by small currents. *Electroencephalography and Clinical Neurophysiology,* 1959, **11,** 823–826.

McFadden, J. T. Metallurgical principles in neurosurgery. *Journal of Neurosurgery,* 1969, **31,** 373–385.

Phillips, C. G., & Porter, R. *Corticospinal neurones: Their role in movement.* New York: Academic Press, 1977.

Silverman, G., Ball, G. G., & Cohn, C. K. A new automatic constant current stimulator and its biological applications. *IEEE Transactions on Biomedical Engineering,* 1975, **BME-25,** 207–211.

Svaetichin, G. Electrophysiological investigations on single ganglion cells. *Acta Physiologica Scandinavica,* 1951, **24,** Suppl. 86, 5–57.

Weinman, J., & Mahler, J. An analysis of electrical properties of metal electrodes. *Medical Electronics and Biological Engineering,* 1964, **2,** 299–310.

Wetzel, M. D., Howell, L. G., & Bearie, K. J. Experimental performance of steel and platinum electrodes with chronic monophasic stimulation of the brain. *Journal of Neurosurgery,* 1970, **31,** 658–669.

Chapter 5

Depth Stimulation of the Brain

José M. R. Delgado

Departamento de Investigación
Centro Ramón y Cajal
Madrid, Spain

ISBN 0-12-547440-7

The depth of the central nervous system is usually reached through the sensory receptors, which are the natural portals of entry of information and excitation into the brain. A flash of light or a click will evoke sensations accompanied by electrical potentials in the occipital or temporal lobes.

The nervous system may be excited directly, without the intermediary of the senses, by means of electrical currents applied through suitable conductors. The use of electricity to explore both peripheral and central nervous systems started long ago with the investigations of Galvani (1791), DuBois Reymond (1848–1849), Fritsch and Hitzig (1870), and other pioneers of neural research. Modern studies of the unanesthetized brain started with the publications of Hess (1932) who demonstrated that reliable motor, autonomic, and emotional manifestations may be evoked in cats by electrical stimulation of specific brain structures.

Therapeutic use of brain stimulation in man originated with the work of Bickford, Petersen, Dodge, and Sem-Jacobsen (1953), Delgado, Hamlin, and Chapman (1952), Heath and the Tulane University Department of Psychiatry and Neurology (1954), and Sem-Jacobsen, Peterson, Dodge, Lazarte, and Holman (1956). More recently electrical stimulation of the brain and the cerebellum have been used for the therapy of dyskinesias, pain, and epilepsy (Brazier, 1971, Cooper, Riklan, & Snider, 1974; Delgado, 1977); see also an editorial in *Lancet* (Anonymous, 1974), Nastuk (1964), Ramey and O'Doherty (1960), Ray, (1974), and Sheer (1961).

Electrical stimulation of excitable tissues requires rapid reduction of the transmembrane neuronal potential from the resting state to a lower critical value. This is accomplished by removing the charges stored and applying a potential through electrodes placed in neuronal structures. At the cathode, positive charges will flow outward across the cell, reducing the transmembrane potential and producing excitation. Part of the applied current may be dispersed while passing through extracellular fluids or nonexcitable tissue, producing potentially damaging electrolysis and heat. To avoid undesirable disturbances, stimulating currents should be of the lowest possible intensity.

Tissue conductivity is related to its water content, which is 75% in muscle, 68% in brain, and 14% in fat. Within the brain, conductivity is heterogeneous in different structures, and preferential paths may channel the applied current in an unpredictable way. In depth stimulation, this problem is minimized by the use of small contacts.

I. Electrodes and Polarization

Electrodes are good conductors, usually metallic, that carry electric current into or out of an electrolyte solution. To stimulate an excitable structure such as the brain, the output of a voltage generator is connected to the tissue by means of electrodes, and a current is passed through the electrode–tissue interface to the extracellular fluid and neuronal membranes to be depolarized. At the metallic tissue contact, there is an active exchange of material particles and ions, with positive charges attracted to the cathode and negative particles accumulating at the anode. A concentration polarization is then produced, opposing electrostatic force to the passage of current. Polarization may be increased by the electrical properties of the metallic electrode immersed in a solution of its own salt.

Polarization at the electrode surface produces a loss of energy, which tends to heat the interface. Polarization of stimulating metal electrodes is related to the kind of material used. With constant current and square pulses applied through platinum electrodes immersed in physiologic saline, the waveform has a fast rising phase followed by a slower capacitor-like charge due to concentration polarization (Greatbatch, 1967). When the pulse is over, the voltage falls slowly without reaching zero level. The remaining voltage is called the postpulse charge and is caused by the disturbance in the concentration of minority carriers that conducted the pulse (Dymond, 1976). This voltage slowly disappears by a diffusion process. Waveforms of galvanostatic charges are different for platinum, silver, and stainless steel. With stainless steel electrodes, higher voltages are required to pass the same amount of current passed with platinum, due to the fact that nonnoble metals are not catalytic to oxygen (Kahn & Greatbatch, 1974). The problem of polarization is complex and still not well-understood (Weinmann & Mahler, 1964).

As shown by Loucks, Weinberg, and Smith (1959), a current intensity as low as 0.1 mA (60 Hz) passing for 3.3 min between two stainless steel electrodes 0.24 mm in diameter and immersed in saline solution, produced considerable erosion of the electrode tip; currents of 2 mA applied for a few minutes through silver, stainless steel, and tungsten electrodes caused considerable destruction of the tips with mushroom-like accretions.

Nonnoble metal electrodes may suffer paradoxic anodal corrosion due to faradic rectification. To avoid this problem in chronic stimulation, cathodic protection should be provided by using a diode that does not permit the cathode electrode to go positive beyond 0.5 V. (Kahn & Greatbatch, 1974). As mentioned later when describing instrumentation, this problem is solved in our hybrid stimulator (Del Pozo & Delgado, 1978).

Another problem is the crevice corrosion. Stainless steel usually develops a protective oxide coating that must be restored whenever it is removed. For this process, there is an abundant amount of oxygen in the tissues. In crevices, however, for example, at the edge between the electrode tip and insulation, oxygen may be exhausted and corrosion may take place. In our laboratory, Parreño (unpublished) has demonstrated that stainless steel electrodes behave in different ways according to their previous use, and the anodal tips of stainless steel electrodes have been cut by crevice corrosion in 10 min by the passage of a 1 mA current (100 Hz, 0.5 msec).

Even in the absence of applied current, some materials may cause tissue reaction. In a systematic study of different metals implanted within the cat brain, Fischer, Sayre, and Bickford (1957) demonstrated that copper and silver produced necrosis while stainless steel was well-tolerated.

In animal experimentation, stainless steel is the most widely used material. Brain implantations in human patients have also been made with stainless steel, but some surgeons prefer gold, platinum, and platinum–iridium (90%–10%); see Adams, Hosobuchi, and Linchitz (1977), Adams and Hosobuchi (1977), Cooper *et al.* 1974), and Delgado *et al.* (1952).

The choice of insulation is also important and the material should have good biological tolerance; high dielectric resistance; endurance to bending and scratching; imperviousness to moisture, enzymes, and heat; and adhesion to metal. In the past, a variety of insulating materials have been used including glass, collodion, rubber, lacquer, Duco cement, varnishes, and enamels (see bibliography in Delgado, 1964a). Plastics and epoxy materials seem to be the present choice, and Teflon insulation is the most widely used.

A. *Chronic Implantation*

Chronic implantation of electrodes within the brain is based on the introduction through the skull of insulated metallic conductors with exposed tips. Anchorage is usually made with plastic cement and small screws. In this way, intracerebral structures are electrically accessible from the outside. The simplest method consists of a stainless steel needle coated with enamel and hammered into the skull (Hoagland, 1940). The inserted bare tip makes contact with the dura of the brain, and the exterior end is electrically connected with a stimulator. A large number of these needles can be implanted in one animal and they are usually well-tolerated. Other methods may be classified as follows:

1. Roving Electrodes

Stereotaxic placement of small metallic tubes in the skull is a procedure of "implanting holes" (Lilly, 1958) through which movable electrodes or cannulae may be introduced for the systematic exploration of cerebral targets at 1 mm steps, for example. Electrodes may be permanently fixed at selected depth after repeated functional exploration.

Our standard procedure for cats and monkeys is to use guides made of 15-mm lengths of #18 stainless steel tubing with a 4-mm length of 1 mm wire soldered perpendicularly to the tube to prevent excessive penetration and to facilitate anchorage. After opening the scalp and cleaning the bone, holes are made in the skull at predetermined points with a stereotaxic drill (for example, with a Kopf instrument [Tijuana, Baja California]). The guide introductor is a metallic bar about 10 mm in diameter ending in a carefully centered tubing that fits the prepared guides. This introductor is driven by the stereotaxic instrument to place each guide in position. After cementation of the guide to the skull, the introductor is removed. As many as 100 guides have been implanted in a single monkey, allowing the exploration of more than 3000 points in each brain (Delgado & Bracchitta, 1972). The roving electrode consists of a length of stainless steel wire insulated with Teflon and protected by a length of stainless steel tubing that fits inside the implanted guides (Fig. 1). Implantation of guides is simpler and more accurate than the use of superstructures originally described by Hess (1932), who was the pioneer and outstanding contributor to brain stimulation in unanesthetized animals; see also Sheatz (1961).

2. Needle and Plate Electrodes

When intracerebral targets are well-established, multilead electrodes may be permanently implanted; see Fig. 2 (Delgado, 1952a, 1955b, 1961,

FIG. 1. (a) Spontaneous threatening and (b) inhibition by electrical stimulation of the caudate nucleus. Needle guides implanted stereotaxically in the skull permit the use of roving electrodes that may be introduced without discomfort in the awake animal.

1964a; Henry, 1949; Marshall, 1953). Twisting two insulated wires together is a simple way to construct a pair of electrodes. However, a more refined procedure to make multilead implantable electrodes is to straighten between two hemostats a piece of Teflon-insulated stainless steel wire 0.12 mm in diameter. Cut this wire in lengths of 100, 97, 94, 91, 88, and 85 mm. Scrape the insulation on each wire for 1 mm at one end and 4 mm at the other. Cement the six wires together with epoxy, spacing the 1 mm bare tips 3 mm apart. With a special tool available in electronic shops, wrap each of the 4 mm bare ends around a subminiature socket. Transistor minisockets or empty minisockets of integrated circuits can be used as electrode terminals. Attach a piece of bare stainless steel wire 100 mm long and 0.4 mm in diameter to one of the pins of the minisocket. This wire is used to anchor the socket to the bone, and also serves as a reference lead for monopolar stimulations. Insulate the electrode connections to the minisocket with epoxy. Check the location of each electrode in the minisocket with an ohmmeter and test the insulation of the leads. Additional information concerning preparation of implantable electrodes may be found in the papers of Delgado (1964a), Maire (1956), Manning (1964), Ninomina, Yonezawa, and Wilson (1976), and Pudenz, Bullara, and Talalla (1975).

Platelike electrodes for exploration of the surface of the brain may be constructed in a similar way as the assembly of needle electrodes, with the difference that all the electrode contacts lie on one side of a polyethylene film about 1 mil thick (0.024 mm) and 10 × 40 mm in surface area (see Fig. 2).

3. Chemitrodes

Some experiments require both chemical and electrical exploration of the depth of the brain and for this purpose, the chemitrode was developed (Delgado, Simhadri, & Apelbaum, 1962). This device consists of two stainless steel #27 tubings soldered together (push–pull cannulae), plus a standard electrode assembly terminating in a minisocket as shown in Fig. 3. Chemitrodes permit the electrical stimulation and recording of several depths and also the delivery and collection of chemicals to and from the brain. This method has proven its usefulness in a variety of studies (DeFeudis, Delgado, & Roth, 1970; Delgado, 1966b; Roth, Allikmets, & Delgado, 1969).

4. Dialytrodes

To prepare a dialytrode, the terminal tips of the chemitrode are enclosed within a polysulfane bag 5 mm in length × 1 mm in diameter (Fig. 3). The dialytrode permits the injection and collection of chemicals

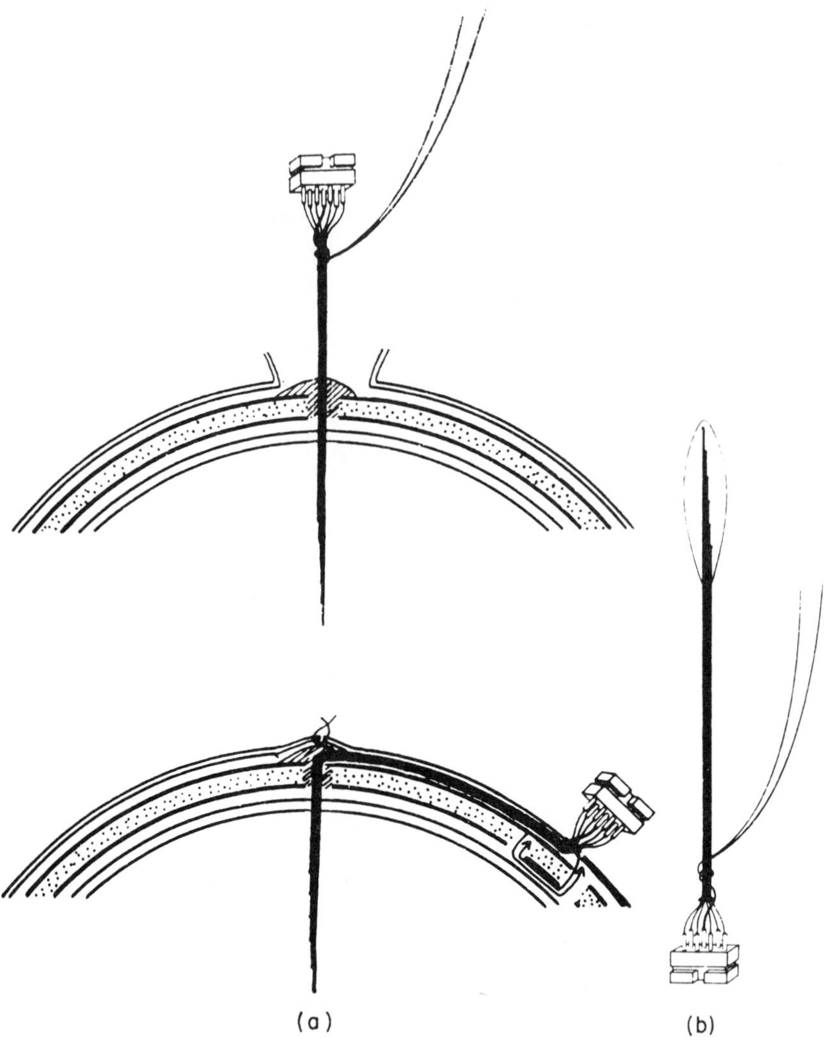

FIG. 2. (a) The assembly of *needle electrodes* permits the exploration of the depth of the brain (Delgado, 1952a, 1955a). (b) The assembly of *plate electrodes* permits exploration of the surface of the brain.

to and from the depth of the brain through the porous bag, avoiding the risk of infection, the clotting of cannulae, and the mechanical disturbance of liquid injection. Glucoproteins and newly synthesized amino acids have been collected from the amygdala and caudate nucleus of unanesthetized monkeys equipped with dialytrodes (Delgado, DeFeudis, Roth, Ryugo, & Mitruka, 1972).

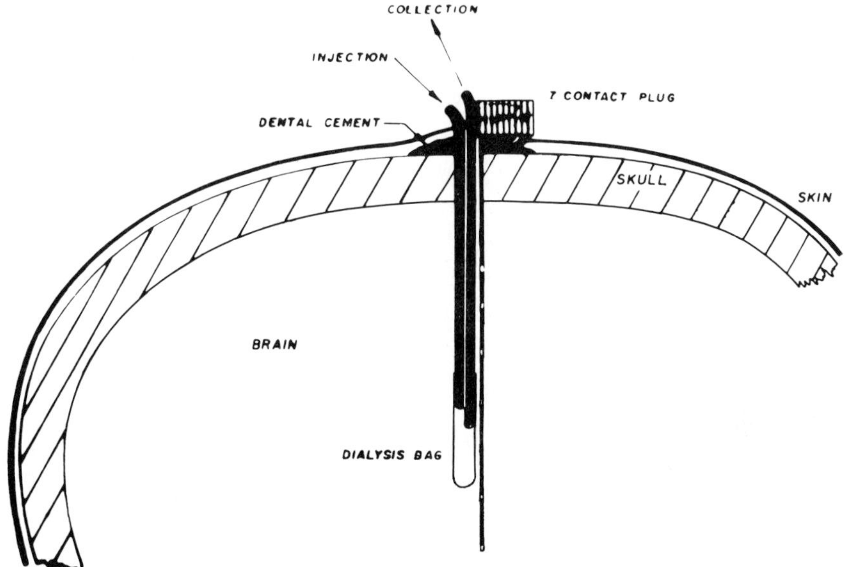

FIG. 3. The dialytrode consists of a push–pull cannula unit ending in a permeable polysulfone bag, plus seven contacts. This instrument permits electrical stimulation and recording, plus chemical injection and collection (Delgado, DeFeudis, Roth, Ryugo, & Mitruka, 1972).

II. Physical Aspects of Brain Stimulation

The types of electrical currents employed by different investigators may be classified as direct or pulsating currents.

A. *Direct Current*

In *direct current* (dc), a potential difference is established between two electrodes, and current passes continuously without changes in polarity. Electrolytic and thermic effects may be of greater magnitude than the stimulating characteristics, and these currents are usually employed to produce lesions in the brain. Application of 3 mA for 30 sec through an electrode 0.12 mm in diameter with a 1 mm exposed tip may produce a destruction of 1 to 2 mm in diameter. Results, however, vary due to unpredictable electrical configuration of field potentials and unknown biological factors. Radio frequency lesions seem to be more reliable.

In some experiments, small dc potentials have been used to study repetitive firing caused by sustained membrane depolarization, including excitatory and inhibitory responses of the neurons of the medullary respiratory center (Burns & Salmoiraghi, 1960). Passing of 1 to 2 μA for 10 to 20 sec has been used by Crow and Cooper (1972) to test possible therapeutic effects of coagulation in the frontal lobes in man. They have also used currents of 10 μA flowing through the medial and lateral frontal lobes for periods of 3 days. The technique of micropolarization, using a few μA or even thousandths of μA has been used therapeutically by Novikova, Russinov, and Semikhina (1952).

B. Pulsating Current

In *pulsating current,* the simplest source of electrical stimulation is the household main line with its voltage reduced by a transformer, and a potentiometer connected across the output terminals. This provides an alternating current (ac) with fixed frequency (60 Hz in United States and 50 Hz in Europe), a fixed pulse duration of 16.6 msec (with 60 Hz), and continuously reversing polarity (biphasic waves). Because of its simplicity, this type of pulsating current is widely used in animal experimentation (Olds, 1960). In other types of pulsating currents, stimulation parameters are better controlled and attention should be paid to the characteristics of electrical current.

C. Voltage and Current

Membrane depolarization of neurons, which is the essential basis for stimulation, requires an amount of current with suitable density and speed to avoid compensatory repolarization phenomena. As expressed by Ohm's law, $I = V/R$, intensity (I) is directly proportional to voltage (V) and is inversely proportional to resistance (R). The resistance of the brain tissue is different in the white than in the gray matter and may be modified by the amount of spinal fluid, circulation, metabolism, and other factors. For these reasons, expression of stimulation values in volts at the stimulator source may be misleading because, if the tissue resistance is low, the nominal voltage also will be lowered while the current may be increased. Commercially available *constant voltage* stimulators have a low output impedance, and therefore, changes in tissue impedance may influence results of stimulation in an unpredictable way.

To increase experimental reliability, many investigators prefer to use *constant current* instruments, which are characterized by a high internal impedance, about 10 times greater than the tissue resistance. In this way, possible changes in the tissue will have a minor influence (below 10%) on the passage of current. Simultaneous monitoring of stimulus voltage and current is essential for proper experimental control and may be performed using a two-channel oscilloscope with the arrangement shown in Fig. 4. Voltage is measured directly in one channel while the other measures the voltage drop across a known resistance placed in series with the output of the stimulating circuit. The value of this resistance should be low with respect to the tissue impedance, and this monitoring also is useful to detect breakdowns in stimulation and changes due to electrode polarization. A disadvantage of this method of monitoring is that the brain is grounded and connected to a high voltage instrument, which is a potential hazard. A safer procedure is to monitor by means of optic sensors of current, as explained in the instrumentation section.

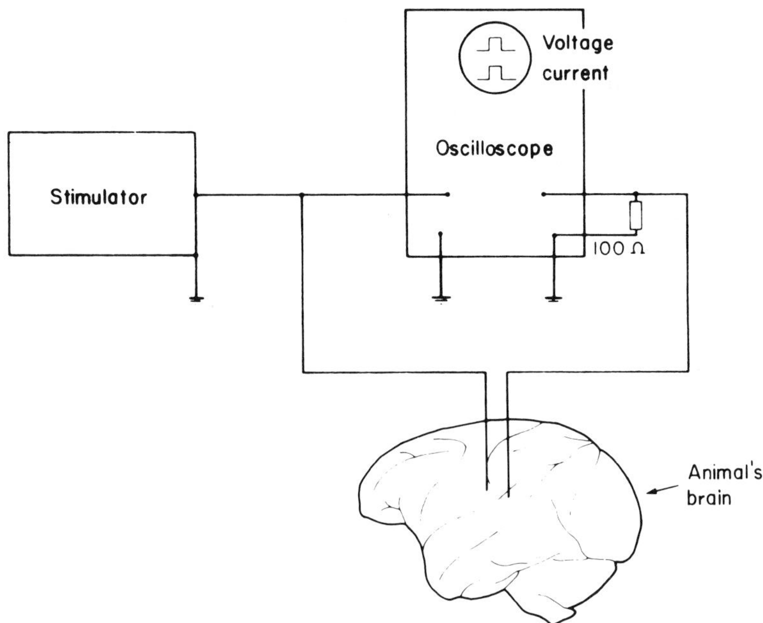

FIG. 4. Circuit arrangement to monitor voltage and current simultaneously during electrical stimulation (Delgado, 1961).

D. *Monopolar and Bipolar Stimulation*

Membrane depolarization requires a specific density of current locally applied to a small surface. The same amount of current applied over a wide area will not reach the local threshold for membrane depolarization. This may be an advantage in *monopolar* stimulation, which allows precise anatomical localization of the excited point. In this case, the active electrode (usually the cathode) has a small exposed surface (for example, 1 mm in a wire 0.1 mm in diameter), while the indifferent electrode (also called the reference or ground) has a much larger surface (for example, a plate of 10 × 10 mm), therefore lacking enough density of current per square millimeter to produce a stimulating effect.

In another experimental arrangement, bipolar stimulation may be used, with two small surface electrodes placed in close proximity. The volume of the current field decreases exponentially with the distance separating the electrode pair, and therefore, two electrodes placed a few millimeters apart stimulate the areas around each contact—preferentially the cathodal region—and not the structures between them. This arrangement is less desirable.

E. *Pulse Phase*

Monophasic pulses change voltage from zero to a given limit without inverting its polarity. The advantage is that a selected structure may be stimulated with a specified polarity that is usually cathodic. The inconvenience is that charges may accumulate locally, thereby increasing polarization. *Biphasic* pulses reverse polarity continuously and, in general, compensate each phase in order to have a zero net current. Lilly, Hughes, Alvord, and Galkin (1955) proposed a special shape of biphasic pulses with very brief (microseconds) cathodic parts, compensated exactly by a second anodic part of longer duration. Displacement of charged particles and tissue injury are thus minimized. Pudenz *et al.* (1975) indicated that biphasic wave forms with balanced charges can be used safely for up to 36 hr of continuous stimulation if the charge per phase does not exceed 0.45 microcoulombs (μC). In our experience with currents below 1 mA (Delgado, 1955b), there was no difference between mono- and biphasic pulses, and Weinmann (1965) disproved the assumption that biphasic pulses caused minimal electrolytic injury. In reality, even in the same contact the electrochemical situation may be considerably asymmetrical for different pulse polarity (see also Wetzel, Howell, & Bearie, 1969).

F. Pulse Shape

The three most common shapes of pulses are sinusoidal, square, and exponential decay. These are ideal shapes generated electronically and visualized in the oscilloscope. However, the brain has filtering components of resistance and capacitance that alter the shape of the applied pulses. Biological effects are less dependent on pulse shape than on other parameters.

G. Pulse Duration

The duration of each pulse is expressed in microseconds or in milliseconds and is easily measured in square waves. In exponential decay waves, the duration is measured from peak to half decay. Investigators have used pulse duration ranging from several microseconds up to 20 or more milliseconds, but short pulses are generally preferred as more effective and less injurious. In our experience, brain stimulation of unanesthetized cats or monkeys with pulse duration between 0.1 and 0.5 msec have proved the most effective for both somatic and autonomic responses (Delgado & Mihailović, 1956). Barry, Walter, and Gallistel (1974) found that short pulse durations (0.1 msec or less) minimize possible deleterious effects of chronic stimulation. By increasing pulse duration above 1 msec, effectiveness reached a plateau, and longer durations did not augment behavioral effects, while they increased the possibility of undesirable effects.

H. Frequency

A single pulse applied to the brain may be used in evoked potential studies, and in some cases may also produce autonomic effects such as slowing down of the heart (Rubinstein & Delgado, 1963). In general, single pulses do not produce detectable autonomic or behavioral responses, and repetitive stimulation is necessary. An obvious limiting factor is the pulse duration, and, for example, with 5 msec pulses the maximum possible frequency is 100 Hz. It is usually accepted that lower frequencies are required to evoke autonomic responses than somatic effects, and also that inhibitory neurons are fired with lower frequencies than excitatory neurons, but these findings are still controversial.

Folkow (1952) reported evoking maximum autonomic effects by stimulation of adrenergic nerves at 20–30 Hz, and frequencies as low as 1

Hz were still effective. According to Kaada (1951), increase in blood pressure was produced by brain stimulation with 40–80 Hz, while decrease was more effective with 15–40 Hz. In our experience, most somatic and behavioral responses in monkeys have been obtained with frequencies of 60–100 Hz, but as shown by many investigators, excitation of the same cerebral point may produce different results depending on the frequency employed. For example, in dogs, stimulation of the same point in the orbital cortex produced slowing down of respiration with 6 Hz, respiratory arrest with 30 Hz, great increase in respiratory amplitude and rhythm with 60 Hz, and no visible effect with 180 Hz (Delgado & Livingston, 1948). Functional studies of the brain therefore require exploration of a wide range of frequencies.

I. Stimulus Isolation

Commercial stimulators usually receive their electrical energy from main lines, and there is a risk of accidental shock to the experimental subject. In addition, when the observed phenomenon requires recording of weak biological electrical signals, powerful amplifiers must be used and their sensitivity may be blocked or disturbed by the relatively high voltage of electrical stimulators. Recording of bioelectrical potentials usually requires grounding of the preparation that may interfere with the grounding of the stimulation source. For these reasons, it is convenient to isolate the stimulation source from the preparation to be stimulated. A simple transformer will accomplish this purpose. A convenient device is the radio frequency isolation unit (Schmitt, 1948), in which the stimulator output energizes a radio frequency oscillator and, through an isolation transformer and rectification unit, is applied to the preparation with low capacity to ground. Stimulus isolation units are supplied with many commercial stimulators such as those of Grass and American Electronics Laboratories (see also Uzzeli & Feezor, 1975).

In battery-operated stimulators such as those described later, the isolation problems are considerably diminished and the shock hazard is absent. To avoid the blocking of recording amplifiers, a good procedure is to disconnect them from the preparation during stimulation time by means of an automatic commutator (Holley & Powell, 1975).

III. Biological Aspects of Brain Stimulation

Because the brain is a reactive structure, its level of excitability and observable behavioral manifestations may vary according to its functional state and previous history. Thus, both physical and biological aspects must be considered in order to evaluate results.

A. *Total Duration of Stimulation*

Electrical stimulation may be applied for periods ranging from a few milliseconds to months, depending on experimental design and local fatigability. Evoked potential studies utilize single shocks. Somatic responses, such as flexion of a limb, require 1 or 2 seconds of cortical stimulation and should not be prolonged for more than 5 to 10 seconds to avoid the possibility of evoking epileptic seizures. Constriction of the pupil has been maintained for weeks by continuous stimulation of the lateral hypothalamus (Delgado & Mir, 1966). The cerebellum has been stimulated for as long as two years in patients, with beneficial results for the control of epileptic seizures (Cooper *et al.*, 1974).

B. *Intervals between Stimulation*

Immediately after the initiation of a propagated response in the axons, there is a refractory period lasting for tenths of a millisecond (Adrian, 1921), imposing a limit on the intervals between repeated stimulations and especially on the maximum frequency that can be effectively used. After the absolute refractory period, excitability rises to control values and may even have a period of supernormal excitability. Prolonged stimulations require taking into consideration the speed of recovery processes including ionic pumping, ATP resynthesis, replenishment of synaptic transmitters, local circulation, and other factors. In the motor cortex, electrical stimulations must be spaced one or more minutes apart in order to recover full excitability. After localized, evoked afterdischarges, control thresholds are reached only following a 4–5 min delay (Mihailović & Delgado, 1956). Generalized afterdischarges lasting for 1–3 min are followed by a long period of slow waves and altered excitability.

C. *Fatigability*

Maintenance of vital functions such as respiration requires rhythmic activation of specialized neuronal structures without fatigue throughout life. Some areas of the brain, such as the motor cortex, fatigue quickly, and the evoked responses fade away after a few seconds of electrical stimulation. Between these two extremes there are other cerebral structures, such as the caudate nucleus, that are able to maintain evoked motor responses such as head-turning for 10–20 min. Brain structures therefore may be classified in three groups: (1) quick fatigue in seconds, such as the motor cortex; (2) slow fatigue in minutes, as in the caudate nucleus and putamen; and (3) indefatigable, as in the lateral hypothalamus, stimulation of which may produce constriction of the pupil indefinitely (Delgado, 1964b). Although little is known about brain fatigability (Delgado, Delgado-Garcia, Conde, & Sanchez-Robles, 1976a), its study is fundamental to our understanding of brain physiology, especially for the use of long-term stimulation experimentally in animals and therapeutically in man.

D. Kindling

Repeated electrical or chemical stimulation of the brain may produce a long-lasting, relatively permanent alteration in brain function, culminating in lowering of thresholds and in the appearance of convulsions whenever the original stimulus is reapplied (Alonso de Florida & Delgado, 1958; Goddard & Douglas, 1976; see review in Wada, 1976). Kindling is produced by application of a few seconds' brain stimulation once a day for several days. This procedures is most effective in the amygdala but also has been observed in other structures such as the hippocampus and caudate nucleus. Experiments requiring daily repetition of brain stimulation should take into consideration the possibility of permanent alteration of brain excitability. Establishment of kindling requires careful administration of stimulation. Under repeated daily brain stimulation, however, local excitability may remain unmodified or may even diminish (Delgado, 1959a; Delgado & Sevillano, 1961; Herberg & Watkins, 1966) have demonstrated in rats that epileptiform seizures induced by hypothalamic self-stimulation were progressively reduced by continuation of the experiments indicating an increased resistance to fits following fits. I propose using the term "negative kindling" to describe the long-lasting increase in thresholds determined by repeated electrical stimulation of the brain with or without induced afterdischarges.

E. Stimulation Programs

In chronic stimulation of fatigable structures, it is necessary to introduce periods of rest for maintenance of effects. The vagus nerve has been activated in dogs for about 7 hr by introducing 1 min of rest after every 4-min stimulation (Ettinger, Hall, & Banting, 1936). During this study, the heartbeat remained at about half the normal rate. In the monkey brain, we have tested several stimulation programs, including 5 sec every min; 1 sec every 5 sec; 5 sec on and 5 sec off; and 5 sec on and 10 sec off (Delgado, Delgado-Garcia, & Grau, 1976b). While results were related to the structure tested and to the evoked effects, the program of 5 sec on, 5 sec off was usually the most effective, for example, to induce lasting inhibition of mobility by caudate stimulation. Suitable programs must be carefully designed and tested when planning long-term experiments. For additional information, reports by Cerf, Van Dale, and Cerf (1976) and Delgado, *et al.* (1976b) may be consulted.

Another objective of programmed stimulation is the production of sequential, organized responses. Pinneo (1966) has described the chronic implantation of up to 200 electrodes in monkeys and the preparation of tape-recorded stimulation programs in order to elicit goal-directed acts such as eating, drinking, grooming, and climbing. Even in a monoplegic animal, Pinneo was able to induce complex movements such as scratching and feeding.

F. Feedback Stimulation and Contingency

Instead of using a fixed stimulation program unrelated to the animal's behavior, it may be preferable to use the occurrence of specific behavior to trigger "on-demand" brain stimulation automatically. For example, in one series of experiments with a rhesus monkey colony, we were interested in controlling animal mobility. Electrodes were implanted in the pallidum where stimulation decreased spontaneous movements. The animals then were equipped with telemetric sensors of spontaneous mobility that relayed information to a computer, which automatically triggered radio stimulation of the pallidum when an animal moved. This feedback and contingent stimulation was 20 times more effective in reducing animal mobility than the best automatic program of 5 sec on, 5 sec off. A selected behavior was thus inhibited by a minimal amount of brain stimulation.

In feedback excitation, detection of the specific phenomenon to be controlled is the triggering element for brain stimulation that is contingent on the presence of the selected phenomenon. In some cases, this contingency factor may be totally essential; for example, in one of our chimpanzees, spontaneous olfactory spindles recorded in the amygdala were detected and used as the triggering signal for automatic feedback stimulation of a negative reinforcing point in the central gray. After 2 hr of contingent stimulation, spindling was reduced 50% and after 6 days of 2-hr sessions daily, spindling practically disappeared (to less than 1%). When this experiment was repeated, however, using not "on line" but previously tape-recorded spindling activity to trigger a similar amount of negative reinforcing stimulation, but without contingency, no modifications were observed in spontaneous amygdala spindling (Delgado, Johnston, Wallace, & Bradley, 1970). In this case, it was evident that contingency between spindling and negative reinforcement was necessary to inhibit the amygdala activity.

G. *Volume of Stimulated Tissue*

Electrical responses may be evoked by stimulation of a single neuron, whereas autonomic and behavioral effects usually require the activation of a large number of cells. For this purpose, many excitable membranes must lie within a minimum density current field. Values, however, do not seem to be too critical, and according to Martin and Lewis (1957), the motor cortex of the cat may be excited with similar current thresholds, using electrodes of between 0.25 and 5 mm^2 surface, although due to their greater impedance, small electrodes needed higher voltage to pass a similar amount of current.

Most investigators (Delgado, 1969b) assume that electrodes with 1-mm exposed tips and currents about 1 mA stimulate cerebral volumes of 1 mm in diameter, allowing precise localization of functions. This estimate has been confirmed by experiments with roving electrodes moving in 0.5- or 1-mm steps (Delgado & Bracchitta, 1972), in which behavioral effects changed or disappeared by moving the position of a contact 1 mm. Further confirmation of the limited area affected by stimulation was provided by chronic studies in monkeys with implanted electrodes in which stimulation of one point in the red nucleus produced a complex sequential behavior including walking, climbing, and threatening, while in the same animal, excitation of another point located 3 mm away produced only yawning (Delgado, 1965).

H. *Local and Distant Effects*

Although the volume of stimulated brain is relatively small, it would be misleading to assume that the observed responses depend on functional systems localized in the stimulated region. One single pyramidal cell of the motor cortex is connected to about 5000 other neurons (Sholl,

1956), each of which has another set of contacts. Behavioral responses are usually multisynaptic. For example, motor effects depend on the organized activation of preestablished mechanisms and the processing of multisensory information that feed back and direct the postural adjustments and complex coordination of the many muscles put into action. As discussed elsewhere (Delgado, 1964a, 1969a), brain stimulation is only a trigger to activate preestablished fragments of behavior but cannot be held responsible for the tremendous complexity of organized behavior. Brain stimulation may provide information about triggering points, but it sheds little light on the many distant mechanisms involved.

The brain has an enormous number of connecting synapses, but neuronal activities circulate through specific pathways without diffusing through the cerebral volume conductor. This is one of the most interesting and lesser known aspects of nervous physiology: the mechanisms that open, close, and select the lines of intracerebral communication. Electrical stimulation of the brain apparently uses these normal mechanisms because the responses are usually as well-organized as normal activities and often may compete with, increase, or diminish them.

I. Delayed Effects

In most cases, brain stimulation effects appear immediately or with only a brief delay. For example, motor cortex stimulation will induce motor responses within 1 or 2 sec. In other cases, however, electrical stimulation seems to leave invisible traces with long-term temporal accumulation, and effects may require hours or days to appear. Typical examples are kindling, which requires one brief stimulation daily, and also excitation of the lateral hypothalamus in the cat, which may be applied for 1 hr without observable effect, although the 24-hr total food intake may increase over 600% above normal (Delgado & Anand, 1953).

J. Anatomical Variability

Placing of intracerebral electrodes generally is based on stereotaxic coordinates using as landmarks the horizontal plane, which passes through both inferior orbital arches, and both auditory canals. The sagittal plane is perpendicular to the horizontal one and is equidistant between the ears. The coronal plane is perpendicular to the other two, passing through the center of the ears. The stereotaxic coordinates theoretically permit an accurate geometric location of any point inside the brain.

Unfortunately, there is considerable variability in the conformation of the skull, and therefore even in animals of the same species, sex, and size, the location of intracerebral nuclei is not identical. This problem is shown in the published maps for the monkey brain in which the position of structures varies as much as 3 to 5 mm (see, for example, Olszewski, 1952; Snider & Lee, 1961). In the human brain, surgical accuracy is more critical, and variability is compounded by genetic differences. Fortunately, intracerebral landmarks such as the anterior and posterior commissures have proved more accurate, and computerized X-ray technology has considerably improved the identification of intracerebral structures (Matsui & Hirano, 1978). Our group has recently developed a computer-stored brain atlas that allows visualization and calculation of selected structures in any chosen plane or rotation (Abraira & Handler, 1978; also Bechtereva (personal communication, June 30, 1978).

K. Functional Variability

When the motor cortex has been exposed in a monkey or patient, the surgeon can predict that its excitation will evoke a contralateral motor response, but the precise location of the muscles involved and the details of motor performance cannot be foreseen. Part of the basic "wiring" of the brain is genetically determined, but a large part of the functional organization depends on individual experience and training. When a dog is conditioned to salivate at the sound of a bell, a new functional connection is established between auditory areas and salivation centers. When a child learns to talk or to play a musical instrument, the brain has been enriched with ideokinetic formulas and memories to be used on demand. Scientists who are aware of anatomical variability often fail to give the deserved importance to functional variability and to the decisive influence of individual history.

In addition to individual experience, there are a number of experimental variables that may decisively influence the effects of brain stimulation, and a good example is the social situation. In monkeys, electrical stimulation of the central gray has produced a reliable offensive–defensive response with baring of the teeth, vocalization, threatening attitude, and launching of well-oriented and coordinated attacks (Delgado, 1955a). Results are very reliable in different animals and on different days, but are highly dependent on the hierarchical status of the stimulated animal. Central gray excitation elicits aggressive behavior when the animal is paired with a submissive partner. However, the same animal stimulated in exactly the same way but in the company of a dominant partner will show only submissive behavior without signs of hostility (Plotnik, Mir, & Delgado, 1971). These experiments emphasize the need to use multiple tests when investigating the effects of brain stimulation, and also show the risk of functional labeling of brain structures.

L. Reliability of Results

The "instability of cortical points" reported by Sherrington (1947) and Penfield and Welch (1949) was probably due to the many variables in their studies performed with exposed brains in which changes occurred in local circulation, local temperature, the amount of spinal fluid, the depth of anesthesia, the pressure and position of the contacts held manually, and other factors.

Other investigators also have reported variability of evoked responses. Horowitz, Adams, and Rutkin (1958) claimed that "no two stimulations at the same anatomical point produced the same images or hallucinations." Cox and Valenstein (1969) indicated that behavior elicited by hypothalamic stimulation could be changed by environmental manipulation. Amygdaloid stimulation in an epileptic patient produced an olfactory and gustatory sensation reported as unpleasant when distressing problems were discussed, and pleasant when the conversation dealt with agreeable topics (Rayport & Ferguson, 1974).

Despite anatomical, functional, and experimental variability, when all experimental conditions are kept constant in the same subject, results of electrical stimulation of the brain (ESB) are very reliable. In our studies with monkeys, we have observed stable responses during periods of more than 4 years (Delgado, 1959b). Thresholds of stimulations and patterns of evoked electrical afterdischarges also have been maintained for months.

M. Histological Location

Stereotaxic placement of electrodes is not completely accurate due to brain variability and possible technical errors. In animal research, anatomical confirmation of precise electrode location is absolutely necessary, and histological study of the stimulated region is convenient for evaluation of possible local modifications of neurons.

The standard procedure in our laboratory is to anesthetize the animal with an overdose of Nembutal and to perfuse it through the heart with physiologic saline followed by a 10% solution of formaline. The head is placed in the stereotaxic instrument, the calvarium removed, and with a stereotaxically oriented knife, coronal sections are made at 0, anterior 10 and 20, or other planes, depending on the experiment. (The stereotaxic Kopf instrument has knife guides originally designed by us.)

Frozen sections may be immediately prepared from the blocks and may be mounted unstained to be used as a photographic negative that gives reasonable contrast for rapid identification of electrode sites (Guzmán, Alcaraz, & Fernandez, 1958); or more preferably, the sections may be stained using the Klüver–Barrera method, for example, for more detailed histological analysis. Identification of the stimulated site may be facilitated by passing a direct current of about 300 μA for 20 sec. For additional information about electrode localization, the works of several researchers may be consulted (Akert & Welker, 1961; Delgado, 1961; Hosco, 1975; Pieri & Hoffmann, 1975; B. W. Robinson, 1962).

N. Histological Effects of Electrical Stimulation

Introduction of electrodes in the brain produces trauma with destruction of neurons, rupture of capillaries, edema, and reactive, reparative processes. The presence of a metallic foreign body produces additional reaction with the formation of glia and encapsulation around the electrodes. Despite all these disturbances, chronic implantation of electrodes is usually well-tolerated, as indicated by the normality of electrical activity, the absence of spikes and other signs of irritation, the reliability of evoked responses, and the histological aspect of the neurons that appear normal in the vicinity of the gliosis limit of the electrode tract (Delgado, 1961). Histopathological changes are minimum with tantalum, platinum, and stainless steel electrodes. Tungsten seems to be a little more toxic, while silver and copper are far more toxic and produce a notable reaction (Collias & Manuelidis, 1957; Fischer *et al.*, 1957; R. F. Robinson & Johnson, 1961; Wetzel *et al.*, 1969).

Most investigators assume that using moderate intensity of stimulation (below 1 mA), no histological disturbances have been produced in the brain beyond the tract of traumatic insertion (Delgado, 1961; Delgado, Rivera, & Mir, 1971). Dodge, Petersen, Sem-Jacobsen, Sayre, and Bickford (1955) reported that a woman who died from natural causes 19 months after having electrodes implanted for 6 days had no detectable residual brain damage. More detailed studies, however, indicate that chronic stimulation may induce changes in the position of the nucleolus, in the amount of cholinesterase and acid phosphatase, and in the ultramicroscopic structure of the neurons (Agnew, Yuen, Pudenz, & Bullara, 1975; Delgado, 1977). Gilman, Dauth, Tennyson, and Kremzner (1975) also have observed that after 205 hr of cerebellar stimulation over a 6-month period in the monkey, there was meningeal thickening and severe loss of Perkinje cells.

O. Instruments for Electrical Stimulation

There are many commercially available stimulators, most of which produce rectangular pulses with controls for pulse width, frequency, voltage, and delay of synchronization with the oscilloscope. Some instruments provide mono- and bi-phasic pulses, timing of stimulation, reverse polarity, and duality of output with independent controls. Stimulators may be classified as *constant voltage,* characterized by low output impedance; and *constant current* with a high output impedance 10 or more times greater than tissue impedance. These are preferred by many researchers because neuronal depolarization is related to current density and constancy of current increases experimental reliability. Simple and miniaturized instruments have been described by Dhume and Gogate (1974) and Silverman, Ball, and Cohn (1975). The inconvenience in most instruments is that, even when using symmetrical charges in biphasic pulses, current-voltage curves are not actually symmetrical due to differences in the chemical kinetics of both anodic and cathodic phases (Faradic rectification), which generate a voltage component related to the remaining postpulse charge (Dymond, 1976). In this case, even with cathodal stimulation and ac coupling, the cathode will become an anode, and paradoxical anodal corrosion of the electrode may occur (Kahn & Greatbatch, 1974).

1. Hybrid Stimulator

To avoid the problems mentioned in the foregoing, we have developed a hybrid stimulator that provides constant current to ensure a reliable depolarization independent of changes in tissue impedance, and during the quiescent phase between pulses, provides a low-resistance path in order to minimize the post-pulse charge. In this way, zero voltage is assured when no current pulse is driven, and there is also a better diffusion process to normalize the original distribution of minority carriers. In addition, the instrument provides cathodal protection (Del Pozo & Delgado, 1978).

To avoid direct connection with the oscilloscope during experimental monitoring of voltage and current, we have added an optocoupler to our stimulator. The output of the instrument energizes an LED (light-emitting diode), and its luminous intensity is detected by a phototransistor. Thus, current monitoring is accurate throughout the experiments without any risk or disturbance for the stimulated brain structure.

2. Radio Stimulators

The presence of sockets anchored to the skull, open wounds, and trailing wires connecting animals and stimulation instruments are the main handicaps for chronic brain stimulation. For experimental research requiring freedom of movements, wireless links with miniaturized instruments carried by the animals have been proposed by several investigators (Alexander & Perachio, 1973; Delgado, 1963, 1969a; Maurus, 1967; Maurus & Ploog, 1971; Maxim & Spelman, 1975; Robinson, Warner, & Rosvold, 1964; Warner, Robinson, Rosvold, Wechsler, & Zampini, 1968). The lack of commercial sources for radio stimulators and the small number of papers published using this technology suggest the existence of difficulties. In our experience, the main problems have been directionality of antennas, standing waves with points of low energy, erratic spikes, interference with unwanted radio signals, thermic sensitivity of components, limit of battery life, and limited distance of transmission.

Some of these problems may be solved with appropriate electronic design, including reduction of battery drain to 1–2 mA, crystal control of radio signals, careful selection of components, antenna testing, and FM coding to control channel selection and parameters of stimulation. The instrument designed by us and presently in use in our laboratory has four channels, measures 40 × 30 × 15 mm, weighs 20 g, and has been tested in field experiments on Hall Island, Bermuda (Fig. 5). Provisions have been made in the logic section to minimize the possibility of interference by spurious radio frequency (RF) signals. The pulse repetition rate is up to 100 HZ, the pulse duration is from 0.1 to 1.0 msec, and the intensity can be regulated between 0.0 and 3 mA for each channel. All parameters may be remotely controlled from the portable transmitting console. The stimulator is totally enclosed in epoxy and is shockproof, waterproof, and practically indestructible (Delgado, Lipponen, Weiss, Del Pozo, Monteagudo, & McMahon, 1975).

3. Head-Mounted Automatic Stimulator

In chronic experiments when parameters and programs of stimulation are preset and kept constant, instrumentation may be simplified with the use of a miniaturized multivibrator anchored directly onto the skull of the animal. The fact that stimulation characteristics are set when the animal is released and do not depend on radio signals may be an ad-

FIG. 5. A gibbon instrumented with intracerebral electrodes, radio stimulator, and telemetric mobility recorder was freely investigated on the island of Hall, Bermuda.

vantage because reliability is increased. The transistor-timed stimulator originally described (Delgado, 1959b) has been used by several investigators (Willey & Freeman, 1968) and is very easy to construct and handle.

4. EXTERNAL STIMOCEIVER

The stimoceiver is an instrument formed by the combination of a multichannel radio stimulator and a telemetric unit for depth EEG (*stimulator* and EEG re*ceiver*); see Delgado *et al.* (1975). It is small enough to be carried on a monkey's collar or in a patient's head bandage, and permits two-way communication to and from the brain in completely unrestricted subjects. Its usefulness has been demonstrated both in animal research (Delgado *et al.*, 1970) and in therapy of temporal lobe epilepsy in man (Delgado, Mark, Sweet, Ervin, Weiss, Bach-y-Rita, & Hagiwara, 1968; Delgado, Obrador, & Martín-Rodriguez, 1973). The advantages of the external stimoceiver over other methods of intracerebral exploration may be summarized as follows: (1) Instrumentation of the patient is very simple, requiring only connection of the stimoceiver to the head sockets. (2) Because the instrument is very small, it may be kept under the head bandage for as long as needed without discomfort. (3) Sending and receiving of radio signals do not disturb spontaneous behavior of the subject. (4) The patient is under continuous medical supervision, and stimulations and recordings can be performed unobtrusively day and night. (5) Studies and medical testing may be carried out during spontaneous social interactions in the hospital environment, without the need of a special testing room, and therefore without introducing factors of anxiety or stress. (6) The brain may be explored in severely disturbed patients without the need of confinement or restraint. (7) The lack of connecting wires, such as those used in standard scalp EEG, avoids the risk of dislodging the implanted electrodes in case of abnormal motor activity of the patient. (8) Therapeutic programmed stimulation of the brain may be continued for as long as necessary with the patient free, while the EEG is continuously monitored. (9) On demand, feedback stimulation of the brain may be established, contingent on the appearance of electrical activity of specified pattern and location.

5. Transdermal Technology

Activation of intracerebral electrodes by miniaturized instrumentation placed underneath the scalp permits chronic stimulation through the intact teguments, avoiding risks of open wounds and discomfort of protruding sockets.

Over forty years ago, Chaffee and Light (1934–1935) used a diode to rectify the waves recorded through the intact scalp, and Harris (1946–1947) implanted coils subcutaneously activated from a distance of several feet by a powerful primary coil. More recently, heart pacemakers were developed to be activated transdermically (Glenn, Hageman, Mauro, Eisenberg, Flanigan, & Harvard, 1964). Percutaneous stimulators have been used in man for pain therapy by dorsal root stimulation, and different types of miniaturized implantable stimulators have been proposed (Gold, Stoeckle, Schuder, West, & Holland, 1974; Terell & Maurer, 1974).

A technique for multichannel transdermal stimulation of the brain has been used in animals (Delgado, 1969b), and later Delgado *et al.* (1973) reported its successful therapeutic application in a patient suffering from intractable pain (Fig. 6). The methodology has been fully described (Delgado *et al.*, 1975) and includes circuitry for both brain stimulation and EEG telemetric recording through the intact teguments. The instrument consists of two disks implanted subcutaneously, connected to electrodes implanted stereotaxically within the brain. As no batteries are used, the life of the instrument is indefinite. Power and information are supplied by radio frequencies. Possibilities of two-way transdermal technology are (1) Long-term depth EEG recording to monitor physiological, pharmacological, and psychological experiments in unrestrained subjects; (2) Long-term electrical stimulation of the brain to elicit or modify auto-

FIG. 6. Psychological testing of a patient with a 4-channel subcutaneous radio stimulator implanted to treat intractable pain by programmed stimulation of the septum–caudate region (Delgado, 1977).

nomic, somatic, and behavioral responses; (3) To provide information directly to the brain, circumvening normal or damaged sensory receptors; (4) Two-way communication between brain and computer for the establishment of artificial links and feedback circuits; and (5) Clinical applications to humans to establish on-demand programs of stimulation triggered by preselected spontaneous electrical waves.

IV. Possibilities and Limitations of Brain Stimulation

Sophistication and miniaturization of electronic technology and development of transdermal two-way communication with the brain allow long-term recording and stimulation of cerebral functions in completely unrestrained subjects. We can therefore investigate the depth of the brain during physiological states, emotional reactions, abnormal activity such as epilepsy and dyskinesias, and administration of psychoactive drugs.

Electrical stimulation of the brain permits elicitation and modification of a variety of autonomic, somatic, and behavioral manifestations that may adjust functional tuning and influence inhibitory mechanisms. The cerebral bases of many aspects of behavior have been investigated in laboratory animals, and some findings have guided therapy in human patients. Some of these aspects are (1) *motility* (Delgado, *et al.* 1976b; Pinneo, 1966); (2) *pleasure* (Crow & Cooper, 1972; Delgado & Hamlin, 1960; Heath & The Tulane University Department of Psychiatry and Neurology, 1954; Olds, 1956; Olds & Milner, 1954; Sem-Jacobsen, 1968; Sem-Jacobsen & Torkildsen, 1960; see also symposium of Wauquier & Rolls, 1975); (3) *punishment* (Delgado, 1952b, 1955a; Delgado, Roberts, & Miller, 1954), (4) *conditioning* (Delgado *et al.,* 1970; Doty & Giurgea, 1961; Galeano, 1963; Wyrwicka, 1964); (5) *aggression* (Delgado, 1964b; Eleftheriou & Scott, 1971; Garattini & Sigg, 1969; Hess, 1928; Hunsperger, 1963; Moyer, 1976; Ploog, Blitz, & Ploog, 1963; Wasman & Flynn, 1962); (6) *food intake* (Anand & Brobeck, 1951; Delgado *et al.,* 1954; Fonberg & Delgado, 1961; B. W. Robinson & Mishkin, 1962); and (7) *social hierarchy* (Delgado, 1967; Plotnik *et al.,* 1971; Pruscha & Maurus, 1976; B. W. Robinson, Alexander, & Bowne, 1969).

V. Conclusions

Brain stimulation will continue to be a very important tool in neurobiological research. One of the as yet little explored possibilities of applying basic research to patient therapy is to provide information directly to sensory pathways or receiving areas of the brain in patients with damaged receptors. Other fields to be explored in the future are the subcutaneous implantation of minicomputers for the establishment of artificial connections between unrelated cerebral areas, and the use of radio links for direct brain-to-brain nonsensory communication (Delgado, 1977).

There is a marked contrast between the many spectacular possibilities of brain stimulation and the limited application of this technology in human therapy. While cardiac pacemakers are widely used, brain pacemakers are seldom applied. One reason is that the heart is a much simpler organ and has only one main response—contraction to eject blood. The brain has an incomparably greater anatomical and functional complexity with many aspects still unknown. Another element hindering brain research is the prejudice and misinformation surrounding the human mind. The risk of loss of life is generally accepted in heart surgery. Possible tampering with structural components of the psyche is rejected by many on religious and emotional grounds. Science fiction also has played a harmful role by inventing radio-controlled individuals and robotized armies. Layperson's fears should be dispelled by accurate reporting to promote an understanding of the real potential and limits of brain stimulation.

Electricity is a monotonous, nonspecific stimulus, able to activate preexisting functions but unable to create them. We may increase a patient's verbal output by temporal lobe stimulation (Higgins, Mahl, Delgado, & Hamlin, 1956), but we cannot introduce words, concepts, or beliefs by applying electricity to the brain. We may increase the aggression of a monkey (or perhaps a human) by central gray stimulation (Delgado, 1966a), but hostility will be oriented in agreement with the subject's past history and cannot be directed by an investigator toward objectives of his or her own choice.

It is generally poorly understood that material and functional structuring of the brain, to a great extent, is influenced by cultural information reaching the neurons through the normal portal of entry: the sensory receptors. Language and beliefs are learned through the eyes and ears but cannot be introduced into the brain by wires and electronics.

With these limitations for use and misuse, electrical stimulation of the brain represents a very important technology, still in full development, holding great promise for research and therapy.

References

Abraira, V., & Handler, P. Computerized stereotaxic brain atlas. *Proceedings of the DECUS Congress,* 1978, **5**, 539–541.

Adams, J. E., & Hosobuchi, Y. Technique and technical problems. *Neurosurgery,* 1977, **1,** 196–199.

Adams, J. E., Hosobuchi, Y., & Linchitz, R. The present status of implantable intracranial stimulations for pain. *Clinical Neurosurgery,* 1977, **24,** 347–361.

Adrian, E. D. *Journal of Physiology (London),* 1921, **55,** 193.

Agnew, W. F., Yuen, T. G. H., Pudenz, R. H., & Bullara, L. A. Electrical stimulation of the brain. IV. Ultrastructural studies. *Surgical Neurology,* 1975, **4,** 438–448.

Akert, K., & Welker, W. I. Problems and methods of anatomical localization. In D. E. Sheer (Ed.), *Electrical stimulation of the brain.* Austin: University of Texas Press, 1961. Pp. 251–260.

Alexander, M., & Perachio, A. A. The influence of target sex and dominance on evoked attack in rhesus monkeys. *American Journal of Physical Anthropology,* 1973, **38,** 543–547.

Alonso de Florida, F., & Delgado, J. M. R. Lasting behavioral and EEG changes in cats induced by prolonged stimulation of amygdala. *American Journal of Physiology,* 1958, **193,** 223–229.

Anand, B. K., & Brobeck, J. R. Hypothalamic control of food intake in rats and cats. *Yale Journal of Biology and Medicine,* 1951, **24,** 123–140.

Anonymous. Electrical stimulation of the brain. *Lancet,* 1974, **2,** 562–564.

Barry, F. E., Walter, M. S., & Gallistel, C. R. On the optimal pulse duration in electrical stimulation of the brain. *Physiology and Behavior*, 1974, **12,** 749–754.

Bechtereva, N. Personal communication, June 30, 1978.

Bickford, R. G., Petersen, M. C., Dodge, H. W., Jr., & Sem-Jacobsen, C. W. Observations on depth stimulation of the human brain through implanted electrographic leads. *Mayo Clinic Proceedings*, 1953, **28,** 181–187.

Brazier, M. A. B. Modern advances in the use of depth electrodes. In A. Winter (Ed.), *The surgical control of behavior*. Springfield, IL: Thomas, 1971. Pp. 5–20.

Burns, B. D., & Salmoiraghi, G. C. Repetitive firings of respiratory neurones during their burst activity. *Journal of Neurophysiology*, 1960, **23,** 27–46.

Cerf, J. A., Van Dale, J., & Cerf, E. A low-cost timing device for increasing the versatility of physiological stimulators. *Physiology and Behavior*, 1976, **16,** 509–512.

Chaffee, E. L., & Light, R. V. A method for the remote control of electrical stimulation of the nervous system. I. The history of electrical excitation. *Yale Journal of Biology and Medicine*, 1934-1935, **7,** 83–128.

Collias, J. C., & Manuelidis, E. E. Histopathological changes produced by implanted electrodes in cat brains; comparison with histopathological changes in human experimental puncture wounds. *Journal of Neurosurgery*, 1957, **14,** 302–328.

Cooper, I. S., Riklan, M., & Snider, R. S. (Eds.). *The cerebellum, epilepsy, and behavior*. New York: Plenum, 1974.

Cox, V. C., & Valenstein, E. S. Effects of stimulation intensity on behavior elicited by hypothalamic stimulation. *Journal of Comparative and Physiological Psychology*, 1969, **69**, 730–733.

Crow, H. J., & Cooper, R. Stimulation, polarization and coagulation using intracerebral implanted electrodes during the investigation and treatment of psychiatric and other disorders. *Medical Progress through Technology*, 1972, **1,** 92–102.

DeFeudis, F. V., Delgado, J. M. R., & Roth, R. H. Content, synthesis and collectability of aminoacids in various structures of the brains of rhesus monkeys. *Brain Research*, 1970, **18,** 15–23.

Delgado, J. M. R. Permanent implantation of multilead electrodes in the brain. *Yale Journal of Biological Medicine*, 1952, **24,** 351–358. (a)

Delgado, J. M. R. Responses evoked in waking cat by electrical stimulation of motor cortex. *American Journal of Physiology*, 1952, **171,** 436–446. (b)

Delgado, J. M. R. Cerebral structures involved in transmission and elaboration of noxious stimulation. *Journal of Neurophysiology*, 1955, **18,** 261–275. (a)

Delgado, J. M. R. Evaluation of permanent implantation of electrodes within the brain. *Electroencephalography and Clinical Neurophysiology*, 1955, **7,** 637–644. (b)

Delgado J. M. R. Prolonged stimulation of the brain in awake monkeys. *Journal of Neurophysiology*, 1959, **22,** 458–475. (a)

Delgado, J. M. R. A transistor timed stimulator. *Electroencephalography and Clinical Neurophysiology*, 1959, **11,** 591–593. (b)

Delgado, J. M. R. Chronic implantation of intracerebral electrodes in animals. In D. E. Sheer (Ed.), *Electrical stimulation of the brain*. Austin: University of Texas Press, 1961. Pp. 25–36.

Delgado, J. M. R. Telemetry and telestimulation of the brain. In L. Slater (Ed.), *Bio-Telemetry*. Oxford: Pergamon, 1963. Pp. 231–249.

Delgado, J. M. R. Electrodes for extracellular recording and stimulation. In N. L. Nastuk (Ed.), *Physical techniques in biological research* (Vol. 5, Pt. A). New York: Academic Press, 1964. Pp. 88–143. (a)

Delgado, J. M. R. Free behavior and brain stimulation. *International Review of Neurobiology*, 1964, **6,** 349–449. (b)

Delgado, J. M. R. Sequential behavior repeatedly induced by red nucleus stimulation in free monkeys. *Science,* 1965, **148,** 1361–1363.

Delgado, J. M. R. Evoking and inhibiting aggressive behavior by radio stimulation in monkey colonies. *American Zoologist,* 1966, **6,** 669–681. (a)

Delgado, J. M. R. Intracerebral perfusion in awake monkeys. *Archives Internationales de Pharmacodynamie et de Therapie,* 1966, **161,** 442–462. (b)

Delgado, J. M. R. Social rank and radiostimulated aggressiveness in monkeys. *Journal of Nervous and Mental Disease,* 1967, **144,** 383–390.

Delgado, J. M. R. *Physical control of the mind: toward a psychocivilized society.* Vol. XLI, World Perspectives Series, R. N. Anshen (Ed.), New York: Harper & Row, 280 pp., 1969. (a)

Delgado, J. M. R. Radio stimulation of the brain in primates and in man. *Anesthesia and Analgesia (Cleveland),* 1969, **48,** 529–543. (b)

Delgado, J. M. R. Therapeutic programmed stimulation of the brain in man. In W. Sweet, S. Obrador, & J. G. Martín-Rodriguez (Eds.), *Neurosurgical treatment in psychiatry, pain, and epilepsy.* Baltimore, MD: University Park Press, 1977. Pp. 615–637.

Delgado, J. M. R., & Anand, B. K. Increase of food intake induced by electrical stimulation of the lateral hypothalamus. *American Journal of Physiology,* 1953, **172,** 162–168.

Delgado, J. M. R., & Bracchitta, H. Free and instrumental behavior in monkeys during radio stimulation of the caudate nucleus. *International Journal of Psychobiology,* 1972, **2,** 233–248.

Delgado, J. M. R., DeFeudis, F. V., Roth, R. H., Ryugo, D. K., & Mitruka, B. M. Dialytrode for long term intracerebral perfusion in awake monkeys. *Archives Internationales de Pharmacodynamie et de Therapie,* 1972, **198,** 9–21.

Delgado, J. M. R., Delgado-García, J. M., Conde, M., & Sánchez-Robles, S. Fatigability of caudate nucleus stimulation in cats. *Neuropsychologia,* 1976, **14,** 11–21. (a)

Delgado, J. M. R., Delgado-García, J. M., & Grau, C. Mobility controlled by feedback cerebral stimulation in monkeys. *Physiology and Behavior,* 1976, **16,** 43–49. (b)

Delgado, J. M. R., & Hamlin, H. Spontaneous and evoked electrical seizures in animals and humans. In E. R. Ramey & D. S. O'Doherty (Eds.), *Electrical Studies on the Unanesthetized Brain,* New York: Hoeber, 1960. Pp. 133–158.

Delgado, J. M. R., Hamlin, H., & Chapman, W. P. Technique of intracranial electrode implacement for recording and stimulation and its possible therapeutic value in psychotic patients. *Confinia Neurologica,* 1952, **12,** 315–319.

Delgado, J. M. R., Johnston, V. S., Vallace, J. D., & Bradley, R. J. Operant conditioning of amygdala spindling in the free chimpanzee. *Brain Research,* 1970, **22,** 347–362.

Delgado, J. M. R., Lipponen, V., Weiss, G., Del Pozo, F., Monteagudo, J. L., & McMahon, R. Two way transdermal communication with the brain. *American Psychologist* (Instrumentation Issue), 1975, **30,** 265–273.

Delgado, J. M. R., & Livingston, R. B. Some respiratory, vascular and thermal responses to stimulation of orbital surface of frontal lobe. *Journal of Neurophysiology,* 1948, **11,** 39–55.

Delgado, J. M. R., Mark, V., Sweet, W., Ervin, F., Weiss, G., Bach-y-Rita, G., & Hagiwara, R. Intracerebral radio stimulation and recording in completely free patients. *Journal of Nervous and Mental Disease,* 1968, **147,** 329–340.

Delgado, J. M. R., & Mihailović, L. Use of intracerebral electrodes to evaluate drugs that act on the central nervous system. *Annals of the New York Academy of Sciences,* 1956, **64,** 644–666.

Delgado, J. M. R., & Mir, D. Infatigability of pupillary constriction evoked by stimulation in monkeys. *Neurology,* 1966, **16,** 939–950.

Delgado, J. M. R., Obrador, S., & Martín-Rodriguez, J. G. Two-way radio communication with the brain in psychosurgical patients. In L. V. Laitinen & K. E. Livingston (Eds.), *Surgical approaches in psychiatry*. Lancaster, England: Medical & Technical Publ., 1973. Pp. 215–233.

Delgado, J. M. R., Rivera, M., & Mir, D. Repeated stimulation of amygdala in awake monkeys. *Brain Research*, 1971, **27**, 111–131.

Delgado, J. M. R., Roberts, W. W., & Miller, N. E. Learning motivated by electrical stimulation of the brain. *American Journal of Physiology*, 1954, **179**, 587–593.

Delgado, J. M. R., & Sevillano, M. Evolution of repeated hippocampal seizures in the cat. *Electroencephalography and Clinical Neurophysiology*, 1961, **13**, 722–733.

Delgado, J. M. R., Simhadri, P., & Apelbaum, J. Chronic implantation of chemitrodes in the monkey brain. *Proceedings of the International Union of Physiological Sciences*, 1962, **2**, 1090.

Del Pozo, F., & Delgado, J. M. R. Hybrid stimulator for chronic experiments. *IEEE Transactions on Biomedical Engineering*, 1978, **BME-25**, 92–94.

Dhume, R. A., & Gogate, M. G. A miniature stimulator for behavioral studies in freely moving cats. *Indian Journal of Physiology and Pharmacology*, 1974, **18**, 123–125.

Dodge, H. W., Jr., Petersen, M. C., Sem-Jacobsen, C. W., Sayre, G. P., & Bickford, R. G. The paucity of demonstrable brain damage following intracerebral electrography: Report of case. *Mayo Clinic Proceedings*, 1955, **30**, 215–221.

Doty, R. W., & Giurgea, C. Conditioned reflexes established by coupling electrical excitations of two cortical areas. In J. F. Delafresnaye (Ed.), *Brain mechanisms and learning*. Springfield, IL: Thomas, 1961. Pp. 133–151.

DuBois-Reymond, E. *Untersuchungen über thierische Elektricität* (2 vols.). Berlin: Reimer, 1848–1849.

Dymond, A. M. Characteristics of the metal-tissue interface of stimulation electrodes. *IEEE Transactions on Biomedical Engineering*, 1976, **BME-23**, 274–280.

Eleftheriou, B. E., & Scott, J. P. (Eds.). *The physiology of aggression and defeat*. New York: Plenum, 1971.

Ettinger, G. H., Hall, G. E., & Banting, F. G. Effect of repeated and prolonged stimulation of the vagus nerve in the dog. *Canadian Medical Association Journal*, 1936, **35**, 27–31.

Fischer, G., Sayre, G. P., & Bickford, R. G. Histologic changes in the cat's brain after introduction of metallic and plastic coated wire used in electroencephalograph. *Mayo Clinic Proceedings*, 1957, **32**, 14–22.

Folkow, H. Impulse frequency in sympathetic vasomotor fibres correlated to the release and elimination of the transmitter. *Acta Physiologica Scandinavica*, 1952, **25**, 49–76.

Fonberg, E., & Delgado, J. M. R. Avoidance and alimentary reactions during amygdala stimulation. *Journal of Neurophysiology*, 1961, **24**, 651–664.

Fritsch, G., Hitzig, E. Ueber die elektrische Erregbarkeit des Grosshirns. *Archiv fuer Anatomie und Physiologie*, 1870, **37**, 300–332.

Galeano, C. Electrophysiological aspects of brain activity during conditioning. A review. *Acta Neurologica Latinoamericana*, 1963, **9**, 395–413.

Galvani, L. De viribus electricitatis in motu musculari. Commentarius. *Proceedings Academia Bologna*, 1791, **7**, 363–418.

Garattini, S., & Sigg, E. B. (Eds.). *Aggressive behaviour*. Amsterdam: Excerpta Med., 1969.

Gilman, S., Dauth, G. W., Tennyson, V. M., & Kremzner, L. T. Chronic cerebellar stimulation in the monkey: Preliminary observations. *Archives of Neurology (Chicago)*, 1975, **32**, 474–477.

Glenn, W. W. L., Hageman, J. H., Mauro, A., Eisenberg, L., Flanigan, S., & Harvard,

M. Electrical stimulation of excitable tissue by radio-frequency transmission. *Annals of Surgery,* 1964, **160,** 338–350.

Goddard, G. V., & Douglas, R. M. Does the engram of kindling model the engram of normal long term memory? In J. Wada (Ed.), *Kindling.* New York: Raven, 1976. Pp. 1–18.

Gold, J. H., Stoeckle, H., Schuder, J. C., West, J. A., & Holland, J. A. Selective tissue stimulation with microimplant·. *Transactions in American Society for Artificial Internal Organs,* 1974, **20,** 430–436.

Greatbatch, W. Electrochemical polarization of physiological electrodes. *Medical Research Engineering,* 1967, 6:2:13.

Guzmán, C. F., Alcaraz, M. V., & Fernandez, A. G. Rapid procedure to localize electrodes in experimental neurophysiology. *Boletin del Instituto de Estudios Medicos y Biologicos* [*Universidad Nacional Autonoma de Mexico*], 1958, **16,** 29–31.

Harris, G. W. The innervation and actions of the neurohypophysis; an investigation using the method of remote-control stimulation. *Philosophical Transactions of the Royal Society of London, Series B,* 1946–1947, **232,** 385–441.

Heath, R. G., & the Tulane University Department of Psychiatry and Neurology (Eds.). *Studies in schizophrenia. A multidisciplinary approach to mind-brain relationships.* Cambridge, MA: Harvard University Press, 1954.

Henry, C. E. A "postage stamp" electrode for subdural electrocorticography. *Digest of Neurology and Psychiatry,* 1949, **17,** 670–680.

Herberg, L. J., & Watkins, P. J. Epileptiform seizures induced by hypothalamic stimulation in the rat: Resistance to fits following fits. *Nature (London),* 1966, **209,** 515–516.

Hess, W. R. Stammganglien-Reizversuche. *Berichte Gesamte weber die Physiologie und Experimentelle Pharmakologie,* 1928, **42,** 554–555.

Hess, W. R. *Beitrage zur Physiologie d. Hirnstammes I. Die Methodik der lokalisierten Reizung und Ausschaltung subkortikaler Hirnabschnitte.* Leipzig: Thieme, 1932.

Higgins, J. W., Mahl, G. F., Delgado, J. M. R., & Hamlin, H. Behavioral changes during intracerebral electrical stimulation. *AMA Archives of Neurology and Psychiatry,* 1956, **76,** 399–419.

Hoagland, H. A. A simple method for recording electrocorticogram in animals without opening the skull. *Science,* 1940, **92,** 537–538.

Holley, J. R., & Powell, D. A. Mercury commutator arrangement for simultaneously stimulating or recording from two small animals in a social situation. *Physiology and Behavior,* 1975, **15,** 741–743.

Horowitz, M. J., Adams, J. E., & Rutkin, B. B. Visual imagery on brain stimulation. *Archives of General Psychiatry,* 1958, **19,** 469–486.

Hosco, M. J. Technique for rapid, permanent documentation of intracerebral electrode sites. *Physiology and Behavior,* 1975, **14,** 367–368.

Hunsperger, R. W. Comportements affectifs provoqués par la stimulation électrique du tronc cérébral et du cerveau antérieur. *Journal de Physiologie (Paris),* 1963, **55,** 45–97.

Kaada, B. R. Somato-motor, autonomic and electrocorticographic responses to electrical stimulation of 'rhinencephalic' and other structures in primates, cat and dog. *Acta Physiologica Scandinavica,* 1951, **24,** Suppl. 83, 1–285.

Kahn, A., & Greatbatch, W. Physiologic electrodes. In C. D. Ray (Ed.), *Medical engineering.* Chicago: Year Book Med., 1974. Pp. 1073–1082.

Lilly, J. C. Electrode and cannulae implantation in the brain by a simple percutaneous method. *Science,* 1958, **127,** 1181–1182.

Lilly, J. C., Hughes, J. R., Alvord, E. C., Jr., & Galkin, T. W. Brief noninjurious electric waveforms for stimulation of brain. *Science,* 1955, **121,** 468–469.

Loucks, R. B., Weinberg, H., & Smith, M. The erosion of electrodes by small currents. *Electroencephalography and Clinical Neurophysiology,* 1959, **11,** 823–826.

Maire, F. W. An adjustable implanted electrode for stimulating the brain of the unanesthetized animal. *Electroencephalography and Clinical Neurophysiology,* 1956, **8,** 337–338.

Manning, G. C. A new miniature multi-contact electrode for subcortical recording and stimulating. *Electroencephalography and Clinical Neurophysiology,* 1964, **17,** 204–208.

Marshall, C. Flexible subdural electrodes for corticography. *Electroencephalography and Clinical Neurophysiology, Supplement,* 1953, **3,** 36.

Martin, A. R., & Lewis, R. S. Variation with electrode size of thresholds for motor responses to cortical stimulation. *Electroencephalography and Clinical Neurophysiology,* 1957, **9,** 726–728.

Matsui, T., & Hirano, A. *An atlas of the human brain for computerized tomography.* Tokyo: Igaku-Shoin, 1978.

Maurus, M. Neue Fernreizapparatur für Kleine Primaten. *Naturwissenschaften,* 1967, **54,** 593.

Maurus, M., & Ploog, D. Social signals in squirrel monkeys: Analysis by cerebral radio stimulation. *Experimental Brain Research,* 1971, **12,** 171–183.

Maxim, P. E., & Spelman, F. A. A radio-controlled constant current biphasic stimulator system for primate studies. *Physiology and Behavior,* 1975, **14,** 663–667.

Mihailović, L., & Delgado, J. M. R. Electrical stimulation of monkey brain with various frequencies and pulse durations. *Journal of Neurophysiology,* 1956, **19,** 21–36.

Moyer, K. E. (Ed.). *Physiology of aggression and implications for control.* New York: Raven, 1976.

Nastuk, N. L. (Ed.). *Physical techniques in biological research* (Vol. 5, Pt. A). New York: Academic Press, 1964.

Ninomina, I., Yonezawa, Y., & Wilson, M. R. Implantable electrode for recording nerve signals in awake animals. *Journal of Applied Physiology,* 1976, **41,** 111–114.

Novikova, L. A., Russinov, V. S., & Semikhina, A. F. Electrophysiological analysis of the conditioning function in the rabbit cortex in presence of a dynamic focus. *Zhurnal Vysshei Nervnoi Deyatel'nosti imeni I. P. Pavlova,* 1952, **2(6),** 844–861.

Olds, J. Pleasure centers in the brain. *Scientific American,* 1956, **195,** 105–116.

Olds, J. Differentiation of reward systems in the brain by self-stimulation techniques. In E. R. Ramey & D. S. O'Doherty (Eds.), *Electrical studies on the unanesthetized brain.* New York: Harper & Row (Hoeber), 1960. Pp. 17–51.

Olds, J., & Milner, P. Positive reinforcement produced by electrical stimulation of the septal area and other regions of the rat brain. *Journal of Comparative and Physiological Psychology,* 1954, **47,** 419–428.

Olszewski, J. *The thalamus of the Macaca Mulatta. An atlas for use with the stereotaxic instrument.* Basel: Karger, 1952.

Penfield, W., & Welch, K. Instability of response to stimulation of the sensorimotor cortex of man. *Journal of Physiology* (*London*), 1949, **109,** 358–365.

Pieri, L., & Hoffman, D. Improved rapid method to check electrode localizations in the brain. *Physiology and Behavior,* 1975, **15,** 113–115.

Pinneo, L. R. Control of purposive behavior by programmed stimulation of the brain. *Physiologist,* 1966, **9,** 276.

Ploog, D. W., Blitz, J., & Ploog, F. Studies on social and sexual behaviour of the squirrel monkey (saimiri sciureus). *Folia Primatologica,* 1963, **1,** 29–66.

Plotnik, R., Mir, D., & Delgado, J. M. R. Aggression, noxiousness and brain stimulation in unrestrained rhesus monkeys. In B. F. Elefthériou (Ed.), *Physiology of aggression and defeat.* New York: Plenum, 1971. Pp. 143–221.

Pruscha, H., & Maurus, M. The communicative function of some agonistic behaviour patterns in squirrel monkeys: The relevance of social context. *Behavioral Ecology Sociobiology,* 1976, **1,** 185–214.

Pudenz, R. H., Bullara, L. A., & Talalla, A. Electrical stimulation of the brain. I. Electrodes and electrode arrays. *Surgical Neurology,* 1975, **4,** 37–42.

Ramey, E. R., & O'Doherty, D. S. (Eds.). *Electrical studies on the unanesthetized brain.* New York: Harper & Row (Hoeber), 1960.

Ray, C. D. (Ed.). *Medical engineering.* Chicago: Year Book Med., 1974.

Rayport, M., & Ferguson, S. M. Qualitative modification by interview content of sensory responses evoked by electrical stimulation of the amygdala in man. *Proceedings of the Congress for Social Biology and Psychiatry,* 1974, pp. 55–56.

Robinson, B. W. Localization of intracerebral electrodes. *Experimental Neurology,* 1962, **6,** 201–233.

Robinson, B. W., Alexander, M., & Bowne, G. Dominance reversal resulting from aggressive responses evoked by brain telestimulation. *Physiology and Behavior,* 1969, **4,** 749–752.

Robinson, B. W., & Mishkin, M. Alimentary responses evoked from forebrain structures in Macaca mulatta. *Science,* 1962, **136,** 260–262.

Robinson, B. W., Warner, H., & Rosvold, H. E. A head-mounted remote-controlled brain stimulator for use on rhesus monkeys. *Electroencephalography and Clinical Neurophysiology,* 1964, **17,** 200–203.

Robinson, R. F., & Johnson, H. T. *Histopathological studies of tissue reactions to various metals implanted in cat brains.* (ASD Tech. Rep. 61-397). Ohio: Wright-Patterson AFB, 1961.

Roth, R. H., Allikmets, L., & Delgado, J. M. R. Formation and release of NA and DOPA. *Archives Internationales de Pharmacodynamie et de Therapie,* 1969, **181,** 273–282.

Rubinstein, E. H., & Delgado, J. M. R. Inhibition induced by forebrain stimulation in the monkey. *American Journal of Physiology,* 1963, **205,** 941–948.

Schmitt, O. H. A radio frequency coupled tissue stimulator. *Science,* 1948, **107,** 432.

Sem-Jacobsen, C. W. *Depth-electrographic stimulation of the human brain and behavior: From fourteen years of studies and treatment of Parkinson's disease and mental disorders with implanted electrodes.* Springfield, IL: Thomas, 1968.

Sem-Jacobsen, C. W., Petersen, M. C., Dodge, H. W., Lazarte, J. A., & Holman, C. B. Electroencephalographic rhythms from the depths of the parietal, occipital, and temporal lobes in man. *Electroencephalography and Clinical Neurophysiology,* 1956, **8,** 263–178.

Sem-Jacobsen, C. W., & Torkildsen, A. Depth recording and electrical stimulation in the human brain. In E. R. Ramey & D. S. O'Doherty (Eds.), *Electrical studies on the unanesthetized brain.* New York: Harper & Row (Hoeber), 1960. Pp. 275–290.

Sheatz, G. C. Electrode holders in chronic preparations. A. Multilead techniques for large and small animals. In D. E. Sheer (Ed.), *Electrical stimulation of the brain.* Austin: University of Texas Press, 1961. Pp. 45–54.

Sheer, D. E. (Ed.). *Electrical stimulation of the brain.* Austin: University of Texas Press, 1961.

Sherrington, C. S. *The integrative action of the nervous system* (2nd ed.). London & New York: Cambridge University Press, 1947.

Sholl, D. A., *The organization of the cerebral cortex.* New York: Wiley, 1956.

Silverman, G., Ball, G. G., & Cohn, C. K. A new automatic constant current stimulator and its biological applications. *IEEE Transactions on Biomedical Engineering,* 1975, **BME-22,** 207–212.

Snider, R. S., & Lee, J. C. *A stereotexic atlas of the monkey brain* (*Macaca mulatta*). Chicago: University of Chicago Press, 1961.

Terell, W., & Maurer, D. Two design approaches to dual channel implantable neuro stimulators. *Proceedings of the 7th Annual Meeting of the Neuroelectric Society*, 1974.

Uzzeli, B. P., & Feezor, M. Dual isolated constant current source for stimulating two brain sites. *Physiology and Behavior*, 1975, **14,** 521–523.

Wada, J. (Ed.). *Kindling*. New York: Raven, 1976.

Warner, H., Robinson, B. W., Rosvold, H. E., Wechsler, L. D., & Zampini, J. J. A remote control brain telestimulator with solar cell power supply. *IEEE Transactions on Biomedical Engineering*, 1968, **BME-15,** 94–101.

Wasman, M., & Flynn, J. P. Directed attack elicited from hypothalamus. *Archives of Neurology* (*Chicago*), 1962, **6,** 220–227.

Wauquier, A., & Rolls, E. T. (Eds.). *Brain-stimulation reward*. Amsterdam: North-Holland Publ., 1976.

Weinmann, J. Biphasic stimulation and electrical properties of metal electrodes. *Journal of Applied Physiology*, 1965, **20,** 787.

Weinmann, J., & Mahler, J. An analysis of electrical properties of metal electrodes. In *Medical electronics*. Liege, Belgium: University of Liege, 1964. Pp. 487–508.

Wetzel, M. C., Howell, L. G., & Bearie, K. J. Experimental performance of steel and platinum electrodes with chronic mono-phasic stimulation of the brain. *Journal of Neurosurgery*, 1969, **31,** 658–669.

Willey, T. J., & Freeman, W. J. Alteration of prepyriform evoked response following prolonged electrical stimulation. *American Journal of Physiology*, 1968, **215,** 1435–1441.

Wyrwicka, W. Electrical activity of the hypothalamus during alimentary conditioning. *Electroencephalography and Clinical Neurophysiology*, 1964, **17,** 164–176.

Chapter 6

Subcortical Stimulation for Motivation and Reinforcement

C. R. Gallistel

Department of Psychology
University of Pennsylvania
Philadelphia, Pennsylvania

ISBN 0-12-547440-7

I. Introduction

The pioneering work of Hess (1954) and Olds and Milner (1954) began a new era in the study of the neural basis of motivation and reinforcement. Hess showed that it was possible to induce motivated behavior sequences by focal stimulation of the brain. Olds & Milner showed that it was possible to produce positively rewarding effects by focal stimulation.

A. Definition of Motivation

Motivated behavior sequences are sequences that involve the conjunction and coordination of many disparate acts to serve a function that is not served when the acts occur in isolation. Neural pathways originating in and around the diencephalon promote the coordinated occurrence of the acts that comprise a motivated behavioral sequence by exerting tonic potentiating and depotentiating effects upon the neural circuits that generate each act. These tonic signals increase the potential for activation in the neural circuits subserving appropriate acts and decrease the potential for activation in other circuits, circuits subserving incompatible acts.

Von Holst and von St. Paul (1963) were the first to analyze the motivational effects of brain stimulation within the conceptual framework just enunciated. The work of Flynn and his collaborators (Bandler & Flynn, 1972; Flynn, 1972; Flynn, Edwards, & Bandler, 1971; MacDonnell & Flynn, 1966; see also Berntson & Beattie, 1975) has provided the most compelling demonstrations of act-specific potentiation induced by motivating brain stimulation. Flynn's experiments show, among other things, that unilateral diencephalic stimulation can induce unilateral potentiation of the elementary reflexes that form part of predatory behavior in cats. A recent experiment by Beagley and Holley (1977) demonstrates unilateral potentiation of an instrumentally conditioned food-seeking act in the rat. Adams (1979) reviews the literature on stimulation and lesions within the brain stem in an attempt to functionally characterize and specify the anatomical locus of the diverse pathways that potentiate various forms of aggressive behavior. Gallistel (1980) gives a book-length development of the concept of selective potentiation and its relation to motivation.

B. Definition of Reward

Positive rewarding effects are effects that induce a goal-directed reorganization of an animal's instrumental behavior. The behavior is reorganized so as to generate the reward effect. Just how these reward effects should be conceived of is unclear. In traditional learning theories, reward effects played a privileged role. It was assumed that if a behavioral sequence did not culminate in a rewarding effect, then no learning occurred. Rewards served to stamp in otherwise evanescent associations. The discovery of the self-stimulation phenomenon gave this conception a new lease on life. It seemed that with rewarding electrical stimulation one directly induced the neural signals that played this stamping in role.

One may doubt the general applicability of traditional theories of learning and in particular the notion that a reward effect is a *sine qua non* for the occurence of learning (cf. Hulse, Fowler, & Honig, 1978). The seemingly essential role of rewards may be an artifact of the traditional paradigms for testing what an animal has learned (cf. Rescorla, 1978). Reward effects may play no privileged role in learning *per se;* rather they may serve to bring what the animal learns into the service of an experimenter-controlled motivational state (cf. Gallistel, 1975). By bringing what the animal learns into the service of a specific motivational state, rewards make what the animal has learned manifest in what it does.

In any event, there is no doubt that some of the neural signals generated by rewarding electrical stimulation yield an engram of some kind—a mnemonic change somewhere in the nervous system—and this engram powerfully redirects the animals instrumental behavior (cf. Gallistel, 1978; Gallistel, Stellar, & Bubis, 1974).

C. The Brain-Stimulation Preparation

The tonic neural signals that underlie naturally motivated behavior and the transient neural signals that mediate natural reward effects have a complex and largely obscure causation under natural conditions. The advantage of inducing these effects by focal brain stimulation is that one bypasses the complex and poorly understood input processes. The motivating and rewarding signals are generated by a single input, the electrical stimulation, and this stimulation is under the experimenter's direct control. Animals implanted with electrodes that yield motivating and rewarding effects constitute preparations in the classic physiological sense of the term, that is, animals in which the behavioral phenomenon one wishes to study has been experimentally simplified in a way that makes it easier to relate the behavior to neurophysiological variables.

One desideratum in a good preparation is that the phenomenon to be studied can be elicited in a highly reproducible manner and more or less to the exclusion of other potentially intrusive phenomena. Motivating and rewarding effects produced by focal brain stimulation have this property. They are powerful and highly reproducible. There is no natural reward that can determine an animal's instrumental behavior trial after trial hour after hour, as can rewarding brain stimulation. This property of the instrumental behavior sustained by rewarding stimulation has made possible the determination of a number of quantitative characteristics of the neural pathways that carry the rewarding signals—their refractory period, strength–duration curves, conduction velocities, span of temporal integration, and so on (see Gallistel, Shizgal, & Yeomans, in press). A similar start has been made in determining characteristics of the neural pathways mediating motivating effects (Beagley, 1976; Halboth & Coons, 1973; Rose, 1974; Shizgal & Matthews, 1977; Yeomans, 1975). This chapter describes modern techniques for making and studying these preparations.

II. Electrodes

A. *Monopolar versus Bipolar*

The majority of investigators use bipolar electrodes, that is, a pair of wires insulated (except at the tip) and twisted together, or glued together by a coat of insulating material. The reason most often cited for choosing this configuration is the belief that the resulting field of excitation will be more circumscribed. It is hard to see any justification for this belief (see, however, Valenstein & Beer, 1961; Wise, 1972). The size of the field of effective excitation is determined by the current intensity and the width of the stimulating pulses (or period, in the case of sinusoidal stimulation). Investigators choose these parameters of stimulation so as to meet or exceed some criterion of behavioral effectiveness. In other words, they increase current intensity and thereby the field of effective excitation until they obtain some desired effect; or they choose a current intensity that previous experience has shown to be effective in most preparations. In either case the size (volume) of the field of excitation is determined by the form and intensity of the stimulation, not by the choice of an electrode configuration.

It is probable that the choice of a bipolar configuration determines the shape of the field of excitation, as opposed to its size. But no one has determined what this shape might be, so considerations of field shape would not appear to offer any reasons for preferring bipolar electrodes. It has been shown that the orientation of a bipolar electrode—whether the tips lie along a rostral–caudal or transverse axis—influences the rewarding effectiveness of a given intensity of stimulation (Szabo & Milner, 1973; Szabo, Nad, & Szabo, 1972).

Despite its popularity, there are a number of reasons for avoiding the bipolar configuration. First, the bipolar configuration, particularly the commonly employed twisted pair of unsharpened wires, damages neural tissue at the time of implantation. A sharpened monopolar electrode, e.g., an insulated insect pin, does not.

Second, with the bipolar configuration, at least one electrode tip must serve as the anode (positive side of the electrical circuit). Usually, the bipolar configuration is used in conjunction with biphasic stimulation (see Section VII-B), which means that each tip serves as the anode half the time. Wetzel, Howell, and Bearie (1969) have shown that anodal stimulation damages neural tissue, unless one goes to the trouble and expense of using platinum–iridium wire. Cathodal stimulation does not damage tissue. Since the damage caused by anodal stimulation occurs at the site of stimulation and grows worse with continued stimulation, the bipolar configuration should be avoided in chronic experiments.

Third, a bipolar electrode presents a more complex form of stimulation to the tissue. The cathodal current at one pole depolarizes the immediately adjacent tissue, while the anodal current at the other pole hyperpolarizes immediately adjacent tissue and perhaps depolarizes more remote tissue. When the phase of stimulation reverses, this complex pattern of hyperpolarizing and depolarizing effects likewise reverses. Thus, for ease of interpretation of the excitatory effect of the stimulation, as well as for the two reasons already mentioned, bipolar electrodes should be avoided in favor of monopolar electrodes. The monopolar electrodes should be used in conjunction with monophasic cathodal stimulation (see Section V-B).

In the monopolar configuration a single wire, insulated except at the tip, is lowered into the brain to the desired site of stimulation. A second, uninsulated wire is layed on the skull, to serve as the current return path.

B. Purchase or Manufacture?

For experiments involving only one or two stimulating electrodes per rat, many North American investigators purchase ready-made electrodes from Plastic Products (Box 12004, Roanoke, Va.). These electrodes come in a variety of sizes, types of wire (nichrome, platinum–iridium, stainless steel), and configurations. The standard model for rat work isMS 303/1. If one wants to use a monopolar configuration, one should order "MS 303/1-A, untwisted, with one insulated and one uninsulated electrode wire." At implantation, the uninsulated wire is bent at right angles to the insulated stimulating electrode and laid along the skull.

The Plastic Products electrodes come attached to a small cylindrical pedestal plug, which is threaded to receive a cap on the connecting cable. The electrical connection with the Plastic Products electrode is not a very good one. When the rat moves around the contact resistance may vary rapidly from a few ohms to a few thousand ohms. If the experimenter is using a constant voltage stimulator, the varying contact resistance will vary the stimulating current. Serious artifacts may result, invalidating whole experiments (Cantor, Beninger, Bellisle, & Milner, 1979). So, the careful investigator should beware. The use of a high-quality constant current stimulator is advisable whenever the electrical contact is of poor quality. Plastic Products also makes a complete line of cables, slip rings, and so forth.

Those who want to make their own electrodes for single or double-electrode implantations, which is cheaper but time consuming, can order No. 00 stainless steel insect pins from Ward Natural Science Establishment (Rochester, N.Y.).

One begins the fabrication by soldering an L-shaped piece of bell wire to the pin about 1 mm above the point where the pin will emerge from the skull. A drop of stainless steel soldering flux must be applied to the pin to promote bonding of the solder. It is also advisable to use solder specially formulated for soldering stainless steel.

Next the electrode is insulated by dipping it in very thick Formvar, a wire insulating varnish obtainable from General Electric industrial supply stores. The electrode should be lowered until the Formvar covers the joint between pin and bell wire and then withdrawn very slowly, so as to prevent the formation of drips on the pin. To harden the varnish, the freshly dipped electrodes must be baked for 2 minutes in a small lab oven at about 100°C. Two or three coats of insulation are recommended.

At implantation, dental acrylic is applied to the skull until it covers the bottom of the bell-wire "L". When the acrylic has thoroughly hardened, the pin is clipped off close to the acrylic, leaving the bell wire protruding above the cement to receive the connector on the cable. Another piece of bell wire laid on the skull before application of the acrylic and bent to protrude up out of the acrylic may serve as the indifferent electrode.

The cable connects to the bell wires by means of bubble-clutch tie pin clasps, which may be purchased from jewelry supply stores. If one has used bell wire thick enough (or piano wire), these bubble-clutch clasps hold fairly securely. However, the quality of the electrical connection is not very good.

Before implantation, scrape the electrode tips bare of insulation to a distance of about 0.5 mm, using an old scalpel blade.

If more than two electrodes are to be implanted in one rat, an electrode assembly should be made using a jig. The jig should be a small block of Lucite or Plexiglas, with holes bored in the sides, to receive the ear bars on a stereotaxic instrument, and a tab, projecting about 1 cm out from the forward face, to rest on the mouthpiece of the stereotaxic instrument. The jig is placed in the stereotaxic and the mouthpiece raised or lowered until the top surface of the jig assumes the same inclination to the horizontal as the top of the animal's skull during implantation. One marks an artificial bregma on the top surface and drills holes relative to this bregma at those loci where one will drill through the skull during implantation. The depth of each hole should be .5–1 mm deeper than the intended depth of the electrode. The holes should be just big enough so that the insulated electrodes fit snugly.

To make a multielectrode assembly, put a piece of cellophane tape over the electrode holes to prevent acrylic adhering to the jig. Then jab the electrodes, with tips already scraped bare, through the tape and all the way down into the holes. Scrape the insulation off of a 2–4 mm segment of the electrodes above the tape, and clip off the electrodes at the top of this segment. Then bend this segment over about 45°, so that it can be rotated into contact with connector leads. Tin the bent segment with solder. Take a multipin microminiature connector plug (e.g., the nine-pin ITT/Canon Model MD1-9P1-1, which makes electrical contacts of excellent quality) and clip the leads down to stubs about 2 mm long, which should be splayed out laterally. Take a mating connector cemented to a narrow strip of sheet metal and place it in the electrode carrier of the stereotaxic instrument to hold the connector that is to be soldered to the electrodes. Lower the connector into position immediately over the array of bent electrode stubs. Rotate each stub into contact with a connector lead and solder. When all the electrodes have been soldered to connector leads, solder a length of stainless steel suture wire to a remaining lead to serve as the skull electrode. Then, embed the solder joints in dental acrylic. When the acrylic has thoroughly hardened, the electrode assembly is raised out of the jig by the carrier.

In this way, one can implant as many as six or eight electrodes in a single rat brain. At implantation, a hole is drilled for each electrode. The electrode assembly is held in the electrode carrier by the same mating connector used during fabrication of the assembly. Initially, the assembly is deliberately positioned so that the electrodes just miss the holes. It is lowered till the deepest electrode tip just touches the skull surface, and the depth reference is noted on the carrier Vernier scale. Then the assembly is positioned directly over the holes and lowered into place. The length of stainless steel suture wire is wound around one or more skull screws, and the assembly is cemented to the skull and the skull screws with dental acrylic.

C. Moveable Electrodes

In mapping studies, where the goal is to study the distribution of sites where stimulation induces a given effect, or to study the threshold for a given effect as a function of electrode locus, the use of a moveable chronic electrode has much to recommend it. The moveable electrode has, for example, recently been put to excellent use in mapping the relation between low-threshold self-stimulation sites and the dopaminergic and adrenergic projections (Corbett & Wise, 1979, 1980). The moveable electrode is a length of straight wire, insulated except at the sharpened tip, and topped by a concentrically mounted Amphenol connector that is threaded externally. A 10 mm long nylon sleave, threaded internally, is cemented to the rat's skull so that the electrode may be inserted into it and screwed down to any desired depth. Details of the fabrication and use are given in Wise (1976).

III. Connecting Cable and Slip Rings

The connecting cable should be made of lightweight flex-resistant wire. The wire used for hearing aids is recommended. The first 20–40 cm of cable above the animal should be passed through a tightly wound spring to prevent the animal chewing on the cable. The next 20–40 cm should be taped to a loosely coiled piano-wire spring to keep a light take-up tension on the cable when the animal is in the apparatus. The cable should connect to a slip ring so that the animal does not twist the cable when it turns. BSR/LVE makes a slip ring; A lightweight seven-circuit slip ring is also available from the Airflyte Electronics Co. (535 Avenue A, Bayonne, N.J.). To prevent premature breakage of the wires, it helps to encase the points of maximum flexing (at the animal end and the slip-ring end of the cable) in a cone of silicone bathtub sealer.

IV. Atlases and Implantation Coordinates

The standard atlases for determining stereotaxic coordinates in the rat are DeGroot (1959), König and Klippel (1967), Pellegrino and Cushman (1967), and Jacobowitz and Palkovits (1974). The angle at which the rat's head is positioned in the stereotaxic instrument varies from atlas to atlas, so each atlas has a different coordinate frame. That is, the coordinates for a given structure are not the same from atlas to atlas. The König and Klippel atlas is perhaps the most frequently used, partly because in its coordinate frame the top of the skull lies very nearly in a horizontal plane (the so-called "level-skull" coordinates). Many investigators find this position of the skull most convenient. The Jacobowitz and Palkovits atlas extends the König and Klippel atlas caudally through the midbrain and well into the hindbrain. It plots the loci of aminergic and cholinergic pathways and cell bodies.

All of the atlases were done using 200–300 g rats, whose skulls unfortunately are somewhat smaller than the skulls of the 350–450 g rats preferred for work with chronic intracranial electrodes. When one derives one's implantation coordinates directly from the atlases, one frequently misses the mark. In our lab, we use the level-skull head position. Table I gives the coordinates we use to hit many of the sites that yield self-stimulation and/or motivational effects. This Table has been supplemented by coordinates supplied by Bartley Hoebel. Table II gives the DeGroot coordinates required to hit various structures. It was supplied by Dale Corbett.

For a fairly recent mapping of self-stimulation sites in the monkey (*Macaca mulata*), see Routtenberg, Gardner, and Huang (1971).

TABLE I

LEVEL-SKULL STEREOTAXIC COORDINATES FOR THE IMPLANTATION OF ELECTRODES AIMED AT REWARD AND MOTIVATION LOCI IN THE 250–450 GRAM MALE CHARLES RIVER RAT (SPRAGUE–DAWLEY STRAIN)

Structure	A–P (referred to bregma)	Lateral (referred to midline)	Depth (referred to skull surface)
Gallistel coordinates			
Dorsal pontine tegmentum (vicinity locus coeruleus)	−0.5 (i.a.[a])	1.3	6.8
Ventral tegmental area of tsai	−5.0 to −6.0	1.2–1.4	8.5–9.5
Posterior lateral hypothalamus[b]	−4.0	1.3–1.5	8.5–9.2
Lateral hypothalamus	−3.0	1.3–1.6	8.3–9.0
Lateral preoptic area	0.0	1.5–1.8	7.5–8.0
Medial septum	0.0 to +1.0	0.6	5.0–6.0
Sulcal cortex	+3.0	0.6	3.8
Hoebel coordinates	(referred to i.a.)		(referred to cortical surface)
Posterior hypothalamus	4.5	1.2–1.5	8.5
Lateral hypothalamus	6.0	1.2–2.0	7.6
Nucleus accumben Septi	9.5–10.0	0.8	5.4

[a] In working this far caudally, one should use the ear bars, that is the interaural line (i.a.), as the A-P reference. Bregma is 10 mm ± 1 mm rostral to the interaural line.
[b] A very reliable self-stimulation site.

TABLE II

DEGROOT COORDINATES FOR THE IMPLANTATION OF ELECTRODES AIMED AT REWARD AND MOTIVATION LOCI IN THE 250–450 GRAM MALE SPRAGUE–DAWLEY RAT[a]

Structure	A-P (referred to Bregma)	Lateral (referred to midline)	Depth (referred to cortical surface)
Cerebellum	−8.5	+0.8	−5.7
Motor nucleus of the trigeminal nerve	−8.0	+1.7	−6.6
Dorsal pontine tegmentum (vicinity of locus coeruleus)	−7.4	+1.3	−6.4
Decussation of the superior cerebellar peduncle	−6.6	+1.3	−6.6
Dorsal raphe	−6.0	+0.0	−6.0
Substantia nigra, pars compacta	−3.5	+2.0	−7.3
Ventral tegmental area of tsai	−3.5	+0.9	−8.3
Lateral hypothalamus	−0.4 mm	+2.7 mm	−8.0 mn

[a] Table supplied by Dale Corbett. DeGroot coordinate frame is established by setting mouthpiece 5 mm above interaural line.

V. Forms of Stimulation

A. *Sinusoidal*

The form of stimulation most easily generated by someone with minimal equipment is 60-cycle sinusoidal. All that is required is a Variac—a continuously variable transformer for stepping down the current available from the nearest wall socket. Since the currents used for sinusoidal stimulation fall in the range of 10 to 100μA, and since the impedance of the electrode/tissue part of the circuit is only a few kilohms, one should not connect the electrodes directly to the output of the variable transformer. One should insert 0.5 MΩ resistors on both sides of the transformer output. These will limit current through the animal to tolerable levels even when the transformer output is maximal and the animal is inadvertently grounded (for example, by touching a grounded metal lever). Not only the animal's safety but also that of the investigator is thereby ensured.

To monitor the current in this simplest of stimulating circuits, connect an oscilloscope across one of the 0.5 MΩ series resistances. If an oscilloscope with differential input (that is, with both sides of the input ungrounded) is not available, then take care to connect across the resistor on the grounded side of the transformer output.

B. *Pulsatile*

Stimulation with short trains of brief cathodal pulses has three advantages: (1) it minimizes the charge that must be delivered to obtain a given effect; (2) it avoids the delivery of anodal current to the site of stimulation; and (3) the mode of excitation is more straightforward and better understood than the mode of excitation by other forms of stimulation.

The choice of pulse sign (+/−) and duration. The charge required to produce a given rewarding effect is minimized by minimizing the pulse width in a train of cathodal pulses (Barry, Walters, & Gallistel, 1974). The same is true for the priming effect in self-stimulation (Matthews, 1977) and probably for other behavioral effects. The current required with brief anodal pulses is about twice that required when cathodal pulses are used (Matthews, 1977).

The choice of pulse frequency. Shizgal, Howlett, and Corbett (see Gallistel, *et al.*, 1981) discovered that, with train duration fixed, the required current intensity is a linear function of the reciprocal of the number of pulses where I is the required current intensity, K is a constant,

$$I = K(1/N) + I_0 \tag{1}$$

and I_0 is the zero intercept, the current required as N becomes indefinitely large. The required charge, where d is pulse duration, is:

$$Q = NdI. \tag{2}$$

Substituting (2) into (1), cancelling, and rearranging terms, yields:

$$Q = d(K + NI_0). \tag{3}$$

It is clear from (3) that choosing lower pulse frequencies (thereby reducing N, the number of pulses in the train) will reduce the total charge required, hence also the charge per second. The constant I_0 is, however, usually so small that reducing pulse frequency below 100 pps has little effect on required charge (Gallistel, 1978). Reducing pulse frequency requires an increase in either current intensity, which can bring in unwanted side effects, or an increase in train duration, which itself wastes charge, so a frequency of about 100 pps is usually best.

The choice of train duration. Gallistel (1978) found that the total charge required to produce a given reinforcing effect was a linearly increasing function of train duration. Unpublished studies by Liran in my laboratory found the same result for the priming effect of stimulation. Hence, the shorter the train duration the less the total charge required to produce a given effect. However, as the train duration gets shorter, the required current increases. Sooner or later this increase will bring in unwanted side effects. Train durations of 0.1–0.5 sec are generally best.

Summary. If one chooses to use cathodal pulses because of their nondestructiveness and their straightforward, well-understood mode of excitation (see the following), then one should use pulses 0.1 msec or less in duration at a frequency of about 100 pps and a train duration of 0.1–0.5 seconds. These choices minimize the charge that must be delivered, as much as one can without bringing in unwanted side effects. Minimizing the charge delivered should minimize electrochemical effects and possible tissue damage.

1. Electrode Polarization

Many investigators who use pulsatile stimulation deliver alternating equal amplitude cathodal and anodal pulses in order to avoid electrode polarization. Electrode polarization is the electrochemical effect of forcing substantial amounts of electric charge across the electrode–tissue junction in one direction only. These electrochemical effects make the junction behave like a battery with an output impedance of many megohms. A difference in electrical potential of as much as several volts develops between the stimulating electrode and an indifferent electrode. This difference decays approximately in an exponential manner over a period of minutes. The rate of decay is unaffected by the existence or nonexistence of any experimenter-supplied shunt between the stimulating electrode and the indifferent electrode. In other words, the decay of electrode polarization is determined by the very high effective impedance of the electrochemical processes at the interface between the electrode and the tissue. However, this electrochemical polarization develops only if a substantial amount of charge (on the order of 1 μC) is made to flow in one direction, with no return flow. The charge contained in one pulse (which is on the order of 50 nC) does not cause any enduring electrode polarization. Thus, electrode polarization is avoided by using alternating equal amplitude cathodal and anodal pulses, because then there is no long-term net flow of charge in either direction.

However, the anodal pulses in a biphasic pulse train deposit metallic ions at the site of stimulation, and they complicate the mode of excitation. It is not necessary to use biphasic stimulation to prevent electrode polarization. One need only design the stimulating circuit so that there is a shunt of moderate resistance between the stimulating and indifferent electrode when no pulse is being delivered. A stimulating circuit with an effective output impedance of less than 50 kΩ (e.g., the Digi-Bit circuit described by Deutsch, 1966) will not cause electrode polarization. The electrode–tissue interface behaves like a capacitor. It is charged by each pulse and discharges through the shunting resistance between pulses.

In our lab, we use constant current stimulators, and we often connect more than one stimulator to the same electrode or to two different electrodes in the same animal. Most constant current-stimulating circuits have a high output impedance. And, if two or more sources of stimulation are to be connected to the same animal, high output impedances are essential to prevent "cross-talk" between the stimulating circuits. ("Cross-talk" occurs when some fraction of the current delivered from one stimulator passes into the other stimulating circuit.) We prevent electrode polarization by inserting an electronic switch on the stimulator output. The programming circuitry switches in a low-resistance shunt whenever none of the stimulators connected to the animal is delivering a pulse.

VI. Stimulators

There are several commercially available stimulators for delivering monophasic or biphasic pulse trains. However, the beginning experimenter with a limited budget should consider constructing his own stimulator out of solid-state programming modules. The current supplied by the outputs of solid-state pulse generators are more than adequate. Self-constructed solid-state stimulating circuits have the additional advantage of being very easily interfaced with solid-state programming equipment. A further advantage is that the stimulating circuitry may be completely isolated from other electrical circuits involving the experimental animal by powering the stimulator from a battery. If footshock is to be delivered to an animal while it is connected to the stimulator, one must take care that some component of the shock current does not pass into the stimulating circuitry. This can be a serious problem if the stimulating circuitry is connected to the wall-socket ground at some point, as is often the case in stimulating circuits that derive their power from ac outlets. With battery powered stimulating circuits, there is no possibility of such cross-talk (provided the oscilloscope that monitors current does not provide a path to ground).

In constructing one's own stimulating circuit, one may use solid-state modules designed specifically for programming behavioral experiments (cf. Deutsch, 1966), or, for much less cost, one may use the solid-state "chips" available from suppliers of electronic components for industry. The cost of these chips is minimal, but their use requires somewhat greater electronic sophistication. Capacitative shunts may be required at the inputs to buffer the circuits against electromagnetic transients. And, the connections between the chips must be carefully made, because solid-state circuits are sensitive to the electrical noise from poor connections.

Figure 1 gives a circuit diagram for an inexpensive constant current, battery-powered, and optically isolated bioelectric stimulating circuit developed by Murray Bloom, formerly in the electronic shop of the Institute of Neurological Sciences at the University of Pennsylvania. Whenever an enable pulse appears at the input, the circuit delivers a constant current output whose intensity is selected by a precision 10-turn potentiometer. The enable pulses may be supplied from a solid-state programming circuit (e.g. Digi-Bits) or from a microprocessor or mini-computer, etc. The electronic switch on the output grounds the output whenever the enable signal is off. Grounding the output between pulses prevents electrode polarization. The circuit is designed in such a way that it draws no current from its batteries except when actually delivering stimulating current, so there is a long battery life. Investigators who do not want to construct their own unit may purchase units from Bloom Associates, Ltd., 1327 Bobarn Drive, Penn Valley, Narbeth, Pa. 19072.

Anyone contemplating a substantial amount of research in brain stimulation should give serious consideration to using a microprocessor.

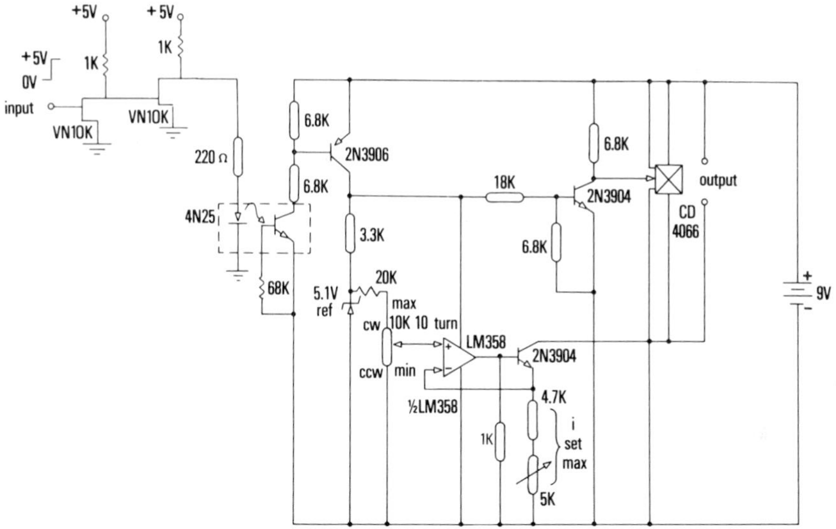

FIG. 1. A constant current stimulating circuit powered by a 9v battery. The electronic switch (CD 4066) on the output short-circuits the output when there is no enable pulse. The circuit draws current from the 9v battery only during stimulation, promoting long battery life. If two or more circuits are to be connected to the same electrode, then the circuit must be modified to place this shunt under the control of a separate enable input. The circuit generates a stimulating current so long as there is +5 V enable at the input (the standard output from microcomputers). The input circuitry (to left of 4N25) requires its own power supply, which may be derived from the computer power supply. Circuit design by Murray Bloom, 1327 Bobarn Drive, Penn Valley, Pennsylvania.

These miniature computers can perform all of the programming functions and data-logging functions heretofore performed by custom-built solid-state or relay programming circuits. They can be programmed to deliver any stimulating waveform via digital-to-analog converters. A microprocessor-driven stimulating circuit is more versatile than commercially available stimulators and should cost only slightly more. When it is remembered that the microprocessor also can program the events in the experiment, log the data, do the statistical computations, and serve as a text processor when it comes to writing up the results, a microprocessor-based experimental setup seems attractive.

VII. Monitoring

In monitoring any form of electrical stimulation, it is essential to determine the current delivered. Inexperienced investigators sometimes report only the voltage of the stimulating pulses. This information is meaningless unless the impedance of the stimulating circuit is known. It is the current delivered that counts, not voltage. Current is determined by monitoring the voltage drop across a known resistance in series with the stimulating electrode. For monitoring this voltage a differential oscilloscope is preferable. With a nondifferential scope, one side of the series resistance is necessarily grounded when the scope is connected. If a scope with differential input is not available, then the series resistance must be placed on the indifferent or current-return side of the stimulating circuit (unless the stimulating circuit is battery-powered). In using a differential scope to monitor the voltage drop across the series resistance, one must consult the scope manual to make sure that the voltage levels at the inputs do not exceed the effective range of differential operation. At high sensitivity settings, most differential scopes cannot handle inputs more than 10 V off of ground. Using a higher known resistance will allow one to work at lower sensitivity settings, hence farther off ground.

In experiments where electric shocks derived from the ac mains are to be delivered while the rat is connected to the stimulating circuitry, it should be borne in mind that the monitoring oscilloscope may provide a path to ground that allows significant cross-talk between the shock circuit and the stimulating circuit.

VIII. Mode of Excitation

The manner in which the electrical current from an intracranial electrode excites neurons in the vicinity of the electrode tip depends upon the electrode configuration (bipolar or monopolar), the stimulating waveform (monophasic or biphasic current), and the type of tissue (cell bodies or axons). The most detailed theoretical and empirical investigation of this topic is by Ranck (1975); see also Chapter 1 in this volume.

A. *Cathodal Pulses*

The simplest case is the application of cathodal pulses from a monopolar electrode to a population of axons. The cathodal sink at the electrode tip sets up depolarizing current fluxes across the membranes of the axons surrounding the sink. Whether or not an axon fires depends on whether the net charge flow across the membrane during the pulse depolarizes the membrane to or beyond the threshold for spike initiation.

On theoretical grounds (see Gallistel, *et al.*, 1981), one might expect that, to a first approximation, the flux to which an axon is exposed would decrease as the inverse square of the distance of that axon from the electrode tip. If so, then the radius of effective excitation should increase as the square root of current intensity. Ranck (1975) reviewed all of the microelectrode studies that permitted an estimate of the relation between the current intensity at the tip of a stimulating macroelectrode and the radius of effective excitation. His plot of log radius as a function of log current intensity is a straight line with slope $\frac{1}{2}$. This plot supports the belief that the radius of effective excitation is proportionate to the square root of the current intensity.

The radius of effective excitation also depends upon pulse duration, since the depolarizing effect of the induced transmembrane flux is cumulative, and also, perhaps, because prolonged pulses may cause some axons to fire more than once (cf. Matthews, 1978). Matthews (1977) determined the trade-off between pulse duration and current intensity for the reward effect, the priming effect, and the motor effect of lateral hypothalamic stimulation. The strength–duration trade-off was approximately hyperbolic, that is, the required current, I, was related to the pulse duration, d, by an equation of the form

$$I = r(1 + c/d),$$

where r is the rheobase (the current required at indefinitely long pulse durations) and c the chronaxie. For the priming and reward effects, the chronaxie was about 1.5 msec; whereas for the motor effect, it was about 0.5 msec.

B. Anodal Pulses

In theory, anodal pulses ought to set up hyperpolarizing transmembrane fluxes in the surrounding neurons, so it is at first sight puzzling that anodal pulses are behaviorally effective. From theoretical (Ranck, 1975 and Chapter 1 in this volume) and empirical (Matthews, 1977, 1978) investigations, it appears that anodal pulses excite in two distinct ways. First, they excite by remote depolarization. The hyperpolarizing currents driven into neurons in the immediate vicinity of the electrode must exit from those same neurons at points more remote from the electrode. These exit currents may depolarize these remote sites sufficiently to fire the neurons. Second, prolonged anodal pulses may cause hyperexcitability of the sodium gates at the site of hyperpolarization. When the hyperpolarizing flux stops, the return to normal membrane polarization may open the hypersensitive sodium gates far enough to initiate an action potential. This phenomenon—"firing-at-break"—was well-known in the days when the nerve–muscle preparation was standard (cf. Hill, 1936). It was demonstrated both theoretically and empirically in the isolated squid axon by Hodgkin and Huxley (1952). Matthews (1977) demonstrated firing at break in the neurons mediating the motor effects of lateral hypothalamic stimulation. He argued from the form of the strength–duration functions for anodal pulses that firing-at-break must also be involved when priming, and reward neurons are excited by anodal pulses lasting longer than 5 msec.

Since anodal pulses hyperpolarize immediately adjacent tissue while cathodal pulses depolarize, one might expect complex interactions when using bipolar electrodes. The hyperpolarization at the anodal tip might extinguish some of the spikes induced by depolarization at the cathodal tip. The magnitude of such effects, as judged by the effectiveness of the stimulation in inducing a given behavior, might depend on the orientation of the tips relative to the behaviorally relevant axon bundle. If the tips lay along the bundle, the spike-extinguishing effect might be greater than if the tips lay athwart the bundle. Szabo *et al.* (1972) have shown that the orientation of bipolar electrodes does indeed affect the rewarding effectiveness of the stimulation.

C. *Biphasic Stimulation*

Hill (1936) gave a theoretical analysis of excitation by sinusoidal stimulation, but his conclusions did not entirely tally with results from nerve–muscle preparations. To what extent his conclusions apply to centrally delivered stimulation has never been evaluated. It should be obvious from the discussion so far that the mode by which biphasic currents applied through bipolar electrodes excite neurons is certain to be complex and hard to analyze. This is a reason for avoiding this method of excitation.

IX. Determining the Locus of the Electrode Tip

The conventional way of determining the locus of the electrode tip is by sectioning the perfused and frozen (or paraffin-embedded) brain at the conclusion of the experiment. There are a number of factors that render this mode of tip localization inaccurate:

If the electrodes are still cemented to the top of the skull when it is cut away to remove the brain, then the electrode tips are unavoidably wiggled back and forth within the perfused brain, leaving a hole around the tip much larger than the *in vivo* track. This may be avoided by placing the perfused head upside down on a wire-mesh platform on the bottom of a head-sized jar. A hole is cut in the center of the mesh platform so that the acrylic that cements the electrodes to the top of the skull projects through this hole. The jar is filled with Formvar thinner to a level that immerses the acrylic but not the rest of the head, and the jar is covered. Formvar thinner (obtained from industrial suppliers of General Electric products) slowly disolves the acrylic. After about two days, one may cleanly and quickly pull out the electrodes, leaving undistorted electrode tracks in the brain.

If the brain is not blocked in the plane of electrode insertion, then when the brain is sectioned, the entire electrode track will not be seen in any one section. Precisely localizing the tip of a track in a series of sections cut diagonally across that track is not easy. One way to block the brain precisely in the plane of electrode insertion is to replace the head in the stereotaxic instrument when the top of the skull has been removed but the brain is still in place. Adjust the height of the mouthpiece so that the head has the same inclination it had at implantation, then block the brain with a scalpel blade held in an electrode carrier. To prevent distortion of the brain in the course of the blocking cut, use the vertical screw on the carrier to saw the scalpel blade up and down while drawing the blade slowly across the brain with the transverse screw.

Even when one employs these procedures for removing the electrodes and blocking the brain, the precise determination of the site where the stimulating current entered the tissue is not easy. The precision of this determination is enhanced if one marks the point of current entry at the time of sacrifice. To do this, one passes a 10-sec-long 0.5 mA anodal current through the stimulating electrode, after the animal has been anesthetized but before the perfusion. Then one perfuses with saline as usual. After the saline perfusion, one perfuses with 10% formalin, to which has been added 3% (by weight) of ferrocyanide, 3% of ferricyanide, and 0.5% of trichloracetic acid. The anodal current deposits ferric and ferrous ions at the site of current entry. The cyanide ions in the just described perfusate react with these, marking the site of current entry with an easily seen blue stain.

X. Determining Which Neural Systems Are Excited

Until recently, there was no way of making this determination. One could only make "guesstimates" based on the site of stimulation. The advent of 2-deoxyglucose autoradiography has greatly improved the prospects for making this very important determination. This technique, while rather expensive, is easier than is generally realized. We have obtained excellent results even after injecting the radioactive 2-deoxyglucose (2-DG) intraperitoneally (rather than via the arterial catheters used heretofore) and perfusing the rat with a weak formalin solution at the time of sacrifice. The present development of this rapidly developing technique is now described,[1] and some illustrations of the results are provided in Figs. 2–4.

A. *Principle*

The 2-DG autoradiography exploits the coupling between neural signaling activity and neural metabolism in order to trace the neural activity generated by some kind or condition of stimulation. The stimulus is delivered to an animal during the period when a pulse of radioactive, unmetabolizable glucose (^{14}C-2DG) injected into the circulatory system is being taken up and phosphorylated by the neurons (and other cells) of the body. After 30–45 min, when all but a small percentage of the radioactive glucose has been taken up by cells, the animal is sacrificed. The brain is removed and rapidly frozen. The brain is then sectioned, and the sections are placed against a photographic emulsion to record the relative concentrations of the phosphorylated radioactive-2-DG. The concentration of the unmetabolizable 2-DG within the cell bodies and nerve terminals of a neural system is an index of that system's metabolic activity: the higher the metabolic activity, the greater the uptake of glucose. Ordinary glucose is metabolized and its carbon constituents are excreted from the cell. But the phosphorylated 2-DG is unmetabolizable; it accumulates in the cell and is excreted very slowly (9–15 hr half-life in brain tissue). The greater the metabolic activity of a neuron, the greater the accumulation of phosphorylated 2-DG within that neuron during the period when the radioactive injection was being taken up by cells. The metabolism of a neuron is fairly closely coupled to its signaling activity, because signaling is work, and work requires energy. Hence, the radiographic images of the brain sections reveal—when compared to suitable controls—the neural systems whose signaling activity was elevated by

[1]The technique was developed by Sokoloff, Reivich, and their collaborators (Sokoloff, Reivich, Kennedy, DesRosiers, Patlak, Pettigrew, Sakurada, & Shinohara, 1977). The methods described here have been worked out by a group doing research in collaboration with Reivich at the University of Pennsylvania. Peter Hand and John Yeomans played a central role in developing some of the refinements.

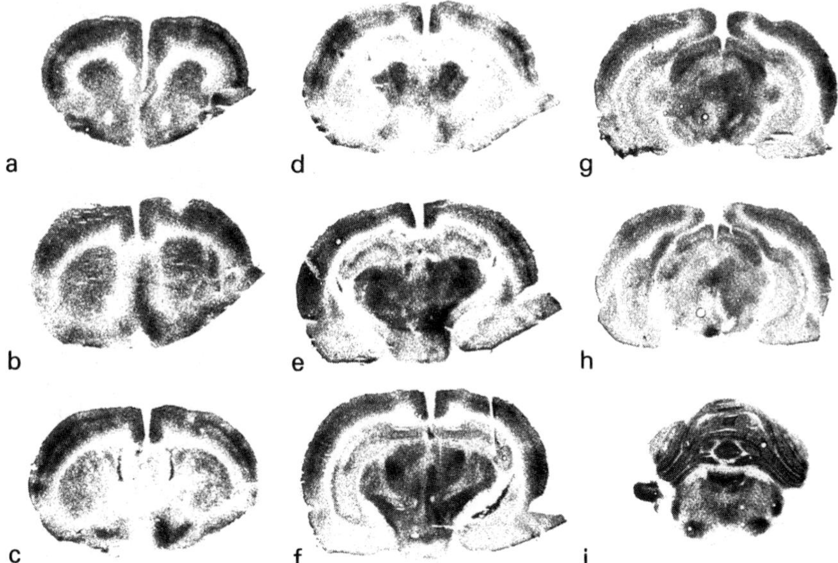

FIG. 2. Autoradiographs from sections of the brain of a rat self-stimulating during the period when a pulse of ^{14}C-2DG was taken up. The electrode tip was in the right zona inserta (see white fleck in section e). For description of the pattern of activation, see text.

the stimulus applied during the 30-min period following the injection of ^{14}C-2DG.

B. Technique

1. PREPARING THE INJECTION

^{14}C-2 deoxyglucose is obtainable from New England Nuclear. It is shipped in small vials and is dissolved in ethanol. It is expensive (approximately \$2/μCi). The dose per animal depends on one's budget and patience, there being, of course, a trade-off between the two. With 400–500 g rats and using a highly sensitive but therefore grainy low-resolution x-ray film, a 50 μCi dose produces easily readable images in 6–7 days; a 30 μCi dose produces similar images in 10–11 days. An x-fold lowering of the dose requires an x-fold increase in exposure time. The experimenter on a tight budget can use the technique, provided he resigns himself to lengthy exposure times.

On the day of injection, the chosen dose is put in a vial, and the ethanol evaporated away in a vacuum chamber, leaving the 2-DG as an

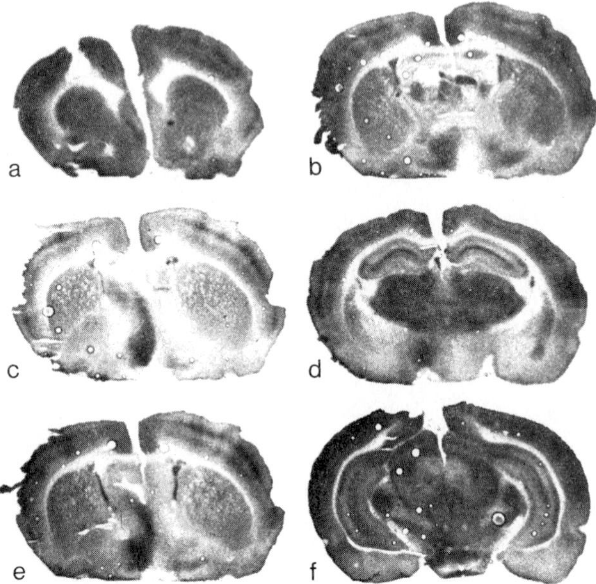

FIG. 3. Autoradiographs from a rat self-stimulating via an electrode on the left in the medial part of the lateral preoptic area. For description of the pattern of activation, see text.

invisible film. Shortly before injection, 1 cc or less of physiological saline is introduced to the vial and swished around to dissolve the 2-DG film. The animal is placed in the self-stimulation setup and set to self-stimulating at the current intensity employed during the behavioral experiments. The saline *cum* ^{14}C-2DG is taken up in a syringe. The animal is removed from the setup, injected intraperitoneally, and replaced immediately. Since the greatest uptake of 2-DG occurs in the first 10 min after injection, it is important that the stimulation be regular throughout this initial period.

2. Perfusion and Brain Extraction

At the end of 45 min, the animal is anesthetized with whatever anesthetic one normally uses. The perfusion procedure omits the initial saline perfusion and uses a weaker than usual solution of formalin (3.3% rather than 10%) in a phosphate-buffered solution with a pH of 7.4. This perfusion fluid is prepared as follows.

The phosphate buffer is made by combining 10.6 g monobasic sodium phosphate, 56 g dibasic potassium phosphate, and 1000 ml distilled water. This yields a 0.4 *M* buffer solution that will keep for weeks. In our

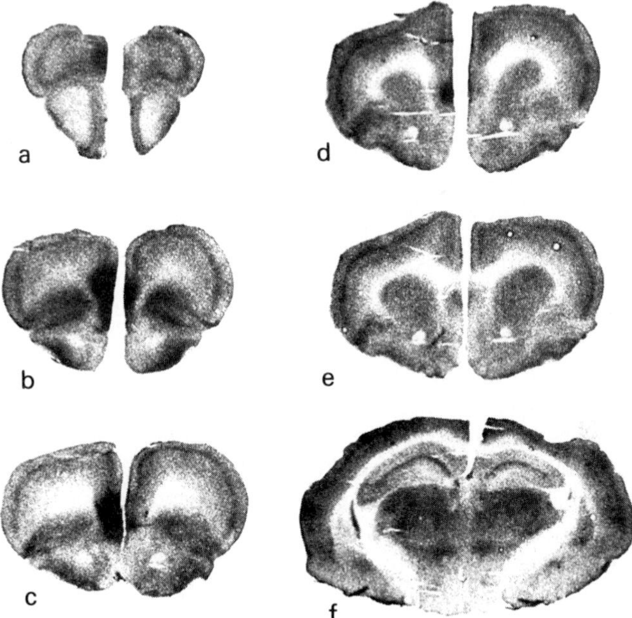

FIG. 4. Autoradiographs from a rat self-stimulating via an electrode on the left in the ventral sulcal cortex. For description of the pattern of activation, see text.

experience, these proportions reliably yield a pH of 7.4, but one should check the pH and adjust it if necessary, using hydrochloric acid or sodium hydroxide. On the day of perfusion, dilute the buffer by adding three parts distilled water to one part buffer, then combine 967 cc of the dilute buffer with 33 cc of Formaldehyde to make 3.3% formalin.

The rat is perfused intracardially with about 250 ml of this solution. Extended perfusion should be avoided, or else the 20μ sections will tend to trap air bubbles when laid on the glass slips. After the brief perfusion, the brain is carefully removed (speed is *not* essential) and lowered into liquid Freon. To promote rapid and even freezing, the brain should be held beneath the surface of the Freon with a fine nylon mesh for the first three minutes.

3. SECTIONING, MOUNTING, AND EXPOSURE

The brain is sectioned at 20 μ on a cryostat chilled to −18°C. The sections are picked up on chilled coverslips and dried on a hot-table at 65°C. When a complete series of dried sections have been obtained, the coverslips are cemented to a sheet of pasteboard with drops of Duco

Household Cement. Mounted in this manner, the dried sections are then pressed against a sheet of x-ray film in an x-ray cassette and left in a dark cupboard for the chosen exposure period. It is important that each section be in tight contact with the film. For quick results, we use Kodak blue-sensitive SB-5 film. The resulting autoradiographs are quite grainy. Noticeably better images are obtained with Dupont Lo-Dose film.

At the end of the exposure time, the sections are removed from the cassette under safe light, and the cassette is taken to an industrial x-ray processing lab for processing. The older 8-min processors yield better results than the newer 90-sec processors. The films may also be developed by hand if a darkroom is available.

4. Staining

To stain the sections from which the autoradiographs were made, cut up the pasteboard into strips the length and width of a microscope slide and place these in dipping trays. Soak the sections (cardboard and all) in absolute alcohol for 2 min, then in xylene for 3 min. Then soak them in absolute alcohol again for 2 min, then in 95% alcohol (2 min), 75% alcohol (2 min), and distilled water (2–5 min). The carboard comes off during the distilled water soak, leaving the sections, which still adhere to the coverslips, ready for staining. To stain sections, we soak them in thionin for 2 min. The stain is made from 1% aqueous thionin (12.5 cc), 0.2 *M* acetic acid (56.6 cc), 0.2 *M* sodium acetate (42.5 cc), and distilled water (138.5 cc); total volume, 250 cc. After the soak in the stain, the slips are dipped three times in 70% alcohol, then three more times in 95% alcohol. Then they are soaked for 2 min in absolute alcohol, followed by 2 min in xylene. Lastly, the coverslips *cum* stained sections are mounted on microscope slides with Paramount.

5. Interpretation of the Autoradiographs

The neural systems excited by the electrical stimulation appear relatively darker on the autoradiographs. The relative darkening is most easily seen in comparing structures on the stimulated side of the brain to the corresponding structures on the unstimulated side.

The pattern of unilaterally activated regions is similar in all the rats with electrodes in or near the medial forebrain bundle (MFB). Figure 2 shows a selection of autoradiographs from a representative rat with an electrode on the right in the zona inserta just dorsal to the MFB at the rostral end of the posterior hypothalamus (Fig. 2e). Figure 3 shows sections from a rat with an electrode on the left at the dorsomedial border of the MFB at the level of the anterior commissure (Fig. 3c). Examination of the complete series of autoradiographs from these two rats reveals essentially no difference in the pattern of unilaterally elevated activity rostral to the posterior hypothalamus. In both cases, unilateral darkening first appears as a thin (about 300 μ), but very distinct layer of activated cells along the lateral border of the septum, at and just rostral to the genu of the corpus collosum (Figs. 2a and 3a). As one moves caudally, one observes very pronounced unilaterally darkening of the band that the tractus striohypothalamicus sweeps through, between the MFB and the lateral septum (Figs. 2b and 3b). At the level of the anterior commissure, the unilateral darkening becomes concentrated in the MFB (Figs. 2c and 3c), where it remains as one continues caudally through the anterior hypothalamus (Figs. 2d and 3d).

However, as one reaches the posterior hypothalamus, where the electrode in Fig. 2 was located, the patterns are no longer the same. In Fig. 3—from the rat with the electrode in the rostral MFB—the darkening is rather sharply confined to the MFB (Fig. 3e and 3f). In Fig. 2, by contrast, the darkening is largely dorsal to the MFB; it extends throughout the zona inserta, the fields of Forel (H_1 and H_2), and the parafascicular nucleus of the medial thalamus (Figs. 2e and 2f). The sections from the rat with the rostral electrode do not show unilateral darkening of the zona inserta or the fields of Forel at any level. There is, however, faint but unmistakable unilateral darkening of the parafascicular nucleus in three successive sections at the extreme posterior hypothalamus (not shown).

The series of sections from the rat with the rostral electrode ends at the rostral tegmentum. However, the series from the rat with the caudal electrode extends well back into the hindbrain. At the level of the rostral tegmentum one sees pronounced unilateral darkening of the ventral tegmental area of Tsai. This darkening engulfs the lemniscus and arches dorsomedially through the reticular system to include the ventral half of the periventricular gray matter (Figs. 2g and 2h). As one moves through the caudal tegmentum and rostral hindbrain, there are little or no perceptible unilateral effects.

Figure 4 presents sections from a rat with an electrode on the left in the sulcal prefrontal cortex (just caudal to section b in Fig. 4). The pattern of unilateral darkening in these sections is radically different from the pattern produced by MFB electrodes. Indeed, there is no discernible overlap. These sections show pronounced darkening of the mid-dorsal sulcal cortex along most of the left side (Figs. 4a–d). The sections in the vicinity of the electrode also show that the current spread to the cortical surface of the right pole (Fig. 4b). Figure 4e shows the caudal-most section in which there was any discernible unilateral effect—in the medial structures of the forebrain a faint darkening on the dorsum of the *medial* septal nucleus. There is no discernible effect in the lateral septum, the striohypothalamic tract, the MFB, or the ventral tegmentum—the areas activated by MFB stimulation. Figure 4f is representative of all sections caudal to the genu of the corpus callosum in that the only discernible unilateral effect is in the claustrum, an area not activated by MFB stimulation.

The determination of which systems were bilaterally activated by the unilateral stimulation is more complex. One must compare similar sections from the brains of stimulated and unstimulated animals. In comparing sections from the brains of different animals, one must keep in mind that the absolute degree of darkening, i.e., the optical density of the autoradiographs over the corresponding areas, is meaningless by itself.

During uptake, the concentration of ^{14}C-2DG "seen" by the brain varies considerably from animal to animal, presumably because the amount taken up by other organs, such as the liver, varies. Consequently, the amount of the tracer taken into neurons with equal metabolic rates varies from brain to brain.

Another factor that has a strong impact on absolute optical density is variation in section thickness. Most cryostats do not cut exactly 20 μ-thick sections every time. The actual thickness of a section may deviate from the nominal thickness by as much as 25%. These deviations in section thickness are readily apparent when one scans a sheet of x-ray film with autoradiographs from many sections. There are noticeable variations in average optical density from image to image, no doubt due to variations in section thickness.

The section-to-section variations in mean optical density make direct comparisons of local optical densities in the images from corresponding sections meaningless. Instead, one must look for differences in relative optical density. Relative optical density is the optical density of a particular point or region relative to the optical densities of other regions in the same section.

Large bilateral increases in the relative optical density of small regions are easily seen, but smaller effects are more difficult to see, and the objectivity of one's judgment comes into question. An objective comparison of bilateral local effects in the images from different sections requires a computerized image processing system.

In a computerized image processing system, the images are scanned by either a scanning microdensitometer or a Vidicon tv camera. The optical density of each spot is digitized and stored in an image-refresh memory. An image-refresh memory is a 256 × 256 × or 512 × 512 memory matrix. Each "cell" in this matrix stores a 5 to 8-bit record of the optical density of a corresponding spot on the image being scanned. This spot-by-spot record of densities is then used to modulate the intensity of the electron beam in a tv tube, as that beam sweeps back and forth across the face of the tube. In this way, the image being scanned is displayed on a tv screen. The fact that the image has been reduced to a digital form in the image-refresh memory makes it easy for a computer to process that information in any of a variety of useful ways.

For example, it is a trivial matter for the computer to scan the cells in the image-refresh memory and compile an optical density histogram. An optical density histogram shows for each discriminable value of optical density the number of cells (i.e., spots on the image) that have that particular value. The relative optical density of a given point or small area is represented by its position on such a histogram.

For example, if the amygdala were bilaterally excited by lateral stimulation, one obtains an objective representation of this fact by scanning comparable sections from stimulated and unstimulated brains and by displaying the optical densities over the amygdalar nuclei of the control and experimental sections against the respective optical density histograms. The optical density of the amygdala nuclei in the experimental sections will lie farther to the right (toward relatively higher optical density) on the histogram.

Displaying the optical densities of localized areas against the optical density histogram for the section normalizes local optical density with respect to the optical densities of all other areas of the section. This procedure removes any factor that has a proportionate effect on all areas, such as, for example, the arterial concentration of the tracer during uptake or section thickness. Such normalization is essential for meaningful comparisons between sections.

Computerized image processing systems are also invaluable in relating the images from the stained sections to the autoradiographic image. The image from the stained section is read into one memory, the image from the autoradiograph into another. Then the two images are alternately flickered on the tv screen, permitting the investigator to align them rapidly. When the images are aligned, one displays the stained image and outlines the structure one is interested in with a cursor—a white spot on the display that may be moved along any trajectory by means of a joystick. The computer stores the outline in memory, superimposes that outline on the autoradiographic image, and computes the mean relative optical density of the area on the autoradiograph within the outline.

Finally, the computer can enhance the contrasts in the original autoradiographic images to make images that are more suitable for publication. Accurate reproduction of continuous tone images in published material is difficult and expensive. Contrast enhancement within density zones that contain the information the investigator wants to convey makes for more effective communication.

XI. Conclusions

Using the techniques just described, one may create preparations that reliably display complex motivated behavior patterns and instrumental learning under the control of a precisely determined, easily manipulatable electrical stimulus, acting at a known and circumscribed site in the central nervous system. Such preparations have played and will play an important role in elucidating the neurophysiological basis for these complex behavioral phenomena.

Three recent technical/methodological developments may promote the productive use of these preparations. The first is the development of behavioral methods for determining quantitative characteristics of the neural systems whose excitation produces the behavioral phenomena (Gallistel, *et al.*, 1981). The second is the development of behavioral methods that convincingly discriminate between nonspecific pharmacological effects on the stimulation-induced behavior and the specific effects of drugs on, for example, the rewarding effect of the stimulation (Edmonds & Gallistel, 1977; Fouriezos & Wise, 1976; Franklin, 1978; Gallistel, Boytim, Gomita, & Klebanoff, submitted). The third is the application of 2-DG autoradiography to the problem of determining which neural systems are excited by the stimulation. I believe that in the not-so-distant future these three developments together promise that the motivating and reinforcing effects of brain stimulation may be convincingly linked to activity in identified neural systems in the central nervous system.

Acknowledgments

The autoradiographic research and the preparation of this chapter were supported by NIH Grant NS 14935 to C. R. Gallistel, P. Hand, and M. Reivich.

References

Adams, D. B. Brain mechanisms for offense, defense, and submission. *The Behavioral and Brain Sciences*, 1979, **2**, 201–242.

Bandler, R., & Flynn, J. P. Visual patterned reflex present during hypothalamically elicited attack. *Journal of Comparative and Physiological Psychology*, 1972, **81**, 541–554.

Barry, F. E., Walters, M. S., & Gallistel, C. R. On the optimal pulse duration in electrical stimulation of the brain. *Physiology and Behavior*, 1974, **12**, 749–754.

Beagley, W. K. Grooming in the rat as an aftereffect of lateral hypothalamic stimulation. *Journal of Comparative and Physiological Psychology,* 1976, **90,** 790–798.

Beagley, W. K., & Holley, T. L. Hypothalamic stimulation facilitates contralateral visual control of a learned response. *Science,* 1977, **196,** 321–322.

Berntson, G. G., & Beattie, M. S. Functional differentiation within hypothalamic behavioral systems in the cat. *Physiological Psychology,* 1975, **3,** 183–188.

Cantor, M. B., Beninger, R. J., Bellisle, F., & Milner, P. M. Brain stimulation reinforcement: implications of an electrode artifact, *Science,* 1979, **204,** 1235–1236.

Corbett, D., & Wise, R. A. Intracranial self-stimulation in relation to the ascending noradrenergic fiber systems of the pontine tegmentum and caudal midbrain. A moveable electrode mapping study. *Brain Research,* 1979, **177,** 423–436.

Corbett, D., & Wise, R. A. Intracranial self-stimulation in relation to the ascending dopaminergic systems of the midbrain: A moveable electrode mapping study. *Brain Research,* 1980, **185,** 1–15.

DeGroot, J. The rat forebrain in stereotaxic coordinates. *Verhandelingen der Koninklüke Nederlandse Akademie van Wetenschappen,* Afdeling Natuurkunde, *Reeks 2,* 1959, **52,** No. 4.

Deutsch, J. A. An electrophysiological stimulator with digital logic. *Journal of the Experimental Analysis of Behavior,* 1966, **9,** 399–400.

Edmonds, D. E., & Gallistel, C. R. Reward versus performance in self-stimulation: Electrode specific effects of AMPT on reward in the rat. *Journal of Comparative and Physiological Psychology,* 1977, **91,** 962–974.

Flynn, J. P. Patterning mechanisms, patterned reflexes, and attack behavior in cats. *In* W. J. Arnold & D. Levine (eds.), (Vol. 20) *Nebraska Symposium on Motivation,* 1972, **20,** Lincoln: University of Nebraska Press, 1972. Pp. 125–153.

Flynn, J. P., Edwards, S. B., & Bandler, R. J. Changes in sensory and motor systems during centrally elicited attack. *Behavioral Science,* 1971, **16,** 1–19.

Fouriezos, G., & Wise, R. A. Pimozide-induced extinction of intracranial self-stimulation. Response patterns rule out motor or performance deficits. *Brain Research,* 1976, **103,** 377–380.

Franklin, K. B. J. Catecholamines and self-stimulation: Reward and performance effects dissociated. *Pharmacology, Biochemistry and Behavior,* 1978, **9,** 813–820.

Gallistel, C. R. *The Organization of Action.* Hillsdale, New Jersey, Lawrence Erlbaum Associates, 1980.

Gallistel, C. R. Motivation as central organizing process: The psychophysical approach to its functional and neurophysiological analysis. In J. Cole & T. Sonderegger (Eds.), *Nebraska Symposium on Motivation,* (Vol. 22). Lincoln: University of Nebraska Press, 1975. Pp. 183–250.

Gallistel, C. R. Self-stimulation in the rat: Quantitative characteristics of the reward pathway. *Journal of Comparative and Physiological Psychology,* 1978, **92,** 977–998.

Gallistel, C. R. Spatial and temporal summation in the neural circuit subserving brain-stimulation reward. In A. Wauguier & E. T. Olds (Eds.), *Brain-stimulation reward.* New York: Am. Elsevier, 1976. Pp. 97–99.

Gallistel, C. R., Boytym, M., Gomita, Y., & Klebanoff, L. Does pimozide block the reinforcing effect of MFB stimulation? The problem of functional specificity in behavioral pharmacology, submitted for publication.

Gallistel, C. R., Reivich, M. S., & Karreman, G. A. [^{14}C]2-deoxyglucose uptake marks systems activated by rewarding brain stimulation. *Brain Research Bulletin,* 1977, **2,** 149–152.

Gallistel, C. R., Shizgal, P., & Yeomans, J. S. A portrait of the substrate for self-stimulation. *Psychological Review,* 1981, in press.

Gallistel, C. R., Stellar, J. R., & Bubis, E. Parametric analysis of brain stimulation reward in the rat. I. The transient process and the memory-containing process. *Journal of Comparative and Physiological Psychology*, 1974, **87**, 848–860.

Halboth, P. H., & Coons, E. E. Behavioral measurements of the neural post-stimulation recovery cycle in the lateral hypothalamic eating system of the rat. *Journal of Comparative and Physiological Psychology*, 1973, **83**, 429–433.

Hess, W. R. *Das Zwischenhirn* (2nd ed.). Basel: Schwabe, 1954.

Hill, A. V. Excitation and accommodation in nerve. *Proceedings of the Royal Society of London, Series B*, 1936, **119**, 305–355.

Hodgkin, A. L., & Huxley, A. F. The dual effect of membrane potential on sodium conductance in the giant axon of *Loliga*. *Journal of Physiology* (London), 1952, **117**, 500–544.

von Holst, E., & von St. Paul, U. On the functional organisation of drives. *Animal Behaviour*, 1963, **11**, 1–20.

Hulse, S. H., Fowler, H., & Honig, W. K. (Eds.). *Cognitive processes in animal behavior*. Hillsdale, N.J.: Larry Erlbaum Associates, 1978.

Jacobowitz, D. M., & Palkovits, M. Topographic atlas of catecholamine containing neurons in the rat brain. *Journal of Comparative Neurology*, 1974, **157**, 13–42.

König, J. F. R., & Klippel, R. A. *The rat brain: A stereotaxic atlas*. Baltimore, Md.: Williams & Wilkins, 1967. Facsimile edition now published by R. E. Krieger, Huntington, New York.

Liran, J. *Electrical self-stimulation of the brain in the rat: Quantitative characteristics of the substrates for priming and reward*. Ph.D. Dissertation, University of Pennsylvania, 1979.

MacDonnell, M. F., & Flynn, J. P. Control of sensory fields by stimulation of the hypothalamus. *Science*, 1966, **152**, 1406–1408.

Matthews, G. Neural substrate for brain stimulation reward in the rat: Cathodal and anodal strength-duration properties. *Journal of Comparative and Physiological Psychology*, 1977, **91**, 858–874.

Matthews, G. Strength-duration properties of single units driven by electrical stimulation of the lateral hypothalamus in rats. *Brain Research Bulletin*, 1978, **3**, 171–174.

Olds, J., & Milner, P. Positive reinforcement produced by electrical stimulation of septal area and other regions of the rat brain. *Journal of Comparative and Physiological Psychology*, 1954, **47**, 419–427.

Pellegrino, L. J., & Cushman, A. J. *A stereotaxic atlas of the rat brain*. New York: Appleton, 1967.

Ranck, J. B., Jr. Which elements are excited in electrical stimulation of mammalian central nervous system: A review. *Brain Research*, 1975, **98**, 417–440.

Rescorla, R. A. Some implications of a cognitive perspective on Pavlovian conditioning. In S. H. Hulse, H. Fowler, & W. K. Honig (Eds.). *Cognitive processes in animal behavior*. Hillsdale, N.J.: Lawrence Erlbaum Associates, 1978.

Rose, M. D. Pain-reducing properties of rewarding electrical brain stimulation in the rat. *Journal of Comparative and Physiological Psychology*, 1974, **87**, 607–617.

Routtenberg, A., Gardner, E. L., & Huang, Y. H. Self-stimulation pathways in the monkey, *Macaca mulatta*. *Experimental Neurology*, 1971, **33**, 213–224.

Shizgal, P., & Matthews, G. Electrical stimulation of the rat diencephalon: Differential effects of interrupted stimulation on on- and off-responding. *Brain Research*, 1977, **129**, 319–333.

Sokoloff, L., Reivich, M., Kennedy, C., DesRosiers, M. H., Patlak, C. S., Pettigrew, R. D., Sakurada, O., & Shinohara, M. The ^{14}C-deoxyglucose method for measurement of local cerebral glucose utilization: Theory, procedure, and normal values in the conscious and anesthetized albino rat. *Journal of Neurochemistry*, 1977, **28,** 897–916.

Szabo, F., & Milner, P. M. Electrode tip alignment and self-stimulation: Influence of anodal hyperpolarization. *Physiology and Behavior*, 1973, **11,** 581–584.

Szabo, F., Nad, E., & Szabo, C. Pole reversals and hypothalamic self-stimulations ascending spread of reward excitation. *Physiology and Behavior*, 1972, **9,** 147–150.

Valenstein, E. S., & Beer, B. Unipolar and bipolar electrodes in self-stimulation experiments. *American Journal of Physiology*, 1961, **201,** 1181–1186.

Wetzel, M. C., Howell, L. G., & Bearie, K. J. Experimental performance of steel and platinum electrodes with chronic monophasic stimulation of the brain. *Journal of Neurosurgery*, 1969, **31,** 658–669.

Wise, R. A. Moveable electrode for chronic brain stimulation in the rat. *Physiology and Behavior*, 1976, **16,** 105–106.

Wise, R. A. Spread of current from monopolar stimulation of the lateral hypothalamus. *American Journal of Physiology*, 1972, **223,** 545–548.

Yeomans, J. S. Quantitative measurement of neural post-stimulation excitability with behavioral methods. *Physiology and Behavior*, 1975, **15,** 593–602.

Chapter 7

Electrical Stimulation as a Tool in Memory Research

Robert F. Berman

Department of Psychology
Wayne State University
Detroit, Michigan

Raymond P. Kesner

Department of Psychology
University of Utah
Salt Lake City, Utah

I. Introduction

The intent of this chapter is to review and discuss the use of localized electrical brain stimulation (EBS) as a tool in the study of neural mech-

ISBN 0-12-547440-7

anisms of learning and memory. Historically, the use of electrical brain stimulation to explore functions of the brain was pioneered by Fritsch and Hitzig (1870), who demonstrated that muscular contractions could be produced by electrical stimulation of cerebral cortex of the dog. The development of chronic electrode implantation enabled investigators to observe the effects of EBS on unanesthetized and relatively unrestrained animals, and the Horsley–Clarke stereotaxic device allowed precise positioning of electrodes within an animal's brain. These developments led to the rapid adoption of EBS as a principal technique for exploring brain function, and the usefulness of the technique remains undiminished today.

As in the early studies by Fritsch and Hitzig (1870), electrical brain stimulation is typically used to elicit various behaviors. Specifically, EBS applied to discrete brain regions has been shown to elicit a number of species-specific behavior patterns, such as sleeping, fighting, feeding, drinking, vocalization, arrest reactions and fearlike responses (Delgado, 1964; Hess, 1957; Kaada, 1972; Penfield & Roberts, 1959; Sterman & Clemente, 1962). However, electrical brain stimulation has also been shown capable of serving as a conditioned stimulus for shock avoidance conditioning (Doty, 1961; Loucks, 1935–1936, 1938), as well as serving as a positive or negative reinforcer in a variety of learning tasks (J. Olds, 1962). More recently, localized EBS has been used to disrupt ongoing neural activity in specific neural regions during or shortly after learning in order to assess the involvement and role of these neural systems in learning and memory processes.

II. EBS as a Tool for the Study of Memory

The rationale for the use of EBS in studies of memory is that electrical stimulation can produce a temporary and reversible interference with ongoing neural activity at the focus of stimulation. That is, appropriately applied low-intensity EBS is seen to act as a reversible and functional lesion by scrambling the normal spatial and temporal patterning of neural impulses within the stimulated region (Doty, 1969; Goddard, 1964). It is further reasoned that an appropriately applied transient of EBS will modify memory to the extent that the stimulated brain region is involved in mnemonic processes. Of course, it is well-known that EBS can also elicit complex, organized behaviors. But the primary effect of stimulation must logically be one of disruption. (Doty (1969) stated this position well:

"while it is seldom stated and there is no direct evidence to prove it, current neurophysiological knowledge makes it essentially axiomatic that the neural organization responsible for (elicitation of stereotyped behavior) lies remote to the neurons stimulated. This principal or axiom follows from the fact that any coordinated movement involving spatiotemporal sequencing of action in motoneuron pools requires equally precise phasing of excitatory and inhibitory control, as does most sensory control. It is impossible to achieve this by electrical stimulation. The current cannot impose upon neurons the spatiotemporal coded and integrated output they normally achieve, it can only drive them in bizarre and nonsensical synchrony. Thus any subtle, highly integrated neural effects resulting from the stimulation must ensue only because the neural systems downstream receiving the nonsense signal are able to transform it into an effective neural code. Were the stimulation inserted into the midst of neurons required to organize a complex action, it could only interfere with, not produce, this action" (p. 292).

A. *Advantages of Electrical Brain Stimulation*

The use of EBS to disrupt ongoing neural activity has several advantages over ablation, electroconvulsive shock (ECS), and intracranial chemical injection techniques. First, EBS allows greater control over onset and duration of action than is possible with ablation or intracranial chemical injection. This is of particular importance, especially if one wishes to investigate temporal characteristics of mnemonic processes. Second, EBS allows greater control over the area and volume of neural tissue affected than is possible with ECS. In fact, relatively precise anatomical localization of effective stimulation sites for memory disruption has been possible with EBS (Livesey, 1975; McGaugh & Gold, 1976; Santos-Anderson & Routtenberg, 1976; Sideroff, Bueno, Hirsch, Weyand, & McGaugh, 1974; Zornetzer, Chronister, & Ross, 1973).

Third, the primary action of EBS appears to be easily reversible with minimal proactive effects. To illustrate, Stamm (1969) demonstrated that stimulation applied to prefrontal cortex (2 or 4 sec) was disruptive only during the first few seconds of a delay period using a delayed response task. Performance was unaffected by stimulation during the intertrial interval or during cue presentation. Similarly, Santos-Anderson and Routtenberg (1976) reported that frontal cortex stimulation interfered with retention of passive avoidance training only when given during the training experience.

Fourth, parameters of EBS, including intensity, duration, and waveform, are readily manipulated by the experimenter.

Fifth, EBS represents a technique whose mechanism of action can be analyzed. This is of importance because it has been assumed that by understanding the mechanism of action of an amnesia-inducing agent (in this case EBS), one can strengthen the understanding of processess associated with memory.

Finally, EBS can be easily applied to freely moving animals under a wide range of training conditions.

Of course, there are also limitations to the use of EBS for memory research. For example, the effects of EBS on behavior may be found to result from spread of stimulation to interconnected neural structures and systems. Also, EBS may produce reinforcing and motivational effects that in turn may mask, alter, or mediate its effects upon memory.

However, ablation, chemical injection, and electroconvulsive shock share the same limitations. With EBS, one can more easily identify and control such "secondary" effects, even to the point of exploiting them. For example, the effects of reinforcing levels of EBS on memory have been examined by several investigators (Destrade & Jaffard, 1978; Huston, Mueller, & Mondadori, 1977; M. E. Olds & Olds, 1961). Indeed, Gallistel, Stellar, and Bubis (1974) have reported fine control over the reinforcing and incentive properties of intracranial electrical stimulation.

III. Electrical Stimulation Parameters

The ideal stimulation parameters for producing memory disruption have never been systematically studied. However, the use of electrical stimulation of the brain to produce temporary localized interference with ongoing neuronal activity logically requires the use of optimal stimulation parameters (i.e., electrode configuration, current intensity, pulse duration, frequency, train duration, and waveform) for exciting neural elements while still using current intensities and electrode configurations that limit spread of current flow, avoid tissue damage, and do not produce competing (e.g., motoric) responses. Precise information concerning such optimal stimulation parameters is presently lacking. However, there is general agreement among investigators concerning the range of useful parameters for memory research, and these are discussed below.

A. Electrode Configuration

A variety of electrode configurations have been used for stimulating the central nervous system in chronically implanted, unanesthetized animals. These configurations include monopolar, bipolar, multipolar, and concentric electrodes (Ervin & Kenney, 1971). However, monopolar and bipolar electrode configurations are most commonly used for studies of brain mechanisms of learning and memory.

Monopolar electrodes consist of a stimulating electrode implanted within the neural region targeted for stimulation and connected to a distant reference lead (usually a skull-screw or an array of skull-screws connected by solder wire). Stimulating current applied to the implanted monopolar electrode is assumed to flow radially outward from the electrode tip with the current density falling off as the square of the distance away from the electrode (Ranck, 1975). Therefore, monopolar stimulation is really a form of bipolar stimulation because intervening regions of the brain tissue between the stimulating and the reference electrode are also stimulated. As a result, monopolar electrodes are not generally used when discrete, localized stimulation is required. Instead, the bipolar electrode configuration described in the following is preferred.

The bipolar electrode is composed of two well-insulated monopolar electrodes cemented or twisted together with bare electrode tips separated by 0.5–1.0 mm. In contrast to the monopolar electrode configuration, the pattern of current flow from bipolar electrodes is concentrated in the region between the two electrode tips (Stark, Fazio, & Boyd, 1962), and neural elements between the two electrode tips are preferentially stimulated (Wetzel, 1972). As a result, the most exact localization of effective action can be obtained with bipolar electrodes where current flow is largely restricted to the tissue between the electrodes (Iggo, 1978). Thus, the effective current spread is less with bipolar than with monopolar electrodes. In addition, lower current thresholds (microamperes) for rewarding brain stimulation are generally (Stark *et al.*, 1962; Valenstein & Beer, 1961), but not always (Gerken & Judy, 1977) reported for bipolar electrodes.

The combination of reduced current spread and lower thresholds for elicited behavior favor the use of bipolar electrode configurations for precise stimulation of the CNS.

1. Waveform

Biphasic waveforms (rectangular or sinusoidal) are typically used in contemporary studies using EBS to investigate brain function. This preference for biphasic over monophasic waveforms undoubtedly has its origin in early studies reporting electrode polarization and tissue injury following long duration pulses of monophasic rectangular waves (Lilly, Austin, & Chambers, 1952). Among the undesirable consequences of electrode polarization are stimulating current hysteresis (Mickle, 1961; Weinmann & Mahler, 1963), deposition of metallic electrode ions at the cathode (Wetzel, Howell, & Bearie, 1969), and the evolution of hydrogen and oxygen at the anode (Greatbatch, Piersma, Shannon, & Calhoon, 1969). Theoretically, the zero net flow of current across an electrode with biphasic stimulation prevents electrode polarization and minimizes the potential tissue destruction (Mickle, 1961). However, EBS thresholds for eliciting behavior with biphasic or monophasic cathodal stimulation appear to be equal (Gerken & Judy, 1977; Mihailovic & Delgado, 1956), and it has been argued that in spite of the possible deleterious effects with monophasic waveforms, their direct effects on neuronal activity are easier to examine (Gerken & Judy, 1977; Ranck, 1975). Both rectangular and sinusoidal biphasic waveforms have been used, and there is little systematic evidence favoring one over the other. However, it has been noted that 50–60 Hz sinusoidal stimulating current is at a frequency at which accomodation would be expected to occur (Ranck, 1975). In any case, neither waveform should be considered more nearly physiological than the other.

2. Frequency

The choice of stimulation frequency has been based largely on the consensus of various laboratories. The most commonly used stimulation frequencies in studies of memory disruption fall within the range of 50–300 Hz. Stimulation frequencies in the vicinity of 100 Hz are by far the most common. This frequency range is similar to the 60–500 Hz range described by Mihailovic and Delgado (1956) as yielding the lowest intensity threshold for stimulation of motor cortex in the monkey. Few studies since have systematically explored the effect of varying frequency within this range. However, there is little doubt that the frequency of stimulation is an important factor. For example, it has been reported that the reticular formation is most effectively excited by frequencies of 100–200 Hz while the most effective frequencies for activating the hippocampus lie between 4–6 Hz (Ervin & Kenney, 1971). Furthermore, the phenomenon known as kindling (Goddard, McIntyre, & Leech, 1969) is frequency-dependent, with 62.5 Hz being the most effective and 3 Hz being ineffective for kindling. In research on memory, Wilburn and Kesner (1972) have reported amnesia in some cats following bilateral stimulation of the caudate nucleus at 3 Hz, while Gold and King (1972) failed to find stimulation effects with caudate stimulation at 60 Hz.

There are only a very few studies that have either varied frequency or train duration. Landfield (1977) demonstrated that low-frequency (7.7 Hz) septal stimulation used to drive cortically recorded hippocampal theta activity facilitates both active and passive avoidance, while theta-blocking higher-frequency stimulation (77 Hz) was ineffective. Gold, Edwards, and McGaugh (1975) reported that 30 sec of post-trial stimulation of the amygdala was more effective than 10 sec in disrupting retention of passive avoidance training in rats.

3. Intensity and Pulse Duration

Stimulation intensity should always be measured and reported in amperes (usually microamperes). The statement of voltage alone is meaningless without some indication of current flow. Therefore, some means of measuring and monitoring both voltage and current is necessary. Most stimulators currently available are constant voltage devices, and the use of constant current-stimulus isolation units is therefore recommended.

With electrical stimulation, the goal is to hold both current and pulse duration to a minimum while still producing the desired behavioral effect (e.g., amnesia, movement, and so on). The two considerations lead to conflict however, because shorter pulse durations require higher current intensities, and vice versa. In turn, higher current levels and longer pulse duration increase the total charge (current × duration) transferred to tissue and can lead to deposition of metallic ions at the anode and gas formation at the cathode. Indeed, the total charge transfer (measured in coulombs) should be seen as more important than either duration or current alone. This problem has been systematically studied by Barry, Walter, and Gallistel (1974). These investigators report that pulse durations 0.1 msec or shorter are optimal for brain stimulation work across a wide range of stimulation frequencies, electrode configurations, and materials, and typically yielded the lowest current thresholds.

These results essentially substantiate earlier reports that pulse durations in the range of 0.1–0.2 msec were the most effective in exciting neural tissue (Mihailovic & Delgado, 1956).

Stimulation intensities are usually in the range of 10 μA to a few hundred μA. These levels are usually chosen to be below the level required to elicit observable changes in behavior. This subthreshold level can be determined by the method of ascending and descending limits (Lilly *et al.*, 1952; Mihailovic & Delgado, 1956). With this technique, stimulation is begun at low intensity and increased until a change in behavior is observed. We typically test animals in a transparent Plexiglas chamber containing dry food pellets, pieces of wood, and a watering tube to allow for observation of "stimulus-bound" behaviors (Berman & Kesner, 1976; Valenstein, Cox, & Kakolewski, 1970). The stimulation level is initially 10 μA and is increased stepwise by 10 μA until a change in behavior is observed. Changes in behavior include orienting to either onset or offset of stimulation, freezing, forced motor movements, defense reactions, changes in activity levels, and stimulus-bound behaviors (i.e., gnawing, eating, grooming, exploratory activity, object carrying, and so forth). We have defined the intensity at which EBS elicits behavioral change as the "behavioral threshold," and the stimulation intensity ultimately used should be below this threshold. This is particularly important in those studies employing EBS during learning or between closely spaced learning trials.

It is also important to determine the presence of reinforcing properties of EBS. Such effects, if present, could easily modify behavior. A simple method for testing for such reinforcing properties of EBS is to study self-stimulation (J. Olds & Milner, 1954). We typically test for reinforcing properties of EBS in rats using a modification of Valenstein and Meyers' (1964) two-platform technique. In this technique, rats are placed into the center of a two compartment chamber, and trains of EBS are delivered as soon as the animal fully enters one of the compartments. No EBS is given when the animal is in the opposite chamber. Total amount of EBS received over successive trials is measured and used as an index of reinforcement effects.

A final consideration is that EBS at high-current intensities may produce seizure after-discharges. They can be most easily detected by recording EEG activity from the stimulating electrodes immediately following stimulation. Seizure after-discharges induced by EBS tend to propagate widely to many neural systems via anatomical pathways or via volume conduction and can produce interference for extended periods of time. It is desirable to eliminate after-discharges by reducing either the intensity or duration of EBS (see Boast & McIntyre, 1977).

4. Unilateral Versus Bilateral Stimulation

Most investigators use bilateral concurrent stimulation of corresponding brain regions, in preference to unilateral stimulation. This is based on the assumption that brain symmetry implies redundant (i.e., bilateral) processing of mnemonic input. Logically, bilateral EBS would be preferred and may even be required to produce maximal interference with memory. There are, however, a few reports of amnesia for shock avoidance training following unilateral, post-trial EBS applied to the amygdaloid region (Bresnahan & Routtenberg, 1972; Gold *et al.*, 1975; McDonough & Kesner, 1971).

B. *Methodological Considerations*

There are a number of methodological issues associated with EBS that must be addressed. First, EBS may elicit involuntary movement in an animal that could compete with the response being measured. Even a slight degree of turning in rats produced by unilateral stimulation of the caudate nucleus can interfere with spatial discrimination tasks (Zimmerberg & Glick, 1975). Movement artifact is frequently observed since movement is seen with stimulation at virtually every brain loci, cortical or subcortical, in the brain of freely moving animals (Doty, 1969) given a high-enough intensity. Fortunately, most undesirable motor effects can be easily identified prior to critical training trials and eliminated by reducing stimulation intensity and duration.

Second, at moderate to high intensities EBS can produce after-discharges. Such after-discharges can occur following amygdaloid stimulation with current intensities as low as 30 μA, and can then propagate widely through the brain via anatomical pathways or via volume conduction. After-discharge activity can be easily detected by recording the EEG from the stimulating electrodes themselves immediately after stimulation or by recording from electrodes in nearby tissue.

It is desirable to eliminate after-discharge activity by reducing current intensity or duration of stimulation.

Third, repeated EBS of many neural regions, particularly the amygdala and other anterior limbic regions, at current intensities initially below seizure threshold often will result in a lowering of threshold and the appearance of after-discharges (Goddard *et al.*, 1969). Goddard *et al.* (1969) have labeled this progressive increase in seizure susceptibility following repeated stimulation trials as "kindling".

Fourth, it is methodologically advisable to include an implanted nonstimulated control group to determine the effect of implantation *per se* on mnemonic processes (Herz, Marshall, & Peeke, 1974). This is important because Boast, Reid, Johnson, and Zornetzer (1976) have reported that electrode implantation alone can produce hemmorrhagic vascular damage that could conceivably confound interpretation of stimulation results. Also, Denti, McGaugh, Landfield, and Shinkman (1970) reported that midbrain reticular formation (MRF) stimulation facilitated active avoidance conditioning when compared to MRF-implanted but nonstimulated control animals, but had no apparent effect when compared to the performance of nonimplanted animals. Similar findings have been reported for post-trial hippocampal (Landfield, Tusa, & McGaugh, 1973) and amygdaloid stimulation (Gold, Macri, & McGaugh, 1973). Care should obviously be taken in interpreting such results.

A fifth consideration is the observation that repeated training-EBS trials become increasingly less effective in disrupting memory (Kesner, McDonough, & Doty, 1970; McDonough & Kesner, 1971; Wilburn & Kesner, 1972). The shorter the training-EBS delay, however, the greater the number of training-EBS trials that will lead to amnesia. One interpretation of these results is that the interference with information processing produced by EBS is partial, allowing some form of "incomplete" or weak memory to be formed. With multiple training-EBS trials the strength of this hypothetical memory trace eventually increases leading to the behavioral expression of memory.

Sixth, it is important to bear in mind that different neural systems may be associated with the processing of mnemonic information specific to a particular learning task. For example, Zornetzer and Chronister (1973) have shown that post-trial EBS of the ventral hippocampus produces amnesia for an appetitive task but not for an aversive one. Similar stimulation of the caudate nucleus produced amnesia for both tasks. Berman and Kesner (1976), Kesner and Conner (1974), and Kesner, Berman, Burton, and Hankins (1975a) have shown that post-trial EBS of the amygdala disrupts long-term retention of passive avoidance and taste-aversion training, but does not disrupt long-term retention of appetitive learning or recovery from neophobia.

IV. Research Strategies with EBS

Electrical brain stimulation can be administered with rather precise temporal control either during or after learning, or just before or during tests for retention of training. In practice, all or a combination of these temporal EBS paradigms are used, and when used in combination they provide a powerful tool for examining various components of memory.

These components of memory have been assessed using EBS within the context of at least six paradigms. These paradigms are called "registration," "short term memory," "consolidation," "short- and long-term memory," "attribute," and "age of memory" (Kesner, in press). The registration paradigm emphasizes the role of specific neuronal substrates with processes associated with registration (e.g., perception, attention) of information.

The short-term memory paradigm places an emphasis upon neuronal substrates involved in processes that modulate or control a short-term memory (STM) system within a short time frame (seconds). The consolidation paradigm, which thus far has received the most attention, emphasizes the role of specific neuronal substrates with processes that control or modulate a long-term memory (LTM) system within a long time frame (seconds to days). The short- and long-term memory paradigm concerns the analysis of neuronal substrates that either exclusively affect STM or LTM systems or play a role in processes that modulate the interactions between the two. The memory attribute paradigm emphasizes the role of specific neural regions in determining the nature of the stored memory trace. Finally, the age of memory paradigm deals with the determination of specific neuronal substrates that affect processes that maintain memory traces over long periods of time (hours, weeks, years). Thus, each paradigm emphasizes a somewhat different aspect of the memory system. Ideally one should apply EBS within as many paradigms as are available, in order to delineate the specific neural substrates associated with memory storage and/or retrieval. Ultimately, selection of a specific paradigm depends upon assumptions one wishes to make concerning the function of the underlying neural substrate, the processes that mediate storage and/or retrieval of mnemonic information, and the nature or structure of the stored memory.

A. *Registration Paradigm*

In the registration paradigm treatments (in this case, EBS) are applied concurrently with a learning trial followed by a long-term retention test (usually 24 hr later). One can also employ a short-term retention test (usually seconds later). This latter procedure will be discussed in the short-term memory paradigm (see next section). It is assumed that registration processes incorporating sensory, perceptual, and selective attention components are operating during exposure to a specific learning experience. Thus, EBS applied during this time might disrupt or facilitate the operation of any of these components resulting in a subsequent alteration of long-term memory.

As an illustration, it has been shown that low-intensity stimulation of the medial frontal cortex, medial or basolateral amygdala, caudate–putamen or substantia nigra pars compacta applied during the acquisition of a step-down passive avoidance task disrupts subsequent long-term retention (Bresnahan & Routtenberg, 1972; LePiane & Phillips, 1978; Routtenberg & Holzman, 1973; Santos-Anderson & Routtenberg, 1976). Of interest is the additional observation that similar levels of stimulation of caudate-putamen and substantia nigra pars compacta during taste-aversion learning failed to produce disruption, while basolateral amygdala stimulation was effective in both learning situations (LePiane & Phillips, 1978).

Even though these results suggest that electrical stimulation of these neural regions might alter long-term retention because of a direct effect upon registration processes, it is first necessary to ensure that EBS did not produce disruption through secondary effects upon long-term processes such as consolidation. Thus, it is necessary to compare the results of stimulation during the learning trial with the effects of similar levels of stimulation applied after the learning trial. Unfortunately, similar levels of stimulation of any of these structures applied post-trial also results in long-term retention deficits. Thus, the possibility that stimulation during acquisition altered a consolidation process cannot be ruled out. Whenever EBS is applied during learning, there is also the possibility that EBS might serve as a detectable event (a cue) or produce a state, i.e., EBS might support a state-dependent effect (Overton, 1977). State dependency refers to the observation that animals trained in one particular state (e.g., under the influence of pentobarbital) may show retention of training only when in the same state, with little or no evidence of training when tested in a different state (e.g., tested in the nondrugged state).

Thus, in order to test for state dependency, it is necessary to apply EBS not only during acquisition but also during the retention test. If there is no retention deficit when EBS is applied both during the learning trial and long-term retention test, in contrast to retention disruption when EBS is applied only during the learning trial, there would be a strong possibility that EBS has cue value or is capable of producing a differential state. Unfortunately, this possibility was not tested in any of the above mentioned studies. There has been only one demonstration of a possible state-dependent effect with low-intensity electrical stimulation of only one neural region (caudate), and only when stimulation was applied just *before* the training trial and *before* the retention test (McIntyre & Gunter, 1979). They showed that rats had impaired retention of passive avoidance training when caudate stimulation was applied either 30 sec before the learning trial or 30 sec before the 24 hr retention test trial (different state). When caudate stimulation was given both 30 sec before the learning trial and 30 sec before retention testing (same state), there was no evidence of memory impairment.

At the present time, it appears that even though a number of neural regions have been stimulated during learning trials resulting in a subsequent long-term retention deficits, it is not possible to interpret the deficits as disruption of registration processes because the same results can be observed with post-trial stimulation and, furthermore, state dependent effects were not tested.

B. Short-term Memory Paradigm

In order to study the operation of a presumed STM system, there has been a revival of tasks such as delayed response, delayed paired comparisons, delayed alternation and delayed-matching-to-sample. Within these tasks, a trial is usually composed of a study phase followed by a delay interval (usually in the order of seconds) and a subsequent test phase. Trials are separated by an inter-trial time interval. It has been assumed that efficient performance in these tasks involves the operation of short-term memory.

Short-term memory has been characterized by a decay process, which functions as a gradual negative gradient with a progressive loss of information with time (seconds). This decay function can be affected by a number of processes (e.g., registration, selective attention, arousal, rehearsal, interference, or retrieval) whose role it is to enhance or reduce by a variety of means the duration of the STM trace. Based on this characterization of STM, it should be possible to identify specific neural regions associated with processes (e.g., interference, registration, selective attention, rehearsal, arousal, or retrieval) necessary for efficient performance as inferred from possible disruptive or facilitatory effects of EBS applied to specific neural regions during the study phase, delay interval, test phase, or inter-trial interval. For example, if EBS disrupts correct performance only when applied during the study phase or early part of the delay period in an STM task, it is reasonable to argue that the stimulated neural structure is critically involved in the encoding process, which incorporates sensory, cue-access, and perceptual and selective attention components. As an illustration, Stamm (1969) applied prefrontal cortex stimulation (2-or 4-sec duration) during discrete portions of a well-learned delayed response task. He reported that electrical stimulation of the middle principalis region (1) disrupted performance completely when applied during the first few seconds of the delay period, (2) disrupted performance somewhat when applied during the final second of cue presentation (study phase) or later portions of delay period, and (3) had no disruptive effect when applied during the inter-trial interval. However, in a more recent study, Kovner and Stamm (1972) have shown that prefrontal cortex stimulation does not produce deficits in a delayed-matching-to-sample task. Thus, it appears possible that the prefrontal cortex is involved in registration processes associated with spatial, but not visual information. However, with humans, it has been shown that electrical stimulation of the posterior frontal lobe near the language production area results in errors on a short-term memory for a names-of-objects task, but only when the stimulation was applied during the recall test (Ojemann, 1978).

It is also reasonable to conclude that a given neural structure is critically involved in retrieval and decision processes, given that EBS disrupts correct performance only when applied during the last part of the delay period and the test phase. As an illustration, Kovner and Stamm reported that in a delayed-matching-to-sample task inferotemporal cortex stimulation applied during the delay (just prior to the match) interfered with correct performance, while stimulation applied during the study phase or at any other time during the task produced no interference in performance. Thus, the inferotemporal cortex appears to be involved with retrieval and decision processes. However, in a different study with humans it has been shown that electrical stimulation of the temporal lobe near the language reception area resulted in errors in a short-term memory for a names-of-objects task when the stimulation was applied during the input phase and delay, but not during the recall test (Ojemann, 1978).

Given that EBS disrupts correct performance only when applied during the delay interval, at least two meaningful patterns could emerge. First, it is possible that EBS disrupts correct performance regardless of when stimulation is given during the delay interval. This would suggest interference with the strength and integrity of the extant STM trace. It is then possible to argue that the specific neural region stimulated might subserve or have access to the STM memory trace. As an illustration, a recent study by Bierley and Kesner (1980) demonstrated that low-intensity electrical stimulation of the midbrain reticular formation (MRF) in rats disrupts short-term memory in a discrete-trial delayed alternation task independent of the temporal application of the stimulation during a 15-sec delay period. The stimulation did not appear (1) to disrupt a possible motor set, (2) to have rewarding or aversive consequences, (3) to alter arousal level significantly, or (4) to affect encoding or retrieval processes. It was suggested that MRF stimulation might alter STM via neuronal and behavioral mechanisms associated with the maintenance of activated memory traces over short periods of time. Second, it is possible that EBS becomes more or less effective in disrupting correct performance as the temporal locus of stimulation approaches the test phase, i.e., EBS produces a positively or negatively graded function. This would suggest possible interference with arousal or rehearsal processes. It is then possible to argue that the specific neural region might subserve arousal or rehearsal processes that in some manner affect the decay of the STM trace. However, this graded pattern of results might also occur if EBS itself produces a STM trace that competes with the STM trace for the stimuli to be remembered in the task.

C. *Consolidation Paradigm*

The most accepted theory of memory to date has addressed itself to the role of the central nervous system in the control of consolidation processes (McGaugh, 1966). The operation of a consolidation process is inferred from a paradigm in which a specific treatment (e.g., EBS) is capable of producing a time-dependent disruption or facilitation in long-term retention of newly acquired experiences. In other words, treatments that are capable of disrupting or facilitating long-term retention when applied immediately after a training experience, but become less effective when delayed a few minutes or a few hours imply the operation of a memory consolidation process.

The pattern of results obtained with this paradigm led to the proposal that memory traces of new experiences initially reside in a labile short-term memory (STM), which decays within hours. This STM serves as the basis for retention of recent experiences and promotes the transfer of information to long-term memory (LTM) by initiating consolidation processes (McGaugh, 1966). This sequential dual-trace hypothesis is similar to that proposed by Hebb (1949).

Subsequent theoretical formulations (McGaugh & Dawson, 1971) assume that both STM and consolidation processes within LTM are initiated by new experiences, but, in addition, information can also be transferred from STM to LTM. Furthermore, it is assumed that even though the duration of the STM trace is limited (information decays within hours), it determines the rate of growth of the trace in LTM.

More recently, Gold and McGaugh (1975) proposed that new experiences initiate consolidation processes within LTM without concurrent activation of traces within a STM system. Instead, there is an immediate or delayed initiation of processes (e.g., arousal) that modulate the consolidation of LTM by either enhancing the strength of the memory trace or preventing interference-induced forgetting.

Kesner (1973) has proposed that experiences independently activate both an STM and an LTM system. It is assumed, further, that akin to the characteristics described for human STM, information within STM decays within minutes rather than hours. The function of STM is not only for immediate recall of an experience, but also to trigger modulatory processes (e.g., rehearsal, higher-order organization). These modulatory processes maintain information in STM and affect the consolidation process of LTM by rendering it stronger and more organized within the existing memory system of the subject. Regardless of the model one proposes for the storage and/or retrieval of information, any EBS treatment that alters long-term retention within the consolidation paradigm can be assumed to change the consolidation process of LTM directly or indirectly via modulation of decay of STM or modulation of some other process such as arousal or rehearsal. However, it should be mentioned that the same pattern of results obtained with the consolidation paradigm has been interpreted by others as reflecting the operation of a retrieval process (DeVietti & Kirkpatrick, 1976; Miller & Springer, 1973; Weiskrantz, 1966). These investigators assume that new information is consolidated immediately, so that treatments applied after learning only affect processes that render information more or less retrievable. However, none of the available experimental paradigms used to study memory provide for a clear separation of storage and retrieval processes. Thus, the issue remains unresolved.

A number of research strategies have been employed in order to delineate the critical neuronal units that subserve the consolidation process. One strategy is to apply post-training electrical stimulation to a number of interconnected neuronal sites using a single training situation and to assess their contribution to the consolidation process. For example, with passive avoidance learning, it has been shown that substantia nigra, pars compacta, caudate nucleus, amygdala, periaqueductal gray, medial and dorsomedial thalamus, ventromedial prefrontal cortex, dorsal hippocampus, and midbrain reticular formation (MRF) may play important roles in memory consolidation since EBS of any of these structures is likely to disrupt long-term retention (Bresnahan & Routtenberg, 1972; Gold *et al.*, 1973, 1975; Kesner & Conner, 1974; McDonough & Kesner, 1971; Routtenberg & Holzman, 1973; Santos-Anderson & Routtenberg, 1976; Wilburn & Kesner, 1974; Wyers & Deadwyler, 1971; Wyers, Peeke, Williston, & Herz, 1968; Zornetzer, 1972; Zornetzer *et al.*, 1973; Kesner & Calder, unpublished); with the exception of the MRF where EBS appears to facilitate retention (Bloch, 1970; Denti *et al.*, 1970). Based on EBS studies, a large number of brain regions (e.g., substantia nigra, pars reticularis, medial lemniscus, red nucleus, locus coeruleus, most of the neocortex, corpus callosum, internal capsule, nucleus accumbens, and lateral geniculate nucleus) apparently do not appear to contribute directly to the consolidation process associated with passive avoidance learning (Routtenberg & Holzman, 1973; Santos-Anderson & Routtenberg, 1976; Wyers, Deadwyler, Hirasuma, & Montgomery, 1973; Wyers *et al.*, 1968).

Somewhat different results are obtained with active avoidance and taste-aversion learning. For example, it has been shown that electrical stimulation of the midbrain reticular formation, dorsal hippocampus, ventral hippocampus, septum, or entorhinal cortex facilitates, while electrical stimulation of the amygdala disrupts long-term retention of active avoidance (Bloch, 1970; Denti *et al.*, 1970; Erickson & Patel, 1969; Gold *et al.*, 1975; Landfield *et al.*, 1973; Martinez, McGaugh, Hanes, & Lacob, 1977). With taste-aversion learning post-illness (apomorphine) electrical stimulation of the amygdala disrupts retention of the taste aversion, but hippocampal, lateral hypothalamic, periaqueductal gray, and midbrain reticular formation stimulation is ineffective (Kesner & Berman, 1977; Kesner, Dixon, Pickett, & Berman, 1975b; Kesner & Calder, 1978; Kesner, Berman, Burton, & Hankins, 1975a). Thus, similar neuronal substrates appear to contribute differentially to long-term retention of specific learning experiences.

There are a number of problems associated with a strategy of varying neural regions within a single learning task. First, it is difficult to equate specific stimulation parameters across a variety of neural regions. This is because of the differential distribution of axons, cell bodies, and dendrites across neural regions, and possible differential responsiveness to specific EBS frequencies. A negative finding could be a function of selection of inappropriate EBS parameters. Second, there is a possibility that different neural systems contribute to the formation of long-term memory because of their involvement with a variety of processes other than LTM consolidation (e.g., short-term memory, reinforcement, arousal, rehearsal).

A second strategy is to stimulate a specific neural region and vary the learning situation. Presumably evidence for general involvement of a given neural region in memory consolidation should be demonstrable across a wide variety of learning situations. However, it has been shown thus far that post-trial stimulation of amygdala can disrupt long-term retention of passive avoidance and active avoidance learning, shock-motivated visual discrimination learning, taste-aversion learning, but not appetitive learning or habituation to a novel flavor (Berman & Kesner, 1976; Bresnahan & Routtenberg, 1972; Gold *et al.*, 1973, 1975; Gold, Rose, Hankins, & Spanis, 1976; Handwerker, Gold, & McGaugh, 1975; Kesner & Berman, 1977; Kesner & Conner, 1974; Kesner *et al.*, 1975a; McDonough & Kesner, 1971). Furthermore, it has been shown that post-trial stimulation of dorsal hippocampus can disrupt or facilitate long-term retention of passive avoidance learning and disrupt appetitive learning, but has no effect on taste-aversion learning or habituation to a novel flavor (Berman & Kesner, 1976; Erickson & Patel, 1969; Kesner & Berman, 1977; Kesner & Conner, 1974; McDonough & Kesner, 1971; Zornetzer *et al.*, 1973). Similarly, EBS of the caudate nucleus has been shown to disrupt long-term retention of passive avoidance learning, maze learning, extinction of a drinking response and habituation, but not taste-aversion learning (Herz, Wyers, & Peeke, 1975; Wilburn & Kesner, 1972).

A variant of this strategy is to manipulate specific contingencies within the same task and test for the effects of EBS. Kapp, Gallagher, Holmquist, and Theall (1978) reported that post-trial stimulation of the hippocampus impaired long-term retention in animals trained in a response-contingent conditioning procedure, but had no effect in animals trained in a noncontingent conditioning procedure. Thus, the effectiveness of hippocampal stimulation depended upon the nature of the associative learning process.

There are a number of problems associated with the second strategy. It is difficult to equate specific stimulation parameters across a variety of learning situations because of variations in strength of associations, duration of action and intensity of specific conditioned and unconditioned stimuli, and motivational conditions. Thus, a negative finding could again be a function of selection of inappropriate EBS parameters for a specific task. Also, it is possible that brain regions implicated in memory consolidation are differentially imvolved in the consolidation of one or more of the various possible attributes (affective component, temporal, spatial, motoric) presumed to comprise a given learning situation.

A third strategy is to vary frequency or intensity of stimulation of a specific neural region given after a learning experience and record electrophysiological changes (EEG, evoked potentials, multiple units, or single units) or biochemical changes in a number of interconnected neuronal systems. Then it is assumed that the electrophysiological or biochemical change reflects the operation of presumably a consolidation process. It is important to ensure that the treatment at one level produces a modulation of the memory system, while at another level there is no effect. One example is provided by Landfield (1977), who demonstrated that post-trial low-frequency (7.7 Hz) stimulation of the septum, which drives a cortically recorded hippocampal theta, is capable of producing facilitation of both active and passive avoidance learning in comparison with post-trial high-frequency (77 Hz) stimulation of the septum, which blocks hippocampal theta. In addition, Landfield *et al.* (1973) have demonstrated that facilitation of active and passive avoidance learning following post-trial stimulation of ventral hippocampus results in an increase in hippocampal theta lasting at least 5 min after stimulation termination. They suggest that cortically recorded hippocampal theta may reflect the ongoing process of consolidation.

Another example is provided by Destrade, Jaffard, Cardo, Ebel, and Mandel (1977). They showed that post-trial stimulation of dorsal hippocampus or lateral hypothalamus not only facilitated retention of an appetitive experience, but also reduced choline acetyltransferase activity within the hippocampus, suggesting that acetylcholine availability in the hippocampus may play an important role in memory consolidation processes.

At the present time very little work has been undertaken using this strategy. Some of the problems associated with this approach pertain to (1) the possibility that a neural or biochemical correlate may be related to processes other than consolidation, and (2) the difficulty of not only selecting the appropriate neural site but also the appropriate electrophysiological or biochemical measure.

D. Short- and Long-term Memory Paradigm

The short- and long-term memory paradigm represents an extension of the consolidation paradigm. In addition to post-trial EBS and a long-term retention test (usually hours after training), a short-term retention test (usually seconds after training) is also employed. The ability to test subjects within seconds after initial learning became a possibility with the advent of low-intensity, short-duration, subseizure-level electrical stimulation. The advantages of this paradigm are that it provides for an assessment of the operation of memory at short time intervals and allows for a comparison of the effects of an identical EBS treatment upon processes associated with short- and long-term retention.

It is assumed that efficient performance on a short-term retention test reflects the operation of a short-term memory system. This STM system consists of a short-term store (STS), in which information that was attended to could persist in the order of seconds (perhaps up to a few minutes), and of a number of operating processes (e.g., selective attention, decay, arousal, encoding, maintenance and elaborative rehearsal, interference, and retrieval). Thus, any EBS-induced alteration in performance observed at a short-term retention test would be a function of some effect upon the operating or control processes associated with the STM system. However, it is also possible that EBS produces short-term proactive changes in performance, which might affect a short-term but not a long-term retention test. One can approach this problem experimentally in two ways. First, it is necessary to demonstrate that the EBS treatment itself does not affect the behavior that is being assessed. Second, it is necessary to demonstrate that there are no changes in performance when the EBS treatment is applied just prior to the long-term retention test.

It is assumed that efficient performance on a long-term retention test reflects the operation of a long-term store (LTS), in which information could persist from seconds to a lifetime, and of a number of operating processes (e.g., elaborative rehearsal, arousal, consolidation, coding, higher-order organization, interference, and retrieval (search)). The possibility for permanent storage of a neural trace in LTS is partially a function of its unlimited capacity and presumably the consolidation or growth of the neural trace through some form of coding, arousal, elaborative rehearsal, or higher-order organization. It is important to note that these characteristics of the LTM system are similar to the formulations of consolidation theory. Thus, any EBS-induced alteration in performance at the long-term retention test would be a function of some effect upon the operating or control processes associated with the LTM system. In addition, this paradigm allows for an analysis of the relationships between STM and LTM systems (e.g., sequential versus parallel).

Extension of the consolidation paradigm to include a STM test lead to the possibility of differentiating specific neural units that are maximally involved in the modulation of these two different stores and their specific operating processes. For example, Kesner and Conner (1972, 1974) implanted rats with bilateral electrodes in the midbrain reticular formation (MRF), hippocampus, and amygdala. The animals were trained to bar-press for sugar water in a Skinner box. After training, they received a 5-mA, 1-sec duration footshock (FS) contingent upon a bar press. Four seconds later, they received 5 sec of bilateral electrical stimulation applied to the MRF, hippocampus, or amygdala. Implanted and unoperated control animals received no brain stimulation. Half of the animals within each group were tested for retention of the FS experience 55 sec after the termination of brain stimulation. The remaining half of the animals were tested for retention 24 hr later. Parameters were adjusted so that the selected treatment stimulation intensities were below the intensity level required to produce (1) an observable behavioral response, (2) an electrographic or behavioral seizure, and (3) a direct interference with an ongoing bar-pressing response.

Control groups demonstrated suppression of bar-pressing at both retention tests, indicating memory for the footshock experience. The MRF-stimulated animals exhibited significantly poorer retention (little suppression of bar-pressing) than did controls at the short-term retention test (55 sec), but retained the aversive experience much as did the controls at the long-term retention test (24 hr). In contrast, the hippocampal-stimulated animals exhibited complete retention of the aversive experience at the short-term, but no retention (no suppression of bar-pressing) at the long-term retention test. The amygdala-stimulated animals exhibited no retention at both short- and long-term retention tests. In order to rule out the possibility that MRF stimulation could have disrupted short-term memory by altering some nonspecific aspect of performance, we were able to demonstrate that (1) MRF stimulation *per se* had no effect upon the level of bar-pressing, and (2) MRF stimulation applied

60 sec prior to the 24-hr retention test had no effect upon long-term retention.

In a somewhat different type of passive avoidance paradigm, Wyers *et al.* (1973) demonstrated that post-trial stimulation of the caudate disrupted retention of a footshock experience at both short-term (2 min) and long-term (24 hr) retention delays. With respect to appetitive learning, we (Berman & Kesner, 1976) took advantage of the fact that water-deprived rats, when placed in a test situation with access to an empty drinking tube, will find the tube quickly, but will lick it only a few times (mean = 7 licks in a 3-min period). If, on the other hand, rats are first allowed 150 licks of a drinking tube containing a sucrose solution, followed by a 90-sec or a 24-hr delay with an empty drinking tube, they will lick the tube on the average 25 times within a 3-min period. Half of the animals with electrodes implanted in the hippocampus received 30 sec of brain stimulation at 25–35-μA intensities commencing 4 sec after completion of a 150-lick sucrose experience and retested for a 3-min period on the empty tube 56 sec or 24 hr after the termination of brain stimulation. The remaining half of the implanted animals underwent the same procedure but received no brain stimulation. The total number of licks taken during the 3-min retest period was used as the main index of retention of the sucrose experience. Results indicated that relative to implanted and unoperated controls, post-trial hippocampal stimulation produced a reliable reduction in total number of licks at the 24-hr test (long-term retention), but did not produce reliable changes at the 90-sec test (short-term retention).

Since the lateral hypothalamus and amygdala have been implicated in the regulation and possible reinforcing effects of food and water intake, additional animals received brain stimulation of the lateral hypothalamus or amygdala immediately after the 150-lick sucrose experience and were tested for retention 90 sec or 24 hr later. Rats that received lateral hypothalamic stimulation showed more licking compared with controls during the short-term but not the long-term retention test. This facilitation of STM may have been influenced by stimulation-induced motivational changes. In contrast, rats that received amygdala stimulation did not exhibit any change in licking relative to controls at either retention test (Berman & Kesner, 1976).

Considered together, the data suggest that the midbrain reticular formation and interconnected neural systems may be associated with processing of information within the STM system at least for aversive experiences, and the hippocampus and interconnected neuronal systems may be associated with processing of information within the LTM system for both appetitive and aversive experiences. Both the caudate and the amygdala appear to be involved with both short and long-term memory for aversive experiences, but the amygdala does not appear to process information triggered by appetitive experiences. The lateral hypothalamus might be involved with processes that modulate STM of appetitive experiences. Finally, the data further suggest that STM and LTM can operate independently.

E. Memory-Attribute Paradigm

The memory-attribute paradigm employs post-trial EBS after original learning and a long-term retention test, followed by presentation of a specific set of cues (composed of some component of the original learning) and a subsequent follow-up long-term retention test. A variant of the memory-attribute paradigm employs presentation of a specific set of cues at some delay after original learning, followed by EBS and a subsequent long-term retention test. This paradigm is similar to the reminder cue and reinstatement paradigms, which were initially designed to test whether EBS treatments alter retrieval rather than storage processes (Miller & Springer, 1973) or affect only active memory traces (Lewis, 1976). These paradigms, however, can also be used to emphasize the possibility that specific neuronal systems could contribute to long-term memory by subserving specific attributes determining the form and nature of the memory for specific experiences.

It is assumed that long-term memory consists of a set or bundle of traces, each representing some attribute or feature of the learning experience (see also Spear, 1976; Tulving & Watkins, 1975). For example, in a passive avoidance training situation the stored memory might be composed of attributes associated with pain, fear, environmental context, motivational states, or feedback from jumping and subsequent freezing responses. This multidimensional scaling of the memory trace contrasts with the assumption that the structure of the memory consists of a monolithic trace, the strength of which can be represented by a unidimensional measure (an assumption usually made in interpreting results obtained from the consolidation paradigm). Thus, it is assumed that an EBS-induced retention deficit is the result of altered storage of some of the necessary attributes, rendering the memory trace as weak, incomplete, and qualitatively different.

In order to test whether different neuronal systems might contribute to the consolidation of specific attributes within a passive avoidance learning situation, the amygdala and hippocampus were selected for study (Baker, Michal, & Kesner, in press).

In the first study, rats received low-level bilateral electrical stimulation of either the amygdala or hippocampus after training in a one-trial passive avoidance task. Rats receiving stimulation showed amnesia when tested 24 hr after training. One hour after the retention test, rats received a footshock reminder cue. Twenty-three hours later, in a second retention test, hippocampus-stimulated animals showed recovery of memory, while amygdala-stimulated rats did not. Stimulated rats that did not receive a reminder footshock remained amnesic. The second study examined the effects of amygdala and hippocampal stimulation applied after the footshock reminder cue. On the second retention test, amygdala stimulation disrupted the reminder effect, while hippocampal stimulation had no deleterious effects. These data suggest that amygdala stimulation might have disrupted attributes associated with emotional consequences of a footshock rendering a subsequent footshock ineffective, while hippocampal stimulation affected different attributes, making it possible for a footshock reminder to interact with the existing memory and thus increase subsequent retention.

F. Age of Memory Paradigm

In the age of memory paradigm, the time between learning and EBS application is varied from hours to days, but the EBS-retention test time interval is held constant. In the consolidation paradigm, usually both the learning-EBS and EBS-retest time intervals are varied. In the more complex version of the age of memory paradigm, not only time but also the subject's specific experiences between initial learning and EBS application are varied, while the EBS-retest delay is still held constant.

The paradigm was developed based on the assumption that information stored into LTM as a unitary or multidimensional trace does not become a static or fixed entity. Instead, there are probably many dynamic changes in the organization, strength, and retrievability of the memory trace. As early as 1887, Ribot suggested that LTM could be separated into *recent* and *remote* memory components. This idea was based on the observation that brain damage affected recent memories more readily than remote memories. More recently, Tulving (1972) has proposed that there are two classes of information stored in long-term memory, namely *episodic* and *semantic*. He suggests that information contained within episodic memory constitutes specific personal experiences that have occurred at particular times in specific places. For example, one's ability to remember what one ate for yesterday's breakfast, lunch, or dinner represents an episodic memory. Most forgetting involves such specific information stored within episodic memory. This forgetting is probably due to the interference of other similar experiences. For example, one's inability to remember what one ate for breakfast, lunch, or dinner two weeks ago might be due to all the other intervening meals since that time. Tulving further suggests that information contained within semantic memory constitutes knowledge of the world and need not be tied to specific spatiotemporal events. The fact that an important ingredient of coffee is caffeine or that there are twelve months in a year are examples of semantic memories, which are probably recalled in the absence of a particular time or place. There is a strong possibility that Ribot and Tulving have described similar phenomena. Thus, one could equate recent with episodic memory, and remote with semantic memory. Episodic or recent long-term memory, then, could be thought of as a set of consolidated memory traces for specific events during a period extending from the present to a few weeks back in time. The development of recent or episodic long-term memory might be subserved by consolidation processes similar to that described in the consolidation paradigm. On the other hand, semantic or remote long-term memory would be composed of more highly organized memory traces resulting in a more permanent kind of memory back to childhood.

Given that little forgetting occurs across the time frame of interest and that the effectiveness of an EBS treatment varies as a function of the age of the memory trace (e.g., EBS might produce a retention deficit one day but not seven days after learning), then it might be reasonable to conclude that the specific neural region affected by EBS is involved in the organization of recent or episodic long-term memory. The opposite pattern of results (e.g., a retention deficit seven days but not one day after learning) might suggest that the specific neural region affected by EBS is associated with remote or semantic long-term memory. Furthermore, the EBS-induced disruption of retention could last for the duration of the EBS treatment or be more permanent. With the former possibility, it is likely that the EBS treatment temporarily blocked the retrievability of the consolidated memory; with the latter, the EBS treatment might have altered, masked, or destroyed the consolidated memory.

Even though the age of memory paradigm has been used extensively by Deutsch (1972) in his work on the role of the cholinergic system in long-term memory, only a few studies have appeared using this paradigm in conjunction with the EBS technique. As an illustration, Kesner *et al.* (1975b) trained animals to bar-press for sugar water in a Skinner box. After reaching a stable level of bar-pressing, the animals received a footshock (FS) contingent upon bar-pressing. Each animal was given the opportunity to bar-press for the remaining 5 min, and most received a second or third FS. Twenty-four hours later, they were tested for retention of the FS experience. After demonstrating complete suppression of bar-pressing, they received unilateral hippocampal stimulation resulting in a seizure after-discharge with retests either 2, 15, 60, or 180 min after the cessation of the primary after-discharge (PAD). Appropriate operated and unoperated controls received no brain stimulation and were tested at 2, 15, 60, and 180 min after the approximate time that experimental groups displayed the end of the PAD. The remaining animals were tested for retention of the FS experience seven days later followed by a hippocampal seizure after-discharge with a retest 2 or 15 min later. Hippocampal after-discharges triggered one day after learning resulted in a temporary amnesic effect (reinstatement of bar-pressing at the 2, 15, or 60-min retest but not at the 180-min retest), but failed to produce an amnesic effect when triggered seven days after learning.

This age of memory-dependent amnesic effect provides for a clear elimination of the possibility that the hippocampal seizures interfered directly with performance by way of enhanced activity, complete disorientation, or increased hunger motivation. If the effect were due to some factor other than an effect upon memory, then hippocampal seizures administered seven days after training should have resulted in an increase in bar-pressing. In other words, with an age of memory-controlled paradigm one can potentially separate performance from memory failures, given that no marked forgetting occurs across the specific time frame of interest. Furthermore, there was an indication of anterograde amnesia in that the bar-pressing behavior that did occur during the immediate retention test did not produce extinction of suppression of bar-pressing on a second 24-hr retest. Additional work has demonstrated that hippocampal seizures can also produce an age of memory-dependent disruption in retention of an active avoidance and bar-pressing habit (Kesner *et al.*, 1975b). These data suggest that the hippocampus and interconnected structures might play a critical role in storage or retrieval of information within recent or episodic LTM, but plays a more limited role within semantic or organized LTM.

In conclusion, EBS can be used as a powerful research tool in the understanding of the neurobiological bases of learning and memory. Even though there are many parameters that can be manipulated with EBS, side effects that need to be controlled, and disagreement concerning the mechanism(s) of action on the central nervous system, there are many important advantages including the reversability of its primary action and the ease of its application before, during, or after training as well as before or during retention tests. From a more theoretical viewpoint the interpretation of EBS effects are primarily a function of the paradigm(s) (e.g., registration, short-term memory, consolidation, short- and long-term memory, attribute, and age of memory) employed and their underlying assumptions concerning the operation of the memory system. Ideally, one should apply EBS within each of these paradigms in order to delineate more precisely the locus of impact of the treatment on mnemonic information processing.

References

Baker, L. J., Kesner, R. P., & Michal, R. E. Differential effects of a reminder cue on amnesia induced by stimulation of amygdala and hippocampus. *Journal of Comparative and Physiological Psychology,* in press, 1981.

Barry, F. E., Walter, M. S., & Gallistel, C. R. On the optimal pulse duration in electrical stimulation of the brain. *Physiology and Behavior,* 1974, **12,** 749–754.

Berman, R. F., & Kesner, R. P. Posttrial hippocampal, amygdaloid and lateral hypothalamic electrical stimulation: Effects upon memory of an appetitive experience. *Journal of Comparative and Physiological Psychology,* 1976, **90,** 260–267.

Bierley, R. A., & Kesner, R. P. Short-term memory: The role of the mid-brain reticular formation. *Journal of Comparative and Physiological Psychology,* 1980, **94,** 519–529.

Bloch, V. Facts and hypothesis concerning memory consolidation. *Brain Research,* 1970, **24,** 561–575.

Boast, C. A., & McIntrye, D. C. Bilateral kindled amygdala foci and inhibitory avoidance behavior in rats: A functional lesion effect. *Physiology and Behavior,* 1977, **18,** 25–28.

Boast, C. A., Reid, S. A., Johnson, P., & Zornetzer, S. F. A caution to brain scientists: Unsuspected hemorrhagic vascular damage resulting from mere electrode implantation. *Brain Research,* 1976, **103,** 527–534.

Bresnahan, E., & Routtenberg, A. Memory disruption by unilateral low level, sub-seizure stimulation of the medial amygdaloid nucleus. *Physiology and Behavior,* 1972, **9,** 513–525.

Delgado, J. M. R. Free behavior and brain stimulation. *International Review of Neurobiology,* 1964, **6,** 349–449.

Denti, A., McGaugh, J. L., Landfield, P. W., & Shinkman, P. G. Effects of post-trial electrical stimulation of the mesencephalic reticular formation on avoidance learning in rats. *Physiology and Behavior,* 1970, **5,** 659–662.

Destrade, C., & Jaffard, R. Post-trial hippocampal and lateral hypothalamic electrical stimulation: Facilitation of long-term memory of appetitive and avoidance learning tasks. *Behavioral Biology,* 1978, **22,** 354–374.

Destrade, C., Jaffard, R., Cardo, B., Ebel, A., & Mandel, P. Effects of hippocampal and lateral hypothalamic electrical stimulation on hippocampal cholinergic mechanisms in BALB/c inbred mice. *Neuroscience Letters,* 1977, **4,** 181–184.

Deutsch, J. A. The cholinergic synapse and the site of memory. In J. A. Deutsch (Ed.), *The physiological basis of memory.* New York: Academic Press, 1972.

DeVietti, T. L., & Kirkpatrick, B. R. The amnesia gradient: Inadequate as evidence for a memory consolidation process. *Science,* 1976, **194,** 438–440.

Doty, R. W. Conditioned reflexes formed and evoked by brain stimulation. In D. E. Sheer (Ed.), *Electrical stimulation of the brain.* Houston: University of Texas Press, 1961.

Doty, R. W. Electrical stimulation of the brain in behavioral context. *Annual Review of Psychology*, 1969, **20,** 289–320.

Erickson, C. K., & Patel, J. B. Facilitation of avoidance learning by post-trial hippocampal electrical stimulation. *Journal of Comparative and Physiological Psychology*, 1969, **68,** 400–406.

Ervin, F. R., & Kenney, G. J. Electrical stimulation of the brain. In R. D. Myers (Ed.), *Methods in psychobiology* (Vol. 1). New York: Academic Press, 1971.

Fritsch, G., & Hitzig, E. Ueber die elektrische erregbarkeit des grosshirns. *Archives fuer Anatomie und Physiologie*, 1870, **37,** 300–332.

Gallistel, C. R., Stellar, J. R., & Bubis, E. Parametric analysis of brain stimulation reward in the rat. I. The transient process and the memory-containing process. *Journal of Comparative and Physiological Psychology*, 1974, **87,** 848–859.

Gerken, G. M., & Judy, M. M. Electrode polarization and the detection of electrical stimulation of the brain. *Physiology and Behavior*, 1977, **18,** 825–832.

Goddard, G. V. Functions of the amygdala. *Psychological Bulletin*, 1964, **12,** 89–109.

Goddard, G. V., McIntyre, D. C., & Leech, C. K. A permanent change in brain function resulting from daily electrical stimulation. *Experimental Neurology*, 1969, **25,** 295–330.

Gold, P. E., Edwards, R. M., & McGaugh, J. L. Amnesia produced by unilateral, subseizure, electrical stimulation of the amygdala in rats. *Behavioral Biology*, 1975, **15,** 95–105.

Gold, P. E., & King, R. A. Caudate stimulation and retrograde amnesia: Amnesia threshold and gradient. *Behavioral Biology*, 1972, **7,** 709–715.

Gold, P. E., Macri, J., & McGaugh, J. L. Retrograde amnesia produced by subseizure amygdala stimulation. *Behavioral Biology*, 1973, **9,** 671–680.

Gold, P. E., & McGaugh, J. L. A single-trace, two-process view of memory storage processes. In D. Deutsch & J. A. Deutsch (Eds.), *Short term memory*. New York: Academic Press, 1975. Pp. 355–378.

Gold, P. E., Rose, R. P., Hankins, L. L., & Spanis, C. Impaired retention of visual discriminated escape training produced by subseizure amygdala stimulation. *Brain Research*, 1976, **118,** 73–85.

Greatbatch, W., Piersma, B., Shannon, F. D., & Calhoon, S. W. Polarization phenomena relating to physiological electrodes. *Annals of the New York Academy of Sciences*, 1969, **167,** 722–744.

Handwerker, M. J., Gold, P. E., & McGaugh, J. L. Impairment of active avoidance learning with posttrial amygdala stimulation. *Brain Research*, 1975, **75,** 324–327.

Hebb, D. O. *The organization of behavior*. New York: Wiley, 1949.

Herz, M. J., Marshall, K. E., & Peeke, H. V. S. Brain stimulation and behavior: Controls and consequences. *Physiological Psychology*, 1974, **2,** 184–186.

Herz, M. J., Wyers, E. J., & Peeke, H. V. S. Caudate stimulation and the production of retrograde amnesia. In T. L. Frigyesi (Ed.), *Subcortical mechanisms and sensory-motor activities*. Amsterdam: Elsevier, 1975.

Hess, W. R. *Diencephalon, autonomic and extrapyramidal functions*. New York: Grune & Stratton, 1957.

Huston, J. P., Mueller, C. C., & Mondadori, C. Memory facilitation by posttrial hypothalamic stimulation and other reinforcers: A central theory of reinforcement. *Biobehavioral Review*, 1977, **1,** 143–150.

Iggo, A. The physiological interpretation of electrical stimulation of the nervous system. *Electroencephalography and Clinical Neurophysiology, Supplement*, 1978, **34,** 335–341.

Kaada, B. R. Stimulation and regional ablation of the amygdaloid complex with reference to functional representations. In B. E. Eleftheriou (Ed.), *The neurobiology of the amygdala*. New York: Plenum, 1972.

Kapp, B. S., Gallagher, M., Holmquist, B. K., & Theall, C. L. Retrograde amnesia and hippocampal stimulation: Dependence upon the nature of associations formed during conditioning. *Behavioral Biology*, 1978, **24**, 1–23.

Kesner, R. P., & Calder, L. D. Rewarding periaqueductal stimulation disrupts long-term memory for passive avoidance learning. *Behavioral Neural Biology*, 1980, **30**, 237–249.

Kesner, R. P. A neural system analysis of memory storage and retrieval. *Psychological Bulletin*, 1973, **80**, 177–203.

Kesner, R. P. Brain stimulation: Effects on memory. In R. F. Thompson & J. L. McGaugh (Eds.), *Neurobiology of learning and memory*. Plenum, New York, in press.

Kesner, R. P., & Berman, R. F. Effects of midbrain reticular formation, hippocampal and lateral hypothalamic stimulation upon recovery from neophobia and taste aversion learning. *Physiology and Behavior*, 1977, **18**, 763–768.

Kesner, R. P., Berman, R. F., Burton, B., & Hankins, W. G. Effects of electrical stimulation of amygdala upon neophobia and taste aversion. *Behavioral Biology*, 1975, **13**, 349–358. (a)

Kesner, R. P., & Conner, H. S. Independence of short- and long-term memory: A neural system analysis. *Science*, 1972, **176**, 432–434.

Kesner, R. P., & Conner, H. S. Effects of electrical stimulation of limbic system and midbrain recticular formation upon short- and long-term memory. *Physiology and Behavior*, 1974, **12**, 5–12.

Kesner, R. P., & Calder, L. D. Rewarding periaqueductal stimulation disrupts long-term memory for passive avoidance learning. Unpublished observations, 1980.

Kesner, R. P., Dixon, D. A., Pickett, D., & Berman, R. F. Experimental animal model of transient global amnesia: Role of the hippocampus. *Neuropsychologia*, 1975, **13**, 465–480. (b)

Kesner, R. P., McDonough, J. H., Jr., & Doty, R. W. Diminished amnestic effect of a second electroconvulsive seizure. *Experimental Neurology*, 1970, **27**, 527–533.

Kovner, R., & Stamm, J. S. Disruption of short-term visual memory by electrical stimulation of inferotemporal cortex in the monkey. *Journal of Comparative and Physiological Psychology*, 1972, **81**, 163–172.

Landfield, P. W. Different effects of posttrial driving or blocking of the theta rhythm on avoidance learning in rats. *Physiology and Behavior*, 1977, **18**, 439–445.

Landfield, P. W., Tusa, R. J., & McGaugh, J. L. Effects of posttrial hippocampal stimulation on memory storage and EEG activity. *Behavioral Biology*, 1973, **8**, 485–505.

LePiane, F. G., & Phillips, A. G. Differential effects of electrical stimulation of amygdala, caudate-putamen or substantia nigra pars compacta on taste aversion and passive avoidance in rats. *Physiology and Behavior*, 1978, **21**, 979–985.

Lewis, D. J. A cognitive approach to experimental amnesia. *American Journal of Psychology*, 1976, **89**, 51–80.

Lilly, J. C., Austin, G. M., & Chambers, W. W. Threshold movements produced by excitation of cerebral cortex and efferent fibers with some parametric regions of rectangular current pulses (cats and monkeys). *Journal of Neurophysiology*, 1952, **15**, 319–342.

Livesey, P. F. Fractionation of hippocampal function in learning. In R. L. Isaacson & K. H. Pribram (Ed.), *The hippocampus* (Vol. 2). New York: Plenum, 1975.

Loucks, R. B. The experimental delimitation of neural structures essential for learning: The attempt to condition striped muscle responses with faradization of the sigmoid gyri. *Journal of Psychology*, 1935–1936, **1**, 5–44.

Loucks, R. B. Studies of neural structures essential for learning. II. The conditioning of salivary and striped muscle responses to faradization of cortical sensory elements, and the action of sleep upon such mechanisms. *Journal of Comparative Psychology*, 1938, **25**, 315–332.

Martinez, J. L., McGaugh, J. L., Hanes, C. L., & Lacob, J. S. Modulation of memory processes induced by stimulation of the entorhinal cortex. *Physiology and Behavior*, 1977, **19**, 139–144.

McDonough, J. F., Jr., & Kesner, R. P. Amnesia produced by brief electrical stimulation of the amygdala or dorsal hippocampus in cats. *Journal of Comparative and Physiological Psychology*, 1971, **77**, 171–178.

McGaugh, J. L. Time-dependent processes in memory storage. *Science*, 1966, **153**, 1351–1358.

McGaugh, J. L., & Dawson, R. G. Modification of memory storage processes. *Behavioral Science*, 1971, **16**, 45–63.

McGaugh, J. L., & Gold, P. W. Modulation of memory by electrical stimulation of the brain. In M. W. Rosenzweig & E. L. Bennet (Eds.), *Neural mechanisms of learning and memory*. MIT Press: Cambridge, MA, 1976. Pp. 549–560.

McIntyre, D. C., & Gunter, J. L. State-dependent learning induced by low intensity electrical stimulation of the caudate or amygdala nuclei in rats. *Physiology and Behavior*, 1979, **23**, 449–454.

Mickle, W. A. The problem of stimulation parameters. In D. E. Sheer (Ed.), *Electrical stimulation of the brain*. Austin: University of Texas Press, 1961.

Mihailovic, L., & Delgado, J. M. R. Electrical stimulation of the monkey brain with various frequencies and pulse durations. *Journal of Neurophysiology*, 1956, **19**, 21–36.

Miller, R. R., & Springer, A. D. Amnesia, consolidation and retrieval. *Psychological Review*, 1973, **80**, 69–79.

Ojemann, G. A. Organization of short-term verbal memory in language areas of human cortex: Evidence from electrical stimulation. *Brain and Language*, 1978, **5**, 331–340.

Olds, J. Hypothalamic substrates of reward. *Physiological Review*, 1962, **42**, 554–604.

Olds, J., & Milner, P. Positive reinforcement produced by electrical stimulation of septal area and other regions of rat brain. *Journal of Comparative and Physiological Psychology*, 1954, **47**, 419–427.

Olds, M. E., & Olds, J. Emotional and associative mechanisms in rat brain. *Journal of Comparative and Physiological Psychology*, 1961, **54**, 120–126.

Overton, D. A. Major theories of state-dependent learning. In B. T. Ho, D. W. Richards, III, & D. L. Chute (Eds.), *Drug discrimination and state dependent learning*. New York: Academic Press, 1977.

Penfield, W., & Roberts, L. *Speech and brain mechanisms*. Princeton, NJ: University of Princeton Press, 1959.

Ranck, J. B., Jr. Which elements are excited in electrical stimulation of mammlian central nervous system: A review. *Brain Research*, 1975, **98**, 417–440.

Ribot, T. H. *Disease of memory*. New York: Appleton, 1887.

Routtenberg, A., & Holzman, N. Memory disruption by electrical stimulation of substantia nigra, pars compacta. *Science*, 1973, **181**, 83–86.

Santos-Anderson, R. M., & Routtenberg, A. Stimulation of rat medial or sulcal prefrontal cortex during passive avoidance learning selectively influences retention performance. *Brain Research*, 1976, **103**, 243–259.

Sideroff, S., Bueno, O., Hirsch, A., Weyand, T., & McGaugh, J. L. Retrograde amnesia initiated by low-level stimulation of hippocampal cytoarchitectonic areas. *Experimental Neurology*, 1974, **43**, 285–297.

Spear, N. E. Retrieval of memories: A psychobiological approach. In W. K. Estes (Ed.), *Handbook of learning and cognitive processes* (Vol. 4). Hillsdale, NJ: Lawrence Erlbaum Associates, 1976.

Stamm, J. S. Electrical stimulation of monkeys' prefrontal cortex during delayed-response performance. *Journal of Comparative and Physiological Psychology*, 1969, **67**, 535–546.

Stark, P., Fazio, G., & Boyd, E. S. Monopolar and bipolar stimulation of the brain. *American Journal of Physiology*, 1962, **203**, 371–373.

Sterman, M. B., & Clemente, C. D. Forebrain inhibitory mechanisms: Sleep patterns induced by basal forebrain stimulation in the behaving cat. *Experimental Neurology*, 1962, **6**, 103–117.

Tulving, E. Episodic and semantic memory. In E. Tulving & W. Donaldson (Ed.), *Organization of memory*. New York: Academic Press, 1972.

Tulving, E., & Watkins, M. J. Structure of memory traces. *Psychological Review*, 1975, **82**, 261–275.

Valenstein, E. S., & Beer, B. Unipolar and bipolar electrodes in self-stimulation experiments. *American Journal of Physiology*, 1961, **201**, 1181–1186.

Valenstein, E. S., Cox, V. C., & Kakolewski, J. W. Reexamination of the role of the hypothalamus in motivation. *Psychological Review*, 1970, **77**, 16–31.

Valenstein, E. S., & Meyers, W. A rate-independent test of reinforcing consequences of brain stimulation. *Journal of Comparative and Physiological Psychology*, 1964, **57**, 52–60.

Weinmann, J., & Mahler, J. An analysis of electrical properties of metal electrodes. *Proceedings of the 5th International Conference on Medical Electronics*, 1963, pp. 487–508.

Weiskrantz, L. Experimental studies of amnesia. In C. W. M. Whitty & O. L. Zangwill (Eds.), *Amnesia*. London: Butterworth, 1966.

Wetzel, M. C. New evidence concerning refractory period in self-stimulation neurons. *Physiology and Behavior*, 1972, **8**, 397–402.

Wetzel, M. C., Howell, L. G., & Bearie, K. J. Experimental performance of steel and platinum electrodes with chronic monophasic stimulation of the brain. *Journal of Neurosurgery*, 1969, **31**, 658–669.

Wilburn, M. W., & Kesner, R. P. Differential amnestic effects produced by electrical stimulation of the caudate nucleus and non-specific thalamic system. *Experimental Neurology*, 1972, **34**, 45–50.

Wilburn, M. W., & Kesner, R. P. Effects of caudate nucleus stimulation upon initiation and performance of a complex motor task. *Experimental Neurology*, 1974, **45**, 61–71.

Wyers, E. J., & Deadwyler, S. A. Duration and nature of retrograde amnesia produced by stimulation of caudate nucleus. *Physiology and Behavior*, 1971, **6**, 97–103.

Wyers, E. J., Deadwyler, S. A., Hirasuma, N., & Montgomery, D. Passive avoidance retention and caudate stimulation. *Physiology and Behavior*, 1973, **11**, 809–819.

Wyers, E. J., Peeke, H. V. S., Williston, J. S., & Herz, M. J. Retroactive impairment of passive avoidance learning by stimulation of the caudate nucleus. *Experimental Neurology*, 1968, **22**, 350–366.

Zimmerberg, B., & Glick, S. D. Changes in side preference during unilateral electrical stimulation of the caudate nucleus in rats. *Brain Research*, 1975, **86**, 335–338.

Zornetzer, S. F. Brain stimulation and retrograde amnesia in rats: A neuroanatomical approach. *Physiology and Behavior*, 1972, **8**, 239–244.

Zornetzer, S. F., & Chronister, R. B. Neuroanatomical localization of memory disruption: Relationship between brain structure and learning task. *Physiology and Behavior*, 1973, **10**, 747–750.

Zornetzer, S. F., Chronister, R. B., & Ross, B. The hippocampus and retrograde amnesia: Localization of some positive and negative memory disruptive sites. *Behavioral Biology*, 1973, **8**, 507–518.

Chapter 8

Brain Stimulation Effects Related to Those of Lesions

Robert L. Isaacson

Department of Psychology
Center for Neurobehavioral Sciences
and
Clinical Campus
State University of New York at Binghamton
Binghamton, New York

I. Introduction

Some 25 years ago, when I was beginning to learn about brain–behavior relationships, I got the impression that lesions and electrical stimulation of a region ought to produce opposite types of behavioral effects, when a region was closely linked to a well-defined behavior. The assumptions were that a lesion eliminates the influence of the region, and the stim-

ISBN 0-12-547440-7

ulation enhances it by "popping" the cells in the area or their efferent fibers. To be sure, there were concerns about the importance of the nature of the electrical pulses used, whether they are square or sinusoidal waves, as well as the interpulse intervals, the frequency of stimulation, and so forth. Nevertheless, the overall view was that stimulation should produce the opposite effects from that of lesions. What is surprising is that this sort of result was sometimes obtained. An example would be the induction of stimulus-bound feeding elicited by stimulation of lateral hypothalamic areas (e.g., Hess, 1949; Miller, 1960) and the lack of eating and drinking produced by lesions in this area (e.g., Anand & Brobeck, 1951). However, the evidence quickly accumulated to show that electrical brain stimulation of a structure often produced effects that were quite similar to those found after lesions. For example, either unilateral or bilateral stimulation of the amygdala (Goddard, 1964; Handwerker, Gold, & McGaugh, 1974) can impair the acquisition of active avoidance problems, a result also found with amygdala lesions. Livesey and his coworkers have reported behavioral effects similar to those found after lesions of the hippocampus with the use of "blocking" stimulation applied to various hippocampal regions (Livesey & Bayliss, 1975; Livesey & Meyer, 1975; Livesey & Wearne, 1973).

There are many physical and physiological effects of lowering a wire into the brain, some of which will be detailed here. The passing of electrical currents of various strengths, waveforms, and frequencies, most of which are totally unnatural, produce consequences unrelated to any natural events. The situation becomes more complicated and unnatural when the possible, and largely unpredictable, effects of induced changes in glia cells and the antidromic stimulation of fibers passing through the stimulated region are considered. The most likely outcome of stimulation would be a disruption of normal activity both in the area stimulated and regions associated with it. The disruption of physiological activities should be associated with the disruption of the functional contributions made by the systems affected.

The consequences of electrical stimulation of the brain begins with the surgery involved with the implantation of the electrodes. These include the effects of the implantation procedures, including presurgical isolation and handling, the trauma of the general anesthesia, the opening of the skull and meninges, the invasion of the brain tissue, the disruptions of the blood–brain barrier and the extracellular fluid compartments, the interruption of the normally sealed cerebrospinal fluid chambers, disruptions of circulation, the disturbance and destruction of neurons and glia cells, the breaking or stressing of capillary networks, the reaction of the tissue to the hemorrhage produced, and the reaction to the metal in the electrodes. On top of these disruptions, the brain often develops infections even by a surgeon using sterile techniques. Very often the use of "clean" technique actually means "dirty"; techniques that if they were used with a less hardy animal than the rat or mouse would inevitably lead to sepsis and cerebromeningitis. The fact that rodents, as a rule, are relatively resistant to cerebral infection and respond well to systemic antibiotics has lead, I believe, to the use of careless procedures on the part of many investigators. Some even fail to use even rudimentary antibacterial agents on the materials to be implanted into the brain. Even with its remarkable resistance to infection, the rat often *does* develop bacterial infections within the brain, both at points of contact with the implanted materials and in the meninges. In addition, infection may occur at a distance from the actual site of implantation due to the interruption of the blood supply to the region. These secondary reactions are often undetected by investigators who examine stained sections of the brain looking for an electrode track. Quite often, sites of infection can be detected at considerable distances from the site of implantation. They may influence the behavior of the animal directly or as an interaction with the electrical or chemical stimulation.

Even if there is no bacterial infection along the electrode track, there will be hemorrhage, leucocytic invasion, astrocytic swelling, alterations in oligondendroglia, and an invasion of capillaries noticeable within the first week (Collins & Mannelidis, 1957). The reaction of fiber bands through which the electrode passes include demyelinization. Brain edema is also likely to occur and may persist for several weeks after implantation.

II. The Effect of Electrode Implantation

When electrodes are placed into the brain of animals, and in particular the rat, the "electrode track" marks the location of a "stab wound." It produces a layer of cell-free necrotic tissue that has entrapped red blood cells and some leukocytes. One day after the lesion, the wound is essentially a fluid-filled elongated hole containing red blood cells. Within two days macrophages begin to appear and become more prominent in the next few days. Two weeks after the insult, the macrophages contain hemosiderin, and this usually helps experimenters to identify the electrode pathway. If the electrode enters the white matter, the damage that appears usually is more extensive with cavitation.

Ramón y Cajál (1928) noted that after stab wounds of the brain, neurons both near and some distance away evidence a granular degeneration that can be observed as early as 24 hr after the insult. Other cellular changes were also described, including eccentric or tangential nuclei and pale or granular dendritic processes, nodes developing in dendritic processes, vacuolation of neuronal soma, pyknotic cells, and cells undergoing chromatolysis. In addition, near the edges of the wound, numerous fibers were noted that had the appearance of newly formed processes and aberrant terminal structure, e.g., clubs, buds, or free balls, which were interpreted to be abortive attempts at axonal regeneration.

The development of the glia cell response to stab wounds has now been studied using an antisera to a brain-specific protein (GFA), which is a major constituent of fibrillary neuroglia (Bigami, 1975). In the intact brain, immunofluorescence to GFA is mainly confined to the glia cells surrounding the surface of the brain and to membranes surrounding blood vessels. Thirty-six to 48 hr after a stab wound, many astroglia become visible by immunofluorescence over wide extents of the neocortical surface receiving the wound or in the striatum when the injury extends this far (Bignami & Dahl, 1976). Fluorescing fibers surrounding the track appear one week after the wound. The fluorescent reaction lasts for a month or longer.

Whether astrocytes normally produce low levels of GFA or whether the degradation proceeds so rapidly as to make levels undetectable by immunofluorescense is unknown. In the former case, injuries would be considered as stimulating GFA production; in the second case, injury would reduce the rate of degradation.

Not only does a stab wound cause a reaction in cells in the area, but also there are changes in the permeability of the blood vessels such as to allow monocytes and polymorphonuclear leukocytes to pass from the bloodstream into the wounded hemisphere in the region of the damage. Monocytes are in the wound area as early as one day after the wound occurs. The macrophages are found in greatest number about three days after the trauma, and elevated numbers are detectable for at least as long as 15 days later. Microglia-like cells slowly increase in the wound area and reach a maximal level at 10–12 days after damage (see Imamoto & Leblond, 1977). It appears that macrophages in the brain are derived from monocytes as has been frequently proposed for both peripheral and central nervous system wounds. It is possible that some local microglia may be converted into macrophages by the damage. This would account for the very early presence of phages in wound region. With time, the number of macrophages declines. Some undoubtedly die, but some may become transformed into microglia-like structures.

The implantation of electrodes onto the surface of the brain or to the surface leads to a growth of connective tissue at the surface of the brain. This connective tissue growth is rapid and apparently reaches a maximal amount at about eight days after the implantation. If cortical electrodes are studied, the connective tissue growth may completely encapsulate the electrode. It is likely that when electrodes made from small screws are used and the tips placed so as to rest on or into the neocortical surface, they will also be encapsulated. This process may lead to pressure on the brain surface and possibly to edema in the underlying tissue (Bernstein, Johnson, Hench, Hunter, & Dawson, 1977). These authors also point out that mechanical injuries due to damage during implantation may be related to the degree of flexibility of the materials implanted, the electrode mass, and the reactions of the meningeal tissues during the implantation process. Furthermore, they point out that gold, rhodium, and carbon should be rejected as materials for long-term electrodes used for stimulation of the central nervous system. Platinum wire was also studied and found to be less toxic than the other substances, but it also had a tendency to corrode. Contrary to the beliefs of some researchers, silver, and silver-chloride electrodes can cause considerable tissue reactions. The toxicity of silver is thought to be due to the formation of metal salts with the protein sulfhydryl or acid groups. Of course, copper, mild steel, or iron cause even greater reactions than silver. A substance that seems to produce minimal reactions in the cat neocortex is tantalum pentoxide (Johnson, Bernstein, Hunter, Dawson, & Hench, 1977). Furthermore, the toxicity of the metal implanted in the brain depends on the amount of electricity passed through the electrodes. When current is applied, the relative toxicities of the metals may change (MacIntyre, Bidder, & Rowland, 1957). It should also be mentioned that most studies of relative toxicity of the metals have used the cat as an experimental subject, and there probably are species differences in toxic reactions to metals or different interactions of metals and currents in inducing toxic reactions. In addition, the pathologic changes found in the brain are dependent on the stimulation parameters (Delgado, 1961; Lilly, 1961; MacIntyre *et al.*, 1957).

It should also be noted that the connective tissue encapsulations of cortical electrodes may actually lift the electrode from the surface of the brain with time. Furthermore, the process of connective tissue reaction going on at the site of puncture of the meninges in deeper electrodes may also tend to move the electrode with time. The reaction at the surface of the brain could also be one of depressing the cortical surface and the creation of mechanical pressures that would drive the electrode deeper into the brain, as well as causing superficial injury.

III. The Effects of Electrical Stimulation on Tissue

Stimulation studies have been undertaken to induce a blockade of neural function in a limited area of the brain. Given that some parameter of stimulation can induce disruption of normal functions, what amount of tissue will be affected? Valenstein (1966) concluded that with bipolar electrodes with insulation removed only at the tips, the field directly influenced was about 1 mm around the tips. This field was thought to hold over a wide range of electrical currents. There is no doubt that the volume stimulated will depend on a wide range of other factors such as the size and material of the electrodes, the nature of the tissue, parameters of stimulation, and so forth.

Ranck's (1975) thoughtful review considers a number of factors related to the technical aspects of brain stimulation. Although based on data from studies using monopolar electrodes, much of the information is useful for people using bipolar electrodes. Of special importance is the observation that only cells that exist within a shell surrounding an electrode tip will be stimulated by the current. Cells in a sphere immediately around the tip that are subjected to currents exceeding eight times their threshold will be blocked. Therefore, only cells outside this maximally stimulated inner core will be activated. The same sort of thing applies to axons passing through the inner core and the outer shell. Fibers that pass through the high-intensity core will *not* likely be activated, whereas those passing through the shell will be. Similarities between the effects of electrical stimulation and lesions have been frequently observed. The classical deficits of impaired delayed response and delayed alternation performance after frontal lobe damage can be found after electrical stimulation of these areas (Stamm, 1969; Weiskrantz, Mihailovíc, & Gross, 1960).

The review of Doty (1969) on the effects of brain stimulation is also of substantial value to researchers in the field or those trying to understand the effects of brain stimulation. It corrects many assumptions that a naive investigator might have about the techniques. The following points are emphasized in the review: (1) The effects of electrical stimulation of a particular brain site are not inevitable and fixed, but depend on the history of the individual, the environment, deprivation level, hormonal levels, and amount of repetition of the stimulus. (2) The organization of behavior depends on timed and patterned neural discharges, impossible to achieve by electrical stimulation. One of the more dramatic examples being the fact that the extirpation of cortical areas from which specific memories have been elicited by stimulation does not affect recall of the memory (Penfield & Perot, 1963). (3) Electrical stimulation can serve as a signal that the organism may use as a conditioned stimulus in acquired behaviors. (4) Movements are a pervasive response to brain stimulation throughout the brain. (5) If stimulation is applied unilaterally, then the homotypic area in the unstimulated hemisphere can act to suppress the stimulation-induced effects, and (6) brain stimulation influencing aggressive or fearful reactions often appears to be highly rewarding. Obviously, any of these factors can confound the analysis of behavioral effects induced by electrical brain stimulation unless careful and often elaborate controls are provided in the experimental design.

Many of the same variables have been shown to confound the analysis of the effects of brain lesions. Perhaps the most exhaustive demonstration of the influence of historical, genetic, dietary, and training factors on the effects of behavioral sequelae of lesions have been done by Donovick and his associates who have studied the effects of septal lesions in rats and mice (e.g., Donovick, Burright, & Bengelloun, 1979; Donovick, Burright, & Bensten, 1975; Donovick, Burright, Fuller, & Branson, 1975; Donovick, Burright, & Swidler, 1973).

In terms of motor effects that are so often found as a consequence of brain stimulation, the effects of lesions often produce subtle and sometimes unexpected results. For example, Castro (1972) demonstrated that lesions of the anterior neocortical surface in the rat interfered with the execution of fine movements of the digits of the forepaw. Unpublished studies in my laboratory by Nick Masi and myself, replicated Castro's results and also suggested that both unilateral and bilateral anterior lesions altered the animals' reactions to the frustration induced by the intermittent obtaining of rewards, possibly indicating secondary reactions to the cortical damage at subcortical sites. Direct evidence describing general changes in systems related to emotional changes subsequent to neocortical damage has been reported (Robinson & Bloom, 1978; Robinson & Coyle, 1979).

Many years ago, Andrew J. Karoly and I (unpublished observations) found that hippocampal lesions in the rat produced an unusual motor disorder. We were training animals to jump on a pole to avoid electrical footshock. The animals with hippocampal lesions failed to acquire the response. However, we noted they had great difficulty in jumping on the pole. Dr. Karoly devised a pole with a wide base that looked like a cone. He trained the animals to climb on it. He then reduced the size of the bottom of the cone slowly. Ultimately, he got the animals to jump on a normal-sized pole. After they were escaping footshock well by this approximation procedure, we were able to show that the lesioned animals acquired the avoidance response at least as rapidly as control animals. Their problems had been in the learning of the motor response required for the pole jump, and not the contingencies related to the avoidance response.

The frequency of the electrical stimulation applied is a critical factor in the determination of effects produced. This is related to the fact that neurons in different regions of the nervous system have different membrane time constants. In the hippocampus, at least for the pyramidal cells, this factor is about 10 msec. The time constant for motor neurons in the spinal cord is substantially less. These membrane time factors determine the frequencies that will be effective in altering cellular activity. Furthermore, repetitive stimulation along some fiber pathways produces changes in the target cell membranes, which produce an inactivation of the spike-generating mechanism (Kandel & Spencer, 1961). It should also be noted that stimulation of certain afferent systems to a structure fails to initiate neuronal action potentials but rather only graduated potentials. An example is the response in the hippocampus to electrical stimulation of the olfactory bulb (Yokota, Reeves, & MacLean, 1970). Furthermore, the stimulation of a fiber system may cause the release of substances such as the monoamines, which may act as neuromodulators, affecting neurons in regions far removed from the actual site of stimulation (e.g., Stein & Wise, 1969; Wang & Aghajanian, 1977).

If repetitive activity is applied to the afferent routes, unusual changes can be produced in the structure. In the hippocampus these include sustained shifts in membrane potentials, changes in graduated potentials, and a long-lasting change in cellular responsiveness (Purpura, 1967; Spencer & Kandel, 1968); some changes occurring after repetitive stimulation reflect the well-known post-tetanic potentiation but others are not. Recently, Andersen and his associates have reported a long-lasting change in the hippocampus arising from stimulation of afferent fibers that seem to be caused by an augmentation of transmitter release (e.g., Andersen, Sundberg, Sveen, & Wigström, 1977). Therefore, when a region of the brain is repeatedly stimulated, the projected effect on recipient areas is likely to be quite inconstant, depending on the nature of the stimulation and the history of stimulation given to the region.

IV. Behavioral Consequences of Punctures, Electrode Implantation, and Stimulation

Many apparently minor interventions with the central nervous system can produce substantial behavioral changes. For example, if the brain is punctured with a scalpel blade or insect pin, a memory impairment for a one-trial inhibitory avoidance task can be produced (Bohdanecka, Bohdanecky, & Jarvik, 1967). These authors found that the memory impairment would result if the cortical puncture was given one hour before, at the time of training, or within one hour after training. No impairment was found in animals receiving the brain puncture six hours or later after training. Dorfman, Bohdanecka, Bohdanecky, and Jarvik (1969) found similar results with punctures of the frontal, medial, or temporal cortex when they were made 30 sec following training. Brain punctures in these regions were ineffective one or six hours after training. When the underlying hippocampus was also disturbed by the puncture, the amnesia was extended to one hour. Puncture of the cerebellum had no effect on retention. Puncture wounds in the cortex of the mouse have also been shown to produce amnesia in a one-trial inhibitory task (Glick & Greenstein, 1972). In this study, however, the wound had to be produced in the middle or anterior regions of the brain to produce measurable effects. Damage to the medial or occipital cortex did not produce detectable deficits. These authors also reported evidence on the basis of the effects of punctures of the brain to indicate that different cortical regions were not involved in short- or long-term retention.

However, even though a puncture may be restricted to one relatively small location of the brain, the effects may be quite widespread. Hudspeth (1973) found that the isoelectric neural activity persisted in the neocortex several minutes after puncture wounds, probably initiating a series of waves of spreading depression. Sharp spike-like discharges can also be found after puncture wounds of the neocortex.

The effects of implanting electrodes into the hippocampus can be to disrupt retention of the one-trial inhibitory task (Zornetzer, Boast, & Hamrick, 1974). Electrodes implanted into the CA_1 field produced retention deficits when measured 15 min after training, while electrodes implanted into the dentate gyrus produced deficits in memory for the task when measured 24 hr later. The effects produced by implantation into the dentate gyrus were reported to be dependent upon the presence of ferric ions in the area at the time of histological evaluation. This was interpreted to be a consequence of the breakdown of hemoglobin by Boast, Zornetzer, and Hamrick (1975). Other reports of disruption of learning and/or memory processes by electrode implantation have been made by Denti, McGaugh, Landfield, and Shinkman (1970); Gold, Hankins, Edwards, Chester, and McGaugh (1975); Landfield, Tulsa, and McGaugh (1973); and Zornetzer *et al.* (1974). However, Destrade and Jaffard (1978) failed to find any "electrode effect" from hippocampal placements on a stepthrough avoidance task or when the animals were performing on a continuous reinforcement schedule in an operant task. Such an effect was found, however, in a discrimination-learning task. These authors believe that the deleterious effects of electrode implantation depend on the complexity of the task and the nature of the response required. It must be added that the location of the implantation wound in the brain must interact with both these behavioral factors. The species of the animal undoubtedly influences these interactions.

A remarkable example of a behavioral deficit arising from the implantation of electrodes comes from a study undertaken by Liang, McGaugh, Martinez, Jensen, and Vasquez (1979). A group of control animals had electrodes placed into the amygdala. No currents were passed through the electrodes in some control groups. In the passive avoidance task being used, these implanted control animals showed significantly less retention at 4, 7, and 12 days after the learning experience than unoperated controls. Extremely large deficits were found in the later retention intervals. Animals that had additional lesions made by the passing of radiofrequency current through the wires were even more impaired. However, at the 7- and 12-day retention intervals, the implanted control animals exhibited remarkably impaired performances. Behavioral effects of the implantation of electrodes have been found in various brain regions. These include the brain stem reticular formation (Denti *et al.*, 1970), the hippocampus (Landfield *et al.*, 1973), and the caudate (Gold, 1970).

If the implantation of electrode-like wires produces lesion effects, progressive changes ought to occur during the postoperative interval, just as is found with intentional lesions of various brain areas. Boast (1976) found such a result. Twisted wire electrodes were placed into the dentate gyrus of the dorsal hippocampus in Swiss/ICR mice. Animals tested in a step-through passive avoidance situation 10 days after the implantation exhibited impaired retention; those tested 60 days after implantation were not.[1]

The stimulation of any neural area must produce its behavioral effects by influences exerted at remote sites, but the problem is how to determine which of the distant locations or systems is producing any given behavioral effect. Indeed, it is likely that stimulation of a fiber bundle of different frequencies and/or intensities could act to produce different effects at different branches of the same axonal system and different

[1]Boast also found that within limits the amount of vascular damage inferred from degree of ferric ion-staining present at sacrifice was relatively independent of electrode wire diameter. This was thought to reflect a probabilistic nature of hitting blood vessels with electrodes of any diameter and the all-or-none reaction if a blood vessel is broken by the wire.

behavioral changes. The remarkable fact that different collateral branches can be selectively activated by stimulation of the same site at different frequencies has been shown.

Furthermore, electrical stimulation can induce morphologic and biochemical changes at axon terminals. For example, electrical stimulation of the ascending catecholamine systems can produce changes both in fluorescence (indicative of the catecholamines) and in the ultrastructure of the catecholamine-containing nerve terminals (Arbuthnott, Crow, Fuxe, Olson, & Ungerstedt, 1970; Koda, Wise, & Bloom, 1978). Even though these studies were undertaken with the animals pharmacologically treated so as to reduce the synthesis of cathecholamines, related changes probably occur in untreated animals. Therefore, it is likely that electrical stimulation may induce changes that are other than transitory and that may modify a large number of neurons. Again, these could be thought of as alterations in neuromodulatory neuronal systems. The observation that brain stimulation may induce very widespread changes in the brain and central nervous system may have special importance for induced changes in behaviors related to learning and memory.

The operation of complex cellular aggregations during the waking state when organized behaviors are being expressed is poorly understood, although in the waking state there is little correlation between the times of discharge of nearby cells (Noda & Adey, 1970; Webb, 1977). During periods of artificially induced or natural quiet sleep there is a correlation among the discharges among cells in isolated neocortical slabs. Burns and Webb (1979) have proposed that the synchronous discharge of nearby cells derives from complex pathways of self re-excitation between them. In the alert animal subcortical areas are thought to act to inhibit certain cells in these re-excitation loops within the neocortex. In essence, the recirculating impulses are broken up by the arrival of impulses from lower regions. Using a cellular conditioning paradigm in Flaxedil-treated cats, O'Brien, Packham, and Brunhoelz (1973) reported that the conditioning of the animal resulted in changes in the background spike discharge activity of cells in the postcruciate gyrus based on the interspike internal analysis. Similar results were found in the amygdala by Ben-Ari and Le Gal La Salle (1972).

This indicates that during learning, subcortical influences go beyond the mere interruption of mutually exciting circuits but impose new rhythms of cellular discharges over wide areas of the brain. Indeed, it is the diffuse "background" changes that are the strongest correlates of the learning process. If these changes are the critical ones for such processes, the effect of electrical stimulation of many regions may be to induce different rhythms, new patterns of activity, and patterns inappropriate to the performance of certain behavioral or mental acts. The changes may represent deviations from an optimal state for memory processing as proposed by Gold, Zornetzer, and McGaugh (1974).

It is possible that the behavioral effects of brain stimulation related to learning and memory are produced by general alterations in "background" activities in widespread areas of the brain. Apparent differences in the effects of stimulation applied to different areas could be the consequence of the ability of the area, when stimulated, to influence large areas of the forebrain, either because of the far-reaching connections of activated cells in stimulated regions or because the stimulation excites fibers near the stimulated region that reaches to widespread regions. The view would be in accord with a similar suggestion of McGaugh and Gold (1976) in their review of the effects of electrical brain stimulation on learning. Areas that would be most effective in disrupting learning or memory processes should be those with greatest access to diffusely activating systems, including the limbic regions, part of whose fibers converge on diencephalic arousal systems, and the brain reticular formation. McGaugh and Gold point out that regions from which memory-modifying results have been most often obtained include the reticular formation, the amygdala, the hippocampus, and the caudate–substantia nigra system. Zornetzer and his associates have demonstrated effects of forebrain projecting norepinephrine systems on retention of learned materials (e.g., Zornetzer, Abraham, & Appleton, 1978). The widespread distribution of catecholamine fibers would make the latter areas prime choices for areas affecting wide regions of the forebrain.

Accounting for the effects of localized electrical brain stimulation effects on the basis of more widespread alterations would also be in line with the fact that a review of the effects of brain lesions on memory processes fails to reveal any strong evidence for the restricted localization of any general memory function (Isaacson, 1976). Coupled with the effectiveness of agents that are known to influence vast areas of the brain (e.g., ECS, inhibition of protein synthesis) in the disruption of memory processes, the case for diffuse storage of memories seems to be strengthened.

V. Summary

Both lesions and electrical stimulation of the brain represent interventions with the normal operation of the brain, and in most cases of forebrain stimulation, the behavioral effects are largely due to secondary reactions occurring at some distance from the intervention site. The observed consequences of both lesions and stimulation follow a complicated time course and depend on a variety of factors, including genetic and historical influences. Therefore, it is impossible to define with certainty the behavioral consequences of either procedure across animals of different constitutional makeup or under different conditions of testing. The effects of electrical stimulation procedures are perhaps more complicated than those of lesion procedures since the implantation procedures and reactions to the materials inserted in the brain are also progressive with time and interact with the electrical stimulation applied through them. In many cases, the electrode implantation alone produces extensive behavioral changes so that the stimulation effects must be seen as a further manipulation of an animal already evidencing lesion-induced changing.

It is unlikely that any electrical stimulation of the brain can produce effects that approach a physiological condition. The stimulation induces a massive onslaught onto cellular and fiber systems that changes over repeated administrations and disrupts the "natural" activities in cells in limited or even widespread regions of the brain. It is likely that stimulation procedures and locations that produce widespread effects in the forebrain are ones that also will produce the effects on the expression of learning and memory processes.

Acknowledgment

Preparation of this chapter was supported in part by NSF Grant BNS-7821682 to Robert L. Isaacson.

References

Anand, B. K., & Brobeck, J. R. Hypothalamic control of food intake in rats and cats. *Yale Journal of Biology and Medicine*, 1951, **24,** 123–140.

Andersen, P., Sundberg, S. H., Sveen, O., & Wigström, H. Specific long-lasting potentiation of synaptic transmission in hippocampal slices. *Nature (London)*, 1977, **266,** 736–737.

Arbuthnott, G. W., Crow, T. J., Fuxe, K., Olson, L., & Ungerstedt, U. Depletion of catecholamines in vivo induced by electrical stimulation of central monoamine pathways. *Brain Research*, 1970, **24,** 471–483.

Ben-Ari, Y., & Le Gal La Salle, G. Plasticity at unitary level. II. Modifications during sensory-sensory association procedures. *Electroencephalography and Clinical Neuarophysiology*, 1972, **32,** 677–679.

Bernstein, J. J., Johnson, P. F., Hench, L. L., Hunter, G., & Dawson, W. W. Cortical histopathology following stimulation with metallic and carbon electrodes. *Brain Behavior and Evolution*, 1977, **14,** 126–157.

Bignami, A. Our present knowledge of the pathology of the dementias. In D. Williams (Ed.), *Modern trends in neurology* (Ser. 6). London: Butterworth, 1975. Pp. 1–16.

Bignami, A., & Dahl, D. The astroglial response to stabbing. Immunofluorescence studies with antibodies to astrocyte-specific protein (GFA) in mammalian and sammalian vertebrates. *Neuropathology and Applied Neurobiology*, 1976, **2,** 99–110.

Boast, C. A. *Neuroanatomical localization of memory disruptive states within the mouse hippocampus*. Unpublished doctoral dissertation, University of Florida, 1976.

Boast, C. A., Zornetzer, S. F., & Hamrick, M. R. Electrolytic lesions of various hippocampal subfields in the mouse: Differential effects on short and long term memory. *Behavioral Biology*, 1975, **14,** 85–94.

Bohdanecka, M., Bohdanecky, Z., & Jarvik, M. E. Amnesic effects of small bilateral brain puncture in the mouse. *Science*, 1967, **157,** 334–336.

Burns, B. D., & Webb, A. C. The correlation between discharge times of neighbouring neurons in isolated cerebral cortex. *Proceedings of the Royal Society of London, Series B*, 1979, **203,** 347–360.

Castro, A. J. The effects of cortical ablations on digital usage in the rat. *Brain Research*, 1972, **37,** 173–185.

Collins, J. C., & Mannelidis, E. E. Histopathological changes produced by implanted electrodes in cat brains. Comparison with histopathological changes in human and experimental puncture wounds. *Journal of Neurosurgery*, 1957, **14,** 302–328.

Delgado, J. M. R. Chronic implantation of intracerebral electrodes in animals. In D. Sheer (Ed.), *Electrical stimulation of the brain*. Austin: University of Texas Press, 1961.

Denti, A., McGaugh, J. L., Landfield, P. W., & Shinkman, P. G. Effects of post-trial electrical stimulation of the mesencephalic reticular formation on avoidance learning in rats. *Physiology and Behavior*, 1970, **5,** 659–662.

Destrade, C., & Jaffard, R. Post-trial hippocampal and lateral hypothalamic stimulation. Facilitation of appetitive and avoidance learning tasks. *Behavioral Biology*, 1978, **22,** 354–374.

Donovick, P. J., Burright, R. G., & Bengelloun, W. A. The septal region and behavior: An example of the importance of genetic and experiential factors in determining effects of brain damage. *Neuroscience and Biobehavioral Reviews*, 1979, **3,** 83–96.

Donovick, P. J., Burright, R. G., & Bentsen, E. O. Presurgical dietary history differentially alters the behavior of control and septal lesioned rats. *Developmental Psychobiology*, 1975, **8,** 13–25. (a)

Donovick, P. J., Burright, R. G., Fuller, J. L., & Branson, P. R. Septal lesions and behavior: Effects of presurgical rearing and strain of mouse. *Journal of Comparative and Physiological Psychology*, 1975, **89,** 859–867. (b)

Donovick, P. J., Burright, R. G., & Swidler, M. A. Presurgical rearing environment alters exploration, fluid consumption, and learning of septal lesioned and control rats. *Physiology and Behavior*, 1973, **11,** 543–553.

Dorfman, L. J., Bohdanecka, M., Bohdanecky, Z., & Jarvik, M. E. Retrograde amnesia produced by small cortical stab wounds in the mouse. *Journal of Comparative and Physiological Psychology*, 1969, **69,** 324–328.

Doty, R. W. Electrical stimulation of the brain in behavioral context. *Annual Review of Psychology*, 1969, **20,** 289–320.

Glick, S. D., & Greenstein, S. Amnesia following cortical brain damage in mice. *Behavioral Biology*, 1972, **7,** 573–583.

Goddard, G. V. Amygdaloid stimulation and learning in rats. *Journal of Comparative and Physiological Psychology*, 1964, **58,** 23–30.

Gold, P. E. *Localization of a memory system for passive avoidance learning*. Unpublished doctoral dissertation, University of North Carolina, 1970. Cited in Gold, Zornetzer, & McGaugh (1974).

Gold, P. E., Hankins, L., Edwards, R. M., Chester, J., & McGaugh, J. L. Memory interference and facilitation with post-trial amygdala stimulation. *Brain Research,* 1975, **86,** 509–513.

Gold, P. E. *Localization of a memory system for passive avoidance learning.* Unpublished doctoral dissertation, University of North Carolina, 1970.

Handwerker, M. J., Gold, P. E., & McGaugh, J. L. Impairment of active avoidance learning with posttraining amygdala stimulation. *Brain Research,* 1974, **75,** 324–327.

Hess, W. R. *Das Zwischenkirn: Syndrome, Lokalisationen, Funktionen.* Basel, Switzerland: Schwabe, 1949.

Hudspeth, W. J. Brain damage and retrograde amnesia on electrographic control. *Behavioral Biology,* 1973, **8,** 131–135.

Imamoto, K., & Leblond, C. P. Presence of labeled monocytes, macrophages, and microglia in a stab wound of the brain following an injection of bone marrow cells labeled with ^{3}H-uridine into rats. *Journal of Comparative Neurology,* 1977, **174,** 255–280.

Isaacson, R. L. Experimental brain lesions and memory. In M. R. Rosenzweig & E. L. Bennett (Eds.), *Neural mechanisms of learning and memory.* Cambridge, MA: MIT Press, 1976. Pp. 521–543.

Johnson, P. F., Bernstein, J. J., Hunter, G., & Dawson, W. W., & Hench, L. L. An *in vitro* and *in vivo* analysis of anodized tantalum capacitive electrodes: Corrosion response, physiology, and histology. *Journal of Biomedical Material Research,* 1977, **11,** 637–656.

Kandel, E. R., & Spencer, W. A. Electrophysiology of hippocampal neurons. II. After-potentials and repetitive firing. *Journal of Neurophysiology,* 1961, **24,** 243–259.

Koda, L. Y., Wise, R. A., & Bloom, F. E. Light and electron microscopic changes in the rat dentate gyrus after lesions or stimulation of the ascending coeruleus pathway. *Brain Research,* 1978, **144,** 363–368.

Landfield, P. W., Tusa, R., & McGaugh, J. L. Effects of post-trial hippocampal stimulation on memory storage and EEG activity. *Behavioral Biology,* 1973, **8,** 485–505.

Liang, K. C., McGaugh, J. L., Martinez, J. L., Jr., Jensen, R. A., & Vasquez, B. J. Time dependent effect of posttrial amygdaloid lesions on retention of an inhibitory avoidance response. *Neuroscience Abstracts,* 1979, **5,** 1051.

Lilly, J. C. Injury and excitation by electrical currents. Part A. In D. Sheer (Ed.), *Electrical stimulation of the brain.* Austin: University of Texas Press, 1961.

Livesey, P. J., & Bayliss, J. The effect of electrical (blocking) stimulation to the dentate of the rat on learning of a simultaneous brightness discrimination and reversal. *Neuropsychologia,* 1975, **13,** 395–407.

Livesey, P. J., & Meyer, P. Functional differentiation in the dorsal hippocampus with local electrical stimulation during learning by rats. *Neuropsychologia,* 1975, **13,** 431–438.

Livesey, P. J., & Wearne, G. The effects of electrical (blocking) stimulation to the dorsal hippocampus of the rat on learning of a simultaneous brightness discrimination. *Neuropsychologia,* 1973, **11,** 75–84.

MacIntyre, W. J., Bidder, T. G., & Rowland, V. The production of brain lesions with electric currents. In *Proceedings of the First National Biophysics Conference, Columbus, Ohio.* New Haven, CT: Yale University Press, 1957.

McGaugh, J. L., & Gold, P. E. Modulation of memory by electrical stimulation of the brain. In M. R. Rosenzweig & E. L. Bennett (Eds.), *Neural mechanisms of learning and memory.* Cambridge, MA: MIT Press, 1976. Pp. 549–560.

Miller, N. E. Some motivational effects of brain stimulation and drugs. *Federation Pro-*

ceedings, Federation of American Societies for Experimental Biology, 1960, **19,** 846–854.

Noda, H., & Adey, W. R. Firing of neuron pairs in cat association cortex during sleep and wakefulness. *Journal of Neurophysiology,* 1970, **33,** 672–674.

O'Brien, J. H., Packham, S. C., & Brunnhoelzl, W. W. Features of spike train related to learning. *Journal of Neurophysiology,* 1973, **26,** 1051–1061.

Penfield, W., & Perot, P. The brain's record of auditory and visual experience—A final summary and discussion. *Brain,* 1963, **86,** 595–696.

Purpura, D. P. Comparative study of dendrites. In G. C. Quarton, T. Melnechuck, & F. O. Schmitt (Eds.) *The neurosciences: A study program.* New York: Rockefeller University Press, 1967. Pp. 372–392.

Ramón y Cajál, S. *Degeneration and regeneration of the nervous system.* London & New York: Oxford University Press, 1928.

Ranck, J. B., Jr. Which elements are excited in electrical stimulation of mammalian central nervous system: A review. *Brain Research,* 1975, **98,** 417–440.

Robinson, R. G., & Bloom, F. E. Changes in posterior hypothalamic self-stimulation following experimental cerebral infarction in the rat. *Journal of Comparative and Physiological Psychology,* 1978, **92,** 969–976.

Robinson, R. G., & Coyle, J. T. Lateralization of catecholaminergic and behavioral response to cerebral infarction in the rat. *Life Sciences,* 1979, **24,** 943–950.

Spencer, W. A., & Kandel, E. R. Cellular and integrative properties of hippocampal pyramidal cell and the comparative electrophysiology of cortical neurons. *International Journal of Neurology,* 1968, **3–4,** 267–296.

Stamm, J. S. Electrical stimulation of monkeys' prefrontal cortex during delayed-response performance. *Journal of Comparative and Physiological Psychology,* 1969, **67,** 535–546.

Stein, L., & Wise, C. D. Release of nonrepinephrine from hypothalamus and amygdala by rewarding medial forebrain bundle stimulation and amphetamine. *Journal of Comparative and Physiological Psychology,* 1969, **67,** 189–198.

Valenstein, E. S. The anatomical locus of reinforcement. In E. Stellar and J. Spague (Eds.) *Progress in Physiological Psychology, Vol. 1.* New York: Academic Press, 1966. Pp. 149–190.

Wang, R. Y., & Aghajanian, G. K. Inhibition of neurons in the amygdala dorsal raphe stimulation: Mediation through a direct serotonergic pathway. *Brain Research,* 1977, **120,** 85–102.

Webb, A. C. Can one detect the presence of orientation columns in the visual cortex of the conscious, mobile cat? *Proceedings of the International Union of Physiological Sciences,* 1977, **13,** 803.

Weiskrantz, L., Mihailović, L., & Gross, C. G. Stimulation of frontal cortex and delayed alternation performance in the monkey. *Science,* 1960, **131,** 1443–1444.

Yokota, T., Reeves, A. G., & MacLean, P. D. Differential effects of septal and olfactory volleys on intracellular responses of hippocampal neurons in awake, sitting monkeys. *Journal of Neurophysiology,* 1970, **33,** 96–107.

Zornetzer, S. F., Abraham, W. C., & Appleton, R. Locus coeruleus and labile memory. *Pharmacology, Biochemistry and Behavior,* 1978, **9,** 227–234.

Zornetzer, S. F., Boast, C. A., & Hamrick, M. E. Neuroanatomical localization and memory processing in mice: The role of the dentate gyrus of the hippocampus. *Physiology and Behavior,* 1974, **13,** 569–575.

Chapter 9

Electroconvulsive Therapy—Who Needs It?*

Duane Denney

Department of Psychiatry
School of Medicine
University of Oregon Health Sciences Center
Portland, Oregon

I. Introduction

All medical and surgical treatments produce combinations of beneficial effects and adverse consequences. Electroconvulsive therapy (ECT) is

*This chapter is dedicated to Paul Hubbard Blachly, a trusted friend and valued colleague, who died in a boating accident in 1977. Many of my ideas and views about ECT have come from innumerable discussions, arguments, agreements, and collaborative research efforts spanning nearly 20 years of close association. His contributions to psychiatry and medicine have been unquestionable, and he is greatly missed.

ISBN 0-12-547440-7

no exception. Provoking a seizure in the human brain, even for a therapeutic purpose, raises some particularly difficult issues for both patients and physicians. Certain dimensions of their dilemma are illustrated by the following two accounts which are fictitious, but typical of events that may occur in clinical practice.

Dear Dr. D—:

I am enclosing the questionnaire that you asked me to fill out with regard to my electric shock treatments last October. Everything has been going well for Bill and me, and a lot of the problems that seemed so serious a year ago are either gone or at least under control now. You can't believe how close I came to "ending it all!"

Your questionnaire made quite a point of asking about memory loss. Actually, I remember practically everything up to about the fourth or fifth treatment, but things are a little fuzzy after that. Since I'm not depressed any more, I feel sharper about little things than I was before.

My friends and relatives all look like they're going to faint every time I mention the word "psychiatrist" or the fact that I've had shock treatment. They seem to expect me to be some sort of zombie. I guess they've all seen "One Flew Over the Cuckoo's Nest."

Thanks for everything. Dr. Smith said he will follow your suggestions about what to do if I have any more trouble, but so far everything looks just great.

Sincerely yours,
Anna M.

Enclosed herewith is an excerpt from a complaint served upon Dr. D. ________ in a case filed in the Circuit Court of the State of ________ for ________ County.

Plaintiff alleges (1) that defendant failed to obtain informed consent for application of electric shock treatments and failed to warn plaintiff against the severe complications ensuant from shock therapy; (2) that defendant negligently and in a cruel and brutal fashion placed electrical contacts on the plaintiff's temples and allowed the passage of potentially lethal amounts of electric current through plaintiff's brain, which led to an epileptic convulsion; (3) that upon awakening from said convulsion, the intellectual processes of plaintiff's mind were severely and permanently damaged; (4) that on five subsequent occasions, defendant negligently forced plaintiff to undergo additional shock treatments, which produced permanent brain damage and loss of memory; (5) that as a direct and proximate result of said negligence only fragments of plaintiff's memory have returned such that plaintiff is unable to function in his profession as mechanical engineer; and (6) because of the direct and proximate result of said negligent conduct by the defendant, plaintiff suffered special damage in the sum of $55,750 and general damages in the sum of $1,500,000.

Physical treatments in psychiatry, neurology, and neurosurgery carry with them implications that go beyond those associated with surgical and medical alterations of other organ systems. The brain is the organ of our uniqueness, or our perception of ourselves as individuals and as members of families, societies, and nations. Deliberately inducing a change of the organ system that not only sustains life, but also makes life meaningful, is quite a different level of biological manipulation to most of us than altering the structure of the heart or its valves, or crippling a patient's immune system to treat a disorder such as lupus erythematosus.

On the other hand, psychiatric disorders are a major source of mortality and morbidity. Suicide is the second highest cause of death in adolescents. Among depressed patients, 15% will ultimately die by their own hand (Avery & Winokur, 1978). Despite major shifts away from hospital treatment, the single diagnostic entity, schizophrenia, still accounts for nearly 25% of *all* hospital bed occupancy in the United States. Perhaps these statistics motivate the continuing search for new ways to help the mentally ill and to improve upon some of the old ones.

I have elected to explore some of the issues relating to the use of ECT not only from a clinician's viewpoint, but also against the background of these cultural and historical facts.

II. A Brief History of Electroconvulsive Therapy (ECT)

Electrical stimulation to the head for treatment of nervous and mental diseases is a very old idea. In 45 A.D., Scribonius Largus treated the Roman Emperor's headaches with the discharge of electric eels. The results of the treatment were not mentioned (F. G. Alexander & Selesnick, 1966, p. 282).

With increasing understanding of electricity and development of techniques to generate current, in 1755 sufficient energy was produced to provoke a convulsion in a human subject (Harmes, 1955). By the latter part of the nineteenth century, electrical therapy for various maladies passed in and out of favor on the basis of increasing knowledge both of the nature of electricity and of the neurobiology of the central nervous system.

According to Sargant and Slater (1963), Weikhardt in 1798 was the first to provoke seizures for therapeutic purposes by injecting camphor intramuscularly in human psychiatric patients. This treatment was reintroduced by Meduna in 1933 because of his observation that schizophrenic patients frequently became less psychotic after spontaneous seizures. Throughout the 1930s other drugs less noxious and unpleasant for the patient were introduced with the same purpose in mind. These included metrazol, picrotoxin (Sargant & Slater, 1963), and most recently, flurothyl (Indoklon) (Esquibel, Krantz, Truitt, Ling, & Kurland, 1958).

Faced with the continuing devastating toll of severe psychiatric disturbance, other means of provoking convulsions were sought. Cerletti and Bini are credited with the first modern clinical application of electroconvulsive therapy (Sargant & Slater, 1963). In a description of the early days of ECT, Cerletti (1950) described the animal research that preceded the first convulsive treatment, as well as some of his personal apprehensions associated with applying the results of animal research to the first human subject.

From 1938 on, ECT became the predominant form of convulsive therapy. It rapidly came to be used indiscriminately in hospitalized psychiatric patients in both Europe and the United States, often with little attention to diagnosis. It was undoubtedly used to subjugate and flatten the affective and motor behavior of disturbed and difficult psychiatric patients (Sargant & Slater, 1963).

Although it is easy to fault psychiatric physicians for this period in medical history, it is important to look at the cultural context in which they worked. Prior to convulsive therapy, no treatment methods had been effective in any psychiatric disorder. Although there were several periods in medical history when humane treatment of individuals was encouraged in mental hospitals, jails, and orphanages, most psychiatric patients lived in deplorable conditions in the early part of this century. Since ECT permitted many patients to escape from such environments, it is not surprising that convulsive therapy was acceptable to patients and physicians alike.

The discovery of the antipsychotic effects of chlorpromazine in the 1950s marked the beginning of a revolutionary change in physicians' attitudes toward psychiatric diagnosis and prognosis. With alternative treatment possibilities available, precise clinical description becomes necessary in order to relate specific therapeutic modalities to specific kinds of pathological behavior. We appear to be entering a new phase of "moral" treatment in psychiatry. Earlier such revolutions stemmed primarily from humanitarian concerns. The new revolution is motivated also by the assumption that treatment modalities are pointers toward an understanding of alterations in brain function that account for abnormal human behavior.

For a variety of reasons, recent use of convulsive treatment shows a marked decline (Asnis, Fink & Saferstein, 1978; Frankel, 1973; Hedlund, Barton, Evenson, Cho, & Hickman, 1978), and ECT in some localities has almost disappeared as a treatment modality. Last year in our own hospital, with 60 inpatient hospital beds and approximately 700 patient admissions, ECT was used only 20 times in seven patients. There are many who feel that ECT is falling from favor for the wrong reasons. To paraphrase the late Paul H. Blachly, ECT started with the wrong disease (schizophrenia) for the wrong reason (presumed antagonism of epilepsy and schizophrenia) and now scarcely can be used for the right disease (depression) for the right reason (it works), a reference to the fact that much of the decrease in ECT is related to cultural, social, and political interference with various aspects of psychiatric practice.

III. Does ECT Work?

Table I lists the variables that need to be controlled to answer the disarmingly simple question, "Does ECT work?" In the succeeding discussion, it will be clear that an ideal efficacy study has not been done.

Most research efforts to evaluate the effectiveness of convulsive therapy can be divided into studies of ECT versus sham ECT or ECT compared to alternate forms of treatment. Evaluation methods include scores

TABLE I

Factors to be Controlled in an Efficacy Study

1. Age, sex, race, socioeconomic class, and "premorbid" level of psychosocial functioning.
2. Psychiatric diagnosis including presence or absence of other medical conditions and whether patient is voluntarily or involuntarily hospitalized.
3. Method of inducing seizures including techniques and instrumentation.
4. Timing, number, duration, and other electrical characteristics of seizures.
5. Assessment measures, including indices of the "therapeutic" as well as the "adverse" effects. Were they assessed blindly?
6. Duration of the follow-up period.
7. "Atmosphere" in which treatment occurs (attitudes and expectations of patient, family, hospital staff, and in the patient's posthospital social network).
8. Medical and psychological therapy during and following treatment including treatment received for concurrent conditions by other physicians.
9. ECT therapist's attitudes and expectations.
10. Patient's pre- and post-treatment self-assessments (of both positive and adverse effects).

on standardized interviews and psychological tests, admission rates, readmission rates of previously treated patients, clinicians' judgments often based on blind assessment, patients' self-assessments, measurement of acute and long-term biochemical and electrophysiological changes, and epidemiological surveys to determine whether treatment has resulted in measurable change in morbidity and mortality.

Barton (1977) reviewed six reports that conformed to his predetermined criteria of scientific acceptability, and five of these represent examples of an ECT versus sham ECT design. A review of the summary data (Barton, 1977, Table I) illustrates the complexity of cross-study comparisons. At the same time, exactly because of these variations in design, the consistently better outcome for 105 treated patients with severe depression versus control groups of 103 with sham shock only is very impressive indeed. In the tenor of the times, sham-shock control groups are probably no longer possible, making these data of particular significance.

Sham-shock comparisons in evaluation of the treatment of schizophrenia are more rare. Twenty schizophrenic patients (Ulett, Smith, & Gleser, 1956) were included in one of the studies reviewed by Barton (1977) and showed improvement similar in degree to that reported for depressed patients when measured by the same criteria. However, an older report failed to show any advantage of ECT over anesthesia alone in catatonic schizophrenics (Miller, Clancy, & Cumming, 1953). These findings are interesting in view of the standard clinical wisdom stating that among the group of schizophrenias, catatonic patients have the best chance of responding to convulsive therapy. Brill, Crumpton, Eiduson, Grayson, Hillman, and Richards (1959) found no differences in sham shock and shock groups one month after treatment. Schizophrenic subtypes were not specified. Approximately 50% of each group showed significant improvement measured with standardized assessment instruments (Brill *et al.*, 1959).

Thus, a brief review of studies with sham-shock controls suggests that ECT is effective in the major depressions. Seizure therapy for schizophrenic patients, including catatonics, must be accepted more cautiously.

There is a much larger literature on the comparative effects of ECT and alternatives such as pharmacological, psychological, and social rehabilitative treatment. Two large studies in the United States (Greenblatt, Grosser, & Wechsler, 1964) and the United Kingdom (Shepherd, 1965) suggest that ECT has significant benefits over pharmacological treatment and placebo. In 250 patients hospitalized for depression in three hospitals in England, subjects were randomly assigned to ECT, imipramine, phenelzine, and placebo treatment groups. Assessment consisted of clinicians' judgments of 15 depressive symptoms scaled for severity and followed over a 6-month period. Raters and patients were initially blind to the type of drug or placebo, but it was impossible to disguise which subjects had received ECT. At the end of 4 weeks, clinicians were free to change treatment modality or to introduce alternative treatment, if necessary, in the placebo group. Physician raters beyond this time were no longer blind. At 4 weeks and at 6 months, both ECT and imipramine were roughly twice as effective as phenelzine and placebo, both in amelioration of symptoms and in permitting hospital discharge. Both ECT and imipramine subsequently improved the majority of placebo and drug nonresponders. ECT showed significant advantages over imipramine in the first 2 months only, and thereafter the treatments were roughly equal in effectiveness.

Greenblatt and his colleagues (1964) studied 281 patients with mixed diagnoses admitted to three Massachusetts hospitals. Multiple assessment measures were used, and most were made blindly and serially over an 8-week treatment period. Again, it was difficult to maintain double-blind conditions for the ECT group. Seventy-six percent of the ECT group showed marked improvement versus approximately 50% of the placebo, imipramine, and phenelzine groups. Isocarboxazid was decidedly less effective than placebo. The incidence of side effects was equal for all groups, including placebo, but the spectrum of side effects was distinctly different for the ECT group.

Both of these studies are widely quoted as proof of the dictum that in endogenous depressive disorders, complete short-term remission of symptoms can be expected in 70 to 90% of patients (Fink, 1974). This is to be compared with a qualitatively similar improvement in 50 to 70% of depressed patients with tricyclic antidepressants, and a placebo and spontaneous remission rate of 30 to 50% (Greenblatt *et al.*, 1964).

Critics of ECT emphasize that with such high spontaneous remission and placebo improvement rates, a much longer time frame is necessary to evaluate therapy.

Avery and Winokur (1976) compared 519 patients with major depressions evaluated retrospectively after three years. Treatment groups included ECT, tricyclic antidepressants in adequate doses, "inadequate" tricyclics, and hospitalization alone ("no ECT/no drug"). They specifically assessed mortality, from both suicide and other causes, and relapse as measured by rehospitalization rates. Both ECT and adequate tricyclics produced a striking decrease in death rates compared to the inadequately treated and no-treatment groups. Two factors are particularly noteworthy. One is the startling lethality of depressive illness. The 3-yr age-adjusted death rate in the under- and non-treated groups was 9–11%, compared to about 2% mortality with treatment. The study also confirmed previous epidemiological findings (Odegaard, 1952) in showing that nonsuicide mortality in depressed patients, especially from heart disease, infection, and malnutrition far exceeds expected population rates. Rehospitalization, a crude measure of 3-yr morbidity, was the same in all groups (5–7%).

In a second analysis of this patient population (Avery & Winokur, 1978), ECT was markedly superior to antidepressant drugs over a 6-month posttreatment period in preventing successful suicide (0% versus 1.5%) and suicide attempts (0.9% versus 4.8%).

Although ECT is effective in mania (Abrams & Taylor, 1976; McCabe & Norris, 1977), the success of lithium salts in both treatment and prophylaxis has decreased the need for it. McCabe and Norris (1977) compared ECT, chlorpromazine, and no-treatment groups in a retrospective study of 84 manic patients hospitalized prior to the availability of lithium salts. As in depression, both treatment modalities were superior to the control group in eliminating active symptoms, shortening hospital stay, and promoting more complete psychosocial recovery. Ten chlorpromazine-treated patients failed to respond to the drug alone but recovered with ECT. There were no treatment failures in the ECT-treated group. Untreated mania was also a highly lethal disorder. Four of 28 patients who received no treatment died, three from exhaustion and one from injuries from physical restraints plus exhaustion.

Comparative studies of ECT and other modalities in schizophrenia are much fewer in number. May, Tuma, Yale, Potepan, and Dixon (1976) followed 228 first-admission schizophrenics with no previous history of treatment. They were randomly assigned to five treatment groups: psychotherapy alone, psychotherapy plus neuroleptics, neuroleptics alone, ECT, and milieu therapy. Interestingly, although a variety of assessment measures were used, those most indicative of overall psychosocial functioning have shown ECT to be better than the other treatment methods and combinations as the study proceeds (now over five years for some patients). This is of particular interest, since conventional clinical wisdom assumes neuroleptics to be the long-term treatment of choice for schizophrenia. In view of the danger of producing tardive dyskinesia with neuroleptic treatment, the decreased rehospitalization rate and number of patient–days in the hospital in the ECT group require reexamination of the popular clinical bias that ECT is useful only for short-term control of flagrant psychotic episodes and catatonia.

Thus, ECT is effective in ameliorating the major signs and symptoms of episodic depressive reactions and mania, and significantly increases survival rates in depression. The usefulness of ECT in schizophrenia is less clear, although a recent prospective study suggests that there are unsuspected long-term benefits, even when short-term improvement cannot always be demonstrated.

IV. Do the Positive Benefits Outweigh the Adverse Effects?

The clinically important factors to be considered in relation to this question by both patient and physician are outlined in Table II. Accepting the evidence that ECT is effective in those conditions in which it is traditionally prescribed, the actual decision to utilize seizure therapy requires serious examination of the short-term and long-term adverse effects.

In the early forties, the use of curare was introduced to modify the intense muscular contractions of the seizures. This eliminated most of the immediate gross morbidity (musculoskeletal injury) and mortality from cardiac arrhythmias (Bernards, 1977). Succinylcholine, an ultra short-acting muscle relaxant, and short-acting barbiturate anesthetics came into widespread use in the late forties and fifties. These two pharmacological modifications are virtually universal parts of ECT technique in this country, and the horror stories about short-term side effects of ECT in its early days are simply no longer applicable (Hurwitz, 1974).

At the same time, the use of a general anesthetic and the requirements

TABLE II

MAJOR EFFECTS OF ECT

	Short Term (1–4 weeks)	Long Term (<5 yr)
Positive	Depression: return to normal function	Measureable decrease in suicide and death rates Measurable decrease in time in hospital
	Schizophrenia: reversal of hallucinations, catatonia, gross affective disturbance	Measurable decrease in time in hospital
Adverse	Confusional states Retrograde amnesia Anterograde amnesia Multiple physical symptoms Increased mortality from anesthesia Social stigma	Usually "patchy" amnesia Potential diffuse brain damage Social stigma

that psychiatrists be familiar with cardiopulmonary support and airway maintenance have introduced some new complications into the field. According to Hurwitz (1974), the majority of the short-term adverse effects are related to complications of anesthesia, particularly prolonged apnea due to pseudocholinesterase deficiency (inability to metabolize succinylcholine), laryngospasm and bronchospasm secondary to barbiturate anesthesia, aspiration, and allergic responses to the pharmacological agents. These all represent increased but generally controllable risks in ECT. The mortality rate of ECT using modern techniques is approximately that of general anesthesia (Blachly, 1968). A host of short-term physical symptoms following one or several seizures are reported by our patients and by others (Greenblatt *et al.*, 1964; Hurwitz, 1974) and include headache, muscle soreness, anorexia and nausea, sore teeth and jaws, apprehension, and malaise. A much more serious and immediate complication is a period of confusion and disorientation that may last from a few minutes to several hours. This is almost invariably remembered by the patient as a very unpleasant experience.

Some patients are embarrassed to admit that they have received electroconvulsive therapy. The sources of this stigma are complex and do not lend themselves to easy analysis or understanding. Clearly, movies and popular novels have painted an unpleasant picture for the patient who is asked by his physician to consider ECT, and positive benefits are rarely discussed in either the popular or the professional nonpsychiatric literature. The psychiatric community itself, responding in part to the same social context and in part to the legitimate question of the ratio of positive and negative effects of the treatment, remains split into two camps. This may further confuse the patient, his family, and nonpsychiatric physicians. This problem is illustrated by the interesting account of D'Agostino (1975), a psychiatrist trained to be generally opposed to ECT, who described the prolonged suffering his father encountered during three hospitalizations for a psychotic depressive reaction. Drug, social, and psychotherapy persistently failed to ameliorate his condition. Finally, a psychiatrist recommended and performed ECT, which promptly relieved all his symptoms.

There is little question that the major adverse effect of induced convulsions in man is related to impairment of memory. All of our patients report retrograde amnesia of varying degrees. For all practical purposes, most patients find this disappears over one to eight weeks. A few patients subjectively report of a persistent defect in memory (Small & Small, 1972) and where symptoms of depression have not been greatly improved or are forgotten, these long-term effects are seen understandably in a very negative light. Varying degrees of anterograde memory loss are also suffered but seem to be less consistently present from patient to patient.

Harper and Wiens (1975) have discussed the methodological problems in evaluation of memory function in human subjects after ECT. Many clinicians and behavioral scientists fail to distinguish defects in learning that are greatly affected by depression, and defects in memory that are produced by ECT. Thus, tests of retrograde amnesia that require a pretreatment learning task will show exaggerated impairment after treatment because of confounding of learning impairments and memory impairments. Anterograde amnesia may be underestimated because of improved posttreatment learning with relief of depression. Recently, techniques for assessment of memory that are free of the requirement for a preliminary learning task have been developed (Brunschwig, Strain, & Bidder, 1971; Squire, Slater, & Chace, 1975). These studies show that long-term memory function is often impaired for several months following a series of ECT treatments. Clinical experience suggests that some patients have a permanent amnesia for certain parts of their past history, a phenomenon that I have termed "patchy" amnesia. This was described by a psychiatrist who suffered from a depressive illness and had ECT (Anonymous, 1965). After the second series of treatments, he lost his ability to image the London subway network, an engram previously easily recalled at will.

Other complex cognitive functions may be affected by ECT. A period of delirium follows immediately after one or several induced or spontaneous seizures. This acute confusional state usually disappears in 1–2 hr. Interestingly, after several hours, a second period of impaired cognition appears. Hargreaves, Fischer, Elashoff, and Blacker (1972) developed a technique that required patients to learn a temporal sequence of alternating level pulls by trial and error. Patients were then tested for retention of the sequence for varying periods of time. Thus, the task required both trial-and-error learning plus short-term memory. At each test session the patient learned a new sequence. Subjects were tested at various times before and after single seizures and for several days after a series of treatments. Impaired performance was maximal 18–24 hr after single seizures. There was no evidence of impairment on this task 10–14 days after the last treatment in a series.

Evidence of long-term cognitive impairment from excessive ECT comes indirectly out of the report of the National Commission for the Protection of Human Subjects of Biomedical and Behavioral Research, a group of experts appointed to examine the medical and ethical issue of psychosurgery and to make recommendations to Congress about any potential federal legislation that might be necessary (Ryan, 1977). The most striking findings of the report related to the virtual absence of measurable intellectual and mnemic impairment from medial cingulotomy. Actual improvement in IQ measures were seen in a number of patients after surgery.

As a by-product of the extensive neuropsychological evaluations done preoperatively, patients who had been previously treated with ECT could be compared with normal controls and with patients who had little or no convulsive therapy. The ECT-treated group (patients with a history of 50 or more convulsive treatments) showed marked deficits in verbal and nonverbal fluency, delayed alternation, tactual maze learning, continuous recognition of verbal material, delayed recall of complex drawings, recognition of faces and houses, and identification of famous public figures. On tests of recent and remote verbal and nonverbal memory, the ECT group were severely impaired compared to the controls and to those with fewer than 50 seizures. It should be emphasized that these patients were severely incapacitated and had been specifically selected because they were refractory to almost every therapy available. Also, many patients had received ECT prior to the use of paralysis and ventilation during seizures. Nevertheless, it is likely that ECT, especially when used repeatedly, produced impaired cognition, and by implication, diffuse cerebral damage in some individuals.

A number of modifications in ECT technique appear to have some bearing on the issue of memory impairment. The introduction of paralysants into ECT procedure marked a significant gain by ensuring that adequate ventilation could be maintained throughout the seizure. Despite a sixfold increase in brain oxygen consumption, blood hyperoxygenation is the rule during and after a seizure when the patient is ventilated with oxygen (Posner, Plum, & van Posnak, 1969). Similarly, with intravenous glucose solution running, hypoglycemia is never present, even during prolonged seizures. This, of course, cannot guarantee that cellular hypoxia and defects in cellular glycolysis may not be present.

Another major technical advance has been the design of stimulus generators that provoke seizures with less power. It is curious that psychiatrists have paid so little attention to the design of instrumentation. This comes partly out of the historical development of convulsive therapy, which implied that the method of provoking a seizure was not critical. Any kind of device that would generate enough current was therefore justifiable. Obviously, very excessive current density, whether it produces a seizure or not, damages nervous tissue (Agnew, Yuen, Pudenz, & Bullara, 1975; L. Alexander & Löwenbach, 1944; Hartelius, 1952). It is equally clear that not all memory effects are secondary to current flow. Seizures induced with flurothyl produce memory effects that do not differ markedly from those seen after ECT with respect to effects on memory (Small & Small, 1972). Nevertheless, common sense demands that seizures be provoked with as little direct application of power to the scalp as possible.

Weaver, Ives, Williams, and Nies (1977) studied clinical response and cognitive function in a group of 20 depressed patients. Half were stimulated with a conventional alternating-current, constant voltage commercial machine (Medcraft B-24) and half with an instrument of their own design that delivered energy in the form of 150 alternating-polarity square pulses. Each pulse was 1 msec in duration with a 10-msec interpulse interval. At 190 V and 550 mA, the total energy delivered was 14.85 J. Stimulus energy from the conventional instrument was about 29 J. There were no significant differences between the two groups on any outcome measure.

A recent review of the characteristics of stimulators was completed by the Utah Biomedical Test Laboratory (Grahn, Gehrich, Convillon, & Moench, 1977). This report emphasized the very broad range of maximal energies available from clinically available devices and the general lack of engineering sophistication that has been devoted to their development. The report ends with the conclusion that a pulse-type generator generally will induce seizures with 25% as much energy as the more commonly used 60-cycle alternating-current generators. According to a survey carried out by the test laboratory, this would in fact eliminate some 90% of the generators currently used in the United States. This group has also published a list of minimal electrical engineering requirements and a set of standards that should be applied to any kind of research directed toward evaluation of the relation between stimulus parameters and outcome variables.

At a different level of abstraction, it is clear that improvement in psychiatric diagnosis will lead to a better fit of available treatment modalities to patients. The considerably greater efficacy of ECT in depressive disorders than in other psychoses can only be expected to improve the effectiveness of ECT by eliminating from therapeutic consideration other patients who do not have such a favorable prognosis.

Lastly, it appears that clinical practice will require more careful physiological monitoring during convulsions, in the interest of early detection of cardiac arrhythmias or failure of a stimulator to provoke a seizure. Prolonged convulsions, which may be obscured by muscular paralysis, can be detected and terminated with reasonable ease by pharmacological means. Most authorities agree that a seizure of very prolonged duration may produce brain damage (Meldrum, Papy, Toure, & Brierly, 1975).

Monitoring has been critical in developing the method of inducing several seizures at brief intervals in anesthetized patients (Blachly & Gowing, 1966). Using this technique, termed "multiple-monitored ECT" (MMECT), patients may have three to five serial convulsions at 5-min intervals and in some cases require no subsequent therapy. More frequently, a second and third series at approximately 4-day intervals are required. Skilled anesthesia support is necessary, but the decrease in hospitalization time and need for multiple successive anesthetic inductions have been appreciated by both our patients and medical staff. The efficacy of this method is still under evaluation and is felt by some to be less than with conventional ECT (Abrams & Fink, 1972). A recent report by Maletzky (1978) suggests that significant antidepressive effects require a minimum of 400–700 sec of seizure time during the course of treatments. Such measurements are nearly impossible to make in a paralyzed patient without EEG or EMG monitoring. Even with incomplete paralysis, gross motor movement stops well before evidence of seizure termination by EEG criteria (Blachly & Gowing, 1966).

Another major innovation in ECT has developed out of studies of the laterality of human brain function. Verbal and symbolic memory is more vulnerable to dominant hemisphere impairment whereas spatial and nonverbal memory is primarily medicated by left-hemisphere activities in most patients. Provoking generalized seizures by primary stimulation of the scalp over the nondominant hemisphere was introduced late in the sixties, and subsequent research consistently has shown that verbal memory is significantly less affected by unilateral electrode placement than with bitemporal stimulation (Squire & Slater, 1978). Universal acceptance of unilateral nondominant stimulation has been slower than expected because of the largely unproven suspicion that unilateral stimulation was less effective. Differences in efficacy are negligible if stimulus intensity is sufficient to produce a generalized seizure by unilateral stimulation (d'Elia, 1974, Table I, p. 23). The recent report by Squire and Slater (1978) demonstrated convincingly that bilateral stimulation produced more dysfunctions of the dominant hemisphere than seizures produced by actual dominant hemisphere stimulation.

Thus, there is every reason to believe that improvement in clinical diagnosis, apparatus design, anesthesia procedures, and introduction of monitoring and unilateral stimulation will make ECT more effective, less aversive, and less destructive to memory. This in no way detracts from the possibility that electrical stimulation leading to a convulsion may lead to permanent memory losses and perhaps some decrease in certain cognitive skills in some patients.

Then how do we answer the question posed earlier: "Does ECT

work?" Clearly, there *is* no one answer, and at this time in history we can expect the controversies and the ethical dilemmas to remain.

V. The Heuristic Contributions of ECT Research

There is a popular misconception that treatment methods develop in medicine as the result of a logical sequence of events. A disorder is first clinically described, and biochemical, anatomical, and physiological mechanisms are clarified. This leads to a specific treatment or a means of prevention, or both. None of the treatment methods in psychiatry can claim such a history. ECT developed because psychiatrists thought schizophrenia and epilepsy were incompatible, and electrical stimulation was an efficient way to induce artificial epilepsy. Lithium was empirically tried in manic patients when it was found to have sedating effects in guinea pigs. Isoniazid produced euphoria in patients with tuberculosis because in addition to its bacteriostatic effects, it was a mild monoamine oxidase inhibitor. Tricyclics developed out of an unsuccessful attempt to produce an improved antipsychotic neuroleptic.

Lithium, neuroleptics, and antidepressant drugs have had enormous influence in psychiatric research. When a specific drug effect can be correlated with a clinical change, a mechanism in a disease process may have been identified. The "dopamine hypothesis" of schizophrenia developed from the observation that all active neuroleptics block dopamine receptors in the nervous system. The "catecholamine hypothesis" of depression grew out of the fact that both monoamine oxidase inhibitors and tricyclics affect the metabolism of dopamine, norepinephrine, and serotonin in various ways.

Only in the very broadest sense can ECT be said to have influenced and expanded our knowledge of the biology of major psychiatric disorders. Seizures have been widely utilized in animals to study memory mechanisms (McGaugh, 1974), but it appears unlikely that the antidepressant effects of ECT are directly linked to the amnesic properties of convulsions. In the first place, the degree of retrograde amnesia produced by ECT is far less predictable among patients than the antidepressant effect. Furthermore, there is little evidence that modified ECT with adequate ventilation produces more or less of an antidepressant effect than older techniques in which hypoxia and attendant amnesia were much more prominent. The most definitive study relating to this question was done by Cronholm and Ottosson (1960). They compared matched groups of patients treated with ECT. Half of the patients had induction of a seizure, followed by immediate termination of the convulsion with lidocaine. There were negligible differences in the amnesic effects in the two groups, but the therapeutic efficacy in patients whose seizures were allowed to run their course was much greater.

In a very large population of patients admitted to northern England hospitals, Roth, Kay, and Kiloh (1966) found that "atypical" schizophrenia responded preferentially to ECT and neuroleptic drugs, that "typical" schizophrenics were largely unresponsive to any treatment procedure, and that clinical distinctions between endogenous and neurotic depressions were confirmed by the latter's refractoriness to both ECT and antidepressants. Thus, conceptually, Roth was using response to treatments that alter brain function as a test of the hypothesis that there were different physiological foundations underlying clinical psychiatric syndromes.

Antidepressant drug actions have focused attention on the possibility that depression and mania are produced by abnormalities in cerebral amine metabolism. Artificial seizures in nonparalyzed, nonventilated animals clearly alter central catecholamines (Kety, Javoy, Thierry, Julou, & Glowinski, 1967; Schildkraut, & Draskoczy, 1974). Repeated daily treatment appears to increase norepinephrine turnover through increased synthesis, which in turn results from increased tyrosine hydroxylase activity. Modigh (1976) has shown that repeated seizures produce sustained increases in norepinephrine turnover selectively, with little alteration in dopamine and serotonin turnover. Recently, electrically induced seizures (as well as intermurine fighting) were found to decrease presynaptic norepinephrine re-uptake and increase the number and affinity of synaptosomal (receptor) sites (Welch, Hendley, & Turek, 1974). Despite these promising results, the search for physiological abnormalities in affective disorders did not come from ECT research as such, but indirectly because of the heuristic value of the "catecholamine hypothesis."

One of the most consistent physiological disturbances in severe depression is alteration in sleep characteristics, particularly those indices involving rapid eye movement (REM) sleep (Cobble, Foster, & Kupfer, 1976). Depressed patients have a shorter latency to the first REM period, greater overall REM sleep as a proportion of total sleep, and increased "rebound" REM sleep after a period of REM sleep deprivation.

There is surprisingly little information on the effects of ECT on sleep characteristics in either animals or man. In one study of eight depressed patients (Mendels, Van de Castle, & Hawkins, 1974), ECT shortened REM latency, an effect opposite to what would generally be predicted from drug treatment effects. Furthermore, an average REM latency before treatment was longer in this group than that usually seen in endogenously depressed patients (Cobble *et al.*, 1976), raising the possibility of diagnostic errors.

Another major area of interest in affective disorders is related to abnormalities in cyclic hormonal rhythms. A number of these are correlated in various ways with clinical disturbances in sexual behavior and drive, food intake regulation, sleep, and activity levels. There has been special interest in the hypothalamic–hypophyseal–adrenocortical axis. Severely depressed patients often have elevated plasma cortisol, and an increased threshold to suppression of the diurnal cortisol rhythm by the synthetic steroid dexamethasone (Carroll, Curtis, & Mendels, 1976).

ECT produces a rapid increase in ACTH and a slower increase of serum cortisol (Allan, Denney, Kendall, & Blachly, 1974). These effects persisted only transiently, even when serial seizures at 5-min intervals were provoked. Growth hormone and thyroid-stimulating hormone were unaffected. Assuming that depressed patients already have evidence of increased adrenocortical function, these effects on ACTH and cortisol would presumably be countertherapeutic, or simply unrelated to the antidepressive effects of ECT.

Thus, research on the effects of ECT on brain neurotransmitter metabolism, sleep, and neuroendocrine function in general have contributed little to our understanding of disordered brain function in major psychiatric disorders. Widespread metabolic and neurophysiological changes are produced by generalized seizures. Looking for a pathogenetic mechanism for depression, mania, or schizophrenia by studying the effects of seizures on the human subject may be analogous to searching for a needle in the haystack with a bulldozer. An understanding of the pathophysiology of severe mental disorders is much more apt to surrender ultimately to the process of picking the haystack apart straw by straw.

VI. The Future of Electroconvulsive Therapy

Intense and vociferous attacks on the rights of physicians to perform ECT has led to the passage of legislation that has nearly abolished convulsive therapy as a treatment modality in several states. Recent developments seem to suggest that a more balanced approach to the whole problem is in the process of developing. Not even the most ardent opponents of ECT can deny that major psychiatric disturbance is a public health problem of enormous importance. In whatever way it may be conceptualized, explained, or understood from an etiological standpoint, it scarcely can be ignored. The public will no longer permit repressive and cruel treatment of psychiatric patients by warehousing them in isolated monolithic asylums. At the same time, it will not tolerate within its ranks severely disabled people who, rightly or wrongly, are seen as a threat to society's welfare and comfort. There is every reason to believe that pharmacological treatment, improvement in social and educational institutions, and continued efforts to develop a science of preventive medicine will lessen the need for ECT and indeed many other potentially harmful therapeutic measures.

For the present, however, ECT has been far too effective in the amelioration of the major symptoms of affective disorders and certain schizophrenic states to disappear altogether until something decidedly better comes along. Much of the objection to ECT may be expected to disappear as improvements in methodology and techniques develop. The general public deserves to be better informed, less fearful, and appropriately realistic about the ratio of positive to adverse effects of the treatment. Physicians themselves must learn to predict more precisely who will benefit from ECT and who will not. What is most to be feared is that irrational public concerns will lead to premature political interference with the process by which all medical therapies have slowly improved over time. This danger is dramatized by the current status of psychosurgery which, despite the National Commission's positive report (Ryan, 1977), has virtually disappeared in this country. It is to be hoped that similar irrationality by a few will not deprive patients of their rights to the benefits of ECT, when their alternatives may be long hospitalization, premature death, or the devastating personal effects of psychotic illness.

References

Abrams, R., & Fink, M. Clinical experiences with multiple electroconvulsive treatments. *Comprehensive Psychiatry*, 1972, **13,** 115–121.

Abrams, R., & Taylor, M. A. Mania and schizo-affective disorder, manic type. A comparison. *American Journal of Psychiatry*, 1976, **133,** 1445–1447.

Agnew, W. F., Yuen, T. G. H., Pudenz, R. H., & Bullara, L. A. Electrical stimulation of the brain. IV. Ultrastructural studies. *Surgical Neurology*, 1975, **4,** 438–448.

Alexander, F. G., & Selesnick, S. T. *The history of psychiatry: An evaluation of psychiatric thought and practice from prehistoric times to the present* (1st ed.). New York: Harper & Row, 1966.

Alexander, L., & Löwenbach, H. Experimental studies on electroshock treatment; the intracerebral vascular reaction as an indication of the path of the current and the threshold of early changes within brain and tissue. *Journal of Neuropathology and Experimental Neurology*, 1944, **2,** 139–171.

Allan, J. P., Denney, D., Kendall, J. W., & Blachly, P. H. Corticotropin release during ECT in man. *American Journal of Psychiatry*, 1974, **131,** 1225–1228.

Anonymous. The experience of electroconvulsive therapy. *British Journal of Psychiatry*, 1965, **111,** 365–367.

Asnis, G. M., Fink, M., & Saferstein, S. ECT in metropolitan New York hospitals: A survey of practice, 1975–1976. *American Journal of Psychiatry,* 1978, **135,** 479–482.

Avery, D., & Winokur, G. Mortality in depressed patients treated with electroconvulsive therapy and antidepressants. *Archives of General Psychiatry,* 1976, **33,** 1029–1037.

Avery, D., & Winokur, G. Suicide, attempted suicide, and relapse rates in depression. Occurrence after ECT and antidepressant therapy. *Archives of General Psychiatry,* 1978, **35,** 749–753.

Barton, J. L. ECT in depression: The evidence of controlled studies. *Biological Psychiatry,* 1977, **12,** 687–695.

Bernards, W. Anaesthesia and ECT. *Convulsive Therapy Bulletin,* 1977, **2,** 38–40.

Blachly, P. H. Electroconvulsive treatment compared to electrocardioversion: A source of ideas. *Comprehensive Psychiatry,* 1968, **9,** 13–30.

Blachly, P. H., & Gowing, D. Multiple monitored electroconvulsive therapy. *Comprehensive Psychiatry,* 1966, 100–109.

Brill, N. Q., Crumpton, E., Eiduson, S., Grayson, H. M., Hillman, L. I., & Richards, R. A. Relative effectiveness of various components of electroconvulsive therapy. *Archives of Neurology and Psychiatry,* 1959, **81,** 627–635.

Brunschwig, L., Strain, J., & Bidder, T. G. Issues in the assessment of post-ECT memory changes. *British Journal of Psychiatry,* 1971, **119,** 73–74.

Carroll, B. J., Curtis, G. C., & Mendels, J. Neuroendocrine regulation in depression. II. Discrimination of depressed from nondepressed patients. *Archives of General Psychiatry,* 1976, **33,** 1051–1058.

Cerletti, U. Old and new information about electroshock. *American Journal of Psychiatry,* 1950, **107,** 440–450.

Cobble, P., Foster, G., & Kupfer, D. J. Electroencephalographic sleep diagnosis of primary depression. *Archives of General Psychiatry,* 1976, **33,** 1124–1127.

Cronholm, B., & Ottoson, J. O. Experimental studies of the therapeutic action of electroconvulsive therapy in endogenous depression: The role of the electrical stimulation and of the seizure studied by variation of stimulus intensity and modification by lidocaine of seizure discharge. *Acta Psychiatrica Scandinavica,* 1960, **35,** Suppl. 145, 69–102.

D'Agostino, A. M. Depression: Schism in contemporary psychiatry. *American Journal of Psychiatry,* 1975, **132,** 629–632.

d'Elia, G. Unilateral electroconvulsive therapy. In M. Fink, S. Kety, J. McGough, & T. A. Williams (Eds.), *Psychobiology of convulsive therapy.* Washington, D. C.: V. H. Winston & Sons, 1974. Pp. 21–34.

Esquibel, A. J., Krantz, J. C., Jr., Truitt, E. B., Jr., Ling, A. S. C., & Kurland, A. A. Hexafluorodiethyl ether (Indoklon): Its use as a convulsant in psychiatric treatment. *Journal of Nervous and Mental Disease,* 1958, **126,** 530–534.

Fink, M. Induced seizures and human behavior. In. M. Fink, S. Kety, J. McGough, & T. A. Williams (Eds.), *Psychobiology of convulsive therapy.* Washington, D.C.: V. H. Winston & Sons, 1974. Pp. 1–17.

Frankel, F. H. Electroconvulsive therapy in Massachusetts: A task force report. *Massachusetts Journal of Mental Health,* 1973, **3,** 3–29.

Grahn, A. R., Gehrich, J. L., Couvillon, L. A., & Moench, L. G. *A study of the safety and performance requirements for electroconvulsive therapy devices* (Final rep.). Salt Lake City, UT: Utah Biomedical Test Laboratory, University of Utah Research Institute, 1977.

Greenblatt, M., Grosser, G. H., & Wechsler, H. Differential response to hospitalized depressed patients to somatic therapy. *American Journal of Psychiatry,* 1964, **120,** 935–943.

Hargreaves, W. A., Fischer, A., Elashoff, R. M., & Blacker, K. H. Delayed onset of impairment following electrically induced convulsions. *Acta Psychiatrica Scandinavica,* 1972, **48,** 69–77.

Harmes, E. The origin and early history of electrotherapy and electroshock. *American Journal of Psychiatry,* 1955, **111,** 932–934.

Harper, R. G., & Wiens, A. N. Electroconvulsive therapy and memory. *Journal of Nervous and Mental Disease,* 1975, **161,** 245–254.

Hartelius, H. Cerebral changes following electrically induced convulsions. An experimental study on cats. *Acta Psychiatrica et Neurologica Scandinavica, Supplement 77,* 1952.

Hedlund, J. L., Barton, J. L., Evenson, R. C., Cho, D. W., & Hickman, C. V. Electroconvulsive therapy in Missouri State facilities: 1971–75. *Journal of Operational Psychiatry,* 1978, **9,** 40–56.

Hurwitz, T. D. Electroconvulsive therapy: A review. *Comprehensive Psychiatry,* 1974, **15,** 303–314.

Kety, S. S., Javoy, F., Thierry, A. M., Julou, L., & Glowinski, J. A sustained effect of electroconvulsive shock on the turnover of norapinephrine in the central nervous system of the rat. *Proceedings of the National Academy of Sciences of the United States of America,* 1967, **58,** 1249–1254.

Maletzky, B. Seizure duration and clinical effect in electroconvulsive therapy. *Comprehensive Psychiatry,* 1978, **19,** 541–550.

May, P. R. A., Tuma, A. H., Yale, C., Potepan, P., & Dixon, W. J. Schizophrenia—a follow-up study of results of treatment, II. Hospital stay over two to five years. *Archives of General Psychiatry,* 1976, **33,** 481–486.

McCabe, M., & Norris, B. ECT versus chlorpromazine in mania. *Biological Psychiatry,* 1977, **12,** 245–254.

McGaugh, J. L. Electroconvulsive shock: Effects on learning and memory in animals. In M. Fink, S. Kety, J. McGaugh, & T. A. Williams (Eds.), *Psychobiology of convulsive therapy.* Washington, D. C.: V. H. Winston & Sons, 1974. Pp. 85–98.

Meldrum, B. S., Papy, J. J., Toure, M. F., & Brierly, J. B. Four models for studying cerebral lesions secondary to epileptic seizures. *Advances in Neurology,* 1975, **10,** 147–161.

Mendels, J., Van de Castle, R. L., & Hawkins, D. R. Electroconvulsive therapy and sleep. In M. Fink, S. Kety, J. McGaugh, & T. A. Williams (Eds.), *Psychobiology of convulsive therapy.* Washington. D. C.: V. H. Winston & Sons, 1974. Pp. 41–46.

Miller, D. H., Clancy, J., & Cumming, E. A comparison between unidirectional current, nonconvulsive electrical stimulation, standard alternating current electroshock (Cerletti method) and pentothal in chronic schizophrenia. *American Journal of Psychiatry,* 1953, **109,** 617–620.

Modigh, K. Long term effects on electroconvulsive shock therapy on synthesis turnover and uptake of brain monoamines. *Psychopharmacology,* 1976, **49,** 179–185.

Odegaard, O. The excess mortality of the insane. *Acta Psychiatrica Scandinavica,* 1952, **27,** 353–367.

Posner, J. B., Plum, F., & van Posnak, A. Cerebral metabolism during electrically-induced seizures in man. *Archives of Neurology (Chicago),* 1969, **20,** 388–395.

Roth, M., Kay, W. K., & Kiloh, L. G. The results of biological (physical) treatment in psychiatry and their bearing on the classification of mental disease. In M. Rinkle (Ed.), *Biological treatment of mental illness.* New York: L. C. Page & Co., 1966. Pp. 71–112.

Ryan, K. J. (Chairman). *Report and recommendations on psychosurgery.* The National Commission for Protection of Human Subjects of Biomedical and Behavioral Research.

Washington, D. C.: U.S. Government Printing Office, 1977. (DHEW Publication No. (OS) 77-0002)

Sargant, W., & Slater, E. *An introduction to physical methods of treatment in psychiatry* (4th ed.). Baltimore, MD: Williams & Wilkins, 1963.

Schildkraut, J. L., & Draskoczy, P. R. Effects of electroconvulsive shock on norepinephrine turnover and metabolism: Basic and clinical studies. In M. Fink, S. Kety, J. McGaugh, & T. A. Williams (Eds.), *Psychobiology of convulsive therapy*. Washington, D. C.: V. H. Winston & Sons, 1974. Pp. 143–170.

Shepherd, M. Clinical trial of the treatment of depressive illness. *British Journal of Psychiatry*, 1965, **111,** 881–886.

Small, J. G., & Small, I. F. Clinical results: Indoklon versus ECT. *Seminars in Psychiatry*, 1972, **4,** 13–26.

Squire, L. R., & Slater, P. C. Bilateral and unilateral ECT: Effects on verbal and nonverbal memory. *American Journal of Psychiatry*, 1978, **135,** 1316–1320.

Squire, L. R., Slater, P. C., & Chace, P. M. Retrograde amnesia: Temporal gradient in very long term memory following electroconvulsive therapy. *Science*, 1975, **187,** 77–79.

Ulett, G. A., Smith, K., & Gleser, G. C. Evaluation of convulsive and subconvulsive shock therapies utilizing a control group. *American Journal of Psychiatry*, 1956, **112,** 795–802.

Weaver, L. A., Jr., Ives, J. O., Williams, R., & Nies, A. A comparison of standard alternating current and low energy brief pulse electrotherapy. *Biological Psychiatry*, 1977, **12,** 525–544.

Welch, B. L., Hendley, E. D., & Turek, I. Norepinephrine uptake into cerebral cortical synaptosomes after one fight or electroconvulsive shock. *Science*, 1974, **183,** 220–221.

Chapter 10

Electrical Stimulation of Peripheral Nerve

John E. Swett

Department of Anatomy
College of Medicine
University of California, Irvine
Irvine, California

Charles M. Bourassa

Department of Psychology
University of Alberta
Alberta, Canada

ISBN 0-12-547440-7

I. Introduction

Electrical stimulation was recommended as a cure for the pains of headache and gout by Roman physicians (McNeal, 1977). The stimulus was supplied by an eel that delivered electrical shocks to the patient. In the eighteenth century, with the development of mechanical and chemical means to produce electrical impulses at will, electrical stimulation became a widely used technique to relieve pain and was said to have miraculous curative powers for a number of conditions ranging from impotence to paralysis (McNeal, 1977). These claims exceeded the bounds of credulity, even for that day, and the use of electrical stimulation as a curative gave way to its use as a tool in diagnosis and physiological experimentation. Electrical stimulation provided a means of testing reflexes and of mapping afferent and efferent connections of peripheral nerve fibers. Early efforts were crude, but with refinements of recording techniques, especially the use of the cathode ray oscilloscope (CRO) (Bishop, 1965; Erlanger, 1964) and microelectrodes (Ling & Gerard, 1949), the detailed analysis of nerve excitation became possible.

Today, electrical stimulation is used extensively for routine medical diagnostic and therapeutic procedures such as evaluating peripheral nerve or neuromuscular disorders, identification of peripheral nerve branches during surgery, testing the efficacy of nerve block procedures, reflex testing, and other applications (Zeh & Katz, 1978). With continued progress in the techniques of stimulation, the situation has turned almost full circle, and use of electrical stimulation is now approaching the level of promise suggested by its earliest proponents, for these means are being used to relieve pain, to restore function to paralyzed organs, and to provide sensory function were this is deficient (e.g., Fields & Leavitt, 1973; Hambrecht & Reswick, 1977).

This chapter deals with techniques of stimulating peripheral nerves with electrical current. As it is not practical to cover all applications of this approach, which range from acute laboratory experiments on animals to chronic stimulation in human subjects, this chapter will focus on the basic considerations essential for any application of electrical stimulation to peripheral nerve. Stimulation of peripheral nerve with electrodes placed on the skin is discussed briefly, but the major emphasis is on electrodes placed directly on nerves. Methods of electrode construction and safety are described, and techniques to achieve selective activation of various fiber types are considered. In addition, consideration is given to methods for quantifying the stimulus and gauging its effectiveness. Although specific applications will be mentioned, the aim is to provide information broadly applicable to a variety of situations.

II. General Principles of Peripheral Nerve Stimulation

This section is concerned with the basic principles and practical considerations of peripheral nerve stimulation. It assumes that the reader is familiar with the fundamentals of classical neurophysiology. Discussion is at the most general level compatible with providing an understanding of the techniques of stimulation presented later. Further details of the ionic mechanisms of nerve excitation are available in various introductory neurophysiology texts. More detailed accounts of the principles of nerve stimulation have been given by McNeal (1977) and Ranck (1965; Chapter 1, this volume).

A. Nerve Morphology

Stimulation of peripheral nerve normally involves stimulation of a major nerve trunk, or one of its branches supplying a specific cutaneous zone, muscle, or both. Although nerve fiber constituents may vary considerably from one nerve bundle to another, it is important to recall that a peripheral nerve has a well-defined generalized structure containing many axons of different diameters. Some of these axons are unmyelinated, and others myelinated; some are sensory and others motor in function. The nerve fiber, by which is meant here the axon, is an extremely elongated cylinder of axoplasm, which forms a good electrical conductor because of its ionic constituents, and is surrounded by its own plasma membrane that serves as an imperfect dielectric having a capacitance of about 1 $\mu F/cm^2$. All axons are additionally closely invested by Schwann cells, whose plasma membranes, when wrapped numerous times about the axon, form the segmented myelin sheath, a much more effective dielectric resistant to the passage of transverse movement of ions. The submicroscopic spaces lying between the plasma membranes of the nerve cell axons and the Schwann cells form longitudinal channels for extracellular current flow, but the larger extracellular space, external to the Schwann cells, offers the least resistance. Individual fascicles of nerve fibers are surrounded by an additional sheath of perineural epithelium within a network of connective tissue (Low, 1976; Shantha & Bourne, 1968). When a peripheral nerve is placed on electrodes for stimulation, the individual nerve fibers are always located varying distances away from the tissue-electrode interface, due to the diameter of the nerve bundle itself, and the nonneural tissues and fluids, which are an integral part of the nerve's structure. In the following description, we will be referring to peripheral nerve in this context. For detailed information on peripheral nerve structure and organization, consult Sunderland (1978) and Landon (1976).

B. Initiation of an Action Potential

A nerve fiber is activated, i.e., caused to propagate or conduct an action potential, when its transmembrane resting potential is reduced to a critical threshold value. Depolarization can be caused by applying a voltage that induces current flow across the axon's membrane. This, in practice, is done by using two electrodes, an anode and a cathode, between which current is made to flow in a controlled manner. The axoplasm within the nerve fibers and the extracellular fluid surrounding the fibers is an aqueous solution of ionized salts and proteins, and the current is carried by the ions. In the region of the cathode, current will flow out of the nerve, thereby depolarizing and bringing the membrane potential closer to its threshold for firing. Two types of excitation thresholds are recognized. The first type is the smallest amount of current that produces an electronic response, that is, a minimal, localized depolarization of nerve membrane that will be insufficient to trigger a conducted action potential. The second and more conventional use of the term is to designate the slightly stronger stimulus intensity which is just capable of initiating a conducted action potential. Here, the term threshold will be used in the latter context.

C. *Anodal Block*

The anode, i.e., positive electrode terminal, will attract negative charge ions, and current will flow across the membrane in an inward direction. This causes hyperpolarization, meaning that the interior of the cell becomes more negative relative to the outside than it was in the resting condition. This displaces the membrane potential further away from the threshold. If hyperpolarization is sufficiently developed over a length of axon, an action potential will fail to be conducted across it, and the nerve is said to be under an anodal block.

D. *Orientation of Electrodes on Nerve*

The foregoing concepts have important implications for the orientation of the electrodes relative to the longitudinal orientation of the nerve to be stimulated. Because a nerve's action potential is most readily elicited at the cathode and, conversely, may be blocked at the anode, for its excitation the cathode should be placed closest to the part of the system from which events are to be observed or recorded. Thus, for the study of sensory inputs, the cathode is placed proximally; for the study of effector responses of nerve excitation, the cathode should be more distal than the anode. Another rule of thumb is that longitudinal current flow is more efficient in producing fiber excitation than transverse current flow. When applying the electrodes to the surface of a nerve, it is better to avoid placing the anode and cathode on opposite sides of the nerve, as larger voltages will be required to produce excitation; anodal and cathode effects will tend to cancel each other. Conditions must favor the longitudinal passage of current within the axoplasm itself (Ranck, Chapter 1, this volume).

E. *Anodal Break Stimulation*

When stimulus pulses are of sufficient duration and amplitude, excitation of fibers can occur beneath the anode on the trailing edge of the stimulus pulse when the direction of current flow is momentarily reversed. This is "anodal break stimulation" (Ranck, 1965, and Chapter 1, this volume). It can lead to complexities in observed events because fibers that were not among those excited at the cathode are likely to be involved at the anode. The spurious action potentials will be delayed by as much as 1–2 msec, confounding interpretation of an event's latency.

If the experimental objective requires activation of the nerve only from the cathode, precautions must be taken to avoid anodal break stimulation by employing brief duration current pulses, correct orientation of the anode and cathode, and weak stimulating currents.

F. Current Density

The effectiveness of current flow in changing the membrane potential will be proportional to local current density. For this reason, the electrode that is to be used to activate the nerve should have a configuration that ensures that the stimulating current will be restricted as much as possible to the region beneath the electrode. If monopolar stimulation with the cathode only contacting the nerve is to be used, the anode should be placed on adjacent tissue in a manner to promote longitudinal current flow, and its surface area should be larger than that of the cathode so as to reduce the current density flowing from it. In this way, the chance of these currents accidentally stimulating structures other than those desired will be minimized. Monopolar stimulation, however, has the disadvantage that severe stimulus artifacts are created that can cause interference if low-level signals are being recorded from a distant site. Where recording is to be done, it is generally advisable to use bipolar methods of stimulation.

G. Accommodation

The rate of change in current flow is important in stimulating a nerve fiber. If the rate of change is too slow, the axon will resist excitation because sodium channel inactivation will counteract the tendency of the fiber to depolarize and initiate an action potential. If slow enough, this process becomes a "cathodal block" or "postcathodal depression." The prolonged subthreshold depolarization will increase the threshold of the axon for initiation of an action potential. Such accommodation can be avoided by using rapid rise-times on the leading edge of the stimulus pulse.

H. Susceptibility of Nerve Fibers to Electrical Stimulation

Due to the so-called cable properties of axons, the largest diameter, fastest conducting fibers have the lowest threshold for electrical stimulation (Jack, Nobel, & Tsien, 1975; Ranck, 1965; Rushton, 1951). This is because longitudinal current flow is proportional to the square of the fiber diameter, and the larger fibers, presenting less resistance to current flow, are more easily influenced by electrical stimulation. Stimulation that is carefully graded in strength, therefore, can be used to selectively activate the largest diameter fibers at the weakest effective stimulus intensities, and, as stimulus intensity is increased, to successively recruit smaller diameter fibers. Because of vagaries in current flow due to the nonhomogeneous architecture of a nerve's cross section, the recruitment of fibers by size may not always be perfectly related to stimulus intensity. Smaller fibers closer to the electrode, for instance, may be activated at weaker stimulus intensities than larger fibers lying more remotely where the current field is less dense.

I. Stimulus Repetition Rates

Stimulus repetition rate is an important variable. Immediately after an action potential is propagated, the axon enters an absolute refractory period when it is incapable of conveying another impulse, however strong the stimulus. With stimulation at rates higher than 500–1000 Hz, the interpulse intervals may become less than the refractory period, and the neuron cannot initiate an impulse with every stimulus pulse. Rapid stimulus rates at high stimulus strength can even be used to block certain fibers that have long recovery periods.

Prolonged repetitive stimulation can lead to polarization effects in which impedance changes develop in the tissue–electrode interface that impair the passage of currents and cause an apparent increase in the thresholds of individual nerve fibers. As a general rule, if repetition rates of more than 100 Hz are to be used, it is advisable to sharply limit the duration of stimulation, so as to reduce the total charge transfer. One way to accomplish this is to use brief, high-rate pulse trains, consisting of 5–10 stimulus pulses of short duration (0.1–0.2 msec) over a 50–150 msec period, interrupted by one or more seconds without stimulation.

With intervals of 2–3 msec or more between stimulus pulses, larger axons in a mammalian nerve will conduct an action potential faithfully on every stimulus pulse for several minutes. If it is a nerve trunk that is being stimulated, then all fibers in it that are depolarized beyond the threshold point will be excited virtually simultaneously with an initial delay of about 70 to 200 μsec, the "initiation" or "set-up time" (Blair & Erlanger, 1933, 1936). This elicitation of a mass discharge is advantageous when recording from nerve for purposes of measuring conduction velocities or evoked potentials. It should be remembered, however, that natural stimuli evoke a very different pattern of firing.

J. Potential Problems

There are several problems that commonly arise with stimulation of peripheral nerve. Perhaps the most common problem is the partial inexcitability resulting from physical trauma due to indelicate surgical procedures (Hershberg, Sohn, Agrawal, & Kantrowitz, 1967). Great care must be exercised in surgically isolating nerve bundles so that they are not stretched, deprived of an adequate blood supply, or exposed unduly to the air. Damage to the nerve can also be caused by electrode materials or excessive stimulating currents. Structures in the central nervous system generally are more vulnerable than peripheral nerve, because the latter is surrounded by protective epithelial coverings and connective tissue; nevertheless, all precautions should be taken to minimize damage due to electrode placement or stimulation (Pudenz, Anew, Yuen, Bullara, Jacques, & Sheldon, 1977–1978).

The electrode materials should be relatively inert to body fluids. Metallic conductors are used in most electrodes, and the contact between salt solution and metal creates an interface where electrochemical reactions may occur even without the imposition of current and may become more vigorous with current flow (Babb & Dymond, 1974; Dymond, 1976). Gold, tantalum, titanium, rhenium, some types of stainless steel, and tungsten are relatively resistant to corrosion and have minimal toxic effects in tissue. Elgiloy, a cobalt–nickel alloy, has been used successfully (Glenn, Hageman, Mauro, Eisenberg, Flanigan, & Harvard, 1964). Copper is toxic. Silver–silver chloride (Ag–AgCl) electrodes and pure silver wire are toxic in long-term use but are acceptable for acute applications (Sawyer & Srinivasan, 1974, pp. 1099–1110). Silver wire can be used successfully for chronic peripheral nerve-stimulating electrodes in animal experiments, provided that the wires have large surface areas and are separated from the nerve by 0.5–1.0 mm (Bourassa & Swett, 1967). Although no material seems perfect, platinun and some of its alloys seem to be the least objectionable choice for electrodes (Bernstein, Johnson, Hench, Hunter, & Dawson, 1977; Brunmer, McHardy, & Turner, 1977; Johnson & Hench, 1977; Wetzel, Howell, & Bearie, 1969; White & Gross, 1974).

Very weak current pulses may transfer charge by a "double layer" or capacitive effect, but at the higher intensities often used for stimulation, the current may cause heating or electrochemical effects, which result in the breakdown of body fluids producing gas bubbles, toxic products, and deleterious pH changes (for details see Brummer *et al.*, 1977; Guyton & Hambrecht, 1973; Johnson & Hench, 1977). Very strong stimulus intensities can cause irreversible nerve block (B. Matthews & Cadden, 1979).

These problems become especially serious with long-term or "continuous" stimulation because by-products of charge transfer at the electrode–tissue interface will accumulate. These consequences can be reduced by using minimal currents and keeping the pulse durations short with respect to the interpulse interval. Weinman and Mahler (1964) suggested that a pulse interval 10 to 15 times the pulse duration should be optimal, but if monophasic current pulses are to be used, even this duty cycle may be excessive. An interpulse interval 100 times greater than the pulse duration gives better assurance of minimizing the consequences of charge transfer.

One commonly used procedure, which in theory should minimize polarization and accumulation of toxic materials, is to employ biphasic pulses (Lilly, 1961) which by reversing the electrochemical processes at the electrode tend to neutralize the net effect of each stimulus cycle (Kaneyuki, Hogan, Glenn, & Holcomb, 1977). The reversal is not perfectly electrochemically balanced (Weinman & Mahler, 1964; Weinman, 1965), but it is sufficient to reduce significantly deleterious effects of using long-term stimulation. Reversing the polarity of the stimulus pulse introduces another complexity, however, in that the compound action potentials seen on recording when using this type of stimulus will appear differently at each half-cycle of stimulation. When during a cycle the distal electrode becomes the cathode, the population of fibers excited may be different in composition and number from those excited when the cathode is proximal, the normal condition for monophasic stimulation. Inevitably, the latencies will differ, one for each half-cycle, due to the slowing effect of anodal block and the greater distance traveled by action potentials elicited by the distal electrode. Because of anodal block, the number of fibers activated will be less when the cathode is distal. It has been claimed that brief audio-frequency stimulus currents can avoid these problems (Wyss, 1967).

Other approaches to minimizing polarization effects with long-term stimulation involve special stimulating circuits (Bartlett, Doty, Lee, Negrao, & Overman, 1977; Delgado, 1977–1978; del Pozo & Delgado, 1978) or electrodes, which do not give a net transfer of electrons thereby greatly reducing electrochemical reactions (Bartlett *et al.*, 1977; Guyton & Hambrecht, 1973; Mauro, 1960). The development of these capacitive electrodes offers considerable promise, but at the present state-of-the-art they tend to be too bulky for certain applications.

Many of these complications resulting from charge transfer can be reduced to acceptable levels by choosing stimulus parameters that are just sufficient to accomplish the desired end, i.e., in principle whether monophasic or biphasic, the stimulus pulses should convey the least amount of charge for the least amount of time (Mickle, 1961). Pulse durations can be made too brief, however, because as pulse duration diminishes below about 100 μsec, the current needed for activation exponentially increases (Lilly, 1961; McNeal, 1973). At durations greater than 300–500 μsec the stimuli tend to aggravate polarization effects and should be avoided. Also, fibers of different diameters respond differently to pulses of a given duration; we have found that a pulse duration of 100–200 μsec is a good compromise for most applications involving myelinated axons. For excitation of unmyelinated axons, longer duration pulses are more efficient (Koslow, Bak, & Li, 1973; Li & Bak, 1976).

Every investigator who uses electrical stimulation should attempt to demonstrate the efficacy of his procedures through biocalibration (Dow, 1978; Upton, 1978), using physiological and/or behavioral indices, e.g., compound action potentials, evoked potentials, muscle twitches, and so forth, to evaluate the effects of stimulation. Biocalibration has other benefits that will be discussed later.

III. Electrodes

Our main concern here will be with chronic stimulation of nerve through implanted electrodes, a method useful for both the research laboratory and some clinical applications. Only brief consideration will be given to stimulation of peripheral nerve by means of surface electrodes, a topic that is to be covered in greater detail elsewhere in this volume.

A. Transcutaneous Electrodes

Transcutaneous stimulation of a nerve can be used for short-term or chronic stimulation. The electrode and skin are smeared with conductive electrode paste to reduce contact resistance to current flow, and the electrodes, which can be conventional surface EEG plate electrodes, are placed a few centimeters apart (Rollman, 1974). Investigators differ in their preference for stainless steel, silver, or nonpolarizable Ag–AgCl contacts. Concentric configurations of bipolar electrodes are often used in order to confine stimulating current to a smaller region near the electrode. The central disk, a plate 1–4 mm in diameter, is surrounded by an annulus with a surface area 4–10 times that of the disk (Saunders, 1974; Sherrick, 1975). The gap between the two electrodes should be greater than 1 mm in order to avoid short circuits. While this arrangement is satisfactory for short-term application, long-term use may be complicated by change in the contact of the electrodes with the skin resulting in altered electrode impedance. Skin irritation can also result (Scott, 1968). A variety of other electrode types have been described to circumvent these difficulties (Burton & Maurer, 1976; Kopman, 1976). Even with short-term stimulation the impedance of the skin may change, especially during the first few minutes of stimulation, and a "warm-up" period is usually required to produce stable conditions (Saunders, 1974).

Electrodes designed to stimulate nerve by passing current through the skin must have a large surface area, if high current densities, which cause pain and skin inflammation, are to be avoided. Spherical or ball-tip electrodes readily shift in their effective surface contact area, and are difficult to maintain with consistent pressure on the skin. For this reason they are not recommended (Kopman, 1976; Lippmann & Fields, 1974). The necessity for a large area of good contact arises because current flows in numerous parallel paths between electrodes and skin. If an area under the electrode should decrease in impedance, current will flow in a concentrated fashion through the region, and this may produce burning (Gibson, 1968; Saunders, 1974).

Electrical fields may interact with the skin in a variety of ways. With large surface-area electrodes placed over dry skin, the impedance will be high, and the skin, acting as one plate of a capacitor, may interact with the electrode in such a way that at high voltages, the skin will actually move to the extent that an audible sound may be heard (M. Meyer, 1931). Even without an excursion great enough to produce sound, a sense of roughness or stickiness may be felt as the electrode is moved on the skin surface (Sherrick, 1975).

Even under the most desirable low-impedance conditions, exactly what local anatomical structures are stimulated with skin electrodes is not entirely clear. If the electrodes are placed on skin regions remote from superficial nerves, sensation is referred to the skin beneath the electrodes. Whether the sensation is produced by direct excitation of axons or specialized sensory endings is not clear. The membranes of sensory endings have been presumed to be nonexcitable electrically (Grundfest, 1957; Paintal, 1959a), but Catton (1966) has argued that some receptors are electrically excitable. The stimulus, more likely than not, activates nerve fibers at a site proximal to the receptors, for such stimulation typically produces very steep functions for absolute detection threshold data in hunans (Rollman, 1974), similar to that seen with direct stimulation of peripheral nerve in cats (Bourassa & Swett, 1967). It is often assumed that the almost quantal nature of the threshold curve is due to by-passing the influence of the receptor's transducer mechanisms, but recent work on the tactile thresholds of the hand of human subjects show that similar threshold functions can be obtained with punctate mechanical deformation of the skin (Vallbo & Johansson, 1976). The possibility exists, of course, that electrical stimulation activates these same fibers at threshold intensities. In general, with direct electrical stimulation the experienced magnitude of sensation grows rapidly with increasing stimulus intensity; it shows limited dynamic range (Rollman, 1974; Rosner & Goff, 1967). With appropriate choice of stimulus parameters, the dynamic range may be markedly increased (Saunders, 1974).

If the electrodes are placed on the skin directly over a superficially coursing nerve bundle, the electrical current can directly activate both the skin and the underlying nerve fibers. This can be established in humans from the fact that resulting paresthesias are referred to the peripheral distribution of the nerve as well as to the skin immediately beneath the electrodes. This inevitably results in a sensory input of indeterminate composition that may render results more difficult to interpret. In other words, it is not always feasible to insure that only the desired nerve trunk will be stimulated. The subject of the most appropriate stimulus parameters has had detailed consideration in the literature (Burton & Maurer, 1976; Butikofer & Lawrence, 1978; Gibson, 1968; Hambrecht & Reswick, 1977; Saunders, 1974).

B. Percutaneous Electrodes

Stimulation of peripheral nerves can be accomplished with somewhat greater precision and with a wider choice of selection when electrodes can be placed closer to the nerve. The percutaneous methods involve necessarily sharp-pointed needle electrodes that are inserted through the skin and advanced close to the nerve to be stimulated. Insulated or uninsulated stainless steel needles are commonly used (Hallin & Torebjork, 1973; Ray & Maurer, 1975). Needles have a much smaller surface area than the skin electrodes, but current required to stimulate the nerve will be reduced because of the closer approximation of the electrode to the nerve and the lower impedance of the body fluids surrounding the nerve. Percutaneous methods of nerve stimulation minimize surgical intervention and allow stimulation of intact nerve trunks while temperature, blood supply, and so on, are normal. Because it is difficult to place needle electrodes near nerves in a predictable and repeatable manner, the percutaneous approach is most suitable for acute testing procedures. It is possible to achieve selective activation of limited groups of fibers by shifting the placement of the electrodes so as to alter current densities on various portions of the nerve. The exact type of fiber or fibers activated must be determined empirically by measurement of conduction velocity or use of some other indicator.

C. *Implantable Electrodes*

The need to investigate the effect of controlled activation of peripheral nerve on sensory and motor behavior in the normal, unanesthetized animal led to the development of implantable electrodes. Hess (1932) was probably the first to insert stimulating electrodes on a peripheral nerve of an awake cat by bringing the electrode wires through the skin to an external current source. Shortly thereafter, a cuff electrode for stimulating the sympathetic trunk was described by Cannon (1933). The method attracted attention of other investigators (Cressman & Blalock, 1939; Kottke, Kubicek, & Visscher, 1945; Manning & Hall, 1937) and led to the development of radiofrequency coupling between an external transmitter and an implanted coil by which means current could be induced across stimulating electrodes thereby eliminating the requirement of bringing wires through skin openings (Fender, 1937; Lafferty & Farrell, 1949; Newman, Fender, & Saunders, 1937). Continuing advances have produced a number of commercially available products for stimulating nerve in research, therapeutic, and prosthetic applications.[1]

Cuff electrodes are designed to wrap around a peripheral nerve bundle. The basic concept is to place the nerve within the most uniform current density field possible by making the stimulus contacts circumferential bands around the nerve. The electrode cuff itself is made of a dielectric in which the metal contacts are embedded on the inner surface. In an acute preparation, electrodes can be applied directly to the surgically exposed nerve, sutured in place, and covered by reclosing the wound,

[1]Avery Laboratories, Inc., 145 Rome Street, Farmingdale, N. Y. 11735; Med General Inc., 10800 Lyndale Avenue 5, Minneapolis, Minn. 55420; M. H. Rhodes, Inc., 99 Thompson Road, Aron, Conn. 06001; Mentor,Division of Codman & Sluntliff, Randolph Industrial Park, Randolph, Mass. 02368; Metronics Associates, Inc., 3174 T Porter Drive, Palo Alto, Calif. 94304; Stimtech, 9440 Science Center Drive, Minneapolis, Minn. 55428.

leaving only flexible wire connections passing through the wound opening to the stimulator. In chronic preparations, the method is similar, except for refinements in materials and surgical techniques.

It is also possible to implant electrodes made of fine wire in the perineurium of a nerve. Such a procedure has been briefly described by McNeal, Waters, & Reswick (1977–1978). The current needed for stimulation is said to be much less than that required with cuff electrodes, and the implant may be tolerated better than the bulkier cuff electrode. At least in theory, this procedure might be developed so as to permit stimulation of a restricted group of nerve fibers as can be done with microstimulation (Abzug, Maeda, Peterson, & Wilson, 1974; Bean, 1974). This approach may ultimately prove superior to the cuff electrode but, at present, experience with this type of electrode is limited, and the discussion will dwell on the more widely used cuff electrode. The following authors have conmented on various types of electrodes for this purpose (Baker, 1971; Barone, Wayner, Aguilar-Baturoni & Guevara-Aguilar, 1979; Brindley, 1972; Bourde, Robinson, Suda, & White, 1970; de Villiers, Nose, Meier, & Kantrowitz, 1964; Dubkin, 1970; Duysens & Stein, 1978; Frank, 1968; Libouban & Aleonard, 1960; McCarty, 1965; Pompeiano & Swett, 1962a; Rosenbaum, Titone, Yagi, & Kantrowitz, 1974; Slaughter & Hahn, 1975; Stein, Dean, Gordon, Hoffer & Jhamandas, 1978; Straw & Mitchell, 1966; Testerman, Hagfors, & Schwartz, 1971; Waters, 1977; Yergler, McNeal, & Perry, 1972). In addition, there is a growing literature on prosthetic applications of peripheral stimulation, in which electrical stimulation has been used for evoking auditory, vestibular, and visual signals, motor control of the extremities, augmented sensory feedback, electrophrenic respiration, control of bladder function, and so forth. Readers interested in knowing more about the technical advantages and limitations of chronic electrical stimulation of these structures should consult recent reviews by Fields and Leavitt (1973) and Hambrecht and Reswick (1977).

Lead wires are carried subcutaneously to some type of connector. In some studies, percutaneous lead wires have been used successfully, but there is always danger of infection where the wires are brought through the skin. More recent work suggests that if the lead wires terminate in a small grommet-like device on the skin, there is little risk of infection (Mooney & Hartmann, 1974; Stein *et al.*, 1978). More commonly in the experimental animal, lead wires are run subcutaneously to the head or some other convenient site, and are wired to an electrical connector that can be attached to the animal by adhesives or resin compounds composed of biologically inert material. In our experience, Kerr Formatray in small quantities is easy to apply and shows no reaction to tissue fluids.

Radiofrequency methods of stimulation may also be used to avoid percutaneous wires. This requires implantation of a subcutaneous antenna (Glenn, Holcomb, Gee, & Rath, 1970) and special stimulating equipment.

In an acute animal preparations, stimulation of nerve is usually done by surgically exposing the nerve and placing on it one or two wire hooks in a bath of warm mineral oil formed by retracted skin flaps and muscle. The mineral oil prevents drying of the nerve and because it is a nonconductor, it serves as a good medium that will permit stimulation of the nerve because the current path is restricted to the nerve bundle. The method, however, has its limitations. It is somewhat tedious if several nerves are to be exposed at the same time, and selection of nerves is restricted by the limited numbers of places where oil pools can be formed. Obviously, the method is unsuitable for chronic or semichronic work. One problem not so obvious is that the nerve bundles do not usually remain in a healthy state in the oil for more than 5–10 hr, even if temperature is maintained and the oil is well-oxygenated. Perhaps because the arterial supply is difficult to maintain, the preparation undergoes progressive deterioration.

1. Considerations in Use of Cuff Electrodes

Chronic implants require that the material of the implant be nonreactive with the body tissues (Hench, 1980). For electrodes themselves, platinum or its iridium alloys seem to be the most satisfactory (Glenn *et al.*, 1964), while as a carrier for the electrodes, plastic sheeting of various types of Silastic is useful. For use in humans it must be recognized that some individuals are sensitive to the materials, and this possibility should be tested before chronic implants are attempted (McNeal *et al.*, 1977–1978). A cuff composed of a flexible plastic sheet 200–300 μm in thickness is of sufficient strength to support the shape of the cuff and the electrodes, while at the same time occupying a minimum amount of space. Much commercially available preformed rubber or plastic tubing has a heavy wall relative to the internal diameter, which makes the electrode cuff either too stiff or bulky.

Extensive investigations of the effect of chronic electrodes on nerve tissue suggest that the major problems are not with electrical parameters, as long as reasonable precautions are taken, but rather with mechanical problems, which involve direct trauma of the nerve by the electrode assembly (deVilliers *et al.*, 1964; Glenn *et al.*, 1970; Hershberg *et al.*, 1967). The cuff lumen must be large enough to initially allow slippage of the nerve in the cuff as well as to allow space for invading connective tissue later. If the cuff is too close-fitting, it can be a source of progressive compression. Any attempt to strip the protective sheaths from the nerve will cause harm. Also, the cuff must be oriented in such a way that it lies naturally within a fascial plane separating muscle groups and aligned with the longitudinal axis of the nerve when the wound is closed so that it does not damage the nerve by causing bending or distortion. Once the electrode is in its proper place, connective tissue will invade available spaces within a few days or weeks to anchor the electrode into place, a process that does not materially interfere with the effectiveness of the electrodes. In the cat, threshold values for nerve excitation stabilize in 2–3 weeks (Bourassa & Swett, 1967; Myers, Hostetter, Bourassa, & Swett, 1974; Pompeiano & Swett, 1962a; Swett & Bourassa, 1967). Changes in impedance or stimulus effectiveness at a later time suggest damage to the nerve or electrodes.

Movement of the animal with constant flexing of the lead wires leads to metal fatigue and eventually to breakage. This can be minimized by using flexible, fatigue-resistant wire (see next section) and by placing the electrode in regions where its movement is restricted. In practice, this usually means the leads should cross as few joints as possible. The subcutaneous leads must have ample scope and traverse each joint in such a way as to be minimally stretched or compressed within the natural range of joint motion. We have found that loops of wire, one placed near the electrode assembly and a second in the back of the neck, by the electrical connector on the head, prevents wire strain and breakage. The possibility of wire breakage requires constant checking to verify that stimulation is actually taking place, and that the conditions of stimulation remain constant.

Another source of difficulty with a cuff electrode can arise when one intends to confine stimulation to functional fiber types in a mixed nerve. For example, the experimenter may intend to activate only sensory fibers, but the stimulus may also activate motor fibers and cause undesirable muscle contractions. In some cases, it may be desirable to tie off the nerve to eliminate the unwanted effect or surgically to isolate a major branch of a nerve with the desired properties.

2. Construction of a Cuff Electrode

Electrodes of superior quality can be purchased from commercial firms (Avery or Medtronic), but they are expensive and large, as they are designed for human applications. Obviously, the physical limitations for stimulating soleus nerve in the rat, or more extreme, the vagus nerve of the rat (Slaughter & Hahn, 1975), is a very different task than stimulating the superficial radial nerve of the cat (Bourassa & Swett, 1967).

We will describe here an electrode that was devised originally for chronic stimulation of peripheral nerve in a study of influences on brainstem arousal and sleep mechanisms (Pompeiano & Swett, 1962a). The current design has been implanted around a peripheral nerve for many months without breakage or damage to the nerve.

The materials and tools used for the electrode are (1) plastic sheeting 0.20–0.30 mm in thickness; (2) platinum or silver wire, 0.20–0.40 mm in diameter; (3) a 20-gauge hypodermic needle; (4) multistrand, Teflon-coated stainless steel wire (Medwire Corp., 316SS 7/44T, 0.2 mm total diameter); (5) a fine-point soldering iron, a damp cleaning sponge, and a high-grade rosin-core silver solder (Ersin); and (6) a pair of hemostats, a scalpel, scissors, and hardened side-cutters for wire.

The first step is to select an electrode size and interelectrode distance that is appropriate for the nerve to be stimulated. Experience by trial and error is the only practical way to determine what size of electrode will be best. Once the size is determined, the supporting cuff is made by cutting a rectangle of soft plastic sheeting. The horizontal dimension determines the interelectrode distance, and the vertical dimension determines the diameter of the cuff when completed (Fig. 1a). In our experience, 10–12 mm is suitable in most applications where bipolar electrodes with an 8–9 mm interelectrode distance is required. The vertical dimension is 8–12 mm for nerves 2.0 mm or less in diameter, whereas larger nerves may require 14–18 mm.

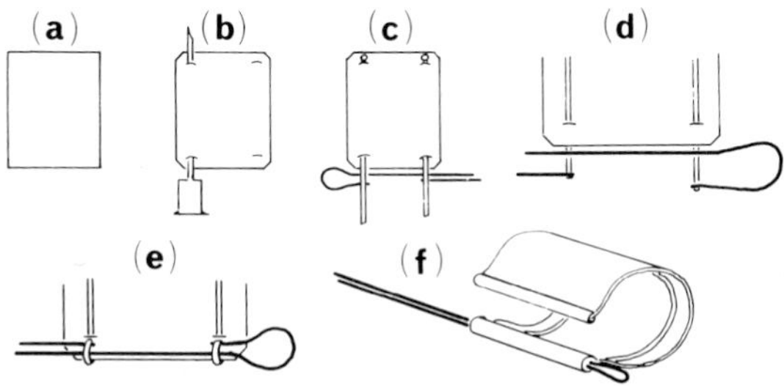

Fig. 1. Stages in fabrication of a cuff electrode. (a) A supple, thin rectangular sheet of plastic is cut to the dimensions suitable for a particular nerve. The vertical dimension is determined by the size of the nerve bundle to be stimulated, while the horizontal dimension governs the interelectrode distance. (b) Sharp corners of the plastic sheet are trimmed away, and a hypodermic needle is inserted as shown. (c) Precut wires, platinum or pure silver, are placed in the holes, and the pretined Teflon-coated stainless steel wire leads are soldered. A loop of lead wire may be used to suture the electrode in place. (d) An enlarged image showing the inside surface of the cuff and arrangement of the lead wires. (e) The stimulating electrode wire is bent into the inner surface of the cuff. (f) Both edges of the cuff are coated with acrylic resin or a similar "cement" that is nonconductile and nontoxic in living tissue. This shows the cuff in its final form ready for implantation.

When the desired cuff size is determined (Fig. 1a), the sharp corners of the plastic rectangle are cut off with scissors, and the hypodermic needle is threaded through the plastic sheet in the manner illustrated in Fig. 1b. The needle pricks should be approximately 1.5–2.0 mm from the two edges of the sheet and near its corners.

Precut and polished electrode wires of platinum or silver, one end of which is melted into a small ball, are then threaded through the plastic sheet (Fig. 1c). The wire should be pulled through until its rounded end fits gently against the slit made by the hypodermic needle, so that it may act as an anchor between the wire and plastic cuff in the last stage of fabrication. For attachment of the lead wires, the cut end of the wires should extend beyond the edge of the plastic sheet by 4 to 5 mm. The point at which the stainless steel wire is to be soldered to the platinum wire is then marked at a point 2.0–3.0 mm out from the edge of the plastic cuff. The cuff is collapsed along the wires, and the marked points are tinned with solder. Use of the hemostat to hold the wire also serves as a heat-sink to prevent the wire from melting or deforming the plastic sheet where the wire penetrates it.

Next, the multistranded stainless steel lead wire is measured in lengths appropriate for the anatomical location of the stimulating cuff on the nerve and the desired exit point through the animal's skin. Usually a wire length of 150–175% of the straight-line distance between these two points is most suitable. With the aid of a dissecting microscope, 1 mm of Teflon insulation is stripped from the cut-wire end, and the wire is tinned with silver solder using stainless steel flux. The tinning process may need to be repeated as many as 10 to 20 times to ensure that the molten solder flows smoothly among the wire strands and appears shiny-bright. A black residue or a crystalline appearance of the solder indicates poor tinning, and tinning should be repeated after scraping the soldered area clean. When the wire end is well-tinned, solder it to the platinum electrode wire, again using the hemostat as a heat-sink.

With both lead wires attached to the platinum electrodes, straighten the plastic cuff so that the electrode assembly appears as in Fig. 1d. At this point, a decision must be made as to whether a "left-handed" or a "right-handed" electrode will be made, a choice that will later prove important when the electrodes are surgically implanted. It may be desirable to fabricate mirror-image pairs of electrodes.

With side-cutters, remove the excess wire and bend the platinum wires over into the inside surface of the electrodes in the manner shown in Fig. 1e. The final step is to insulate with acrylic resin all wire surfaces except those exposed between the slits in the plastic sheet. The electrodes may be stored flat in individual paper envelopes until ready for use. They can be sterilized by steam or chemical treatment, preferably the latter. At the time that they are implanted in the animal, they are curved by wrapping them around small cylinders slightly larger in diameter than the nerves to be stimulated (Fig. 1f).

IV. Stimulus Intensity

The word "intensity" is a somewhat imprecise term used to indicate the stimulus parameter of amplitude or strength, without implying any particular set of units. It may be expressed in volts or milliamperes, or in units such a coloumbs or watts, but however expressed, sufficient information must be provided so that other investigators can judge its intensity and if necessary, replicate the stimulus and its reported effects. It is important to monitor and report stimulus parameters, but even when most of the electrical parameters are reported, there may still be some uncertainty about the effectiveness of the stimulation. Therefore, we recommend a further step that involves not only reporting the stimulus parameters, but also reporting the effectiveness of the stimulation in terms of some biological indicator.

A. Absolute Intensity Scaling

Many stimulators have amplitude controls in the form of rotating potentiometers with calibrated dials that may lack the precision necessary for critical applications. Apart from reading errors due to parallax or insufficiently scaled divisions, the actual values of voltage or current applied to the electrode may be very different from those indicated by the dials. As standard operating procedure, every investigator should monitor the voltage and/or current of the pulse waveforms delivered to the electrodes (Becker, Peacock, Heath & Mickle, 1961; Mickle, 1961). One method is to display the waveforms on a well-calibrated oscilloscope (CRO), so that the intensity of the stimulus pulse can be measured directly from the CRO. Voltage across the stimulating electrodes can be measured with less than 5% error, provided that the input impedance of the vertical amplifier of the CRO is high, 1 MΩ or greater. Current can be measured readily by observing the voltage drop across a precision resistor wired in series with the path of current flow across the stimulating electrode. The resistor should have a value of 5% or less of the tissue–electrode impedance. The vernier adjustment on the vertical amplifier gain control of the CRO can be adjusted to display convenient values per graticule division. Current-measuring probes or chassis-mounted devices are available with some oscilloscopes and can provide an accurate measure of stimulating current. If voltage and current are routinely monitored, it is possible to calculate (using Ohm's law) a useful estimate of tissue–electrode resistance for routine applications. More accurate methods for measuring tissue–electrode impedance are available but require special instrumentation (Babb & Dymond, 1974; Dymond, 1976; Johnson & Hench, 1977; Pollack, 1974a, 1974b).

While reporting voltages or currents is necessary, it is important to recognize that their values can be misleading because of the large numbers of variables that influence the amount and pattern of the current flow across the nerve itself. Because of their influence on the biological effectiveness of an electrical stimulus, some of the additional factors that must be reported are (1) type of stimulator used and its output impedance characteristics; (2) geometry and physical characteristics of the electrode's conductors; (3) pulse waveform, duration, and repetition rates; (4) the location and orientation of the electrodes in relation to the nerve; (5) the physical environment in which the stimulus is applied (skin, saline, oil, and so on); and (6) type and composition of the nerve stimulated.

As these factors all influence the effectiveness of the stimulation, it can be seen that there is an unpredictable relationship between absolute intensity values and their biological consequences. For example, because of slight differences in the electrodes and their relation to the nerve, an identical biological effect seen in animal *A* may not be reproduced at precisely the same parameters of stimulation in animal *B*. In fact, current and voltage alone have limited value for determining in advance what to expect with the application of the stimulus. Comparisons of the effectiveness of stimuli used in several laboratories, where differences exist in the electrode types, pulse waveforms, and repetition rates, becomes difficult or impossible. Such comparisons are possible, however, if a relative intensity scaling is used.

B. Biocalibration (Relative Stimulus Intensity Scaling)

Some of the serious drawbacks of absolute intensity scaling can be circumvented by use of biocalibration (Dow, 1978; Upton, 1978). The principle is simple. Stimulus intensity is scaled relative to a biological event evoked by the stimulus. In the simplest case, an easily recordable neural or behavioral event, which is linked to the stimulation (e.g., an evoked potential of a given amplitude or threshold of a muscle contraction), serves as an indicator of the effectiveness of stimulation. The advantage of this method is that it normalizes stimulus intensities in terms of biological effectiveness and minimizes the differences that would result with changes in electrode configurations and impedances from site to site or from animal to animal.

Another advantage of biocalibration is that it automatically monitors the effectiveness of the stimulation and will quickly reveal any changes due to equipment failure, breakage of a lead wire, inappropriate stimulus parameters, and so forth. In addition, monitoring a biological response is an aid in choosing stimulus parameters that are just adequate rather than excessive.

A more elaborate form of biocalibration can be used with stimulation of certain CNS structures (Swett & Bourassa, 1967, 1980) and is particularly useful for the control of peripheral nerve stimuli (consult also Section V-A,6: Graded Stimulus Intensity). The procedure involves normalizing the stimulus intensity with respect to minimal activation of the nerve. With a good quality stimulator, oscilloscope, and amplifier, one can convert easily from absolute values to relative intensity scaling. In order to determine this, one must place recording electrodes on the peripheral nerve stimulated, or record from known CNS structures whose responses accurately reflect minimal activation of the nerve (Bourassa & Swett, 1967; Swett & Bourassa, 1967). The intensity is adjusted until a just-noticeable electrophysiological response is recorded. Signal averaging may be used as a more sensitive method of identifying this value. The voltage (and/or current) is monitored as before and given the value of 1.00 *T*, the "*T*" signifying that the value is relative to a biological threshold. The vernier on the CRO may be adjusted so that the pulse amplitude is precisely equal to one graticule division. Intensities greater than 1.00 *T* are then expressed as multiples or fractions thereof of the intensity applied. A stimulus of 2.00 *T* will represent a pulse amplitude of two graticule divisions, and so on.

This procedure is slightly more cumbersome than the one required for measuring absolute values because absolute values must be converted to values relative to the weakest effective stimulus. This may require the aid of a slide rule or calculator, if it is not possible to make such measurements directly from the graticule of the CRO.

There are rapid ways to adjust relative intensity scaling so that its calibrated values can be read directly from dial settings. This eliminates the need to measure or compute relative intensity values each time a new stimulus intensity is used. One solution is to design and build a special output stage from a pulse generator (Mills & Swett, 1965), or to design and build a stimulator that will incorporate both absolute and relative intensity controls (Taylor & Swett, 1972).

A schematic version of the output stage we employ is shown in Fig. 2. A rectangular monophasic pulse of fixed amplitude with a preselected duration and repetition rate is delivered to the stimulator output circuit through an optical coupler. This coupler isolates the animal from ground in order to reduce undesirable ground currents that can produce stimulus artifacts when recording low-level signals.

The driving pulse, V_{in}, from the stimulator activates a light-emitting diode (LED). The current through the LED is controlled by R_1 and the open collector buffer, IC. The circuit provides a -12-V drop across R_2 and R_3, and R_2 is adjusted so that precisely 10 V (V_{ref}) occurs across R_3. The voltage occurring between the wiper-arm of R_3 and the isolated common is V_{base}, the voltage used to calculate absolute stimulus intensities. It can be varied from 0 to 10 V. This voltage is attenuated or amplified, depending on the ratio of R_5/R_4. The amplifier is a special purpose high-voltage unit used in the operational feedback mode. The feedback resistance circuit, R_5, has a total value 10 times greater than R_4 to provide a maximum gain of 10 times the V_{base} voltage, a V_{out} of 100 V. It is arranged in three decades, each decade being controlled by a Digitran (#29004) lever–thumb wheel switch. When the reading is changed from 0.01 on the dial (100Ω) to 9.99 (99,900 Ω), the gain is varied from .01 to 9.99 times the value of V_{base} applied to the input of the amplifier.

The design of this system makes relative intensity scaling as convenient to use as absolute scaling. The thumb wheel decade switches (R_5) are adjusted to read 1.00 while recording from the peripheral nerve. R_3 is adjusted until a just-noticeable response of the compound action-potential is observed, so that this value on the thumb wheel decades then represents 1.00 *T*. After the dial of R_3 is locked into position, any change in the dial settings of R_5 will represent stimulus intensity relative to minimal activation of the nerve, e.g., with a setting of 2.84 *T* on the R_5 thumb wheel switches, the stimulus intensity is 2.84 times the voltage (V_{base}) required for minimal activation of the nerve. Because the dial reading on R_3 represents the absolute preset value (in millivolts) required for 1.00 *T*, the product of the two dial settings will give the absolute intensity value for any relative intensity chosen. For example, a V_{base} of 170 mV and a relative scale setting of 2.84 *T* will have an absolute value of 0.84 V.

Stimulation intensities can be rapidly adjusted and recorded with this system using relative intensity values. Its convenience, repeatability, and

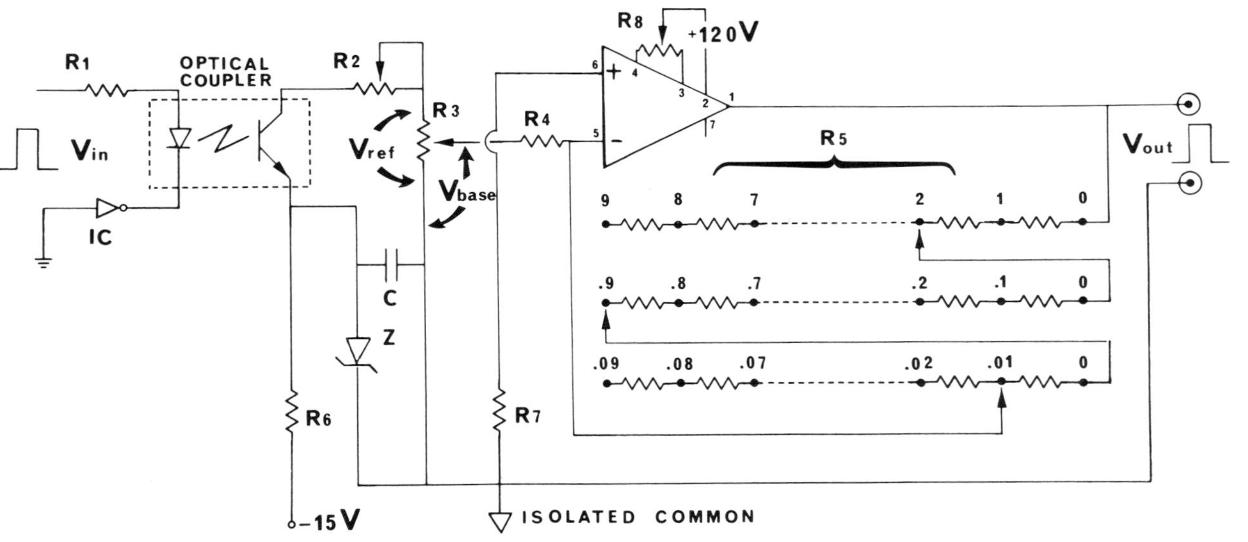

FIG. 2. Wiring schematic of an optically coupled, isolated output stage of a stimulator. All controls on the output stage are arranged to give values for relative and absolute intensity scaling. The optical coupler (H11A1) prevents unwanted ground currents. Pulse durations and repetition rates are governed by the stimulator (not shown), which delivers a pulse of fixed amplitude, V_{in} (5 V), to the output stage. Resistor R_1 (150 Ω) limits the driving current of the light-emitting diode (LED), which excites the phototransistor portion of the optical coupler. Components R_6 (330 Ω), C (100 μF) and Z (IN4742) supply the emitter of the optical coupler with a regulated, decoupled −12 V referenced to an isolated common. When the phototransistor is enabled −12 V will appear on the collector, and a voltage drop will occur across R_2 (1 k Ω) and R_3 (10 k Ω), a precision 10-turn potentiometer (Amphenol, 4101B). The operational amplifier (Burr–Brown 3583 AM) can deliver a maximum of 100 V and 75 mA of load current. The ratio of $R5$ (100 k Ω)/R_4 (10 k Ω) determines the amplitude of V_{out}. R_7 (5 k Ω) is selected to compensate for input currents at nominal gain of 1.0. The balancing potentiometer, R_8 (100 k), is adjusted for minimum voltage output at a gain of 10 (9.99 on dial of R_5) while stimulator is in the *off* mode.

accuracy become apparent with use. There is one source of serious potential error, however, that must be guarded against at all times—a drift in stimulus–response conditions so that 1.00 on the thumb wheel settings may no longer accurately reflect the threshold 1.00 *T*. In acute or semichronic conditions, when the peripheral electrodes have not had time to settle to a stable relationship with the nerve, it is necessary to recalibrate frequently to assure that the V_{base} value is correct and that the 1.00 *T* setting on the relative intensity control switches corresponds to the biological event that one has selected for normalizing stimulus intensity. In acute and semichronic stimulus applications, it may be necessary to redetermine the base voltage periodically until it is apparent that the drift is negligible. In chronic applications, such drift will occur while the electrode is "growing in," and thereafter base voltage (V_{base}) settings should not require further adjustment for weeks or months.

C. *Advantages and Disadvantages of Absolute and Relative Intensity Scaling*

Absolute scaling is the most frequently used, least costly in terms of apparatus, and most convenient (and abused) method for scaling stimulus intensity, but the information obtained may have little value unless the stimulating conditions are described in detail. For example, the wide discrepancy among the intensities, which have been reported to produce analgesia with repetitive stimulation of peripheral nerve (Ignelzi & Nyquist, 1976; G. A. Meyer & Fields, 1972), probably simply reflects the use of various stimulation conditions from one laboratory to another. Absolute intensity scaling would be of greater value if numerous variables in the stimulus condition could be simplified by adoption of a set of conventions governing electrode configurations, waveforms, accuracy standards, and essential parameters for description, but as the potential applications and conditions for stimulation of peripheral nerve are myriad, there appears to be no practical way of achieving realistic consensus on how absolute intensity scaling should be used.

Relative intensity scaling (biocalibration), by comparison, is more costly to implement and slightly more time-consuming to employ on a routine basis. Moreover, it can only be used under conditions in which a sharply defined biological event can be measured with objective recording procedures. Where usable, however, relative intensity scaling provides more meaningful information about the biological effect of the stimulus than does absolute intensity scaling. An incidental benefit of using this method is that it obligates the investigator to be much more aware of stimulus–response conditions and encourages him or her to use weak but sufficient stimuli, rather than overwhelming ones. The inherent danger of relying upon absolute intensity scaling is that it can be employed too casually, for example, with inadequate control; relative intensity scaling will not work properly unless it is rigorously applied.

Perhaps the greatest advantage of relative intensity scaling is its inherent ability to standardize. For example, repeatability and predictability of the stimulus–response relationships can become so well defined that behavioral response curves for sensory detection thresholds of different subjects are nearly superimposable (Bourassa & Swett, 1967; Swett & Bourassa, 1967).

V. Selective Activation

Previous sections dealt with general procedures for stimulation of peripheral nerve. This section deals with the methods used to achieve activation of selected fiber types contained within a peripheral nerve. Originally, interest in selective activation was spurred by the oversimplified concept that modalities of sensation might be directly linked with fibers of specific diameters (consult Heinbecker, Bishop, & O'Leary, 1934; Melzack & Wall, 1962; or Sinclair, 1955, 1967). As later techniques for recording neural activity became more refined, selective activation of peripheral fibers provided a tool for understanding central connections of identifiable types of sensory input. On the efferent side, selective activation of peripheral fibers made it possible to distinguish between the effects of the alpha and gamma components of the motor system (Leksell, 1945), and to permit description of the contractile behavior of different types of motor units (W. Burke & Ginsborg, 1956; Kuffler & Vaughan Williams, 1953).

Most of the methods for selective activation involve stimulation of a nerve in conjunction with a procedure for blocking transmission in a selected group of fibers. For a general discussion of clinical applications of nerve blocks, consult Levy (1977). The following discussion will focus on the research applications of nerve block, the difficulties peculiar to each method, and some general considerations in interpreting the effectiveness of selective activation.

Details on the historical development and use of the classification systems (Fig. 3) used to describe peripheral nerve can be obtained from Somjen (1972), Paintal (1973); or Boyd & Kalu (1979). Briefly, nerve fibers are classified on the basis of diameters or conduction velocities,

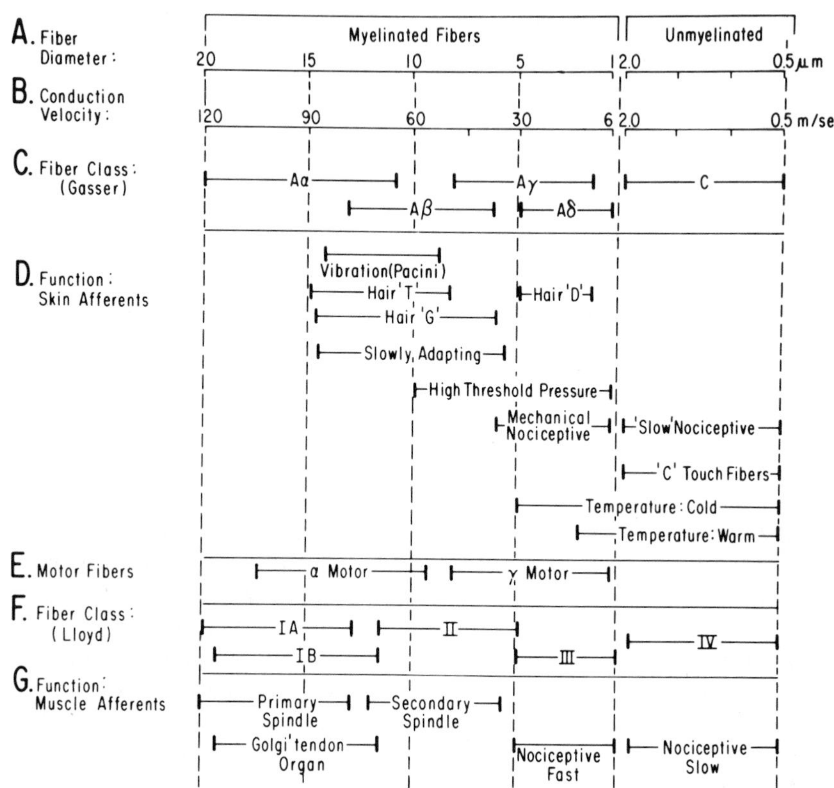

FIG. 3. Summary of fiber sizes and conduction velocities, showing fiber diameters and conduction velocities on the horizontal scale. Hursh's (1939) conversion factor has been applied to relate conduction velocity and fiber size. Although commonly used, this conversion involves some inaccuracy (for a detailed consideration of conversion factors, consult Boyd and Kalu, 1979). The data in the table should be taken as approximations. They refer to average values in small laboratory animals such as rats, rabbits, and rhesus monkeys. Recent data on human mechanoreceptors also neatly fit the diagram. Data from Hunt (1954); Hunt and McIntyre (1960); Wuerker, McPhedran, and Henneman (1965); Iggo (1968, pp. 84–111); and Burgess, Petit, and Warren (1968). (Diagram and caption based on Somjen, 1972; reprinted with permission of Plenum Publishing Corporation.)

on presence or absence of a myelinated sheath, and on functional modality. As the various factors are related, it is possible to shift from one classification system to another.

From Fig. 3 it may be noted that there is considerable overlap in the fiber sizes associated with the different types of receptors. This emphasizes that selective activation by fiber size need not result in activation of fibers exclusively from one type of receptor. Although selective activation of single receptor types is briefly covered, the major emphasis in this section is on selective activation of fibers of differing sizes or conduction velocities. It is important to realize that the fiber diameter spectrum and functional components of peripheral nerves vary greatly from one nerve to another in the same animal. Moreover, the composition of homologous nerves in different species differ greatly (Boyd & Davey, 1968; Brown & Hayden, 1971; Brown & Iggo, 1967; Willis & Coggeshall, 1978). Thus, effectiveness of selective stimulation requires an appropriate choice of nerves and species. In addition, some form of procedure is necessary in order to demonstrate that activation, in fact, has been selective for the fibers desired.

A. *Methods for Selective Activation*

1. Local Anesthetic

Activation of a select group of fibers can be accomplished by blocking conduction in adjacent axons of known size while continuing to stimulate the remaining fibers. Among the more successful procedures is the application of a local anesthetic agent, such as procaine, lidocaine, cocaine, and so on, to a peripheral nerve (deJong & Wagman, 1963; Franz & Perry, 1974). With proper concentrations of anesthetic agent covering an appropriate length of nerve, conduction can be impaired differentially in time with blockage occurring first in smaller diameter fibers. This concept was introduced by von Anrep in the 1880s when he reported the effects of cocaine on nerve conduction (Dixon, 1905). Gasser and Erlanger (1929) made an extensive study of the relation of a selective block to fiber size and found that fiber susceptibility was not strictly dependent on fiber size. The anesthetic appears to impede ionic mechanisms necessary for the depolarization of the membrane potential (Ritchie, 1979; Strichartz, 1976). In myelinated fibers, blockage occurs at the nodes of Ranvier. The electrical current produced by depolarization of one node is ordinarily sufficient to produce activation at least two nodes distant. To achieve conduction block, the anesthetic must influence a critical length of neuron encompassing more than two adjacent nodes, i.e., in a large caliber neuron, several millimeters. The nodes of Ranvier are more closely spaced on smaller-diameter myelinated axons, and thus, local anesthetic applied to a nerve will influence its smaller fibers first because they have shorter length constants. This is true in the motor system as well so that the smaller myelinated gamma motor axons seemed to be blocked sooner than the larger alpha motor axons (Landau, Weaver, & Hornbein, 1960; P. B. C. Matthews & Rushworth, 1957, 1958).

Similar arguments concerning a critical length apply also to continuous conduction in unmyelinated fibers (Franz & Perry, 1974; Strichartz, 1976). On the basis of present knowledge, it is not possible to predict the relative susceptibility of unmyelinated and myelinated fibers to anesthetic block. It has been empirically reported that *C*-fibers are blocked before or at about the same time as the smaller myelinated fibers, which means that it may be impossible to block only the unmyelinated fibers (Franz & Perry, 1974; Nathan & Sears, 1961). In the autonomic system, however, the small myelinated preganglionic axons (usually called *B*-fibers, but see Paintal, 1973) may be far more sensitive to lidocaine than the unmyelinated postganglionic *C*-fibers (Heavner & deJong, 1974).

Blocking of neural conduction by local anesthetic does not occur in strict accordance with fiber diameter. One reason is that if segments of the nerve trunk longer than about 4 mm are bathed by the anesthetic, the critical length for all fiber sizes will be exceeded; all fibers will tend to be blocked at the same time (Franz & Perry, 1974). Also, some large fibers may reside more superficially in the nerve trunk than some smaller fibers; hence, differential diffusion rates and local concentrations of blocking agents will influence the large fibers before reaching the small fibers at the center of the nerve trunk (Franz & Perry, 1974). These factors reduce selectivity. Another complication is that a slowing in conduction velocity takes place prior to the blocking effect so that neural activity responses will change even before blocking occurs, and interpretations can be misleading (Franz & Perry, 1974).

In chronic studies a complete, prolonged block of nerve conduction can be obtained by gradual diffusion of the local anesthetic agent from a silastic cuff impregnated with the drug and placed around the selected nerve. Stimulating electrodes can be installed in the cuff to test the efficacy of the block (Benoit & Changeaux, 1978; Robert & Oester, 1970). The possibility of developing a system using circulating fluids to obtain partial block in chronic experiments, might be worth considering. Complete reversible blocks can also be obtained by injection of the anesthetic agent near a peripheral nerve, but this is not a reliable technique for obtaining selective blocks because of poor control over the amount and concentration of anesthetic reaching the nerve (Mackenzie, Burke, Skuse, & Lethlean, 1975; Torebjork & Hallin, 1973).

In acute studies, controlled application of local anesthetic can be obtained by using iontophoretic injections (Gangarosa, Park, & King, 1977), or extrusion of an agar–procaine solution through micropipettes (Kater, Fountain, & Hadley, 1976). More typical, however, is the topical application of filter paper soaked in the anesthetic solution (P. B. C. Matthews & Rushworth, 1957) or the use of a chamber in which the nerve is surrounded by the anesthetic solution (Franz & Perry, 1974; Nathan & Sears, 1961). These latter methods allow repeated applications of and recovery from the anesthetic.

To obtain selective blockade, weak concentrations of blocking agent must be applied to the nerve, so the time required to obtain the block will be prolonged (deJong & Wagman, 1963; Nathan & Sears, 1963). There will be a period of time when conduction in most of the smaller fibers will be impaired, but larger fibers will be able to conduct in an unhindered fashion.

Other chemical approaches to selective nerve block have been suggested but not explored in the same detail as anesthetics. Decreases in sodium concentration may block conduction in smaller fibers before large fibers are blocked (Nathan & Sears, 1962). Lack of oxygen appears to have a similar effect (Heinbecker, 1929). Phenol initially was reported to produce a selective block in a manner similar to local anesthetics, but more recent work indicates that there may be no selective effect (Fisher, Cress, Haines, Panin, & Paul, 1970).

2. Pressure

Gasser and Erlanger (1929) found that pressure applied directly to frog nerve tends to selectively block conduction in the larger fibers while smaller ones continue to function. Later studies verified and extended these observations to include *C*-fibers (Bishop, Heinbecker, & O'Leary, 1933). Leksell (1945) used a pressure clamp, and even more effectively his fingers, to reveal the selective influence of gamma motoneurons on intrafusal muscle fibers through blockade of larger alpha motoneurons. It is difficult to calibrate the pressures so as to obtain uniform results from one preparation to another. Moreover, some damage to the nerve results, so that the effects are not fully reversible.

In humans and with other chronic preparations, pressure can be applied to superficial nerves by compressing the overlaying skin with a thin edge. Such a pressure block should not be confused with an ischemic block, which has a different effect on neural conduction (see the next section).

By application of pressure it is possible to eliminate activity in myelinated fibers while leaving *C*-fiber activity intact, but to obtain a clear separation between components of the myelinated fiber groups is difficult or usually impossible. Nevertheless, the procedure has had a long history of use in studies of sensory function in man, dating back at least to Herzen in 1886 (Zotterman, 1933). Pressure block of *A*-fiber components was successfully used to show that *C*-fiber activity in normal humans gives rise to the experience of pain (Dyson & Brindley, 1966; Mackenzie *et al.*, 1975). The possibility of permanent damage to axons (Moldaver,

1954), and poor selectivity within the *A*-fiber groups suggest that pressure block may have limited applications.

3. Ischemia

Ischemia causes preferential blockade of conduction in small fibers before larger ones (Fox & Kenmore, 1967; Heinbecker, 1929). It is seldom put to deliberate use in acute experiments as a means of selective fiber block, but may be inadvertently produced. It can also induce pain. Ischemia is sometimes used on man, because it can be easily produced with a pressure cuff inflated above systolic blood pressure (Horowitz & Ginsberg-Felner, 1979). Paresthesias occur within 1 to 3 min, peak at 3–4 min, and wane over the next 3–5 min (Horowitz & Ginsberg-Felner, 1979; Sinclair, 1948). Insofar as possible, care must be taken to prevent any compression of the underlying nerves, as this would result in pressure block (Sinclair, 1948). Ischemia may produce a transient increase in neural excitability (Seneviratne & Peiris, 1968; Weddel & Sinclair, 1947). Complete block of all fibers will occur after 20 to 30 min, and restoration of blood flow will quickly restore normal function. Although studies of sensory function in humans with ischemic block have been widely used to draw psychophysical conclusions about the relations between sensory experience and fiber diameters, few studies have had independent physiological measures to determine which fibers were actually blocked (Mackenzie *et al.*, 1975; Willer, 1977). In addition, in many studies the stimuli used to test different sensory functions are not equivalent (Sinclair & Glasgow, 1960).

4. Cooling

Gasser (1931) noted that cooling a frog nerve reduced the height of the compound action potential to a low level. There was a gradual loss of height when the temperature was reduced from about 30 to 15°C, after which the spike amplitude decreased sharply, approaching a minimum as the temperature dropped to about 5°C.

Current evidence suggests that conduction in mammalian myelinated axons is blocked completely but reversibly at temperatures between 5 to 7°C, while *C*-fibers still conduct, although at reduced velocities (W. Douglas & Malcolm, 1955; Franz & Iggo, 1968; Paintal, 1965, 1967). At temperatures around 4°C conduction block of *C*-fibers can be produced. Any selective blocking action on conduction within the myelinated group seems unlikely. During cooling, the *A*-delta elevation of the compound action potential disappears while the elevation due to activity in the larger diameter fibers remains visible. Recordings of single fibers, however, demonstrate that the *A*-delta fibers still conduct, and the decreased

A-delta elevation is due to temporal dispersion caused by a slowing of conduction velocity (Franz & Iggo, 1968; Paintal, 1965). The unit studies suggest that all sizes of myelinated fibers block at about the same low temperature (Franz & Iggo, 1968; Paintal, 1967), but this remains debatable (Byck, Goldfarb, Schaumburg, & Sharpless, 1972).

Cooling of human peripheral nerve can be accomplished by cooling the skin with running chilled water where a nerve runs close beneath its surface (Sinclair & Hinshaw, 1951). Thermodes with circulating fluids have been used for cooling of more limited areas of skin or exposed nerve. In acute work with exposed nerves, cuff-shaped thermodes have been constructed so that cooling may be applied directly to the circumference of a nerve bundle (Byck *et al.*, 1972; W. Douglas & Malcolm, 1955; Franz & Iggo, 1968).

A newer cooling technique makes use of the Peltier effect, which allows the temperature to be controlled as a function of applied voltage. The polarity of the voltage determines whether the thermode's surface will be warmed or cooled. These devices have been described in detail for use on cerebral cortex (Reed & Miller, 1978), deep structures of the brain (Hayward, Ott, Stuart, & Cheshire, 1965), the skin (Gordon & Kay, 1960; Lele, 1962; Wolf & Basmajian, 1973), and for blocking of conduction in exposed nerves (Layman, 1971; Roberts & Blackburn, 1975). The Peltier thermode provides an easy and accurate means of temperature control, and also allows the use of multiple probes and convenient timing control with electronic devices readily available in most laboratories. The speed with which the temperature changes, however, may be somewhat slower with a Peltier device (about 1°C per second) than with fluids, and the voltages needed to operate the system may cause electrical interference under certain recording conditions.

Cooling is a relatively simple method for producing temporary nerve block, but it seems to provide little differentiation between myelinated fibers, and may influence conduction in *C*-fibers when *A*-fibers are completely blocked. In addition, cooling or warming fibers may cause initiation of neural activity at temperatures that must be traversed to produce blocking. In myelinated fibers, warming tends to excite smaller fibers before the larger ones, and cooling has the reverse effect (Dodt, 1953; Granit & Lundberg, 1947; von Euler, 1947). One should be aware that some sensory receptors may respond to cooling (Michalski and Sequin, 1975). From our experience, cold block has some limitations. The nerve does not recover rapidly after a period of brief (10–15 min) cooling; 30–60 min of recovery time may be required before the compound potential recovers its original form after rewarming. Repeated cooling further delays full recovery and leads us to suspect that some amount of permanent injury may occur with cooling. One should be aware that cooling can produce circulatory changes and other complications that could influence interpretation of changes that follow cooling procedures (Sinclair, 1967).

5. Ultrasound

Ultrasound has been used to produce a selective, reversible block of the smaller fibers of frog nerve (Young & Henneman, 1961). This technique seldom has been used and, therefore, is difficult to evaluate.

6. Graded Stimulus Intensity

The use of carefully graded increases in stimulus intensity to activate the largest diameter fibers in a nerve trunk and gradually to recruit smaller fibers as intensity is increased has been briefly described in Section II-H. Some of the advantages of this procedure and details of an appropriate stimulator are given in Sections III-B and C.

Use of graded stimulus intensities has proven especially valuable in investigation of the central influence of the Group I afferent projections from muscle spindles (Bradley & Eccles, 1953). With stimulation of muscle nerve, the weakest effective stimulus will exclusively activate Group I fibers. Depending upon the muscle nerve being stimulated, Group II fibers may be recruited with stimulus intensities of 1.3 to 2.0 *T* (Brock, Eccles, & Rall, 1951; J. C. Eccles, Oscarsson & Willis, 1961; R. M. Eccles & Lundberg, 1959; Giaquinto, Pompeiano, & Swett, 1963; Pompeiano & Swett, 1962b; Swett & Bourassa, 1967). Group I activity continues to increase and reaches a maximum around 2.0 to 2.5 *T*. Group II recruitment tends to be complete when intensities are raised to about 5.0 *T* (Oscarsson, 1959). Group III fibers in muscle nerves begin to be recruited at or above 5.0 *T* (Brock *et al.*, 1951). Using graded stimulation, Bradley and Eccles (1953) were able to distinguish between Group Ia and Ib fibers in some nerves.

In afferent nerves lacking the large-diameter Group I afferents, minimal stimulus intensities activate fibers in the A-beta range. In stimulation of human cutaneous nerve the A-delta fibers begin to be recruited at 3–6 *T* (D. Burke, Mackenzie, Skuse, & Lethlean, 1975; Collins, Nulsen, & Randt, 1960). All myelinated fibers appear to be activated at intensities of about 10 *T*. Intensities required to activate *C*-fibers are significantly higher, such as 15–20 *T* (D. Burke *et al.*, 1975) or even more (Collins *et al.*, 1960). These values differ according to the nerve or methods used, because D. Burke *et al.* (1975) report that with radial nerve stimulation *C*-fibers became active at 5.0 to 7.0 *T*.

One of the difficulties in use of graded stimulus intensities is the great variability in composition of peripheral nerves between species (Brown & Hayden, 1971; Brown & Iggo, 1967). Unless the composition of the nerve is known, it is not possible to state exactly which fiber groups will be activated by a stimulus at a given value above the minimally effective intensity. To establish which fiber types are activated by graded stimulation, one can be guided by observations of previous investigators, but, in order to increase the degree of certainty, the conduction velocity of the fibers in question should be determined (Chambers, Eggett, & Eldred, 1970). If a correlation is desired between the fibers activated and their functional classifications (e.g., receptor types, and so on), then because of the overlap in fiber size of different types of receptors, conduction velocities alone are an insufficient guide. Some other means, preferably single unit recordings, coupled with natural stimuli must be used to establish the functional identity of the fiber types (Burgess & Perl, 1973).

Recruitment by fiber size will reliably occur if the electrode configuration creates a uniform electrical field across the entire cross section of the nerve. If one part of the nerve trunk is influenced more than another by the electrical field, the subset of neurons activated at very low intensities will contain only a small fraction of largest fibers but may possibly also include a few small-diameter fibers that lie in closer proximity to the electrode–nerve interface where current densities will be greatest.

Weak stimuli can also cause longer latencies because of slower rise-times in the induced electrotonic potentials. As stimulus intensity is raised, latencies will decrease to a stable, minimum value. A decrease in latency, however, can also result because higher stimulus intensities may cause a spread in current that will activate nodes of Ranvier situated further away from the stimulating electrode (Rushton, 1949; Wiederholt, 1970a, 1970b). A decrease in latency does not necessarily mean that smaller fibers were recruited before larger ones; conduction velocity measurements are more reliable indicators of fiber size and should be used to resolve uncertainties.

Electrodes producing a nonuniform field of current around a nerve trunk can be used to advantage when one wishes to stimulate only a portion of the fibers in a nerve. This can be accomplished by using commercially available electrodes consisting of a group of small wires or a cuff with a number of small electrodes, each with its own lead wire. This approach has been valuable in stimulating mixed human nerves. A particular electrode combination may produce painful and distracting motor contractions while another combination may produce, at lower thresholds, paresthesias instead of motor effects. At the time of implantation various combinations of electrode pairs can be tested until the configuration of current flow is such that the stimulus will operate most effectively on the combination of fibers desired by the experimenter.

With appropriate electrodes, configurations, impedance matching, and precise control of pulse parameters, graded stimulation is one of the most useful and reliable means of selectively activating large-diameter nerve fibers.

7. "Double-volley" and "Collision" Techniques

There are two methods for obtaining specific information about nerve fibers that take advantage of the absolute refractory period of axons: the "double-volley" and "collision" techniques.

The "double-volley" technique depends upon the delivery, with one or two pairs of electrodes, of two stimuli of different amplitudes, separated in time by 0.3 to 1.0 msec. By exploiting the principle that the largest diameter fibers are recruited at the weakest suprathreshold intensities, it is possible to separate in time the central actions of a group of higher threshold components by removing the lower threshold component. The first stimulus, the conditioning stimulus, is the weaker of the two and is adjusted in amplitude to activate most or all fibers of the lowest threshold fiber group. The second stimulus, the test stimulus, is of greater amplitude and is adjusted to recruit the same group of fibers plus one or more higher threshold fiber groups of smaller diameter. The delayed test stimulus is timed to occur during the absolute refractory period of the fibers activated by the first shock. The test stimulus will succeed in activating only those fibers that had not first been activated by the conditioning shock. The "double-volley" technique was a valuable tool for determining the identities of Group Ia and Ib fibers in muscle nerves and their respective synaptic actions within the spinal cord (Bradley & Eccles, 1953; J. C. Eccles, Eccles, & Lundberg, 1957). More recently this method was used to expose the central actions of higher threshold muscle afferents in the spinal cord with microelectrode field-potential analysis (Fu, Santini, & Schomburg, 1974).

The "collision" technique is not a selective activation technique *per se,* but rather a method to assess activity in selective fiber populations. This technique has proved useful for measuring conduction velocities in small-diameter fibers and *C*-fibers. It is an indirect method that may require one to three pairs of stimulating electrodes, depending upon the objectives of the experiment. Electrically induced antidromic volleys are recorded while naturally or electrically induced orthodromic activity occurs in the same nerve bundle. When two action potentials collide in a fiber they are annihilated. W. W. Douglas and Ritchie (1957) applied a stimulus, supramaximal for whatever components were to be studied, to the proximal end of a cut visceral nerve. A recording electrode was placed distally between the site of stimulation and the visceral sensory receptors. If any sensory fibers are conducting action potentials centrally, their axons will be in an absolute refractory state at some point between the stimulating and recording electrodes. The amplitude of the antidromically conducted compound action potential will be inversely proportional to the amount of orthodromic impulse traffic. By appropriate positioning of the stimulating and recording electrodes and by use of discrete natural stimuli, it is possible to obtain quantitative measure of small fiber activity. A variation on this procedure was developed by Iggo (1958) for measuring conduction velocities in identifiable *C*-fibers in the vagus nerve. The method has been used successfully to assess activity in visceral nerves of humans (Guz & Trenchard, 1971a).

These methods require exacting experimental conditions and considerable care in utilization, for they can yield information that is sometimes difficult to interpret. The "double-volley" technique has the drawback that the test stimulus can precondition events that are to be analyzed centrally. Antidromic volleys may affect sensory receptors (Paintal, 1959b). Thus, these procedures can be used best only when prior conditioning can be safely excluded as a contaminant in the events under observation. When properly used and controlled, these methods can yield valuable information.

8. Stimulus Frequency

Bishop (1932) found that Faradic (make-and-break) stimulation applied to a nerve caused a reversible block. With careful application large-fiber input could be selectively blocked while smaller fibers remained functional (Bishop & Heinbecker, 1935). A burst of Faradic stimulation 6–12 sec in duration produces a block lasting 2–4 min, which can be repeated up to 30 times (Collins & Randt, 1960). It is possible to use pulses of 0.3–0.5 msec in duration applied to the nerve at 30 Hz for short periods of time (Laporte & Montastruc, 1957). These stimuli produced total block, but the small fibers recovered before the large ones, and their effects could be assessed for brief periods before activity in the large fibers resumed.

The use of alternating currents of about 5 kHz (Muller & Hunsperger, 1967), or even higher frequencies of 20 kHz, can also be used to produce blocks (Tanner, 1962). Force of muscle contraction can be regulated by applying a 600-Hz blocking stimulus between a driving stimulus to the muscle and the muscle itself. McNeal & Reswick (1976) argue that neural transmission is prevented at frequencies of 300–700 Hz due to depletion of the synaptic neurotransmitter at motor end plates. At higher frequencies of stimulation (1000 Hz), a true nerve block exists, i.e., a region of nerve in which nerve impulses cannot pass. Paintal (1959b) suggest that the antidromic activity induced by short-duration bursts, less than 1 sec of high-frequency stimulation, does not cause a nerve block, but rather acts by depressing the excitability of sensory receptors.

Voltages needed for this form of blocking are high, from 10 to 40 V (Laporte and Montastruc, 1957; Tanner, 1962). While this technique is simple, it has some of the same drawbacks found with other electrical techniques. It is not useful in separating myelinated fiber groups. High-frequency blocking pulses also stimulate and, therefore, the result is a barrage of input to the CNS before the impulses of interest arrive (Woo & Campbell, 1964). Although with continued stimulation, a true block might be established, events under study could be preconditioned by this barrage.

9. Inability to Follow

The activity in some fibers can also be eliminated by stimulating at rates too high for fibers to follow. It has been reported that in humans, larger myelinated fibers can follow at rates of at least 50 Hz, although slower-conducting *A*-fibers may begin to show evidence of block at this frequency. *C*-fibers, however, block at stimulus frequencies from 2 to 10 Hz and, in general, any burst of activity nay lead to blocking of these fibers (Torebjork & Hallin, 1973, 1974). It should be noted that in the cat, *C*-fibers are able to follow at much higher rates of stimulation (Brown, Hamann, & Martin, 1975). As with the preceding techniques, this one also has the disadvantage of producing large amounts of neural activity, even in the fibers to be blocked, and therefore can only be employed when such activity will not disturb the phenomenon to be investigated.

10. Anodal Block

Pflüger is said to be the first to report that nerve impulses sometimes had difficulty in passing the anodal electrode (Accornero, Bini, Lenzi, & Manfredi, 1977). This is because the resting potential under the anode is displaced to a level that will fail to sustain the action potential. Larger fibers are more readily hyperpolarized in the region of the anode than smaller fibers, and will tend to be blocked first (Accornero *et al.*, 1977). By using graded stimulus intensities, anodal block can be used in an attempt to achieve selective fiber blockade.

Mendell and Wall (1964) elaborated a technique to analyze afferent activity similar to that first proposed by Kuffler and Gerard (1947). A set of polarizing electrodes is attached to the nerve, the anodal side of the polarizing electrodes being proximally placed. A dc current controlled by a potentiometer is passed through the polarizing electrodes. As the current is increased, large fibers are blocked first, followed by smaller ones. The current required for blocking depends on a number of factors, but values of 50 to 500 μA have been reported. Although there is general agreement that larger fibers block before smaller ones, it is not clear to what degree selective fiber excitation can be achieved. Kuffler and Gerard (1947) expressed disappointment with the selectivity of dc blocking currents. There is evidence that myelinated fibers will block before unmyelinated ones (but see Dawson, Merrill, & Wall, 1970), and alpha fibers before gamma fibers (Fukushima, Yahara, & Kato, 1975; Kato & Fukushima, 1974). Fukushima and Kato (1975) claimed that Group I afferents may be blocked while permitting Group II afferents to conduct. In general, however, the sequence of blocking within the myelinated fiber spectrum does not always appear to be well-correlated with fiber diameter (Casey & Blick, 1969; Manfredi, 1970). In some cases *A*-delta fibers may be affected before or simultaneously with larger *A*-fibers (Brown & Hamann, 1972; Whitwam & Kidd, 1975).

Disadvantages of dc blocking currents are the risk of rapid deterioration of the nerve (Brown *et al.*, 1975; Guz & Trenchard, 1971b) and evidence that the current itself causes the supposedly blocked nerve fibers to initiate action potentials in an asynchronous manner that may lead to spurious effects (Campbell & Woo, 1966; Cangiano & Lutzemberger, 1972; Sassan & Zimmerman, 1973). These observations suggest that the method has severe limitations and is of questionable value.

A number of variations aimed at overcoming some of these technical difficulties with dc anodal blocking have been suggested. They include reversing the position of the anode and cathode (Zimmerman, 1968), but this does not appear to be uniformally successful (Dawson *et al.*, 1970; Manfredi, 1970). Another variant is to straddle the standard bipolar stimulating electrode with a polarizing pair of electrodes whose anode lies between the stimulating cathode and the recording site (Fukushima *et al.*, 1975). With dc anodal blocks, some authors suggest the use of ramp-shaded leading and trailing edges of the blocking current to minimize unwanted neural excitation (Cangiano & Lutzemberger, 1972; Kato & Fukushima, 1974; Manfredi, 1970; Zimmerman, 1968).

Another variation of the anodal block technique was suggested by Kuffler and Vaughn Williams (1953) who described a method requiring brief pulses and only one set of electrodes. An impulse originating at the cathode, with the correct choice of electrode separation and pulse duration, will be blocked at the anode. If the anodal block is removed at the appropriate instant, impulses arriving later in slowly conducting fibers will pass unhindered. By simply reversing polarity, both large and small fibers can be activated simultaneously, thus allowing combined effects to be studied. Kuffler and Vaughn Williams (1953) thought that the method was not applicable to a whole nerve bundle with its intact protective sheaths because current paths cannot be adequately controlled. There were also obvious constraints on stimulus pulse parameters. Nevertheless, this method has been used successfully to obtain selective activation of the smaller motoneurons innervating slowly contracting motor units (W. Burke & Ginsborg, 1956). Harley (1977) has suggested a possible modification of this method for use with prosthetic devices.

While applications of brief-duration dc blocking currents avoid some of the difficulties associated with long-duration dc currents, other complications are introduced; the possibility of anodal break stimulation is intensified (Manfredi, 1970; Mendell & Wall, 1964; Whitwan & Kidd, 1975). In order to avoid this problem, trapezoidal waveforms with slowly rising and declining edges are useful (W. Burke & Ginsborg, 1956; Koizumi, Collin, Kaufman, & Brook, 1970). This problem seems to have been best resolved by Accornero *et al.* (1977). They employed a "triangular pulse" with a steeply rising leading edge and an exponentially decrementing trailing edge. The nerve is stimulated with bipolar (or tripolar) electrodes. These authors observed that tripolar electrodes with a central cathode and distal and proximal anodes worked well on intact nerve bundles. The rectangular pulse from the stimulator is shaped by a diode and resistance–capacitance circuit whose time-constant allows the trailing edge of the pulse to fall exponentially to zero over a period of several milliseconds. The cathode initiates action potentials in the normal way; these are then blocked by the prolonged hyperpolarization induced by the gradually decaying anodal currents. By adjusting the time-constant and amplitude of the pulse, it is possible to selectively block larger-diameter fibers while permitting activity in the smaller fibers to pass through the zone of blockade. The circuit described by Accornero *et al.* (1977) works well in high impedance conditions but must be modified with appropriate impedance-matching devices, such as an operational amplifier, to be effective in low impedance conditions. The technique has the advantage of producing selective blockade without eliciting activity that can contaminate CNS activity prior to the time of arrival of the desired afferent input. There are still constraints on pulse rates, because of the long duration of the stimulating–blocking pulse.

Another method, which combines the anodal block principle with the collision technique, has recently been described. It allows higher rates of stimulation and unidirectional conduction of evoked action potentials. The method was devised as a means of evoking antidromic activity in motor nerves at rates that, using the collision concept, would cancel naturally occurring orthodromic impulses in motor axons without evoking muscle contractions (Van den Honert & Mortimer, 1979). An asymmetric tripolar stimulating electrode is used in which a central cathode is placed closer to one of the two anodes. A pulse with an abrupt onset, short plateau phase (350 msec), and exponential falling phase is used to initiate neural activity. Propagation in one direction is prevented by the more positive anode, whereas the less positive anode permits propagation in the opposite direction. This type of "blocking" electrode may have certain advantages. The neural activity thus produced can be "collided" with neural-occurring neural activity or with activity imitated from another set of electrodes and thus provide selective conduction in smaller-diameter fiber groups. Some of the problems usually associated with anodal block techniques may be largely circumvented by this novel approach. It is not yet known whether this method could be employed successfully to study the central effects of uncontaminated small-fiber afferent inputs to CNS structures.

11. Other Techniques

Selective activation can be obtained by subdividing nerve bundles until only a single fiber remains on the stimulating electrodes. This method is useful for only special types of preparations. It is tedious but highly effective if the fiber's functional identity is to be confirmed (Kuffler & Gerard, 1947).

Selective activation of functional classes of afferent fibers can be achieved by using natural stimulation. This topic is beyond the scope of this review, but it should be noted that natural stimulation may often be the least ambiguous way to insure activation of functionally similar afferent fibers (R. E. Burke, Rudomin, Vyklicky, & Zajac, 1971; Kuffler & Gerard, 1947; Schmidt, 1969).

B. Evaluations of Selective Excitation Techniques

The extent to which selective excitation or blocking is effective is frequently evaluated by measuring amplitude and conduction velocities of subcomponents of the electrically evoked compound action potential. Decreases in amplitude or disappearance of particular subcomponents of interest is taken to indicate the establishment of the block. This conclusion, however, is unwarranted. Blocking by cooling, local anesthetic, or anodal currents may cause differential slowing of conduction velocities in fibers within the region of the block. Such slowing causes an increase in the dispersion of the conduction velocities. This dispersion can significantly reduce the amplitude "signatures" of fiber subcomponents and give the appearance of a partial, or even complete, block when many unwanted action potentials may still be conducted. Slowing and dispersion affects the smaller fibers to a greater degree than the larger ones, so that the *A*-delta elevation of the compound action potential, for example, is more likely to disappear than are the larger, less dispersed elevations associated with the larger, more rapidly conducting *A*-fibers. This probably accounts for some of the disagreement in the literature on whether the *A*-delta group is actually blocked before the *A*-beta fiber group under certain conditions.

Another source of difficulty in evaluating the extent of blocking is the possibility that although the block appears to be present, the means of producing it may elicit additional unwanted neural activation in "blocked" fibers. This kind of activity can result from collision and double volley techniques, high-frequency blocking, temperature changes, and anodal break excitation. As the neural firing is asynchronous, it will not be observable if the compound action potential is the only measure used to monitor effectiveness of the block; single-unit studies, or recordings from small populations of spinal root fibers, must be carried out to make quantitative estimates of the completeness of the block. Analysis of central events known to be caused by the supposedly blocked fibers may also serve as a useful control (Bradley & Eccles, 1953; Casey & Blick, 1969). One or both of these precautions are necessary before it can be assumed that blocking was satisfactory.

In addition to the factors mentioned previously, there are still other complications that may result from nerve block and selective activation techniques. These topics fall outside the scope of this chapter, but a few can be briefly mentioned. Electrical stimulation is likely to produce quite unnatural patterns of neural activity including simultaneous activation of axons from functionally different receptor types. This results in central processing that might be far different from that occurring in normal conditions (R. E. Burke *et al.,* 1971; Loeb, Bak, & Duysens, 1977). Peripheral nerve stimulation also can directly and indirectly influence the autonomic nervous system, which, in turn, may influence sensory function (Kline, Yeung, & Calaresu, 1968; Sato & Schmidt, 1973). Any kind of blocking will change not only the total and relative amounts of neural activity, but also will change any conditioning influences normally exerted by the blocked fibers. For a detailed discussion, consult Melzack and Wall (1962).

Many of the techniques for selective activation of peripheral nerve fibers have been applied to human subjects (for example, Kellgren & McGowan, 1948), often for the purpose of exploring physiological mechanisms of sensory experience. One major difficulty in interpreting sensory loss due to nerve block in humans is the frequent failure to match the test stimuli in terms of sensory magnitudes (Sinclair & Glasgow, 1960). It also should be clear that results of studies which rely on psychophysics, rather than on direct recording of neural activity to indicate blocking or activation of certain nerve fibers, may produce reliable sensory data but cannot be interpreted in terms of neural mechanisms (W. W. Douglas & Ritchie, 1962; Sinclair, 1967). Along with the difficulties of getting adequate separation on the basis of fiber size, axons from different kinds of mechanoreceptors in humans, as in animals, have overlapping fiber sizes that further increase the difficulty in analyzing the sensory results in terms of receptor types (Knibestol, 1973, 1975). If the blocking procedures cause asynchronous firing, then central effects would be complex and probably not interpretable as simple loss of activity in one group of afferent fibers. Recently, it has become possible to record single units from awake humans, and this procedure will be useful in providing some of the necessary controls (Mackenzie *et al.*, 1975; Torebjork, 1979; Torebjork & Hallin, 1973; Vallbo & Johansson, 1979).

The role of receptor specificity and labeled-lines in sensation is not completely resolved; many central neurons receive convergent input, and natural stimuli will usually cause activity in axons of more than one type of mechanoreceptor. If the resulting sensation is due to this complex input rather than the activation of one type of receptor, then selective activation will be less useful than previously believed in revealing the neural mechanisms of sensation.

VI. Concluding Comments

We have attempted to review the basic techniques of electrical stimulation of mammalian peripheral nerve and have intentionally restricted our survey to general principles and advantages and disadvantages of certain procedures. Precluded was any consideration of the admittedly important topic of the commercially available electronic equipment designed for the purpose of stimulating excitable tissues. These instruments differ in quality, accuracy, pulse-delivery characteristics, and safety features. One instrument may be suitable for one set of applications and unsuitable for others, and the applications intended and their requirements must be defined before an intelligent choice of the instrument can be made. One consideration often not given proper attention is the adaptability of the instrument to relative intensity scaling with minimal hardware modifications.

Peripheral nerve stimulation with electrical pulses is subject to an almost limitless number of variables, all of which influence the biological effectiveness of the stimulus. The variables (stimulator designs, electrode configurations and physical characteristics, stimulus environment, pulse waveforms, and timing parameters) would seem to defy universal standardization. It is frequently difficult (and sometimes impossible) to interpret, verify, or reconcile published observations of different laboratories because of poorly documented descriptions of the stimulus–response conditions. This need not be the case. We believe that some degree of standardization can be imposed on the techniques for electrical stimulation for a wide variety of routine uses. Application of two principles, relative intensity scaling and minimal net charge transfer per unit-time, would be a rational step toward standardization. Relative intensity scaling normalizes stimulus strength in relation to a sharply defined biological event and minimizes the variables in stimulus–response conditions. It permits reliable comparisons between subjects and observations of different laboratories. Whether electrical stimulation is to be applied to nerves in man or animals, every effort should be made to use relative intensity scaling (biocalibration) whenever possible. Net charge transfer can be minimized by using minimal pulse durations (but not less than 50 to 100 μsec durations), lower frequencies, and interrupted pulse trains in lieu of continuous stimulus rates and, where applicable, biphasic pulses.

With improvements in biomaterials and the exploration of the use of peripheral nerve stimulation for behavioral studies in animals and therapeutic, prosthetic, and neural augmentive applications in man, the electrical stimulation of nerve assuredly will become an even more increasingly effective tool in research and medicine.

Acknowledgments

This work was supported by the National Institutes of Health Grant NS13751. We wish to thank Professor Earl Eldred, Department of Anatomy, University of California, Los Angeles, for his constructive review of the manuscript, and also Mrs. Sherril Sharp and Ms. Cecile Woodcock for their indefatigable efforts in preparing it.

References

Abzug, C., Maeda, M., Peterson, B. W., & Wilson, V. J. Cervical branching of lumbar vestibulospinal axons. *Journal of Physiology (London)*, 1974, **243,** 499–522.

Accornero, N., Bini, G., Lenzi, G. L., & Manfredi, M. Selective activation of peripheral nerve fibre groups of different diameter by triangular shaped stimulus pulses. *Journal of Physiology (London),* 1977, **273,** 539–560.

Babb, M. I., & Dymond, A. M. *Electrode implantation in the human body.* Brain Information Service/Brain Research Institute, University of California, Los Angeles, 1974.

Baker, M. A. Spontaneous and evoked activity of neurones in the somatosensory thalamus of the waking cat. *Journal of Physiology (London),* 1971, **217,** 359–379.

Baron, F. C., Wayner, M. S., Aguilar-Baturoni, & Guevara-Aguilar, R. A bipolar electrode for peripheral nerve stimulation. *Brain Research Bulletin,* 1979, **4,** 421–422.

Bartlett, J. R., Doty, R. W., Sr., Lee, B. B., Negrao, N., & Overman, W. H., Jr. Deleterious effects of prolonged electrical excitation of striate cortex in macaques. *Brain, Behavior and Evolution,* 1977, **14,** 46–66.

Bean, C. P. A. A theory of microstimulation of myelinated fibres. *Journal of Physiology (London),* 1974, **243,** 514–522. (Appendix to Abzug *et al.,* 1974)

Becker, H. C., Peacock, S. M., Jr., Heath, G. G., & Mickle, W. A. Methods of stimulation control and concurrent electrographic recording. In D. E. Sheer, (Ed.), *Electrical stimulation of the brain.* Austin: University of Texas Press, 1961. Pp. 74–90.

Benoit, P., & Changeux, J. P. Consequences of blocking the nerve with a local anesthetic on the evolution of multiinnervation at the regenerating neuromuscular junction of the rat. *Brain Research,* 1978, **149,** 89–96.

Bernstein, J. J., Johnson, P. F., Hench, L. L., Hunter, G., & Dawson, W. W. Cortical histopathology following stimulation with metallic and carbon electrodes. *Brain, Behavior and Evolution,* 1977, **14,** 126–157.

Bishop, G. H. Action of nerve depressants on potential. *Journal of Cellular and Comparative Physiology,* 1932, **1,** 177–194.

Bishop, G. H. My life among the axons. *Annual Review of Physiology,* 1965, **27,** 1–18.

Bishop, G. H., & Heinbecker, P. The afferent function of non-myelinated or C fibers. *American Journal of Physiology,* 1935, **114,** 179–193.

Bishop, G. H., Heinbecker, P., & O'Leary, J. L. The function of the non-myelinated fibers of the dorsal roots. *American Journal of Physiology,* 1933, **106,** 647–669.

Blair, G. A., & Erlanger, J. A comparison of the characteristics of axons through their individual electrical responses. *American Journal of Physiology,* 1933, **106,** 524–564.

Blair, G. A., & Erlanger, J. On the process of excitation by brief shocks in axons. *American Journal of Physiology,* 1936, **114,** 309–316.

Bourassa, C. M., & Swett, J. E. Sensory discrimination thresholds with cutaneous nerve volleys in the cat. *Journal of Neurophysiology,* 1967, **30,** 515–529.

Bourde, J., Robinson, L. A., Suda, Y., & White, T. T. Vagal stimulation. I. A technic for repeated stimulation of the vagus on conscious dogs. *Annals of Surgery,* 1970, **171,** 352–356.

Boyd, I. A., & Davey, M. R. *Composition of peripheral nerves.* Edinburgh: Livingstone, 1968.

Boyd, I. A., & Kalu, K. U. Scaling factor relating conduction velocity and diameter for myelinated afferent nerve fibres in the cat hind limb. *Journal of Physiology (London),* 1979, **289,** 277–297.

Bradley, K., & Eccles, J. C. Analysis of the fast afferent impulses from thigh muscles. *Journal of Physiology (London),* 1953, **122,** 462–473.

Brindley, G. S. Electrode arrays for making long-lasting electrical connexion to spinal roots. *Journal of Physiology (London),* 1972, **222,** 135P–136P.

Brock, L. G., Eccles, J. C., & Rall, W. Experimental investigations on the afferent fibres in muscle nerves. *Proceedings of the Royal Society of London, Series B,* 1951, **138,** 453–475.

Brown, A. G., & Hamann, W. C. DC-Polarization and impulse conduction failure in mammalian nerve fibres. *Journal of Physiology (London)*, 1972, **222,** 66–67.

Brown, A. G., Hamann, W. C., & Martin, H. F. Effects of activity in non-myelinated afferent fibers on spinocervical tract. *Brain Research,* 1975, **98,** 243–259.

Brown, A. G., & Hayden, R. E. The distribution of cutaneous receptors in the rabbits hindlimb and differential electrical stimulation of their axons. *Journal of Physiology (London),* 1971, **213,** 495–506.

Brown, A. G., & Iggo, A. A quantitative study of cutaneous receptors and afferent fibers in the cat and rabbit. *Journal of Physiology (London),* 1967, **193,** 707–733.

Brummer, S. B., McHardy, J., and Turner, M. J. Electrical stimulation with Pt electrodes: trace analysis for dissolved platinum and other dissolved electrochemical products. *Brain, Behavior and Evolution,* 1977, **14,** 10–22.

Burgess, P. R., & Perl, E. R. Cutaneous mechanoreceptors and nociceptors. In A. Iggo (Ed.), *Somatosensory system.* New York: Springer-Verlag, 1973. Pp. 29–78.

Burgess, P. R., Petit, D., & Warren, R. M. Receptor types in cat hairy skin supplied by myelinated fibers. *Journal of Neurophysiology,* 1968, **31,** 833–848.

Burke, D., Mackenzie, R. A., Skuse, N. F., & Lethlean, A. K. Cutaneous afferent activity in median and radial nerve fascicles: A microelectrode study. *Journal of Neurology, Neurosurgery and Psychiatry,* 1975, **38,** 855–864.

Burke, R. E., Rudomin, P, Vyklicky, L., & Zajac, F. E. Primary afferent depolarization and flexion reflexes produced by radiant heat stimulation of the skin. *Journal of Physiology (London),* 1971, **213,** 185–214.

Burke, W., & Ginsborg, B. L. The electrical properties of slow muscle fiber membrane. *Journal of Physiology (London),* 1956, **132,** 586–598.

Burton, C. V., & Maurer, D. D. Solvent-activated current passing tape electrodes for transcutaneous electrical stimulation of peripheral nervous system. *IEEE Transactions on Biomedical Engineering,* 1976, **BME-23,** 346–347.

Butikofer, R., & Lawrence, P. D. Electrocutaneous nerve stimulation. I. Model and experiment. *IEEE Transactions on Biomedical Engineering,* 1978, **BME-25,** 526–531.

Byck, R., Goldfarb, J., Schaumburg, H. H., & Sharpless, S. K. Reversible differential block of saphenous nerve by cold. *Journal of Physiology (London),* 1972, **222,** 17–26.

Campbell, B., & Woo, M. Y. Further studies on asynchronous firing and block of peripheral nerve conduction. *Bulletin of the Los Angles Neurological Societies,* 1966, **31,** 63–71.

Cangiano, A., & Lutzemberger, L. The action of selectively activated group II muscle afferent fibers on extensor motoneurons. *Brain Research,* 1972, **41,** 475–478.

Cannon, B. A method of stimulating autonomic nerves in the unanesthetized cat with observations on the motor and sensory effects. *American Journal of Physiology,* 1933, **105,** 366–372.

Casey, K. L., & Blick, M. Observations on anodal polarization of cutaneous nerve. *Brain Research,* 1969, **13,** 155–167.

Catton, W. T. A comparison of frog skin receptors to mechanical and electrical stimulation. *Journal of Physiology (London),* 1966, **187,** 23–33.

Chambers, G., Eggett, C., & Eldred, E. Graphic aid for relating axon classification with conduction delay and distance. *Brain Research,* 1970, **23,** 259–260.

Collins, W. F., Jr., Nulsen, F. E., & Randt, C. T. Relation of peripheral nerve fiber size and sensation in man. *Archives of Neurology (Chicago),* 1960, **3,** 381–385.

Collins, W. F., Jr., & Randt, C. T. Midbrain evoked responses relating to peripheral unmyelinated "C" fibers in cat. *Journal of Neurophysiology,* 1960, **23,** 47–53.

Cressman, R. D., & Blalock, A. Experimental hypertension—effects of kieselguhr injection and splanchnic stimulation. *Proceedings of the Society for Experimental Biology and Medicine,* 1939, **40,** 258–260.

Dawson, G. D., Merrill, E. G., & Wall, P. D. Dorsal root potentials produced by stimulation of fine efferents. *Science,* 1970, **167,** 1385–1387.

deJong, R. H., & Wagman, I. H. Physiological mechanisms of peripheral nerve block by local anesthetics. *Anesthesiology,* 1963, **24,** 684–727.

Delgado, J. M. R. Instrumentation, working hypotheses, and clinical aspects of neurostimulation. *Applied Neurophysiology,* 1977–1978, **40,** 88–110.

del Pozo, F., and Delgado, J. M. R. Hybrid stimulator for chronic experiments. *IEEE Transactions on Biomedical Engineering,* 1978, **BME-25,** 92–94.

deVilliers, R., Nose, Y., Meier, W., & Kantrowitz, A. Long-term continuous electrostimulation of a peripheral nerve. *Transactions of the American Society for Artificial Internal Organs,* 1964, **10,** 357–365.

Dixon, W. E. The selective action of cocaine on nerve fibres. *Journal of Physiology (London),* 1905, **32,** 87–94.

Dodt, E. Differential thermosensitivity of mammalian A-fibres. *Acta Physiologica Scandinavica,* 1953, **29,** 91–108.

Douglas, W. W., & Malcolm, J. L. The effect of localized cooling on conduction in cat nerves. *Journal of Physiology (London),* 1955, **130,** 53–71.

Douglas, W. W., & Ritchie, S. M. A technique for recording functional activity in specific groups of medulated and non-medulated fibres in whole nerve trunks. *Journal of Physiology (London),* 1957, **138,** 19–30.

Douglas, W. W., & Ritchie, J. M. Mammalian nonmyelinated nerve fibers. *Physiological Reviews,* 1962, **42,** 299–334.

Dow, R. S. Summary and evaluation of chronic cerebellar stimulation in man. In I. S. Cooper (Ed.), *Cerebellar stimulation in man.* Raven, New York, 1978. Pp. 207–212.

Dubkin, C. A constant-contact stimulating electrode for nerves. *Journal of Applied Physiology,* 1970, **28,** 350.

Duysens, J., & Stein, R. B. Reflexes induced by stimulation in waking cats with implanted cuff electrodes. *Experimental Brain Research,* 1978, **32,** 213–224.

Dymond, A. M. Characteristics of the metal-tissue interface of stimulation electrodes. *IEEE Transactions on Biomedical Engineering,* 1976, **23,** 274–280.

Dyson, C., & Brindley, G. S. Strength-duration curves for the production of cutaneous pain by electrical stimuli. *Clinical Science,* 1966, **30,** 237–241.

Eccles, J. C., Eccles, R. M., & Lundberg, A. Synaptic actions on motoneurons in relation to the two components of the group I muscle afferent volley. *Journal of Physiology (London),* 1957, **136,** 527–546.

Eccles, J. C., Oscarsson, O., & Willis, W. D. Synaptic action of group I and II afferent fibres of muscle on the cells of dorsal spinocerebellar tract. *Journal of Physiology (London),* 1961, **158,** 517–543.

Eccles, R. M., & Lundberg, A. Synaptic action in motoneurones by afferents which may evoke the flexion reflex. *Archives Italiennes de Biologie,* 1959, **97,** 199–221.

Erlanger, J. A. A physiologist reminisces. *Annual Review of Physiology,* 1964, **26,** 1–14.

Fender, F. A. Prolonged splanchnic stimulation. *Proceedings of the Society for Experimental Biology and Medicine,* 1937, **36,** 396–398.

Fields, W. S., & Leavitt, L. A. (Eds.). *Neural organization.* New York: Intercontinental Medical Book Corp., 1973.

Fisher, E., Cress, R. H., Haines, G., Panin, N., & Paul, B. J. Evoked nerve conduction after nerve block by chemical means. *American Journal of Physical Medicine,* 1970, **49,** 333–347.

Fox, J. L., & Kenmore, P. I. The effect of ischemia on nerve conduction. *Experimental Neurology,* 1967, **17,** 403–419.

Frank, K. Some approaches to the technical problem of chronic excitation of peripheral nerve. *Annals of Ontology, Rhinology, & Laryngology,* 1968, **77,** 761–771.

Franz, D. N., & Iggo, A. Conduction failure in myelinated and non-myelinated axons at low temperatures. *Journal of Physiology (London),* 1968, **199,** 319–345.

Franz, D. N., & Perry, R. S. Mechanisms for differential block among single myelinated and non-myelinated axons by procaine. *Journal of Physiology (London),* 1974, **236,** 193–210.

Fu, T. C., Santini, M., & Schomburg, E. D. Characteristics and distribution of spinal focal synaptic potentials generated by Group II muscle afferents. *Acta Physiologica Scandinavica,* 1974, **91,** 298–313.

Fukushima, K., & Kato, M. Spinal interneurons responding to Group II muscle, afferent fibers in the cat. *Brain Research,* 1975, **90,** 307–312.

Fukushima, K., Yahara, O., & Kato, M. Differential blocking of motor fibers by direct current. *Pfluegers Archiv,* 1975, **358,** 235–242.

Gangarosa, L. P., Park, N. H., & King, G. Iontophoresis of lidocaine in frog sciatic nerve fibers. *Life Sciences,* 1977, **21,** 885–890.

Gasser, H. S. Nerve activity as modified by temperature changes. *American Journal of Physiology,* 1931, **97,** 254–270.

Gasser, H. S., & Erlanger, J. The role of fiber size in the establishment of a nerve block by pressure or cocaine. *American Journal of Physiology,* 1929, **88,** 581–591.

Giaquinto, S., Pompeiano, O., & Swett, J. E. EEG and behavioral effects of fore- and hindlimb muscular afferent volleys in unrestrained cats. *Archives Italiennes de Biologie,* 1963, **101,** 133–148.

Gibson, R. H. Electrical stimulation of pain and touch. In D. R. Kenshalo (Ed.). *The skin senses.* Springfield, IL: Thomas, 1968. Pp. 223–261.

Glenn, W. W. L., Hageman, J. H., Mauro, A., Eisenberg, L., Flanigan, S., & Harvard, M. Electrical stimulation of excitable tissue by radio-frequency transmission. *Annals of Surgery,* 1964, **160,** 338–350.

Glenn, W. W. L., Holcomb, W. G., Gee, J. B. L., & Rath, R. Central hypoventilation, long-term ventilatory assistance by radiofrequency electrophrenic respiration. *Annals of Surgery,* 1970, **172,** 755–773.

Gordon, G., & Kay, R. H. A thermo-electric "cold" stimulator. *Journal of Physiology (London),* 1960, **153,** 3–5.

Granit, R., & Lundberg, A. Heat- and cold-sensitive mammalian nerve fibres. Some somatic reflexes to thermostimulation. *Acta Physiologica Scandinavica,* 1947, **13,** 334–346.

Grundfest, H. Electrical inexcitability of synapses and some consequences in the central nervous system. *Physiological Reviews,* 1957, **37,** 337–361.

Guyton, D. L., & Hambrecht, F. T. Capacitor electrode stimulates nerve or muscle without oxidation-reduction reactions. *Science,* 1973, **181,** 74–76.

Guz, A., & Trenchard, D. W. Pulmonary stretch receptor activity in man: A comparison with dog and cat. *Journal of Physiology (London),* 1971, **213,** 329–343. (a)

Guz, A., & Trenchard, D. W. The role of non-myelinated vagal afferent fibers from the lungs in the genesis of tachypnoea in the rabbit. *Journal of Physiology (London),* 1971, **213,** 345–371. (b)

Hallin, R. G., & Torebjork, H. E. Electrically induced A and C fibre responses in intact human skin nerves. *Experimental Brain Research,* 1973, **16,** 309–320.

Hambrecht, F. T., and Reswick, J. B. (Eds.). *Functional electrical stimulation.* New York: Dekker, 1977.

Harley, P. Monopolar stimulation in a volume conductor allows the selective excitation of small nerve fibers. *Journal of Electrophysiological Techniques,* 1977, **6,** 31–37.

Hayward, J. N., Ott, L. H., Stuart, D. G., & Cheshire, F. C. Peltier biothermodes. *American Journal of Medical Electronics*, 1965, **4**, 11–19.

Heavner, J. E., & deJong, R. H. Lidocaine blocking concentrations for B- and C-nerve fibers. *Anesthesiology*, 1974, **40**, 228–233.

Heinbecker, P. Effect of anoxemia, carbon dioxide and lactic acid on electrical phenomena of myelinated fibers of the peripheral nervous system. *American Journal of Physiology*, 1929, **89**, 58–83.

Heinbecker, P., Bishop, G. H., & O'Leary, J. Analysis of sensation in terms of the nerve impulse. *Archives of Neurology and Psychiatry*, 1934, **31**, 34–53.

Hench, L. L. Biomaterials. *Science*, 1980, **208**, 826–831.

Hershberg, P. I., Sohn, D., Agrawal, G. P., & Kantrowitz, A. Histologic changes in continuous, long-term electrical stimulation of a peripheral nerve. *IEEE Transactions on Biomedical Engineering*, 1967, **14**, 109–114.

Hess, W. R. *Beitrage zur Physiologie des Hirnstammes*. Leipzig: Thieme, 1932.

Horowitz, S. H., & Ginsberg-Fellner, F. Ischemia and sensory nerve conduction in diabetes mellitus. *Neurology*, 1979, **29**, 695–704.

Hunt, C. C. Relation of function to diameter in afferent fibers of muscle nerves. *Journal of General Physiology*, 1954, **38**, 117–131.

Hunt, C. C., & McIntyre, A. K. An analysis of fibre diameter and receptor characteristics of myelinated cutaneous afferent fibers in cat. *Journal of Physiology (London)*, 1960, **153**, 99–112.

Hursh, J. B. Conduction velocity and diameter of nerve fibers. *American Journal of Physiology*, 1939, **127**, 131–139.

Iggo, A. The electrophysiological identification of single nerve fibers, with particular reference to the slowest-conducting vagal afferent fibres in the cat. *Journal of Physiology (London)*, 1958, **142**, 110–126.

Iggo, A. Electrophysiological and histological studies of cutaneous mechanoreceptors. In D. R. Kenshalo (Ed.), *The skin senses*. Springfield, IL: Thomas, 1968. Pp. 84–111.

Ignelzi, R. J., & Nyquist, J. K. Direct effect of electrical stimulation on peripheral nerve evoked activity: Implications in pain relief. *Journal of Neurosurgery*, 1976, **45**, 159–165.

Jack, J. J. B., Noble, D., & Tsien, R. W. *Electrical current flow in excitable cells*. London & New York: Oxford University Press, 1975.

Johnson, P. F., & Hench, L. L. An *in vitro* analysis of metal electrodes for use in neural environment. *Brain, Behavior and Evolution*, 1977, **14**, 23–45.

Kaneyuki, T., Hogan, J. F., Glenn, W. W. L., & Holcomb, W. G. Diaphragm pacing: Evaluation of current waveforms for effective ventilation. *Journal of Thoracic and Cardiovascular Surgery*, 1977, **74**, 109–115.

Kater, S. B., Fountain, R. L., & Hadley, R. D. Reversible procaine block of activity in selected nerve trunks. *Journal of Electrophysiological Techniques*, 1976, **5**, 30–34.

Kato, M., & Fukushima, K. Effect of differential blocking of motor axons on antidromic activation of Renshaw cells in the cat. *Experimental Brain Research*, 1974, **20**, 135–143.

Kellgren, J. H., & McGowan, A. J. On the behavior of deep and cutaneous sensibility during nerve blocks. *Clinical Science*, 1948, **7**, 1–11.

Kline, R. L., Yeung, K. Y., & Calaresu, F. R. Role of somatic nerves in the cardiovascular responses to stimulation of an acupuncture point in anesthetized rabbits. *Experimental Neurology*, 1978, **61**, 561–570.

Knibestol, M. Stimulus-response functions of rapidly adapting mechanoreceptors in the human glabrous skin area. *Journal of Physiology (London)*, 1973, **232**, 427–452.

Knibestol, M. Stimulus-response functions of slowly adapting mechanoreceptors in the human glabrous skin area. *Journal of Physiology (London)*, 1975, **245,** 63–80.

Koizumi, K., Collin, R., Kaufman, A., & Brook, C. McC. Contribution of unmyelinated afferent excitation to sympathetic reflexes. *Brain Research*, 1970, **20,** 99–106.

Kopman, A. F. A safe surface electrode for peripheral nerve stimulation. *Anesthesiology*, 1976, **44,** 343–345.

Koslow, M., Bak, A., & Li, C. L. C-fiber excitability in the cat. *Experimental Neurology*, 1973, **41,** 745–753.

Kottke, F. J., Kubicek, W. G., & Visscher, M. B. The production of arterial hypertension by chronic renal artery-nerve stimulation. *American Journal of Physiology*, 1945, **145,** 38–47.

Kuffler, S. W., & Gerard, R. W. The small-nerve motor system to skeletal muscle. *Journal of Neurophysiology*, 1947, **10,** 383–394.

Kuffler, S. W., & Vaughan Williams, E. M. Small-nerve junctional potentials. The distribution of small motor nerves to frog skeletal muscle and the membrane characteristics of the fibres they innervate. *Journal of Physiology (London)*, 1953, **121,** 289–317.

Lafferty, J. M., & Farrell, J. F. A technique for chronic remote nerve stimulation. *Science*, 1949, **110,** 140–141.

Landau, W. M., Weaver, R. A., & Hornbein, T. F. Fusimotor nerve function in man. *Archives of Neurology (Chicago)*, 1960, **3,** 10–23.

Landon, D. N. (Ed.). *The peripheral nerve*. New York: Wiley, 1976.

Laporte, Y., & Montastruc, P. Role des différents types de fibres afférentes dans les réflexes circulatoires généraux d'origine cutanée. *Journal of Physiology (Paris)*, 1957, **49,** 1039–1049.

Layman, D. B. A cooling device for the cold blocking of nerves. *Medical and Biological Engineering*, 1971, **9,** 395–400.

Leksell, L. The action potential and excitatory effects of the small ventral root fibers to skeletal muscle. *Acta Physiologica Scandinavica*, 1945, **10,** Suppl. 31, 1–84.

Lele, P. P. An electrothermal stimulator for sensory tests. *Journal of Neurology, Neurosurgery and Psychiatry*, 1962, **25,** 329–331.

Levy, B. A. Diagnostic, prognastic, and therapeutic nerve blocks. *Archives of Surgery (Chicago)*, 1977, **112,** 870–879.

Li, C. L., & Bak, A. Excitability characteristics of the A- and C-fibers in a peripheral nerve. *Experimental Neurology*, 1976, **50,** 67–79.

Libouban, S., & Aleonard, P. Sur un mode d'implantation d'électrodes à demiure chez le rat permettant l'observation du même animal pendant plusieurs mois. *Comptes Rendus des Séances de la Société de Biologie et de Ses Filiales*, 1960, **154,** 540–543.

Lilly, J. C. The balanced pulse-pair waveform. In D. E. Sheer (Ed.), *Electrical stimulation of the brain*. Austin: University of Texas Press, 1961. Pp. 60–64.

Ling, F., & Gerard, R. W. The normal membrane potential of frog sartorious fibers. *Journal of Cellular and Comparative Physiology*, 1949, **34,** 383–396.

Lippmann, M., & Fields, W. A. Burns of the skin caused by a peripheral nerve stimulator. *Anesthesiology*, 1974, **40,** 82–84.

Loeb, G. E., Bak, M. J., & Duysens, J. Long-term unit recording from somatosensory neurons in the spinal ganglia of the freely walking cat. *Science*, 1977, **197,** 1192–1194.

Low, F. N. The perineurium and connective tissue of peripheral nerve. In D. N. Landon (Ed.), *The peripheral nerve*. New York: Wiley, 1976. Pp. 159–187.

Mackenzie, R. A., Burke, D., Skuse, N. F., & Lethlean, A. K. Fibre function and perception during cutaneous nerve block. *Journal of Neurology, Neurosurgery and Psychiatry*, 1975, **38,** 865–873.

Manfredi, M. Differential block of conduction of larger fibers in peripheral nerve by direct current. *Archives Italiennes de Biologie,* 1970, **108,** 52–71.

Manning, G. W., & Hall, G. E. An apparatus for prolonged stimulation experiments in unanesthetized animals. *Journal of Laboratory and Clinical Medicine,* 1937, **23,** 306–310.

Matthews, B., & Cadden, S. W. Conduction block in peripheral A and C fibers following electrical stimulation. *Neuroscience Abstracts,* 1979, **5,** 306.

Matthews, P. B. C., & Rushworth, G. The relative sensitivity of muscle nerve fibres to procaine. *Journal of Physiology (London),* 1957, **135,** 263–269.

Matthews, P. B. C., & Rushworth, G. The discharge from muscle spindles as an indicator of γ efferent paralysis by procaine. *Journal of Physiology (London),* 1958, **140,** 421–426.

Mauro, A. Capacity electrode for chronic stimulation. *Science,* 1960, **132,** 356.

McCarty, L. P. A stimulating electrode for nerves. *Journal of Applied Physiology,* 1965, **20,** 542.

McNeal, D. R. Peripheral nerve stimulation—superficial and implanted. In W. S. Fields & L. A. Leavitt (Eds.), *Neural organization.* New York: Intercontinental Medical Book Corp., 1973. Pp. 77–99.

McNeal, D. R. 2000 years of electrical stimulation. In F. T. Hambrecht & J. B. Reswick (Eds.), *Functional electrical stimulation.* New York: Dekker, 1977. Pp. 3–35.

McNeal, D. R., & Reswick, J. B. Control of skeletal muscle by electrical stimulation. *Advances in Biomedical Engineering,* 1976, **6,** 209–256.

McNeal, D. R., Waters, R., & Reswick, J. Experience with implanted electrodes at Rancho Los Amigo's Hospital. *Applied Neurophysiology,* 1977–1978, **40,** 235–239.

Melzack, R., & Wall, P. D. On the nature of cutaneous sensory mechanisms. *Brain,* 1962, **85,** 331–356.

Mendell, L. M., & Wall, P. D. Presynaptic hyperpolarization: A role for fine afferent fibres. *Journal of Physiology (London),* 1964, **172,** 274–294.

Meyer, G. A., & Fields, H. L. Causalgia treated by selective large fibre stimulation of peripheral nerve. *Brain,* 1972, **95,** 163–168.

Meyer, M. Hearing without cochlea. *Science,* 1931, **73,** 236–237.

Michalski, W. J., & Seguin, J. J. The effects of muscle cooling and stretch on muscle spindle secondary endings in the cat. *Journal of Physiology (London),* 1975, **153,** 341–356.

Mickle, W. A. The problems of stimulation parameters. In D. E. Scheer (Ed.), *Electrical stimulation of the brain.* Austin: University of Texas Press, 1961. Pp. 67–73.

Mills, L. W., & Swett, J. E. Precise control of stimulation parameters in low impedance conditions. *Journal of Applied Physiology,* 1965, **20,** 334–338.

Moldaver, J. Tourniquet paralysis syndrome. *AMA Archives of Surgery,* 1954, **68,** 136–144.

Mooney, V., & Hartmann, D. B. Percutaneous passage. In H. A. Miller & D. C. Harrison (Eds.), *Biomedical electrode technology: Theory and practice.* New York: Academic Press, 1974. Pp. 329–339.

Muller, A., & Hunsperger, R. W. Reversible Blockierung der Erregungsleitung im Nerven durch Mittelfrequenz-Daverstrom. *Helvetica Physiologica et Pharmacologica Acta,* 1967, **25,** CR211–CR213.

Myers, D. A., Hostetter, G., Bourassa, C. M., & Swett, J. E. Dorsal columns in sensory detection. *Brain Research,* 1974, **70,** 350–355.

Nathan, P. W., & Sears, T. A. Some factors concerned in differential nerve block by local anesthetics. *Journal of Physiology (London),* 1961, **157,** 565–580.

Nathan, P. W., & Sears, T. A. Differential nerve block by sodium-free and sodium deficient solutions. *Journal of Physiology (London),* 1962, **164,** 375–394.

Nathan, P. W., & Sears, T. A. The susceptibility of nerve fibres to analgesics. *Anaesthesia,* 1963, **18,** 467–476.

Newman, H., Fender, F., & Saunders, W. High frequency transmission of stimulating impulses. *Surgery (St. Louis),* 1937, **2,** 359–362.

Oscarsson, O. Further observation on ascending tracts activated from muscle, joint, and skin nerves. *Archives Italiennes de Biologie,* 1959, **96,** 199–215.

Paintal, A. S. Intramuscular propagation of sensory impulses. *Journal of Physiology (London),* 1959, **148,** 240–251. (a)

Paintal, A. S. Facilitation and depression of muscle stretch receptors by repetitive antidromic stimulation, adrenaline and asphyxia. *Journal of Physiology (London),* 1959, **148,** 252–266. (b)

Paintal, A. S. Block of conduction in mammalian myelinated nerve fibres by low temperatures. *Journal of Physiology (London),* 1965, **180,** 1–19.

Paintal, A. S. A comparison of the nerve impulses of mammalian non-medullated nerve fibers with those of the smallest diameter medullated fibres. *Journal of Physiology (London),* 1967, **193,** 523–533.

Paintal, A. S. Conduction in mammalian nerve fibres. In J. E. Desmedt (Ed.), *New developments in electromyography and clinical neurophysiology* (Vol. 2). Basel: Karger, 1973. Pp. 19–41.

Pollack, V. Computation of the impedance characteristics of metal electrodes for biological investigations. *Medical and Biological Engineering,* 1974, **12,** 460–464. (a)

Pollack, V. Impedance measurements on metal needle electrodes. *Medical and Biological Engineering,* 1974, **12,** 606–612. (b)

Pompeiano, O., & Swett, J. E. EEG and behavioral manifestations of sleep induced by cutaneous nerve stimulation in normal cats. *Archives Italiennes de Biologie,* 1962, **100,** 311–342. (a)

Pompeiano, O., & Swett, J. E. Identification of cutaneous and muscular afferent fibers producing EEG synchronization or arousal in normal cats. *Archives Italiennes de Biologie,* 1962, **100,** 343–380. (b)

Pudenz, R. H., Agnew, W. F., Yuen, T. G. H., Bullara, L. A., Jacques, S., & Sheldon, C. H. Adverse effects of electrical energy applied to the nervous system. *Applied Neurophysiology,* 1977–1978, **40,** 72–87.

Ranck, J. B., Jr. Electrical stimulation of neural tissue. In R. F. Rushmer (Ed.), *Methods in medical research.* Chicago: Year Book Med., 1965. Pp. 262–269.

Ranck, J. B., Jr., Extracellular stimulation. Present Volume.

Ray, C. D., & Maurer, D. D. Electrical neurological stimulation systems: A review of contemporary methodology. *Surgical Neurology,* 1975, **4,** 82–90.

Reed, O. J., & Miller, A. D. Thermoelectric Peltier device for local cortical cooling. *Physiology and Behavior,* 1978, **20,** 209–211.

Ritchie, J. M. A pharmacological approach to the structure of sodium channels in myelinated axons. *Annual Review of Neuroscience,* 1979, **2,** 341–362.

Robert, E. D., & Oester, Y. T. Absence of supersensitivity to acetycholine in innervated muscle subjected to prolonged pharmacologic nerve block. *Journal of Pharmacology and Experimental Therapeutics,* 1970, **174,** 133–140.

Roberts, J. N., & Blackburn, J. G. Cold block of peripheral nerve fiber activity using a Peltier biothermode. *Journal of Electrophysiological Techniques,* 1975, **4,** 40–43.

Rollman, G. B. Electrocutaneous stimulation. In F. A. Geldard (Ed.), *Cutaneous communication systems and devices.* Austin, TX: Psychonomic Society, 1974. Pp. 38–51.

Rosenbaum, A. T., Titone, C., Yagi, S., & Kantrowitz, A. A subcutaneously implantable electrode for intermittent vagal stimulation on dogs receiving cardiac allografts. *Journal of Surgical Research,* 1974, **16,** 62–65.

Rosner, B. S., & Goff, W. R. Electrical responses of the nervous system and subjective scales of intensity. In: *Contributions to Sensory Physiology*, 1967, **2,** 169–221.

Rushton, W. A. H. The site of excitation in the nerve trunk of the frog. *Journal of Physiology (London)*, 1949, **109,** 314–326.

Rushton, W. A. H. A theory of the effects of fibre size in medullated nerve. *Journal of Physiology (London)*, 1951, **115,** 101–122.

Sassen, M., & Zimmerman, M. Differential blocking of myelinated nerve fibres by transient depolarization. *Pfluegers Archiv*, 1973, **341,** 179–195.

Sato, A., & Schmidt, F. Somatosympathetic reflexes: Afferent fibers, control pathways, discharge characteristics. *Physiological Reviews*, 1973, **53,** 916–947.

Saunders, F. A. Electrocutaneous displays. In F. A. Geldard (Ed.), *Cutaneous communication systems and devices*. Austin, TX: Psychonomic Society, 1974. Pp. 20–26.

Sawyer, P. N., & Srinivasan, S. Metals and implants. In C. D. Ray (Ed.), *Medical engineering*. Chicago: Year Book Med., 1974. Pp. 1099–1110.

Schmidt, R. F. Spinal cord afferents: Functional organization and inhibitory control. *UCLA Forum in Medical Sciences*, 1969, **11,** 209–229.

Scott, R. N. Myoelectric control systems. *Advances in Biomedical Engineering and Medical Physics*, 1968, **2,** 45–72.

Seneviratne, K. N., & Peiris, D. A. The effect of ischemia on the excitability of human sensory nerve. *Journal of Neurology, Neurosurgery and Psychiatry*, 1968, **31,** 338–347.

Shantha, T. R., & Bourne, G. H. The perineural epithelium—a new concept. In G. H. Bourne (Ed.), *The structure and function of nervous tissue* (Vol. 1). New York: Academic Press, 1968. Pp. 379–459.

Sherrick, C. E. The art of tactile communication. *American Psychologist*, 1975, **30,** 353–360.

Sinclair, D. C. Observations on sensory paralysis produced by compression of a human limb. *Journal of Neurophysiology*, 1948, **11,** 75–92.

Sinclair, D. C. Cutaneous sensation and the doctrine of specific energy. *Brain*, 1955, **78,** 584–613.

Sinclair, D. C. *Cutaneous sensation*. London & New York: Oxford University Press, 1967.

Sinclair, D. C., & Glasgow, E. F. Dissociation of cold and warm sensibility during compression of the upper limb. *Brain*, 1960, **83,** 668–676.

Sinclair, D. C., & Hinshaw, J. R. Sensory changes in nerve blocks induced by cooling. *Brain*, 1951, **74,** 318–335.

Slaughter, J. S., & Hahn, W. W. A chronic electrode for peripheral nerve stimulation: Application for vagal stimulation. *Psychophysiology*, 1975, **12,** 110–112.

Somjen, G. *Sensory coding in the mammalian nervous system*. New York: Appleton, 1972.

Stein, R. B., Dean, R., Gordon, T., Hoffer, J. A., & Jhamandas, J. Impedance properties of metal electrodes for chronic recording from mammalian nerves. *IEEE Transactions on Biomedical Engineering*, 1978, **25,** 532–537.

Straw, R., & Mitchell, C. A simple method of implanting electrodes for long-term stimulation of peripheral nerves. *Journal of Applied Physiology*, 1966, **21,** 712–714.

Strichartz, G. Molecular mechanisms of nerve block by local anesthetics. *Anesthesiology*, 1976, **45,** 421–441.

Sunderland, S. *Nerves and nerve injuries* (2nd ed.). New York: Longmans, Green, 1978.

Swett, J. E., & Bourassa, C. M. Comparison of sensory discrimination thresholds with muscle and cutaneous nerve volleys in the cat. *Journal of Neurophysiology*, 1967, **30,** 530–545.

Swett, J. E., & Bourassa, C. M. Detection thresholds to stimulation of ventrobasal complex in cats. *Brain Research*, 1980, 313–328.

Tanner, J. A. Reversible blocking of nerve conduction by alternating current excitation. *Nature (London)*, 1962, **195,** 712–713.

Taylor, G. G., & Swett, J. E. A versatile, precision constant voltage stimulator. *Proceedings of the 25th Annual Conference on Engineering and Biology*, 1972, 191.

Testerman, R. L., Hagfors, N. R., & Schwartz, S. I. Design and evaluation of nerve stimulating electrodes. *Medical Research Engineering*, 1971, **10,** 6–11.

Torebjork, H. E. Activity in C nociceptors and sensation. In D. R. Kenshalo (Ed.), *Sensory functions of the skin of humans*. New York: Plenum, 1979. Pp. 313–325.

Torebjork, H. E., & Hallin, R. G. Perceptual changes accompanying controlled preferential blocking of A and C fibre responses in intact human skin nerves. *Experimental Brain Research*, 1973, **16,** 321–332.

Torebjork, H. E., & Hallin, R. G. Responses in human A and C fibres to repeated electrical intradermal stimulation. *Journal of Neurology, Neurosurgery and Psychiatry*, 1974, **37,** 653–664.

Upton, A. R. M. Neurophysiological mechanisms in modification of seizures. In I. S. Cooper (Ed.), *Cerebellar stimulation in man*. New York: Raven, 1978. Pp. 39–57.

Vallbo, A. B., & Johansson, R. S. Skin mechanoreceptors in the human hand: neural and psychophysical thesholds. In Y. Zotterman (Ed.), *Sensory function of the human skin in primates*. Oxford: Pergamon, 1976. Pp. 185–198.

Vallbo, A. B., & Johansson, R. S. Coincidence and cause: A discussion on correlations between activity in primary afferents and perceptive experience in cutaneous sensibility. In D. R. Kenshalo (Ed.), *Sensory functions of the skin of humans*. New York: Plenum, 1979. Pp. 299–311.

Ven den Honert, C., & Mortimer, J. T. Generation of unidirectionally propagated action potentials in a peripheral nerve by brief stimuli. *Science*, 1979, **206,** 1311–1312.

von Euler, C. Selective responses to thermal stimulation of mammalian nerves. *Acta Physiologica Scandinavica*, 1947, **14,** Suppl. 45, 1–75.

Waters, R. Electrical stimulation of the peripheral and femoral nerves in man. In F. T. Hambrecht & J. B. Reswick (Eds.), *Functional electrical stimulation: Application in neural prostheses*. New York: Dekker, 1977. Pp. 55–64.

Weddell, G., & Sinclair, P. C. "Pins and needles": Observations on some of the sensations aroused in a limb by the application of pressure. *Journal of Neurology, Neurosurgery, and Psychiatry*, 1947, **10,** 26–46.

Weinman, J. Biphasic stimulation and electrical properties of metal electrodes. *Journal of Applied Physiology*, 1965, **20,** 787–790.

Weinman, J. & Mahler, J. An analysis of electrical properties of metal electrodes. *Medical Electronics and Biological Engineering*, 1964, **2,** 299–310.

Wetzel, M. C., Howell, L. G., & Bearie, K. J. Experimental performance of steel and platinum electrodes with chronic monophasic stimulation of the brain. *Journal of Neurosurgery*, 1969, **31,** 658–669.

White, R. L., & Gross, T. J. An evaluation of the resistance to electrolysis of metals for use in biostimulation microprobes. *IEEE Transactions on Biomedical Engineering*, 1974, **BME-21,** 487–490.

Whitwam, J. G., & Kidd, C. The use of direct current to cause selective block of large fibres in peripheral nerves. *British Journal of Anesthesia*, 1975, **47,** 1123–1133.

Wiederholt, W. C. Threshold and conduction velocity in isolated mixed mammalian nerves. *Neurology*, 1970, **20,** 347–352. (a)

Wiederholt, W. C. Stimulus intensity and site of excitation in human median nerve sensory fibers. *Journal of Neurology, Neurosurgery and Psychiatry*, 1970, **33,** 438–441. (b)

Willer, J. C. Comparative study of perceived pain and nociceptive flexion reflex in man. *Pain*, 1977, **3,** 69–80.

Willis, W. D., & Coggeshall, R. E. *Sensory mechanisms of the spinal cord.* New York: Plenum, 1978.

Wolf, S. L., & Basmajian, J. V. A rapid cooling device for controlled cutaneous stimulation. *Physical Therapy,* 1973, **53,** 25–27.

Woo, M. Y., & Campbell, B. A. Asynchronous firing and block of peripheral nerve conduction by 20 KC alternating current. *Bulletin of the Los Angeles Neurological Societies,* 1964, **29,** 87–94.

Wuerker, R. B., McPhedran, A. M., & Henneman, E. Properties of motor units in a heterogeneous pale muscle (m. gastrocnemius) of the cat. *Journal of Neurophysiology,* 1965, **28,** 85–99.

Wyss, O. A. Nervenreizung mit mittle frequency-Stromstossen. *Helvetica Physiologica et Pharmacologica Acta,* 1967, **25,** 85–102.

Yergler, W. G., McNeal, D. R., & Perry, J. Muscle response to internal stimulation of the peroneal nerve in hemiplegic patients. *Clinical Orthopaedics and Related Research,* 1972, **86,** 164–167.

Young, R., & Henneman, E. Reversible block of nerve conduction by ultrasound. *Archives of Neurology (Chicago),* 1961, **4,** 83–89.

Zeh, D. W., & Katz, R. L. A new nerve stimulator for monitoring neuromuscular blockade and performing nerve block. *Anesthesia and Analagesia (Cleveland),* 1978, **57,** 13–17.

Zimmerman, M. Selective activation of C-fibers. *Pfluegers Archiv,* 1968, **301,** 329–333.

Zotterman, Y. Studies in the peripheral nervous mechanism of pain. *Acta Medica Scandinavica,* 1933, **80,** 185–242.

Chapter 11

Grid and Peripheral Shock Stimulation

Fred A. Masterson

Department of Psychology
University of Delaware
Newark, Delaware

ISBN 0-12-547440-7

I. Introduction

Since its introduction in the early 1900s, electric shock has remained the most widely used stimulus for producing controlled amounts of discomfort in animals. Shock is easier to control than, for example, loud noise, bright light, air blasts, and hot or cold temperatures, and its motivational potency does not habituate over time (Masterson, 1965, 1969).

A major factor in the popularity of electric shock is the ease with which controlled amounts of shock can be administered to unrestrained animals with grid-floor apparatus (Sections II-A and II-B). Lack of physical restraint permits the study of ecologically meaningful escape and avoidance reactions such as running away from noxious stimulation or from the potential threat of noxious stimulation. Indeed, this chapter's heavy emphasis on grid-floor shock reflects the widespread use of grid-floor apparatus in studies of escape, avoidance, and punishment.

We have tried to organize the following sections so that they can be read in whatever order best suits the needs of the individual reader. To guide the nonsequential reader, we have used relatively self-explanatory section and subsection headings, and we have made substantial use of cross-references between the sections. These references elucidate relationships between material in different sections that the nonsequential reader might otherwise miss. In addition, references to earlier sections guide the nonsequential reader to definitions or arguments that are used in later sections. However, an important exception to this policy is the widespread use of the shock source design nomenclature introduced in Section VI-A. Thus, a reading of this section is essential for comprehension of later sections.

We shall now provide an outline or overview of the following sections in order to allow readers to select those sections most relevant to their interests.

A. *Overview*

Section II describes the basic electrode systems used to deliver motivating electric shock to animals: grid-floor electrodes, fixed external electrodes, subcutaneous electrodes, and parallel plate electrodes for delivering shock to fish. A description of optimal designs for grid-floor apparatus occupies a major portion of this section.

Section III describes additional equipment needed for grid-floor shock applications. A grid polarity scrambler is required to prevent animals from discovering "safe" grid positions. Direct current (dc) and alternating current (ac) short-detection circuits are required to check for possible alternate shock paths that can shunt the shock away from the animal and thus decrease the aversiveness.

Section IV examines the electrical parameters of animal subjects. Animals present a resistive load to the shock source. Furthermore, an animal's resistance decreases as a function of increasing shock intensity. Knowledge of this relationship is essential for the design or selection of optimal shock sources.

Section V presents a classification of shock sources in terms of their abstract properties, e.g., whether the shock is ac or dc, and the capability of the source to regulate current, voltage, or power. Considerable attention is paid to the suitability of the general types of sources for grid-floor applications.

Section VI describes two popular ac shock source designs: the fixed impedance ac (FIAC) source, and the constant current, fixed voltage ac (FVAC) source. These sources are simple, yet effective. Complete circuit specifications are given for a 150-kΩ FIAC source and a 500-V FVAC constant current source. These are optimal sources for rats and grid shock, in the sense that they produce minimal variations in shock aversiveness (as explained in Section VII).

Section VII discusses the problem of minimizing the variations in grid-floor shock aversiveness that inevitably occur when an animal moves about on the grids. The original approach to solving this problem was to select a shock source that regulates (holds constant) that electrical parmeter which is best correlated with aversiveness. Unfortunately, proponents of this solution could not reach complete agreement on the best electrical correlate—voltage, current, or power. More recently, B. A. Campbell and Masterson (1969) devised a technique for measuring the variability of a shock's aversiveness and used this technique to delineate a set of optimal, minimally variable sources. These sources are described, and their common features are discussed. Finally, it is argued that the variety of optimal sources indicates that neither voltage, current, nor power, as measured at the shock source terminals, are particularly good correlates of grid-floor shock aversiveness.

Section VIII presents *equal aversion functions* for translating between levels of one noxious stimulus to equally aversive levels of another noxious stimulus. Functions are presented that translate rat grid-floor shock levels between different types of shock sources. An equal aversion function is described that translates levels of rat grid-floor shock into equivalent levels of rat subcutaneous shock. Functions are then presented that convert rat grid-floor shock intensities into equally aversive levels of loud noise and bright light. Finally, the transituational validity of the equal aversion functions is discussed.

Section IX discusses methods for ascertaining the range of usable shock intensities. The lower limit of the range is assessed by measuring aversion thresholds and escape thresholds. The upper limit is established by measuring tetanization thresholds, and also by measuring the point past which escape performance deteriorates with increasing shock intensity. These limits are presented for several shock sources used with rats and grid floors. In addition, a practical lower limit is imposed on rat grid-floor shock escape experiments by the suppression of locomotor activity at low shock intensities. Recent experiments documenting this suppression effect are summarized, and it is hypothesized that rats learn to restrict their movements at low shock levels in order to avoid transient peaks in current density. Section IX also presents upper and lower limits for rat subcutaneous shock and for aquatic shock with goldfish. Finally, a method is described for partitioning the usable range of rat grid-floor shock intensities into *Just Aversive Differences* (JADs): successive shock levels that are just barely discriminated by the rat as being unequal in aversiveness. This partitioning proves useful for optimal selection of several shock levels in any parametric study of shock intensity.

Section X provides a general outline of the measurement techniques used to produce many of the results cited in earlier sections of this chapter. The techniques are presented in the order they would be utilized in a research program addressing the specification and control of shock motivational stimuli for a new situation or species.

Several of this chapter's conclusions are based on the article by B. A. Campbell and Masterson (1969). The date will be omitted in the many citations of this article that follow.

II. Apparatus for Delivering the Shock to the Subject

In this section we shall describe various methods for applying aversive shock stimuli to animal subjects. First, we will cover techniques that present the shock through some ubiquitous aspect of the subject's environment—for example, shocking rats through a grid-bar floor, or shocking fish through the surrounding water. Second, we will describe methods that use electrodes that are fixed to the animal's skin. Finally, we will give some examples of the use of subcutaneous electrodes.

A. *Grid Floors: Material, Size, and Spacing of the Grid Bars*

The most common method of delivering shock to unrestrained animals is the grid-floor apparatus. The floor of the apparatus consists of a network or grid of parallel, uniformly spaced metal bars. The optimal cross-sectional shape, size, and spacing of the bars depends on the age and species of the animal subject. A good grid bar material is stainless steel, since it is highly resistant to corrosion by the chemicals in urine and feces. A 316 grade of stainless steel is commonly used.

While there have been no systematic investigations of the optimal grid shape, size, and spacing for particular species, there are a few obvious design considerations. Round grid bars appear to work best with animals whose paws are developed for grasping small objects—e.g., mice, rats, hamsters, gerbils, guinea pigs, monkeys, and so forth. Other animals, such as dogs or cats, may gain more stable support from flat bars. The bars should be just large enough to provide the animals with an easy perch. Adjacent bars should be sufficiently far apart so that boluses fall through the grid. This is especially critical for automated experiments where bolus shorts are usually not detected by the experimenter until the end of the session.

(Before we describe the grid-bar dimensions commonly employed with various species, we would like to emphasize that a surprisingly large number of articles fail to describe these basic dimensions. A minor but related point involves the procedure of specifying grid floor geometry indirectly by listing the make and model number of a commercial chamber. Trying to decode such information can be a nuisance when model numbers change or when the manufacturer has gone out of business.)

Two grid designs are most commonly used for rats: $\frac{3}{32}$-in. diameter bars spaced $\frac{1}{2}$ in. center-to-center, and $\frac{1}{8}$-in. diameter bars spaced $\frac{9}{16}$ in. center-to-center. Infrequently, one sees relatively large grid bars employed with rats (e.g., Dinsmoor, 1958). One might imagine that the wide spacing would make it more difficult for rats to move around. Be that as it may, it seems unwise to use an atypical design of unproven superiority.

Of the two designs commonly used with rats, the $\frac{1}{8}$-in. diameter, $\frac{9}{16}$ in. center-to-center spacing design has a lower probability of bolus shorts due to the wider spacing. However, the smaller $\frac{3}{32}$-in. diameter, $\frac{1}{2}$ in.

center-to-center spacing design allows the experimenter to work with immature rats, as young as 30 days old, as well as adults. Below 30 days of age, smaller grids and narrower spacing should be used (Kirby, 1963).

Guinea pigs can be shocked with the standard rat grid floors. For smaller rodents, such as mice, gerbils, or hamsters, $\frac{3}{32}$-in. round bars spaced $\frac{3}{8}$ in. center-to-center are commonly used.

A popular dog apparatus, the Solomon and Wynne (1953) shuttlebox, uses 1-in. wide stainless steel channel bars with $\frac{1}{2}$-in. spaces between the bars. Cats have been shocked with $\frac{1}{2}$-in. wide flat bars and $\frac{1}{2}$- to $\frac{3}{4}$-in. spaces. While not as resistant to corrosion as stainless steel bars, the $\frac{1}{2}$-in. wide galvanized steel wall standards used in conjunction with bracket-mounting bookshelf systems provide an inexpensive and readily available material. Squirrel monkeys have been shocked with rat-sized grid floors. Larger monkeys, including young male rhesus monkeys, can be used with grid floors having the dimensions recommended for dogs or cats.

The electrified floor has not been a popular method of shocking pigeons because the scaly tissue on the feet can present resistances of over 100 MΩ (Azrin, 1959). A conducting paste applied to the feet has been used to reduce the resistance (Azrin, 1956; Ferster & Skinner, 1957). However, Walker and Bitterman (1968) note that the reduction in resistance produced by electrode paste is relatively brief. These authors treated their pigeons' feet with a callous remover four days prior to experimentation.

For pigeons, a simple alternative to a grid-bar floor is described by Bresler and Bitterman (1974). In their design, closely spaced rivets are secured in a $\frac{1}{4}$-in.-thick piece of Plexiglas. The pigeons walk on the heads of the rivets. Alternate rivets are wired to opposite polarities. The shafts of the rivets are coated with an insulating material to prevent shorts when the animals evacuate.

B. *Grid Floor Construction*

It is difficult to comprehend why the majority of commercial grid-floor apparatuses have the grids supported by the walls of the enclosure. A subject's urine rapidly accumulates on these walls, and the salts in the urine conduct current between adjacent grids, thus decreasing the shock felt by the subject. The easy solution to this problem is to mount the grids in a recessed framework unexposed to the subject's urine.

The grid bars should be mounted in a frame that is independent from and that extends beyond the walls of the apparatus. This is illustrated in Fig. 1. The grids are suspended between two parallel pieces of in-

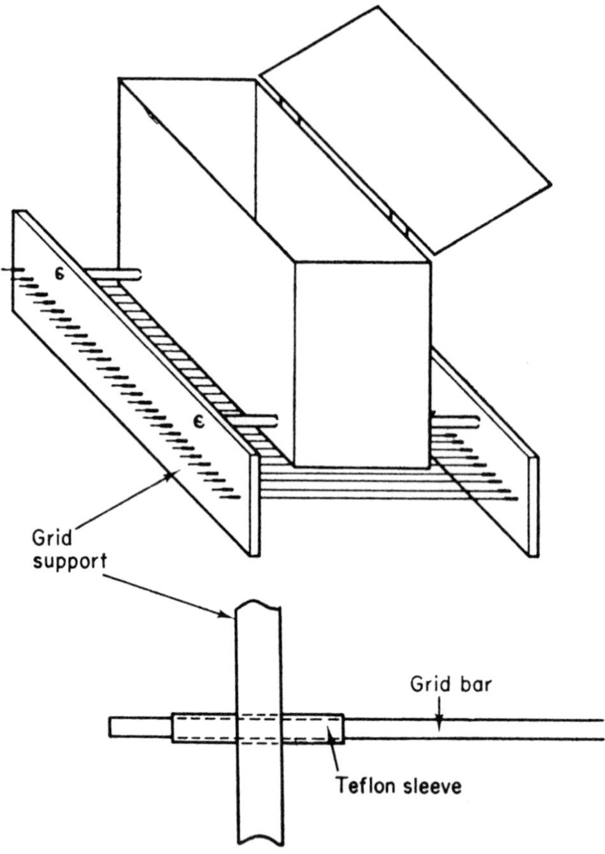

FIG. 1. An example of a grid-floor apparatus for use with small manmals. (From Masterson & Campbell, Fig. 1, 1972, p. 24.)

sulating material such as Plexiglass or Bakelite. The important advantage of this design is that it is impossible for urine to reach the grid-bar supports.

Another important feature shown in Fig. 1 is the use of Teflon sleeves, which insulate the grid bars from the grid supports. This is a useful precaution against electrical shorting due to moisture condensing on the grid supports during conditions of high humidity. Size-12 Teflon thin-wall spaghetti tubing makes a good fit over $\frac{3}{32}$-in. diameter grid bars. In the grid supports, one should drill holes that are just large enough to permit insertion of the Teflon sleeves, then insert the grid rods through the sleeves. Optimal choice of size of the drilled holes will result in firm grid support. In case a loose fit allows a rod and sleeve to slip back and forth, the rod can be firmed by dabbing plastic cement on the sleeve-support junction.

A good way to connect wires to small grid bars is by solder, but before soldering the wires to the ends of the grids, the ends should be roughened with a file. Then the wires are crimped around the ends of the grids. Special solder and flux designed for stainless steel will greatly facilitate soldering the wires to the grids; however, it then will be necessary to clean spattered flux off the surrounding area with a grease solvent such as denatured alcohol.

This information applies to grid floors for rodents or the squirrel monkey. The flat grids used for dogs or cats may be bolted down to an external supporting frame. Electrical connection can be made with spade lugs attached to the bars with machine screws inserted in holes that are drilled in the bars and tapped to accept the screw thread.

Finally, it is highly desirable to electrify the walls of the apparatus. Otherwise, animals may learn to place their hindpaws on the same grid bar and lean on a wall with their forepaws (rats are fairly clever this way). Thus, the walls must be metal and should be connected to one pole of the shock source. In particular, the metal walls should be connected to the pole or side of the source that is electrically grounded (Sections VI-B and VI-C).

Many commercial grid-floor apparatuses use metal walls parallel to the grids, but plastic walls perpendicular to the grids. This arrangement works fairly well because animals with hindpaws on the same grid bar are less likely to lean on the plastic walls on either side than to lean on the metal wall in front of them. (We assume the metal walls are connected to the grounded pole of the shock source.) Yet animals in this position sometimes discover they can lean on one of the plastic side walls to avoid shock. Therefore, it is a good precaution to electrify all four walls. Plastic walls are easily metallisized by covering them with $\frac{1}{32}$-in. aluminum sheets, which are easy to cut with tin shears.

C. *Water Shock for Aquatic Animals*

Electric current can be delivered to aquatic animals through the surrounding water. The shock source is connected to a pair of parrallel conducting plates mounted to opposite walls of an aquarium (Bitterman, 1966; Horner, Longo, & Bitterman, 1960, 1961; Scobie & Herman, 1972). The ions liberated from metal electrode plates do not appear to have an adverse effect on fish subjects in short-term experiments (Horner *et al.*, 1961). Less reactive electrodes can be constructed by coating opposite walls of the aquarium with a low-resistance mixture of carbon and Styrofoam in methyl-ethyl-ketone (Bitterman, 1966).

Scobie and Herman (1972) have studied the problem of measuring and controlling electrical shock for goldfish. They point out that large electrodes have the virtue of producing a more uniform electric field than that produced by smaller electrodes. In addition, they address the problem of the best electrical correlate of the behavioral effects of aquatic shock. One candidate is the spatial voltage gradient: the voltage applied to the electrodes divided by the distance separating the electrodes. Another candidate is the density of current in the aquatic medium: the amount of current flowing through a unit-area parallel with the electrodes. In terms of the shock's capacity to elicit small body movements (twitching or dorsal-fin extension), they show that the voltage gradient is a better correlate than aquatic current density.

Scobie and Herman also measured reaction, detection, and escape thresholds for the goldfish, as well as the shock intensity past which escape performance deteriorates as a function of increasing intensity (Section IX-E).

Etscorn (1974) has described an aquatic shuttlebox in which the electrodes are inserted in the fish's home tank. A novel feature of this system is that banks of parallel stainless steel rods are used in place of solid, flat metal plates. The electric field should be highly similar, provided the bars are spaced sufficiently close to one another.

D. *Fixed External Electrodes*

With rats, fixed external shock electrodes usually have been employed in conjunction with some method of keeping the rats from biting or pulling off the electrodes. One method is to partially restrain the subjects (Bijou, 1942; Hall, Clayton, & Mark, 1966). Azrin, Hopwood, and Powell (1967) used tail electrodes on rats that were confined in a relatively cramped test chamber. A rat was placed in the chamber with its tail leading out of a hole and taped to a restraining bar behind the chamber. Another procedure for discouraging rats from biting the electrode is to wrap the leads with a coil of uninsulated wire. One of the electrodes is permanently connected to the uninsulated coil. If a rat bites at the coil, he closes the circuit and gets punished.

J. Weiss (1967) has described a tail electrode assembly for the rat that does not require either body or tail restraint, and he has cited its use in one-way and shuttle avoidance learning situations.

Fixed external or subcutaneous electrodes are often used to shock pigeons, since the high resistance of the scaly tissue of their feet (Azrin, 1959) can interfere with foot shock. The use of subcutaneous electrodes to shock pigeons will be discussed in the next section. Hoffman and Fleshler (1959) have used an external electrode system in which shock is delivered to a loop of wire snugly wrapped around the base of each wing. A practical system for making temporary connections to the loops has been described by Hoffman (1960). More recently, Hoffman and Ratner (1974) have described a similar wing-loop system for newly hatched precocial birds.

There are many ways in which to attach electrodes to the legs of larger animals. Church, LoLordo, Overmier, Solomon, and Turner (1966) and Overmier and Seligman (1967) shocked the hindfeet of dogs restrained in a Pavlovian harness using brass-plate footpad electrodes. Also in conjunction with a restraining harness, Overmier (1966) attached copper alligator clips to the backs of the hindlegs of his canine subjects. Plumer (1971) used a pair of women's earrings to present shocks to the hindlegs of cats. The earrings were secured to the weblike skin folds on either side of one of the claws on the foot. Lubow (1964) has used a modified cable clamp to deliver leg-flexion unconditioned stimuli to goats and sheep.

Surface electrodes have been used to shock monkeys in restraining chairs. Commenting on the defects of the method where the shock is applied between the seat of the chair and the footrest, B. Weiss and Laties (1962) described the use of an electrode "shoe" placed on the subject's foot. Hake and Azrin (1963) have reported the use of a monkey-tail electrode for use in conjunction with a restraining chair, and Findley and Ames (1965) used a shock collar with an unrestrained chimpanzee.

E. *Subcutaneous Electrodes*

Subcutaneous shock electrode systems are described for rats by B. A. Campbell and Moorcroft (1970), and for cats by Kelly and Glusman (1964). These authors present aversion thresholds obtained with the electrodes (see Section IX-D).

B. A. Campbell and Moorcroft found subcutaneous shock to be less aversive to rats than footshock by a factor of about 10. For example, a 3-mA subcutaneous shock was equal in aversiveness to a 0.2-mA grid-floor shock from the 500-V constant current FVAC source described in Section VI-C.

The electrodes used by B. A. Campbell and Moorcroft were $\frac{3}{8}$-in. solid silver rings implanted in the necks and hind-ends of the rats. Pulsed shock (133 msec *on*, 67 msec *off*) was used because pilot work had indicated that pulsed shock produced less physical damage and disruption than continuous shock. However, even with this precaution, evidence of tissue damage and/or muscular tetanization occurred above 5 or 6 mA, corresponding to an equally aversive grid-floor shock intensity of only .6 mA.

B. A. Campbell and Moorcroft conclude that subcutaneous shock is not suitable for general use with rats. The surgery is lengthy, expensive, and can incur a poor recovery rate. The current levels required are higher than those required for grid-floor shock. Finally, the highest safe current that can be used is equally aversive to what is generally considered to be an *intermediate* level of grid-floor shock.

The usefulness of subcutaneous electrodes with rats also may be restricted by unconditioned response to internal shock. Azrin *et al.* (1967) report that their attempts to use subdermal electrodes in avoidance learning situations were thwarted by the rat's freezing response to subdermal shock. However, in some situations, these freezing responses would not be a hindrance. Thus, de Toledo and Black (1965) report the successful use of implanted electrodes to present shock in a conditioned suppression situation. Barfield and Sachs (1968) used safety pins to deliver shock in a study of the facilitative effects of shock on the male rat's sexual behavior.

Given the difficulty of using grid-floor shock with pigeons, the most popular method of shocking pigeons is one devised by Azrin (1959). In this method, wire loops are implanted around the bird's pubis bone. While Azrin used gold wire, Coughlin (1970) describes the satisfactory use of inexpensive stainless steel wire. Lydic and Anson (1974) have modified Azrin's technique for quail.

Granda, Matsumiya, and Stirling (1965) have used electrodes implanted in the jaw of the turtle to present shock unconditioned stimuli for head retraction.

III. Additional Equipment Required for Grid-floor Shock

Unlike the other applications in Section II, grid-floor shock requires equipment in addition to the shock delivery electrode system and the electric shock source. A grid polarity scrambler is required to keep the subjects from discovering "safe" grid combinations. Dc- and ac-leakage path detection circuits are required. Finally, if the scrambler is several feet away from the grid-floor apparatus, specially constructed low-capacitance cables may be required.

A. *Shock Scramblers*

The simplest way to connect grid bars to a shock source is to wire alternate grid bars to each output terminal of the source. This method is still used in the construction of student Skinner boxes. Anyone who has watched these boxes in operation with shock will be familiar with the fact that rats often discover how to escape the shock by putting all their weight on grid bars of the same polarity. Once a rat learns this trick, it is extremely difficult to shape the official escape or avoidance response.

A scrambler is a switching device that changes the pattern of connections from the two poles of the shock source to the grid bars. By continuously changing the grid polarity pattern, one eliminates permanently safe grid-bar combinations.

An important fringe benefit of grid polarity scrambling is a reduction in the seriousness of bolus shorts. Without scrambling, a bolus lying across adjacent grids will continue to short out the current until it is removed. With a grid polarity scrambler, the source will be shorted out only during those scrambler patterns where the two shorted grids are assigned opposite polarities, that is, about half the time. The subject will continue to receive shock, even though at a diminished frequency.

We shall describe two classes of scrambling devices. The first class consists of relatively sophisticated devices designed to produce a widely varying sequence of polarity patterns. The second or economy class consists of considerably less-sophisticated devices that appear to do an adequate job inexpensively.

Scramblers in the first category produce a repeating sequence of polarity patterns. Each pattern makes a specific assignment of polarities to between 12 and 16 grid-bars. Additional bars in the grid floor are wired up in such a way that they repeat the basic pattern. Each pattern should contain an approximately equal representation of the two shock source poles, and should avoid clustering of like polarities over adjacent grids. Successive patterns should differ as much as possible. Finally, over the entire sequence of patterns, any two grids should be at opposite polarity in approximately half of the patterns. In practice, we suggest that one begin by randomly assigning polarities to each successive pattern, subject to the criterion that each pattern contain equal representation of either pole. Then one should edit his or her results subject to the other criteria. Trial and error will then lead to a reasonable sequence of patterns.

The scrambler switching frequency is the rate at which successive patterns are presented. In practice, this rate varies between a few to a few dozen per second. Relatively slow rates will prolong the life of electromechanical switching components. On the other hand, in punishment or conditioned suppression situations in which brief shocks of controlled duration are administered, the switching frequency should be relatively high. For a given position of the subject on the grid bars, there will be a wide variation in the effectiveness of the different scrambler polarity patterns, ranging from no contact at all, when the subject occupies safe grids, to good contact. The scrambler frequency should be high enough so that several patterns are sampled during individual shocks of controlled duration.

B. A Survey of Scrambling Systems

In practice there are several ways to vary the grid-bar polarity pattern. Motor driven rotary switches have been used (Skinner & Campbell, 1947; Wycoff & Page, 1954). Alternately, one can use a stepping rotary switch activated by periodic 28-V dc pulses (B. A. Campbell and Teghtsoonian, 1958). A group of relays, properly sequenced, can deliver a series of grid polarity patterns (Hoffman & Fleshler, 1962; modified by J. M. Campbell & Jerison, 1966; Snapper, 1966). Mercury switches displaced by eccentric cams have been used to switch grid polarities (Owen & Kellermeier, 1966). An unusual system designed by Parks and Sterritt (1964) changes the polarity pattern only when the subject is not conducting current.

The first all-electronic (no moving parts) scramblers appeared in the mid-1960s (England, 1964; Markowitz & Saslow, 1964). Their complexity made them relatively unattractive compared to simpler mechanical switching circuits. However, the "solid-state revolution" has changed this picture, so that all-electronic and nearly all-electronic scramblers are readily commercially available. They have the advantage that they make little or no noise.

Concerning the selection of a scrambler design, either to be bought or built, our primary reservation concerns scramblers that deviate from the guidelines put forward in the last two paragraphs of Section III-A. In particular, one should avoid scramblers that change the polarity of one grid at a time, while all other grids have likely polarity. In each polarity pattern of this type of scrambler, all the grid bars, save one, are connected to the same pole of the shock source. The identity of the "odd grid bar" is changed from pattern to pattern. This arrangement is needlessly inefficient. For example, suppose each polarity pattern encompasses 12 grid bars. Suppose further that the animal is resting its weight on two grid bars. In this case, the subject will receive shock a mere 16.7% of the time. In contrast, a sequence of 12-grid polarity patterns designed in accordance with the rules mentioned earlier will deliver shock to the subject about 50% of the time. It seems probable that shock aversiveness is affected by the percentage of the time the scrambler delivers shock to the subject, and that scramblers with low percentages will significantly attenuate the aversiveness. Bolles (1966) has presented evidence along these lines.

The scrambling patterns of electronic scramblers should be carefully scrutinized. Some electronic scramblers produce the "one odd grid" patterns criticized in the preceding paragraph. Another type of electronic scrambler repeatedly samples random "bits," in order to determine the polarities of successive grid bars. A commercially available version of this design rejects patterns with all grids at the same polarity; it then samples another bit pattern. Unfortunately, it allows patterns in which *nearly all* the grid bars have the same polarity—that is, patterns in which only a few (one or two) bars are different. Such patterns occur often enough to seriously compromise the efficiency of shock delivery. Given the low cost of microcomputer hardware, an inexpensive system could be devised to make a more exhaustive check on the quality of each newly sampled polarity pattern, rejecting it and resampling if necessary.

Another caution regarding electronic scramblers concerns the possibility of attenuation of the shock at low levels. This should be checked. One way to guarantee the absence of attenuation is to use electromechanical relays to actually switch the grid bar polarities. Thus we arrive at a hybrid design: an electronic circuit controlling a bank of polarity-switching electromechanical relays.

Yet another consideration concerning electronic scramblers is that malfunctions may be subtle and not readily detected, and that the repair will require a higher degree of sophistication in electronics than is required to fix an electromechanical scrambler.

C. A Simple Electromechanical Scrambler

Having a great deal of experience with stepping rotary switch scramblers, we can testify to their reliability and long life. Malfunctions are easy to detect because they tend to be all-or-none, i.e., the switch stops stepping. The only drawback is the noise the stepping switch makes.

One will probably wish to construct a small sound-isolation box for housing the unit. Mount the stepping switch in a 4 × 5 × 3-in. steel utility box (e.g., Bud CU 728). Wrap the utility box in foam rubber, Fiberglas, or some other sound-absorbing material and insert it inside a larger wooden box. This construction is quite effective in hushing the clicks made by the stepping switch. Instead of a wooden outer box, one of the smaller-sized aluminum picnic chests can be used for the outer enclosure.

Our stepping switch scrambler has as its main component an Automatic Electric Type-80 rotary 10-point stepping switch with 12 nonbridging levels. By analogy with selector switch terminology, this switch has 12 poles (levels) and 10 positions (points). It can be advanced one position at a time by feeding the stepper coil a 28-V dc pulse. The twelve grid bars of the basic polarity pattern are connected to the 12 rotating contacts. Each of the stationary contacts is connected to one side or the other of the shock source output, in accordance with the rules previously mentioned for constructing a good sequence of polarity patterns.

The 28-V dc pulses used to step the rotary switch are easily produced via a cam-operated microswitch. A wide range of stepping rates can be selected, depending on the shape of the cam and the revolution rate of the motor driving the cam.

The rotary stepping switch should be ordered with lc *interrupter* contacts. This is a single set of SPDT contacts similar to that on a SPDT relay. The contacts are switched by the same coil that advances the rotary switch contacts. They should be incorporated into the coil operate circuit as shown in Fig. 2. With this circuit an initial 28-V dc activating pulse is fed unobstructed to the stepper coil. However, once the coil is activated, the interrupter contacts switch a 30 Ω, 10-W resistor into the

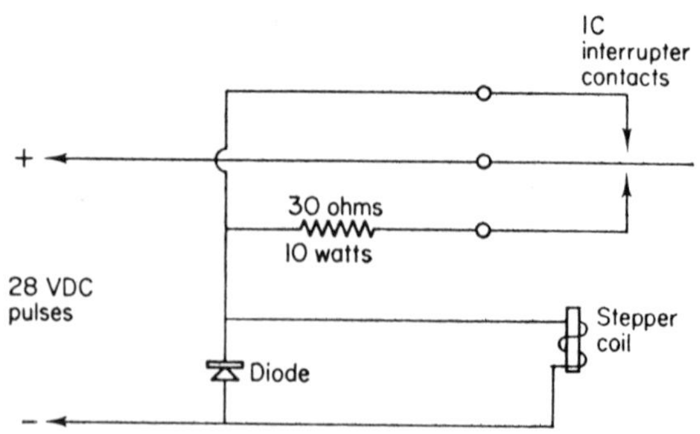

FIG. 2. Coil operation circuit for a rotary stepping-switch scrambler. (From Masterson & Campbell, 1972, Fig. 6, p. 44.)

coil circuit. This reduces the coil current to a level that is just sufficient to keep the stepping switch activated. This arrangement prolongs the life of the coil in situations in which the pulses fed to the coil are longer than needed to switch the rotary contacts.

The stepping switch coil should be spark-suppressed. This can be accomplished by connecting a diode across the coil leads, as shown in Fig. 2. Ordinary diodes may limit the speed with which the stepping switch can be operated. To obtain fast stepping speeds, one should use a 50-V zener diode.

Finally, the Automatic Electric switch comes with *off-normal* contacts. These contacts are not used in the present system. Thus, any choice of off-normal contacts is suitable (e.g., lc off-normal contacts).

The Automatic Electric Type-80 rotary switch, configured as above, has the part number PW-187003-CDAA (available from Automatic Electric, 400 N. Wolf Road, Northlake, Ill., 60164).

D. Inexpensive Scramblers

We have encountered two inexpensive methods for preventing rats from finding safe grids. We have found that both methods give reasonably satisfactory results, and one or the other might be incorporated in a student lab apparatus or in experiments where the greater degree of control provided by more sophisticated scramblers is not thought to be important. The success of these simple devices implies that the rat's ability to discriminate safe grid combinations is relatively limited.

The circuit of the first device is shown in Fig. 3. It acts like a primitive scrambler with two patterns (+, −, −, and 0, −, +) and has a switching rate of 120 per second. Using the alternating polarity pattern found on

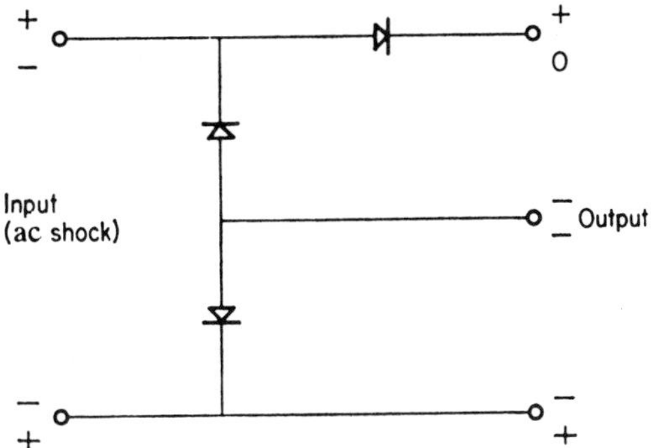

FIG. 3. An inexpensive scrambler. The upper and lower output polarities correspond to the upper and lower input polarities. (From Masterson & Campbell, 1972, Fig. 7, p. 45.)

student apparatus with grid bars spaced every half inch, permanently safe grid pairs occur at multiples of 1-in. spacing. With this device and the same grids, permanently safe pairs occur at multiples of 1-$\frac{1}{2}$ in. spacing. Apparently this is enough to confuse rats.

The second device is not really a scrambler. It consists of a motor-driven cam switch that pulses the shock every 0.6 sec, with a cycle consisting of 0.3 sec *on* and 0.3 sec *off*. Apparently, periods of safety due to the brief occupation of safe grids are masked by the 0.3-sec safe periods produced by the cam switch. The author has never seen a rat find permanently safe grids using this device, even in the early phase of bar-press escape training, where relatively long escape latencies are the rule.

E. *Equipment for Detecting Current Leakage Paths*

With grid shock, care must be taken to ensure that all the current leaving the shock source actually travels through the subject. There are two major ways some of the current can get diverted. First, leakage pathways may arise from the build-up or urine, moisture, or grime on the structures supporting the grid bars, or from boluses lying across two or more adjacent grids. Both ac and dc current can flow through a resistive leak. Second, stray electrical capacitances, such as cable capacitance, can provide capacitative leakage paths. Only ac current can flow through a capacitative leak.

F. *Resistive Leakage Paths*

Resistive leaks can be readily detected with a sensitive ohmmeter or with the inexpensive meter circuit shown in Fig. 4. The leads from the shock source should be unplugged from the scrambler, and the meter leads connected in their place. When the scrambler is turned on, the meter will be successively connected to each of the different grid polarity patterns in the scrambling cycle and will indicate if any of these patterns are shorted out. It should be noted that rapidly cycling scramblers may not dwell on shorted polarity patterns long enough to produce a deflection of the meter needle. If this is the case, a push button may be wired into the scrambler circuit permitting the experimenter to manually cycle the scrambler at a slower rate.

Any significant meter deflection should occasion a search for the leak's cause. Failing to find an obvious cause, such as a bolus, one should

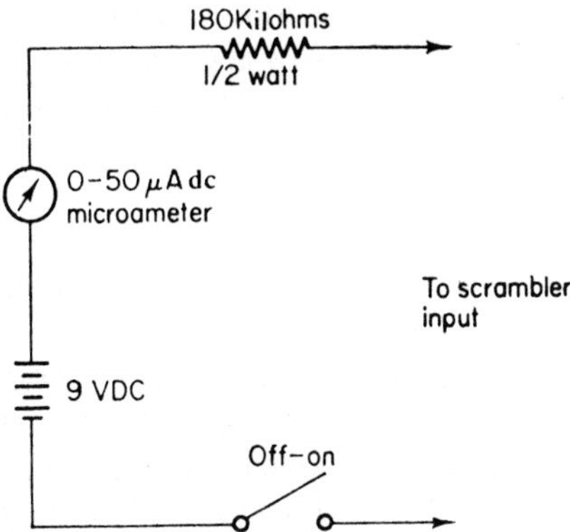

FIG. 4. An inexpensive meter for detecting resistive leaks. A full short (0 Ω) will produce full-scale deflection (50 μA). A 1-mΩ leak will produce an 8.5-μA deflection. (From Masterson & Campbell, 1972, Fig. 8, p. 46.)

wash the grid bars and support junctions. Drying may be accelerated with a hair dryer. We recommend making a leakage check prior to running each subject.

The commercial practice of mounting grids to the wall of behavioral apparatuses makes the development of urine leakage paths inevitable. Apparatus of this design should be routinely cleaned and dried.

G. *Capacitative Leakage Paths*

Most of the capacitance in a shock system is of negligible value. Thus, the capacity of the scrambler or of the grids is usually not a serious problem. The case is different for cable capacity, especially the residual capacity of the multiconductor cable that connects the scrambler's output to a grid-floor apparatus. Depending on the type of cable and its length, a significant proportion of current may be shunted through the capacitance of the cable (Section III-H).

A new installation can be checked for excessive capacitative leakage paths using the following simple procedure. Disconnect the leads to the scrambler input from the shock source output terminals, and instead connect them to the secondary of a doorbell transformer. As shown in Fig. 5, a 10 kΩ resistor and a capacitor of at least 0.25 μF should be connected in series with one of the leads running to the scrambler input. The purpose of the capacitor is to block dc currents, and thus to eliminate the influence of resistive leakage paths. Consequently, the resulting measurements should reflect only the presence of capacitative leakage paths.

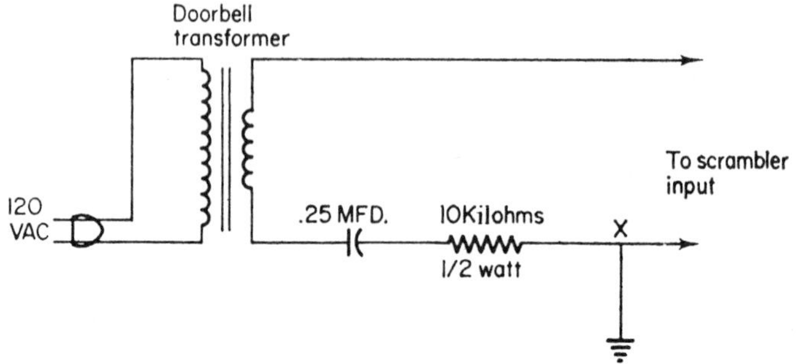

FIG. 5. System for measuring capacitative leaks. To avoid accidental injury, a low-voltage doorbell transformer is used as the voltage source. A filament transformer would also serve the purpose. (From Masterson & Campbell, Fig. 9, 1972, p. 48).

Plug the primary of the doorbell transformer into a 120-V ac line socket, and measure the voltage drop across the 10 kΩ resistor, using an ac VTVM or oscilloscope having an input impedance of 1 MΩ or more. This measurement should be made with the scrambler in operation.

If an ac VTVM is used, and if the scrambler normally cycles at a high speed, it may be necessary to manually cycle the scrambler at a lower speed (as in Section III-F). If the voltage readings vary over the scrambler positions, record the maximum voltage reading. Divide this voltage by 10. This will give the maximum capacitative leakage current (in mA) for any of the scrambler positions. Now divide the secondary voltage of the doorbell transformer by the just-derived current value (in mA). The result gives the approximate impedance (in units of kilohms) of the maximum capacitative leak associated with the various scrambler positions. This value should be in excess of several thousand kilohms.

As Fig. 5 shows, point *X* should be grounded, in order to simulate the normal ground relation recommended in Sections VI-B and VI-C. if the ac VTVM or oscilloscope has an internally grounded input lead, that lead should be connected to point *X* when measuring the voltage across the 10-kΩ resistor.

H. Low Capacitance Cable for Connecting the Grids to the Scrambler

The multiconductor cable required to connect the scrambler to the shock grids may introduce significant capacitative current leaks. Consider the case where a 12-conductor cable is used. At each position of the scrambler, about six of the cable's conductors will be connected in the scrambler to one side of the shock source, the other six to the other side. We have measured the capacitance between several random selections of two groups of six conductors each in a standard 12-conductor cable (Beldon 8457). The average capacitance was about 100 micro-μF per foot of cable. With a 60-Hz shock, this corresponds to a capacitative impedance of 26,000 kΩ per foot. Since the capacitative impedance of a cable is inversely proportional to its length, a 10-ft cable would have a capacitative impedance of 2600 KΩ, which can cause significant attenuation of the ac current passing through the subject, especially when the subject is in relatively poor contact with the grid floor. (For a description of the rat's resistance in a grid-floor apparatus, see Section IV.)

The easiest solution to this cable capacitance problem is to mount the scrambler close to the grid-floor apparatus, thus minimizing cable length. An alternate solution is to make a low-capacity multiconductor cable out of separate wires with plastic spacers to hold the wires apart from one another. A spacer can be made by drilling small holes around the circumference of a 2- or 3-in. diameter plastic disk. The wires are then threaded through these holes. Spacers should be placed every foot or so along the wires.

IV. Electrical Properties of the Animal

The first step in the standardization of shock motivation is the measurement of the average resistance of the subject as a function of the stimulating shock level. The functional properties of shock sources depend not only on the source's resistance but also on the average subject resistance. Thus, knowledge of the subject's resistance is required for an understanding of shock source functioning.

A. Consistent Changes in the Animal's Resistance in Response to Shock

There is a systematic relation between the electrical resistance of a subject and the current flowing through the subject. Figure 6a shows this relation for rats when foot shock is delivered from a constant current, 500-V FVAC source (B. A. Campbell & Teghtsoonian, 1958; see Section VI-C for a description of this source). At each current level, the median of 60 separate measurements was obtained for each rat, and the medians of the different rats were averaged with arithmetic means. Thus the

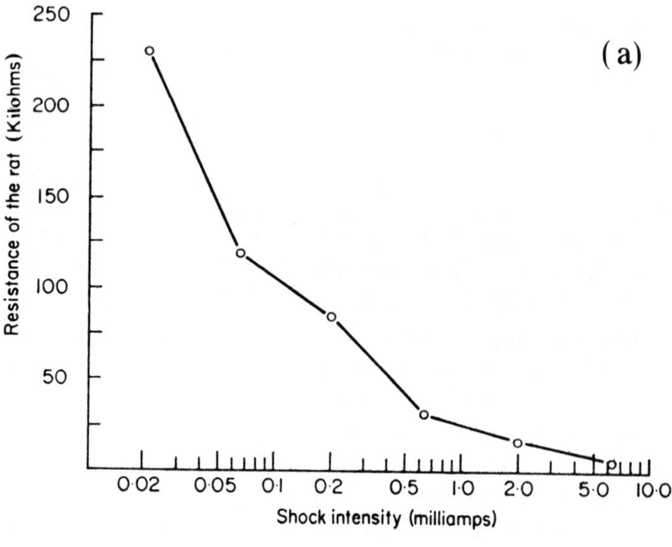

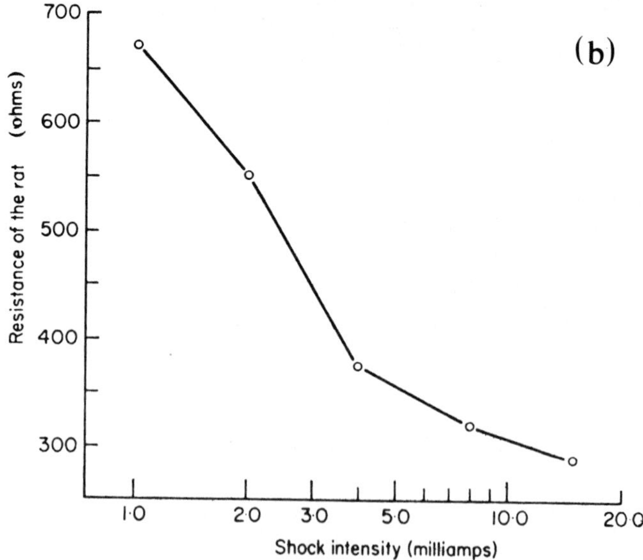

FIG. 6. Average resistance of the rat as a function of the intensity of current from a constant current ac source. (a) Grid-floor shock (data from Campbell & Teghtsoonian, 1958). (b) Subcutaneous shock (edited data from Messing & Campbell, 1971). (From Masterson & Campbell, Figs. 2a,b, 1972, p. 30).

momentary fluctuations due to the rats' movements on the grids were effectively "averaged out." What remains is a systematic effect of shock intensity on the animal's resistance. The resistance ranges from above 200 kΩ at 0.02 mA (below the rat's "aversion threshold"—see Sections IX-A, IX-B) to below 10 kΩ at 6.3 mA.

A similar systematic variation of subject resistance as a function of ac current has been measured in a single rat using subcutaneous electrodes and pulsed shock (Messing & Campbell, 1971). As seen in Figure 6b, the resistance is much lower, and the proportional variation is considerably smaller with implanted electrode shock than with the grid-floor shock. However, the shape of the function is essentially the same.

According to Fig. 6a, the resistance of a rat suddenly exposed to a 2-mA, 60-Hz constant current grid shock stimulus should drop from a resting level of about 200 kΩ to a value near 20 kΩ. How fast is this change? Measurement with electrodes bound to the paws of anesthetized rats indicated that the change is completely obscured by the 60-Hz sinusoidal waveform (B. A. Campbell, unpublished study). This suggests that the change takes no more than a few milliseconds. A study with human subjects by Gibson (1965) obtained similar results. For practical purposes, the response of the subject's resistance to a sudden change in current flow is instantaneous.

In the familiar light of Ohm's law, where current flow is determined by resistance, the dependence of the subject's resistance on current flow depicted in Figs. 6a and 6b may seem like the tail wagging the dog. However, such a dependence is a familiar state of affairs in electrical engineering and would be described by saying that the subject behaves electrically like a nonlinear resistor.

B. *The Interaction of Ohm's Law with the Inverse Relationship between the Animal's Resistance and Current*

To elucidate the interaction of Ohm's law and the relationship shown in Figs. 6a and 6b, imagine the general shock circuit shown in Fig. 7a. The secondary of a step-up transformer provides a voltage V_{source}, which we shall call the source voltage. The subject is connected to the transformer secondary through a resistor R_{source}, which we shall call the source resistance or alternately, the source impedance. By Ohm's law, the current $I_{subject}$ flowing through the subject is

$$I_{subject} = \frac{V_{source}}{R_{source} + R_{subject}} \tag{1}$$

where $R_{subject}$ is the resistance of the subject. The functional dependence of the subject's resistance on current depicted in Fig. 6a or 6b may be described by the relation

$$R_{subject} = \frac{A}{I_{subject}} + B \tag{2}$$

which is a good approximation so long as $I_{subject}$ remains above a minimum value of 0.2 mA for the footshock case and about 2 mA for the case of subcutaneous shock. The values of the constants A and B are 15.4 and 11.3, respectively, for the Campbell–Teghtsoonian rat footshock data, and 515 and 256, respectively, for the Messing–Campbell rat subcutaneous shock data.[1] It should be kept in mind that $I_{subject}$ and $R_{subject}$ are time-averaged quantities, so that momentary fluctuations due to the subject's movements have been cancelled out.

Equations 1 and 2 are perfectly consistent, and their simultaneous solution determines the values of the subject shock parameters $I_{subject}$ and $R_{subject}$ that result with a particular setting of the shock source parameters V_{source} and R_{source}:

$$I_{subject} = \frac{V_{source} - A}{R_{source} + B} \tag{3}$$

$$R_{subject} = \frac{AR_{source} + BV_{source}}{V_{source} - A} \tag{4}$$

According to Eq. 3, the time-averaged current I flowing through the subject may be increased either by decreasing the source resistance R_{source} or by increasing the source voltage V_{source}.

Similar equations for $V_{subject}$, the voltage drop across the subject, and $P_{subject}$, the power dissipated in the subject, follow from Ohm's law:

$$V_{subject} = I_{subject}R_{subject} = \frac{AR_{source} + BV_{source}}{R_{source} + B}$$

$$P_{subject} = I_{subject}V_{subject} = (V_{source} - A)\frac{AR_{source} + BV_{source}}{(R_{source} + B)^2}.$$

[1]The grid-shock values of A and B were determined by fitting Eq. 2 to the constant current ac source and matched-impedance ac (150-kΩ) source data in Fig. 1 of Campbell and Teghtsoonian (1958). Currents were inferred for the 150-kΩ source by means of Ohm's law. Only currents ranging between about 0.2 and 2.0 mA were used. The subcutaneous shock values of A and B were determined by fitting Eq. 2 to Fig. 3 of Messing and Campbell (1971), excluding the 1.0-mA data point. The curve-fitting procedure minimizes the sum of the squared *proportional* deviations of predicted $R_{SUBJECT}$ from the data.

C. *A New Equation That Better Fits the Rat Resistance Data*

Equation 2 fits the relationship between resistance and current for all but the lowest current levels, and provides a simple illustration of the interaction of this relationship with Ohm's law. However, Eq. 2 fails at the lowest current levels because it allows $R_{subject}$ to approach infinity as $I_{subject}$ approaches zero. A more realistic equation would be

$$R_{subject} = \frac{A}{I_{subject} + C} + B \tag{5}$$

The inclusion of a new parameter in the denominator of the fraction serves to limit $R_{subject}$ to a value of $A/C + B$ when $I_{subject}$ approaches zero.

Equation 5 provides a good fit[2] of the Campbell–Teghtsoonian grid-floor data with $A = 21.0$, $B = 8.37$, and $C = .0835$, and it nicely fits the Messing–Campbell subcutaneous function when $A = 522$, $B = 258$, and $C = .206$. Unlike eq. 2, Eq. 5 can be applied to the entire range of intensities shown in Figs. 6a and 6b.

V. Classification of Shock Sources by General Properties

A. AC *versus* DC *Sources*

Dc sources are undesirable for fixed electrode placements since a polarization or electrolytic breakdown in the subject's tissue causes a gradual increase in the tissue's resistance (Lilly, 1961; Mickle, 1961). This effect is avoided in ac sources by the rapid alternations in polarity.

Dc sources are also undesirable for grid-floor stimulation. Campbell and Masterson found that low-intensity grid shocks from a dc source produce more variation in aversiveness than do equally aversive shocks from an analogous ac source (see Section VII-D). The greater variability may be due to the storing up of electric charge in the electrical capacitances of the scrambler contacts, cables, grids, as well as in the source's

[2]Parameters A, B, and C were obtained by fitting Eq. 5 to the same data sets used for the fits of Eq. 2, except that none of the lower current values were excluded. The fitting technique minimizes the sum of the squared proportional deviations between the predicted $R_{subject}$ and the data.

filter capacitors when the animal occupies "safe" grids, and also to the subsequent discharge of this abnormally large accumulation when the subject later occupies "hot" grids (B. A. Campbell & Masterson, 1969). This repeating cycle of accumulation and discharge cannot occur with a 60-Hz ac source.

A final strike against dc sources is that they tend to be more complex and more expensive than their ac counterparts. For example, translation of the ac source designs recommended in Section VI to dc analogs would require additional rectification and filtering circuits.

B. Constant Current Sources

A constant current source is one that keeps variations in current flow within a narrow range despite large fluctuations in the subject's momentary resistance.

Constant current sources are among the most popular used with grid-floor apparatuses, where the movements of the subject produce large variations in momentary resistance (Section VII-A). This popularity is partly due to the mistaken belief that good current regulation is necessary in order to minimize variations in the aversiveness of grid-floor shock. The fallaciousness of this belief is demonstrated by the existence of sources that do an optimal job minimizing variations in grid-floor shock aversiveness, yet do a relatively poor job regulating current (see Section VII-E).

Far from being essential for optimal control of grid-shock stimuli, a very high degree of current regulation can lead to serious problems. Consider the case in which an animal with three paws planted on grids with the same polarity begins to lift the fourth paw off a grid of opposite polarity. As the paw begins to lift, the constant amount of current will be forced through a smaller and smaller contact area, resulting in increasing levels of current density. It is quite likely that concentration of current into a small area is more painful than the same current spread over the entire paw. Consequently, one might expect an animal to learn to avoid these current density peaks by remaining relatively immoble on the grids. This expectation is supported by the observation that rats minimize their locomotor activity at low shock intensities (Section IX-C). However, activity suppression is not a common feature of higher shock intensities, possibly because these intensities elicit innate flight reactions that largely dominate the rat's response repertoire (Bolles, 1970; Masterson, Crawford, & Bartter, 1978).

At medium to large current levels, highly current-regulated sources may produce tissue damage when the animal is in minimal contact with "hot" grids. The animal's resistance will be extremely high with minimal contact, and the voltage impressed across the subject must rise proportionately in order to hold current constant. As a result, power—the mathematical product of voltage and current—will increase, even though the paw contact area is minimal, and an abnormally large amount of power will be dissipated in the small contact area. Since power is dissipated as *heat*, high concentrations of power in small areas can lead to physical trauma.

Taken to greater extremes, very highly current-regulated sources can produce physical trauma by continuing the flow of current via an electrical arc after paw contact is broken. As mentioned previously, the voltage impressed across the animal must rise in proportion to the animal's resistance in order to maintain a constant current level. If the voltage is allowed to rise above several hundred volts, small air gaps between a paw and a "hot" grid become ionized and pass an electric discharge or spark. This would be the case if the animal's other paws were all touching grids of the opposite polarity.

To avoid possible tissue damage due to excess power density and sparking, an upper limit should be imposed on the voltage that the source can drop across the subject. In practice, this upper limit is set by the *source voltage*, or V_{SOURCE}, defined as the voltage across the source's output terminals when the source is not connected to a load. In terms of the simple ac source circuit shown in Fig. 7a, the source voltage V_{SOURCE} is simply the voltage developed across the secondary of the step-up transformer.

An indication of the limits on V_{SOURCE} required to avoid sparking is provided by Dunlap (1931). He compared two constant current sources, one with a source voltage of 450 V to one with a source voltage of 1500 V. He observed sparking with the higher voltage source but not with the lower voltage source. Staying on the conservative side of this range, we recommend keeping V_{SOURCE} in the neighborhood of 500 V or less in order to avoid sparking effects.

Given these considerations, it is remarkable that several commercial vendors offer constant current shock sources with source voltages in excess of 2000 V. Our recommendation is that the source voltage be 500 V or less. Optimal control of grid-floor shock aversiveness can be achieved with source voltages in this range (Section VII-D), so there is no need to risk the physical trauma that can occur with higher voltages.

Constant current sources are very popular, and as a result, *current* has become a major electrical parameter for specifying shock intensity. Hence, new workers have been motivated to purchase or build constant current sources to facilitate comparison of their shock intensities with those used in other laboratories. However, it should be noted that in one particular case—that of grid-floor shock and rats—current can be directly compared to voltage levels of the fixed impedance sources described in Section VI-B. Campbell and Masterson derived equal aversion functions for translating between equally aversive current and voltage levels of the respective types of sources. These functions are presented in Section VIII-B.

The easiest and most popular way to achieve good current regulation in an ac source is by using the general circuit of Fig. 7a, with values of R_{SOURCE} several times larger than the average subject resistance, R_{SUBJECT}. In this case, momentary variations in the subject's resistance about the average value will cause negligible proportional changes in the total series resistance $R_{\text{SOURCE}} + R_{\text{SUBJECT}}$, and hence, by Ohm's law (Eq. 1), negligible proportional changes in the total current flowing through the subject.

These considerations can be expressed more precisely by the formula:

$$\%I_{\text{subject}} = -\frac{1}{0.01 + \dfrac{r+1}{\%R_{\text{subject}}}} \tag{6}$$

where $\%R_{\text{SUBJECT}}$ is any momentary percentage change in the subject's resistance away from the average value R_{SUBJECT}; $\%I_{\text{SUBJECT}}$ is the momentary percentage change in current flow caused by the change in resistance; and r is the ratio of R_{SOURCE} to the average subject resistance, that is, $r = R_{\text{SOURCE}}/R_{\text{SUBJECT}}$.

Equation 6 shows that for a given momentary percentage change $\%R_{\text{SUBJECT}}$, the resulting momentary percentage change in current is a decreasing function of the ratio r. That is, the greater the ratio of R_{SOURCE} to R_{SUBJECT}, the better the current regulation. Let us consider a concrete example. Suppose the subject's momentary resistance increases by 100%—that is, it doubles. We set $\%R_{\text{SUBJECT}}$ equal to 100 in the formula. If $r = 40$ (R_{SOURCE} is 40 times as large as the average subject resistance R_{SUBJECT}), this 100% momentary change in subject resistance will cause a percent change in current flow of $\%I_{\text{SUBJECT}} = -2.4$ (*minus* because it is a decrease), which represents a high degree of current regulation. If $r = 10$, the equation indicates that $\%I_{\text{SUBJECT}} = -8.3$, which represents relatively good regulation. Finally, if R_{SOURCE} equals the average subject resistance (the case of a matched impedance source; see Section V-E), then $r = 1$ and $\%I_{\text{SUBJECT}} = -33.3$, which represents relatively poor current regulation. These examples illustrate the role played by the ratio of source resistance to average subject resistance in the circuit shown in Fig. 7a. The simplest strategy for designing a constant current source is to make this ratio large enough to achieve good current regulation.

For grid-floor shock, this strategy is limited by our earlier warnings concerning traumatic peaks in current density and power density, and electrical arcs drawn between an animal's paw and a "hot" grid. To eliminate these problems, we recommended using source voltages in the vicinity of 500 V or less. A detailed practical circuit for a constant current source—an elaboration of Fig. 7a with V_{SOURCE} = 500 V—is presented in Section VI-C.

More sophisticated circuits can achieve better current regulation without resorting to higher values of V_{SOURCE}. One type uses a large internal voltage in conjunction with Zener diodes to limit the output voltage. The other type uses electronic feedback to control current fluctuations. Both types have in common the feature that current regulation is quite good so long as the output voltage remains below a particular value, e.g., 500 V. When the contact of the animal with the grid floor is so poor that more than this voltage is required to maintain the desired current level, current regulation deteriorates.

The first type of circuit follows the genral plan of Fig. 7a, except that a series chain of back-to-back Zener diodes is connected across the output terminals. A large transformer secondary voltage (and therefore a larger series resistor) can be used to achieve better current regulation within the output voltage limit imposed by the Zener diodes. When that limit is reached, regulation falls off. For example, Ali and Reiter (1977) used a 2400-V transformer and four Zener diodes to limit the output voltage. The diodes were connected in series across the source's output, with two of them connected in one direction and the other two connected in the opposite. Since each of Ali and Reiter's Zener diodes had a Zener voltage of 100 V (the voltage at which the diode begins to conduct in the "reverse" direction), the resulting voltage limit was 200 V. Within this 200-V limitation, the source displays the current regulation capacity of a 2400-V version of the circuit in Fig. 7a; yet the source voltage, that is, the output voltage of the source with no load, is a mere 200 V.

The second type of circuit can achieve virtually perfect regulation up to a limit imposed by the maximum available voltage. The principle behind this type of source is negative feedback. A discrepancy between actual and desired current flow changes the momentary resistance of a transistor or vacuum tube in just the right amount to resolve the discrepancy. Current regulation is excellent up to the point where the transistor or tube approaches its minimum resistance. Past that point, current regulation deteriorates. Far from undesirable, this deterioration prevents the spark discharges and the excessive current density and power density peaks mentioned earlier. Muenzinger and Walz (1934) presented a pentode feedback circuit for a dc source, and B. A. Campbell and Teghtsoonian (1958) used an updated version of this pentode circuit. A similar update has been described by Davidon and Boonin (1956). Stewart and Campbell (1970) describe a feedback circuit that can deliver ac as well as dc shock. Reus, Houser, and Paré (1971) have described a feedback-type source that is specialized to deliver well-regulated 60-Hz square wave shocks at very low current levels (.015–.2 mA). Such a source is useful for aversion threshold determinations (Section X-C).

Are these more sophisticated circuits necessary? They cost more than sources based on the simpler circuit shown in Fig. 7a. However, their main superiority may be in the owner's aesthetic appreciation of the more sophisticated electronics. As mentioned earlier, good current regulation is not a necessary requirement for optimal control of grid-shock aversiveness. Poorly regulated sources can achieve equally good control (see Section VII-E). And fixed electrode applications avoid the necessity of very good current regulation because the proportional fluctuations in R_{SUBJECT} are likely to be relatively small.

C. *Constant Voltage Sources*

A constant voltage source maintains a constant voltage drop across the animal regardless of shifts in the resistance the animal presents to the source. A constant voltage ac source is easily realized by replacing the source resistor R_{SOURCE} in the general circuit of Fig. 7a with a wire, that is, $R_{\text{SOURCE}} = 0$. Because the other components of the circuit, such as the transformer windings, have virtually zero resistance, the voltage delivered to the animal will remain constant.

Shocks from a constant voltage source can produce a chain reaction culminating in tetanization. B. A. Campbell and Teghtsoonian (1958) noted that a 40-V shock initially produced mild annoyance in rats, but over the course of 1–2 min, the shock elicited increasingly intense emotional behavior and, eventually, tetanization. These changes were paralleled by a gradual drop over 1–2 min in the average resistance of the rats, from an initial 70 kΩs down to 4 kΩ. These gradual changes in R_{SUBJECT} are different from the virtually instantaneous changes of R_{SUBJECT} as a function of current flow I_{SUBJECT} discussed in Section IV. Campbell and Teghtsoonian tentatively speculated that a circular process occurs in which shock produces an emotional reaction that in turn lowers the animal's resistance. The lowered resistance of the animal then permits more current to flow through the animal, thereby increasing the intensity of the emotional reaction—and so forth. Certainly, some kind of positive feedback process seems to be involved. Most other sources evade this problem because they have an internal series resistance, R_{SOURCE}, which places an upper limit on current flow, thus breaking the postive feedback process.

Obviously, this is a shock source to be avoided. Yet, it still crops up. For example, one manufacturer sells a student-operant conditioning control station with a built-in constant voltage source.

D. Constant Power Sources

Interest in constant-power shock sources stems from a group of studies in which the size of fixed external electrodes varied and power dissipation was found to be the best correlate of the pain sensations reported by human subjects (Forbes & Bernstein, 1935; Green, 1962; Hill, Flanary, Karnetsky, & Wikler, 1952).

True constant power sources must incorporate a feedback system that continuously adjusts the current $I_{SUBJECT}$ in order to keep the product $V_{SUBJECT}\ I_{SUBJECT}$ constant (Green, 1962; Hurwitz & Dillow, 1966). The type of circuitry involved is considerably more complex than that used in the previously mentioned sources. This added complexity is probably one reason that constant power sources have not been used to any significant extent.

In addition to its complexity, another drawback of the constant power source is that it probably promotes the dramatic *"chain-reaction"* lowering of subject resistance observed by B. A. Campbell and Teghtsoonian (1958) for the case of a constant voltage source. In the present case, a gradual lowering of $R_{SUBJECT}$ will cause an effective increase in $I_{SUBJECT}$ in order that power, $I_{SUBJECT}^2\ R_{SUBJECT}$, remain constant. In turn, the increase in $I_{SUBJECT}$ will cause a further decrease in $R_{SUBJECT}$, causing yet another increase in $I_{SUBJECT}$, and so forth. In the context of this chain-reaction problem, the significant similarity between the constant power and constant voltage sources is that neither source has a fixed resistor R_{SOURCE} to limit the vicious circle of decreases in $R_{SUBJECT}$ and increases in $I_{SUBJECT}$.

Good power regulation presents problems for grid-floor applications similar to those examined in Section V-B for the case of the constant current source. With minimal paw contact, the constant power intensity will be dissipated in a small area, possibly causing burns at high-shock levels. Furthermore, excessive power regulation necessitates the use of large voltages, which might lead to spark discharges between the animal's paws and the grids.

E. *Matched Impedance Sources*

Good power regulation is beyond the means of the simple ac source shown in Fig. 7a. However, such a source does its *best* job regulating power when the source resistance equals the subject's average resistance, $R_{SOURCE} = R_{SUBJECT}$. This special case is called a *matched impedance source*.

Since the subject's resistance decreases with increasing shock intensity (Section IV), the value of R_{SOURCE} required to match $R_{SUBJECT}$ will likewise decrease as a function of shock intensity.

In the context of grid-floor shock and rats, B. A. Campbell and Teghtsoonian (1958) referred to the 150 k Ω source described in Section VI-B as a "matched impedance source" because it matched the rat's resistance at low-intensity shocks. Unfortunatlely, this terminology has often been used without the qualification that it applies only to low shock levels. In fact, the 150-k Ω source drastically mismatches $R_{SUBJECT}$ at medium-to-high shock intensities.

VI. Practical AC Source Designs

A. *General Circuit Plan*

We shall now describe two simple, effective, and very popular designs for ac shock sources. Both are elaborations on the circuit shown in Fig. 7a. The major difference in the two designs depends on the methods of varying shock intensity. In the *fixed voltage* ac (FVAC) source, V_{SOURCE} is internally fixed, and the intensity is controlled by varying R_{SOURCE} (Fig. 7b). This arrangement is particularly useful for designing simple constant current ac sources (see Section VI-C). In the *fixed impedance* ac (FIAC) source, R_{SOURCE} is internally fixed, and the shock intensity is controlled by varying V_{SOURCE} (Fig. 7c). Because of its greater simplicity, the fixed impedance design will be discussed first.

B. *The Fixed Impedance* AC *(FIAC) Source*

These sources use a fixed R_{SOURCE} resistor and manipulate the shock intensity by varying V_{SOURCE}. In practice, V_{SOURCE} is best varied with a variable transformer, as shown in Fig. 7c.

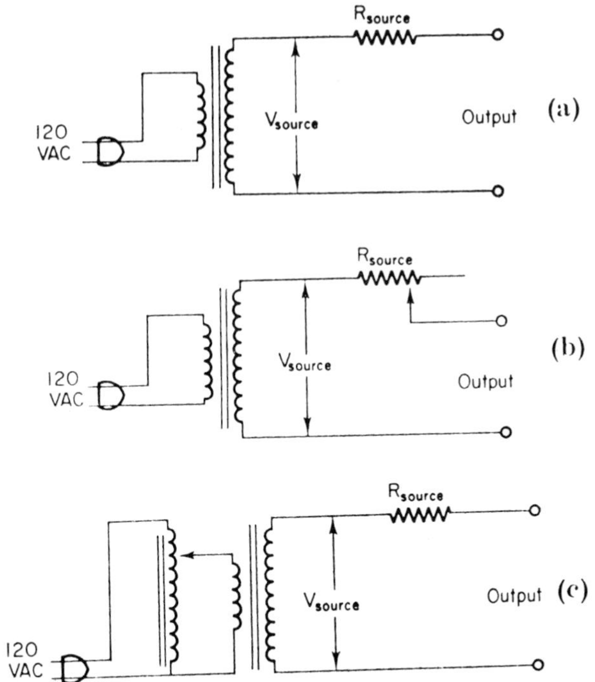

FIG. 7. Basic shock source designs. (a) General circuit; (b) fixed-voltage ac (FVAC) source; (c) fixed-impedance ac (FIAC) source. (From Masterson & Campbell, Figs. 3a–c, 1972, p. 33.)

Figure 8 shows a practical circuit for a FIAC source. Adjustment of the variable transformer (T_2) produces a range of from 0 to 120 V that is fed to the primary of a step-up transformer (T_1). Several manufacturers sell variable transformers that convert 120-V ac from a standard ac power outlet to a variable 0–120-V output (e.g., Powerstat Type 10B). The step-

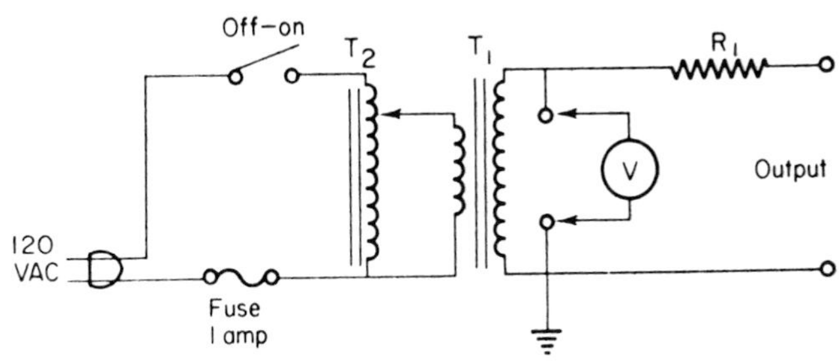

FIG. 8. Practical circuit for a fixed-impedance ac (FIAC) source. In the case of the 150-kΩ source recommended in the text, R_1 is a 150-kΩ, 3-W resistor. (From Masterson & Campbell, Fig. 5, 1972, p. 37).

up transformer multiplies the variable transformer's output by a fixed ratio to produce the source voltage V_{SOURCE}. In order to realize the full range of usable shock intensities, the step-up transformer should transform 120 V to the V_{SOURCE} value which produces maximum subtetanizing shocks (see Section IX-B).

The source voltage is monitored by an ac voltmeter connected across the step-up transformer secondary. Since the impedance at the transformer secondary is virtually zero, a relatively inexpensive low-impedance volt–ohmmeter (VOM) or a fixed-range panel-mounting ac voltmeter will work just as well as more expensive electronic voltmeters featuring high-input impedances.

We recommend grounding the bottom end of the step-up transformer secondary. Most electronic voltmeters measure voltage from ground. Should such a meter be used, its grounded lead should be connected to the grounded end of the transformer secondary. One advantage of this hookup is that the bottom end of the step-up transformer secondary will remain grounded whether or not an internally grounded voltmeter is employed (or when no voltmeter is connected), thus preventing variations in stray capacitances that occur whenever grounding relations are altered. Another advantage is that permanently grounding the bottom leg of the step-up transformer secondary will help prevent groundloops.

For grid-floor apparatus and rats, we recommend using a fixed impedance value of $R_{SOURCE} = 150\ \text{k}\Omega$. A 150-kΩ FIAC source does an optimal job controlling shock aversiveness (Section VII-D). In addition, its highest usable voltage level of about 500 V (Section IX-B) is not high enough to produce spark discharges to the animals paws (see Section V-B). To realize this maximum usable voltage, the circuit requires a step-up power transformer (T_1) that transforms the maximum 120-V output of the variable transformer (T_2) to 500 V. The current capacity of the transformer secondary can be determined by a "worst case" analysis: what would happen if the output leads of the source were shorted together while V_{SOURCE} was set to the 500-V maximum? By Ohm's law, the current flow will be 500-V/150 kΩ, or 3.33 mA. Hence, we might conservatively rate our maximum current requirements at 5 mA. Power transformers with a 120:500 step-up factor and with secondary maximum current ratings of 5 mA or more are easy to find (e.g., Allied Electronics type 6K88VG or Thordarson type 24R90).

The 150-kΩ R_{SOURCE} should be a precision resistor with a power rating of 3 W or more. This rating is arrived at by continuing the "worst case" analysis begun in the preceding paragraph. In the event of a dead short across the output terminals, the maximum voltage of 500 V will be dropped across R_{SOURCE}. Since the current flow was determined to be

3.33 mA, the power dissipated in R_{SOURCE} is 500 V × .00333 A, or 1.67 W. Staying on the safe side of this figure, we recommend a power rating of 3 W or more for the 150-kΩ R_{SOURCE} resistor.

A general word concerning the selection of the R_{SOURCE} resistor—and, for that matter, any resistors used in the construction of ac sources. The resistors should be of the *carbon composition* type, or, if wire-wound, the winding type should be *noninductive* as opposed to *inductive*.

C. A Simple Constant Current AC Source: The Fixed Voltage AC (FVAC) Source

Fixed voltage ac (FVAC) sources use the general circuit plan in Fig. 7b. The source voltage V_{SOURCE} is fixed, and the shock intensity is manipulated by varying R_{SOURCE} with a variable resistor.

With a sufficiently large fixed V_{SOURCE}, the fixed voltage design provides a simple but effective constant current source. This is because a reasonably large $R_{SOURCE}/R_{SUBJECT}$ ratio (source resistance divided by the time-averaged subject resistance) can be maintained over a wide range of current levels, thus guaranteeing relatively good current regulation (Section V-B). At low current levels, R_{SOURCE} must be set to a very large value, generally many times larger than $R_{SUBJECT}$, producing a large $R_{SOURCE}/R_{SUBJECT}$ ratio and good current regulation. One might expect this ratio to suffer at higher current levels where lower R_{SOURCE} settings are required. However, the average subject resistance $R_{SUBJECT}$ likewise decreases at higher current levels, as shown in Fig. 6a. As a result, the ratio $R_{SOURCE}/R_{SUBJECT}$ remains at a relatively high value. Thus, the success of the fixed voltage design as a constant current source is partly due to the inverse relation between $R_{SUBJECT}$ and the current flowing through the subject.

For rats and grid floors, we recommend using a fixed V_{SOURCE} value of 500 V. A 500-V source voltage does a reasonably good job regulating current at all usable intensities (as we shall see), does an optimal job controlling shock aversiveness (Section VII-D), and keeps V_{SOURCE} within our recommended upper limit of 500 V (Section V-B).

Some examples will illustrate the current regulation capacity of the 500-V source for rat grid-floor shock. To produce a small 0.1-mA shock, the total resistance $R_{SOURCE} + R_{SUBJECT}$ must be 5000 kΩ. The value of $R_{SUBJECT}$ may be determined by Eq. 5: when $I_{SUBJECT}$ = 0.1 mA, $R_{SUBJECT}$ = 123 kΩ. By subtraction, R_{SOURCE} must be set to 4877 kΩ. To assess current regulation, we evaluate the ratio $R_{SOURCE}/R_{SUBJECT}$ = 4877/123 = 39.7, or nearly 40. As we have seen in Section V-B, a ratio of 40 produces good current regulation. Moving to the other end of the shock level scale, let us consider the case of a 3-mA shock, representative of the highest grid-shock levels used with rats. Equation 5 reveals that R_{SUBJECT} will be 15.2 kΩ at this current level. By Ohm's law, the *total* series resistance $R_{\text{SOURCE}} + R_{\text{SUBJECT}}$ must be 166.7 kΩ, so that R_{SOURCE} must be set to 151.5 kΩ. In this case, the ratio is 151.5/15.2 = 9.97, or nearly 10. As we have noted earlier in Section V-B, a ratio of 10 provides fairly good current regulation.

A practical circuit for the FVAC source is shown in Fig. 9. A step-up transformer T_1 transforms the 120-V line voltage to the fixed value desired for V_{SOURCE}. The variable resistor R_2 is used to adjust the shock level, and a fixed resistor R_1 limits the maximum possible current that would flow if the output leads of the source were shorted together while R_2 was set at 0 Ω.

Current levels are monitored by a high-impedance (1 MΩ or higher) electronic voltmeter connected across a small series resistor R_3. Current levels can be inferred from the voltage measurements. For example, if R_3 = 1000 Ω, the number of volts read on the voltmeter will correspond exactly to the number of milliamperes flowing through the circuit.

In order to calibrate a particular current level, the animal's average resistance must be simulated by temporarily connecting a "dummy subject" resistor across the output terminals of the source. For rats and grid floors, the appropriate value of this resistor may be calculated with Eq. 5.

We recommend grounding the right side of R_3. Most high-impedance electronic ac voltmeters measure voltage from ground and should be connected across R_3 so that the internally grounded meter lead is connected to the grounded side of R_3. One advantage of this hookup is that the right side of R_3 remains grounded whether or not the voltmeter is

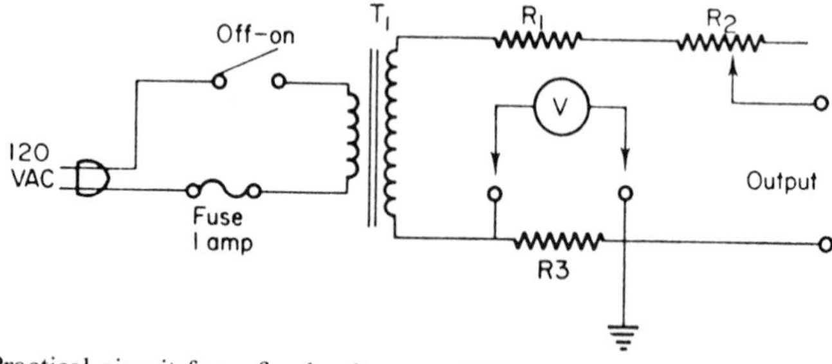

Fig. 9. Practical circuit for a fixed-voltage ac (FVAC) source. With a sufficiently large series resistance ($R_1 + R_2 + R_3$), this circuit approximates a perfect constant current source. (From Masterson & Campbell, Fig. 4, 1972, p. 35.)

connected, thus preventing variations in stray capacitances that tend to occur whenever grounding relationships are altered. Another advantage is that permanently grounding the right side of R_3 will prevent groundloops.

Let us now consider the practical problem of circuit component selection. Using $V_{SOURCE} = 500V$, as recommended for rats and grid floors, we select a transformer T_1 that can step the 120-V ac line voltage up to 500 V. The maximum secondary current capacity should be 5 mA or greater to comfortably accommodate the highest nontetanizing current levels (the 5% tetanization threshold for this source proves to be 3.8 mA; see Section IX-B). Several transformers are commercially available with these specifications (e.g., Allied Electronics type 6K88VG or Thordarson type 24R90).

The purpose of R_1 is to limit the current flow in the "worst case" of shorting the source's output terminals when the variable resistor R_2 is set at 0.0 Ω. A choice of 100 kΩ for R_1 will limit the flow to 5 mA—a value comfortably in excess of the highest subtetanizing current levels, as mentioned previously. Power dissipation for this "worst case" will be 500 V × .005 A = 2.5 W, so R_2 should have a maximum power dissipation rating of 3 W or more.

We recommend a precision multiturn potentiometer for the variable resistor R_2, since the resolution provided by the multiple-turn feature allows one to return to a previously calibrated current level without the need of recalibration. The resistance across the total span of the potentiometer should be large enough to produce the lowest desired current levels. A value of 5 MΩ will enable current levels down to 0.1 mA, the lowest employed with rats in grid-floor apparatus (the aversion threshold is 0.041 mA—see Section IX-B). A Beckman–Helipot type SE-613 has 10 turns and a maximum resistance value of 5.298 MΩ (available from Beckman–Helipot, 2500 Harbor Blvd., Fullerton, Calif. 92634). Another approach would be to use a selector switch with precision 1% 500 kΩ resistors wired in series to make coarse adjustments, combined in series with a 500 kΩ 10-turn potentiometer (e.g., Bourns Model 3501S-1) to make fine-grain adjustments. An advantage of this alternative is that 500 kΩ multiturn potentiometers are considerably less expensive (e.g., $23) than the 5.298-MΩ unit ($130).

Finally, we recommend a 1 kΩ resistor for R_3 because, as already explained, it produces the convenient "1 V = 1 mA" correspondence between the ac voltmeter scale and the current flow. R_3 should be a 1% tolerance precision resistor because of its crucial role in calibrating current levels. The power dissipated in R_1 will be negligible, so a $\frac{1}{2}$-W power rating will be more than sufficient.

All the resistors used in this or any other ac source design must be of the *composition carbon* type, or, if wire-wound, the winding type must be *noninductive* as opposed to *inductive*.

D. Convenience

Though convenience should be a minor consideration, it might play a role in choosing between two otherwise equally meritorious shock sources. For example, the constant current 500-V FVAC source and the 150 kΩ FIAC source both minimize variability in aversiveness of grid-floor shock for rats (see Section VII-D), but the 500-V source is harder to calibrate. Unlike the 150 kΩ source, the 500-V source requires the use of "dummy subject" resistors during calibration, as well as the use of more expensive electronic voltmeters (see Section VI-C).

VII. Sources That Minimize the Variability of Grid-floor Shock

A. The Inherent Variability of Grid Shock

Unlike fixed electrode shock, grid-floor shock is highly variable. As an animal changes position, the resistance it presents to the grids can vary from a few thousand to several million ohms, causing proportional variations in current flow, voltage drop, and/or power dissipation (depending on the type of generator used). An imaginary analogy from human psychophysics would be a vision experiment in which subjects move about, view the visual display from different distances and angles, and even look away from time to time!

Even though some variability is inevitable, we can search for sources that minimize variation in shock aversiveness. Two main strategies have been used to guide this search.

B. Minimizing Variability: The Best Electrical Correlate Strategy—and Why It Failed

Sources can be designed to hold constant either the total current flowing through the subject, the voltage dropped across the subject, or the power dissipated in the subject (Section V). When any one of these three parameters is held constant, the other two will vary as the subject's resistance varies. The electrical correlate strategy holds constant the electrical parameter that is best correlated with shock aversiveness.

Unfortunately, agreement is lacking concerning the best electrical correlate of shock aversiveness. While current may be the most popular candidate, power has attracted significant support. In addition, while no one has formally extolled the virtues of voltage, constant voltage sources are still in use.

The basic difficulty with the best-correlate approach is the absence of a model linking such *macro* parameters as total current flow, total voltage drop, or total power dissipation to the *micro* electrical and neurological events that ultimately determine the aversiveness of grid-floor shock. Without such a model, selection of the best correlate must rely on unformalized intuitions. No wonder, then, that different researchers have made different selections.

Lack of an adequate model of grid-shock aversiveness appears to be due to the complexity of the underlying processes. Imagine the total area of contact between the subject and the grids as being divided into a large number of tiny regions. The rate of firing of discomfort and pain receptors in any one of these regions probably depends on the *current density* flowing through that region (i.e., the current flowing through the region divided by the area of the region). Current density, in turn, depends on the skin conductivity and the electric field intensity at the region. Finally, the total discomfort or pain sensation produced by the shock depends on the quantitative rule by which the pain receptor activities in all the tiny regions spatially summate to produce the momentary overall level of discomfort.

So far, we have examined some of the factors needed to predict a single momentary sensation of discomfort. As the subject moves about, these factors must be reanalyzed for each successive small interval of time, yielding a temporal series of discomfort sensations. Finally, this temporal series must be averaged in some fashion to predict the overall subjective time-averaged discomfort of the shock stimulus. A model of grid-shock aversiveness must specify the mathematical properties of this temporal averaging process.

The complexity of this analysis suggests that the myriad *micro*-electrical and neurological processes underlying shock aversiveness are poorly reflected in gross *macro*-parameters such as total current flow, voltage drop, or power dissipation as measured from the output terminals of the shock source. It is probably fair to say that while one of these three macro parameters may be a better correlate of aversiveness than the others, none of them are particularly good correlates in an absolute sense. We shall present concrete evidence for this conclusion in Section VII-E.

C. *Minimizing Variability: Campbell and Masterson's Empirical Strategy*

Concluding that the electrical correlate strategy was a dead end, Campbell and Masterson (1969) used an empirical strategy for finding least variable shock sources. They presented rats with pairs of footshocks from a given source and measured the rats' ability to discriminate which shock was more aversive. It was assumed that the difficulty of such a discrimination is positively related to the size of the momentary fluctuations in the aversiveness of the shocks. Thus, the difficulty of the discrimination provides an index of the variability of the source in the region of shock intensities being tested. Applying this measurement procedure to several different shock sources, Campbell and Masterson identified a set of *least variable* sources—that is, sources that promoted the best discrimination performance over their entire range of usable shock intensities.

The notion that stimulus discriminability is negatively related to stimulus variability lies at the heart of most theories of discrimination performance (e.g., Torgerson, 1958). The novel aspect of Campbell and Masterson's application is that the major source of variability results from the subject's movements. In human psychophysical experiments, a constant spatial relationship is maintained between the subject and the source of stimulation (visual display, loudspeaker, earphones, and so on), and the major portion of variability is presumed to occur in the subject's sensory apparatus and nervous system. As mentioned earlier, a closer analogy to the grid-shock situation would be a human vision experiment in which subjects constantly move around the room, causing large variations in viewing distances and angles.

A more detailed description of Campbell and Masterson's discrimination measurement technique is presented in Section X-F. The result of their survey of different shock sources is presented in the following section.

D. *Some Least Variable Sources for Grid-floor Shock with Rats*

Using their discrimination measurement technique, Campbell and Masterson identified a set of least-variable shock sources for use with rats and grid floors. Since all the sources in this set are equally good in terms of stimulus control, the choice of any one will depend on such considerations as ease of construction, ease of calibration, and so on.

Campbell and Masterson studied FIAC sources with source impedances of 0, 35, 150, and 600 kΩ. The 150 and 600 kΩ FIAC sources showed minimal variability over their entire usable intensity ranges. The 35 kΩ FIAC source showed significantly higher variability at low-shock intensity (specifically, levels with $V_{SOURCE} < 40$ V, corresponding to an equally aversive current level about .3 mA—see Section VIII-B), and minimal variability at higher intensities. The 0 kΩ FIAC source—a constant voltage source (Section V-C)—produced very high variability across its entire intensity range. This result, and also the gradual "chain reaction" current escalation described in Section V-C, indicate that the 0-kΩ constant voltage source is unacceptable for grid-shock applications.

Campbell and Masterson studied ac and dc constant current sources. The ac constant current source was the 500-V FVAC source described in Section VI-C, and the dc constant current source was the electronically regulated source used by B. A. Campbell and Teghtsoonian (1958). The 500-V constant current ac source proved to be a minimally variable source: variation in shock aversiveness was minimal over the entire usable range of current intensities. By contrast, the constant current dc source produced significantly higher variability at low (less than .3 mA) intensities, but minimal variability at higher intensities.

As mentioned in Section V-A, Campbell and Masterson speculated that this increased variability at low current intensities may be due to the alternate build-up and discharge of dc charges as the animal alternates between "safe" and "unsafe" grid combinations.

The set of least variable sources discovered by Campbell and Masterson for rats and grid-floor shock may thus be summarized: FIAC sources with R_{SOURCE} between 150 kΩ and 600 kΩ, and constant current FIAC sources with V_{SOURCE} in the neighborhood of 500 V. What do these least variable sources have in common? One commonality is that the source resistance R_{SOURCE} is never much lower than the time-averaged subject resistance $R_{SUBJECT}$ (or, in the terminology presented in Section V-B, the *ratio* $R_{SOURCE}/R_{SUBJECT}$ never drops much below a value of 1). R_{SOURCE} can be as low as $R_{SUBJECT}$ without raising variability, as illustrated by the minimal variability of low-intensity shocks from the 150-kΩ FIAC source where R_{SOURCE} = 150 kΩ approximately matches the subject's average resistance. However, when R_{SOURCE} is much lower than $R_{SUBJECT}$, variability rises above the minimum possible value. This is nicely illustrated by the 35 kΩ source, where the variability of low shock intensities is greater than minimal. The transition from nonminimal to minimal variability occurs at a level of about 40 V, that is, when the subject's average resistance is about 60 kΩ (Eq. 4). This suggests that the ratio $R_{SOURCE}/R_{SUBJECT}$ can drop as low as 0.5 before the variability in aversiveness significantly rises above the minimum possible value.

Another commonality of the least-variable sources is that, with one exception, the value of V_{SOURCE} never exceeds 500 V. (The exception occurs with high-intensity settings of the 600 kΩ FIAC source, where V_{SOURCE} approaches 1000 V.) Campbell and Masterson avoided larger V_{SOURCE} values because of the possibility of spark discharges when a subject breaks contact with the grids (Section V-B). It seems likely that this sparking effect would increase the variability of shock sources that use excessively high values of V_{SOURCE}.

E. *The Best Electrical Correlate Strategy Revisited*

At the end of Section VII-B, we suggested that none of the three *macro*-electrical parameters (total current, voltage, or power) were very good correlates of grid-shock aversiveness, and in Section VII-C, we opted for an empirical approach to shock source variability. Now that the results of the empirical approach have been described (Section VII-D), what do they tell us about the degree of correlation between aversiveness and these three basic *macro*-parameters?

The wide variety of least-variable sources substantiates the earlier argument that neither current, voltage, nor power, as measured at the shock source terminals, correlates very well with grid-shock aversiveness. Voltage is the most easily discredited: The constant voltage source was the most variable of all those tested. The poor correlation of current with shock aversiveness follows from the fact that minimal variability in aversiveness is relatively independent of good current regulation. In Section VII-D we found that ratios of $R_{SOURCE}/R_{SUBJECT}$ as low as 1.0 or even 0.5 led to minimal variability despite the fact that these ratios produce relatively poor current regulation (Section V-B).

While the minimal requirements for the value of R_{SOURCE} suggests that a bare modicum of current regulation is essential for minimal variability of shock aversiveness, there is an intriguing alternate explanation. Consider the positive feedback process operating with the constant voltage source, where $R_{SOURCE} = 0$ (Section V-C). Perhaps the importance of a minimal series source resistance R_{SOURCE} is that it limits total current flow, thus putting a break on the runaway increases in current flow observed with the constant voltage, 0 kΩ source.

Finally, the Campbell–Masterson results suggest that power is not a very good correlate of shock aversiveness. At 0.065 mA, the 150 kΩ

FIAC source matches the average resistance of the rat (by Eq. 5), so power variations will be smaller than with the 600 kΩ FIAC source or the 500-V FVAC source, where R_{SOURCE} mismatches $R_{SUBJECT}$. Yet the latter two sources are no more variable than the 150 kΩ source at equivalent low-shock levels. Similarly, at 0.705 mA, the 35 kΩ FIAC source matches the average resistance of the rat, yet is no less variable than the 150 kΩ, 600 kΩ, or 500-V sources at equivalent levels (where the latter three sources mismatch the rat's resistance).

VIII. Translating between Different Sources and Situations: Equal Aversion Functions

A. *The Grid-shock "Tower of Babel"*

Once upon a time there was hope, in some quarters, that a single source would emerge as the obvious choice for delivering shock to subjects via grid floors. This has not happened. As shown in Section VII-D, there are several sources that are equally desirable for grid-floor shock in the sense that they reduce variability in aversiveness to the same *minimal* value. Thus, it appears that proliferation of shock sources is a permanent, rather than temporary, state of affairs.

The main problem posed by the proliferation of shock sources is that of translation. How is one to compare voltage levels between two different FIAC sources or a current level of a constant current source with a voltage level of a FIAC source? One could try to use the equations in Section IV, but the results would not be accurate. Those equations were formulated in terms of the *time-averaged* subject resistance, $R_{SUBJECT}$. To predict shock aversiveness, one would need a dynamic model encompassing the factors mentioned in Section VII-B, including a quantitative rule specifying how the animal averages momentary sensations of discomfort to arrive at the overall subjective aversiveness.

As in the case of the variability problem (Sections VII-B and VII-C), an empirical solution comes to our rescue. Using a simple forced-choice measurement technique, we can in a sense "ask the animals" which of two shocks from two different sources is more aversive. From the animals' "answers," we can construct equal aversion functions relating the two sources.

In general, an *equal aversion function* is an equation that can be used to transform an intensity value for one noxious stimulus into a corresponding, equally aversive intensity value for another noxious stimulus (for more details, see Section X-E). In the remainder of this section, we shall present equal aversion functions relating different sources of grid-floor shock. Then we shall discuss an equal aversion function comparing grid shock to subcutaneous shock. Equal aversion functions relating shock to noise and light then will be presented.

B. *Equal Aversion Functions Relating Different Sources of Grid-floor Shock for Rats*

Campbell and Masterson selected the 150-kΩ FIAC source as a "standard" to be compared with several other sources. Each comparison yielded an equal aversion function relating levels of the comparison source to levels of the 150-kΩ standard source.

1. Translating between Fixed Impedance AC Sources

Campbell and Masterson reported an equal aversion function for transforming 150-kΩ source voltages V_{150} into V_{SOURCE} voltages for another FIAC source with source resistance R_{SOURCE}. An algebraically equivalent but simpler form of their equation is given by:

$$V_{\text{SOURCE}} = \frac{R_{\text{SOURCE}} + 38.7}{188.7}(V_{150} - 16.5) + 16.5. \quad (7)$$

A more general version of this function would relate equally aversive voltage levels V_{SOURCE} and V'_{SOURCE} for two FIAC sources with resistances of R_{SOURCE} and R'_{SOURCE}, respectively. Such a function can be derived from Eq. 7:

$$V'_{\text{SOURCE}} = \frac{R'_{\text{SOURCE}} + 38.7}{R_{\text{SOURCE}} + 38.7}(V_{\text{SOURCE}} - 16.5) + 16.5. \quad (8)$$

For example, let us determine the voltage from a 250-kΩ FIAC source that is equal in aversiveness to a 450-V shock from a 600-kΩ FIAC source. Setting $R_{\text{SOURCE}} = 600$ kΩ $V_{\text{SOURCE}} = 450$V, and $R'_{\text{SOURCE}} = 250$ kΩ, Eq. 8 shows that $V'_{\text{SOURCE}} = 212$ V.

The equal aversion equations (Eqs. 7 and 8) were derived from data spanning a range of intensities of 45–300 V from the 150-kΩ source. We do not recommend applying these functions to shock levels for which the equally aversive 150-kΩ source voltages fall very far outside this range.

Equation 7 does an excellent job summarizing those levels of other

FIAC sources that were measured to be equally aversive to preselected levels of the 150-kΩ source. Noting that fact, Campbell and Masterson proposed a simple mathematical model that predicts Eq. 7 as one of its consequences. A description of that model and its good and bad points may be found in B. A. Campbell and Masterson (1969, pp. 27–30).

2. Translating between an FIAC Source and the Constant Current 500-V FVAC Source

Campbell and Masterson reported an equal aversion function that converts V_{150}-volt shocks from the 150-kΩ FIAC source to equally aversive milliampere current levels I from the constant current 500-V source:

$$I = .000268(V_{150})^{1.56} \tag{9}$$

To translate other FIAC sources into 500-V constant current source levels, first use Eq. 8 to find the equally aversive 150-kΩ source voltage (set R_{SOURCE} = 150 V), then insert that value as V_{150} in Eq. 9.

To convert 500-V source currents I (in milliamperes) to equally aversive voltages V_{150} of the 150-kΩ source, use the formula

$$V_{150} = 195(I)^{0.641} \tag{10}$$

If desired, V_{150} then can be transformed to an equally aversive voltage from a different FIAC source with the aid of Eq. 7.

The equal aversion Eqs. 9 and 10 are based on data spanning a range of 150-kΩ ac source levels of 45–300 V, or equivalently (by Eq. 9), a 0.10–1.96 mA range of intensities of the 500-V ac source. Therefore, we do not recommend applying them to shock levels that fall very far outside of these ranges.

C. *Equal Aversion Functions Relating Grid-floor Shock to Subcutaneous Shock for Rats*

B. A. Campbell and Moorcroft (1970) derived an equal aversion function relating grid-floor shock to subdermal shock. The constant current 500-V FVAC was used for both types of shock, but the subdermal shocks were pulsed (133 msec *on*, 67 msec *off*) to reduce physical trauma (see Sections II-E and IX-D). The electrodes were $\frac{3}{8}$-in. solid silver rings implanted in the necks and hind-ends of the rats.

The resulting equal aversion function shows an abrupt change in shape between grid-floor intensities of 0.57 mA and 0.80 mA, which the authors attribute to tissue damage and/or tetanization caused by the subdermal shocks (see Section IX-D).

D. *Equal Aversion Functions Relating Grid-floor Shock to Loud Noise and Bright Light for Rats*

Campbell and Bloom (1965) present graphs of equal aversion functions equating voltage levels V_{150} from the 150-kΩ FIAC source to dB levels N of pink noise (1200–4800 Hz) in terms of their aversiveness to the rat. The equations corresponding to these graphs were reported by Masterson (1965):

$$N = 1.95\ V_{150} + 21.6$$
$$N = 1.93\ V_{150} + 31.0$$

The first function was obtained from the first 30 min of a total 100-min session, while the second is based on the final 30 min. These functions were based on data spanning a noise range of 45–115 dB and a shock range of V_{150} of 10–45 V, and therefore should not be applied to levels very far removed from these ranges.

The highest noise level used by Campbell and Bloom was 115 dB (higher levels would have risked damage to the rat's inner ear). This 115-dB level is equivalent to a footshock 150-kΩ source voltage of 48 or 44 V, depending on whether the first or second function is used, respectively. The equally aversive constant current 500-V FVAC source levels are .11 and .098, respectively (Eq. 9). As described in Section IX-B, these levels fall at the bottom end of the range of usable footshock intensities. Thus, the maximum prolonged sound levels that can be safely applied to rats are equivalent to the lowest usable grid-floor shock intensities.

One possible reason for the relatively low level of aversiveness of prolonged loud noise, as evidenced by the above result, is auditory fatigue. Masterson (1965, 1969) has shown that the motivational potency of loud noise drastically decreases over a 1-hr experimental session, suggesting that rats adapt to the noise. Since Campbell and Bloom used a relatively long experimental session, it is likely that their rats were similarly adapted to loud noise.

Messing (1970) determined an equal aversion function linking footshock to bright-light stimuli for rats. She found that the aversiveness of the light—as indexed by the equally aversive footshock level—*decreased* above 50 fc of illumination, a phenomenon she attributed to retinal damage. The maximally aversive 50 fc level was equaled in aversiveness by a footshock current of 0.10 mA. Here, as in the case of loud noise, the maximum aversiveness matches the lowest usable levels of grid-floor shock (Section IX-B).

These results make it clear why experiments in noise escape (e.g.,

Masterson, 1969) and light escape (e.g., Kaplan, Jackson, & Sparer, 1965) have measured such low levels of performance in comparison to those typically obtained with shock. The most aversive usable levels of noise and light are equivalent in noxiousness to the least-aversive usable levels of grid-floor shock.

E. *Transituational Validity of the Equal Aversion Functions*

Do these equal aversion functions, based on the forced-choice procedure, generalize to other situations? Can they predict equal levels of performance of other behaviors? The equal aversion function for translating between fixed impedance ac sources do a good job predicting equal learning rates and asymptotic performance levels in the runway avoidance situation. Likewise, the equal aversion functions predicted equal behavior levels in a punishment experiment, and also in a tilt-cage measure of shock-induced activity. These results are presented in detail in Campbell and Masterson (1969, 1972).

IX. The Usable Range of Aversive Shock Intensities

A. *Defining the Limits*

The lower limit of useful shock is determined by the *aversion threshold,* which is the intensity that is just strong enough to motivate a simple avoidance reaction. Specifically, the aversion threshold is the intensity of shock that animals avoid 75% of the time in a forced-choice situation.

A lower bound on the useful shock intensities for escape learning situations is provided by the *escape threshold,* that intensity from which animals will actively escape 50% of the time.

The upper limit of useful grid-floor shock is determined by the onset of tetanization (characterized by a chronic grasping of the grids). Campbell and Masterson reported 50%-tetanization thresholds—intensities at which half the subjects show symptoms of tetany. A more useful index is the 5%-tetanization threshold, where only 5% of the animals evidenced such symptoms. The 5% threshold better pinpoints the *onset* of tetany with increasing shock level.

Another way to estimate the upper limit of usable shock is to measure the shock level above which an animal's performance deteriorates (Scobie & Herman, 1972).

The techniques for measuring these upper and lower limits of usable shock intensities are discussed in Sections X-C and X-D.

B. *Limits for Rat Grid-floor Shock*

Table 1 shows aversion thresholds, runway escape thresholds, and 50% and 5% tetanization thresholds for several sources used to deliver grid-floor shocks to rats (these sources are described in Section VI).

Those familiar with grid shock for rats are apt to be surprised by the low values of the aversion thresholds. These intensities are lower than those used to motivate such commonly studied responses as bar-pressing and runway traversal. One of the best features of the forced-choice preference technique used by Campbell and Masterson is that it is sensitive to extremely small differences in aversiveness.

Interestingly, the aversion thresholds in Table 1 are the same as independently measured shock *detection* thresholds (Campbell & Masterson, 1969). For a rat, there are no "neutral" levels of footshock: if a rat can feel it, the rat does not like it.

Paré (1969) found no statistically significant differences between the footshock aversion thresholds of Long–Evans, Sprague–Dawley, and Wistar rats. He did find a significant sex difference, as well as a significant difference between age groups. However, an analysis of covariance showed that the key variable was body weight: the heavier the rat, the higher its aversion threshold. When the variance produced by the weight variable was factored out, the sex and age differences were not significant.

The runway escape thresholds shown in Table 1 provide a lower bound for shock levels useful in experiments on active escape training (Mas-

TABLE I

AVERSION, ESCAPE, AND TETANIZATION THRESHOLDS FOR FIVE SHOCK SOURCES

Shock source	Aversion threshold	Runway escape threshold	50% tetanization threshold	5% tetanization threshold
500–V FVAC	0.041 mA	.22 mA	5.5 mA	3.8 V
0-kΩ FIAC	8.5 V	—	57 V	44 V
35-kΩ FIAC	12 V	25 V	220 V	160 V
150-kΩ FIAC	14 V	45 V	680 V	540 V
600-kΩ FIAC	14 V	128 V	1300 V	830 V

terson, 1981). These thresholds were determined in our laboratory at the University of Delaware using the fixed-trial titration technique described in Section X-C. On each of 50 trials, a subject had 30 sec during which it could escape by traversing a 6-ft runway. If the animal escaped, a lower shock level was used on the subsequent trial; however, if the animal failed to escape in the alloted time, the trial was terminated and a higher level was used on the subsequent trial. For the 150-kΩ FIAC source, the titration levels were 0, 30, 37, 45, 55, 68, 83, 100, 122, and 150 V. Equally aversive titration levels were determined for the other sources using the equations in Section VIII-B. The thresholds were computed from the last 30 trials of the 50 trial sessions.

These runway escape thresholds should be regarded as lower bounds rather than practical guidelines. They represent levels at which rats escape *within 30 sec on half of the trials*. Often, one is interested in obtaining more consistent escape performance. In that case, the data presented in Section IX-C should be useful.

The reader may have noted that the aversion thresholds in Table 1 are not equally aversive in terms of the equal aversion functions presented in Section VIII-B. The same is true of the tetanization thresholds. This is not surprising, since the equal aversion functions were determined for a narrower range of intensities—that is, roughly 45–300 V from the 150-kΩ FIAC source, or 0.1–2 mA from the 500-V FVAC source—and should not be expected to produce accurate results much below or much above this range.

The case is different for the runway escape thresholds shown in Table 1. These thresholds fall within the jurisdiction of the equal aversion functions, yet application of the functions shows the thresholds to be *unequal* in aversiveness. This anomaly can be explained in terms of a learned immobility reaction by means of which rats avoid painful transient peaks in current density. This explanation is covered in the following section.

C. *Suppression of the Rat's Locomotor Activity at Low Intensities of Grid-Floor Shock*

A practical lower intensity limit for *active* escape responses is imposed by the rat's tendency to remain relatively immobile at low shock intensities. The escape thresholds reported in the last section are relatively poor indexes of these limits, since they were based on a loose response criterion (escape within 30 sec) and on a 50% escape rate. What are the limits for a more typical escape learning situation.?

The lowest shock intensity used in Trapold and Fowler's (1960) study of the effects of shock intensity on runway escape speeds was 120 V delivered from a 250-kΩ FIAC source. Following the equations in Section VIII-B, this proves equivalent in aversiveness to a 0.27-mA current from the constant current 500-V FVAC source. The authors reported a failure to obtain escape performance at a lower level. Similarly, Masterson (1970) was unable to shape bar-press escape responses with shock intensities below 90 V delivered from the 150-kΩ FIAC source—equivalent to a 0.30-mA current from the constant current 500-V source. The rats evidenced distress at the lower levels, but refrained from moving, making it impossible to shape a bar-approach response.

Recently, we have systematically explored this activity suppression effect for the case of the 150-kΩ FIAC source (Masterson, 1981). We measured the activity of rats subjected to 6 min of inescapable shock in a box with a tilting grid floor. The small tilts of the floor about a central pivot were accumulated as a measure of small-scale activity (SSA). This measure appears to be especially sensitive to small movements such as startle reactions or, when the subject is directly over the central pivot line, the redistribution of weight over the four paws. Large-scale activity (LSA) was a count of the number of times the subject made a substantial change in location of several inches.

Figure 10 shows activity as a function of shock intensity: SSA in Fig. 10(a) and LSA in Fig. 10(b). It is clear that SSA is an increasing function of shock intensity, in agreement with data presented by Campbell and Masterson. However, LSA is a U-shaped function of shock level, with minimum LSA occurring at 30 V during the first 2-min block of the experimental session. During the second 2-min block, LSA is likewise a U-shaped function of shock level, but the minimum LSA value occurs at 68 V. The results for the third 2-min block are identical to those of the second, suggesting a stable or asymptotic pattern.

We obtained the same results when we measured the effect of low-shock intensities on the LSA of rats in a 6-ft runway. These data are shown in Fig. 11. After 2 min, there is a pronounced suppression of LSA at intermediate voltages, with maximum suppression occurring at 68 V.

The point of maximum suppression in both experiments—68 V—is equal in aversiveness to a 0.19-mA current from the constant current 500-V FVAC source. Taking the Trapold and Fowler, and Masterson observations as a guide, it appears necessary to use levels of around 0.3 mA or more (equivalent to around 90 V from the 15-kΩ source) in order to train reliable active escape responding.

The fact that the U-shaped function relating LSA to shock level requires a minute or two to stabilize is consistent with the hypothesis that rats *learn* to minimize their LSA as a result of exposure to intermediate low

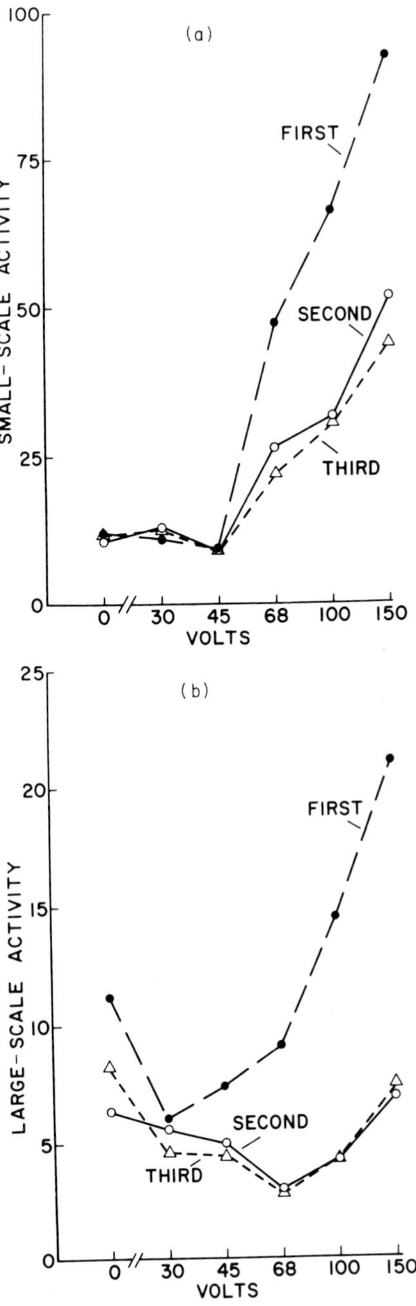

FIG. 10. The rat's activity in a tilt cage as a function of grid-floor shock intensity. The data are plotted in successive 2-min blocks. (a) Small-scale activity; (b) large-scale activity (From Masterson, 1981).

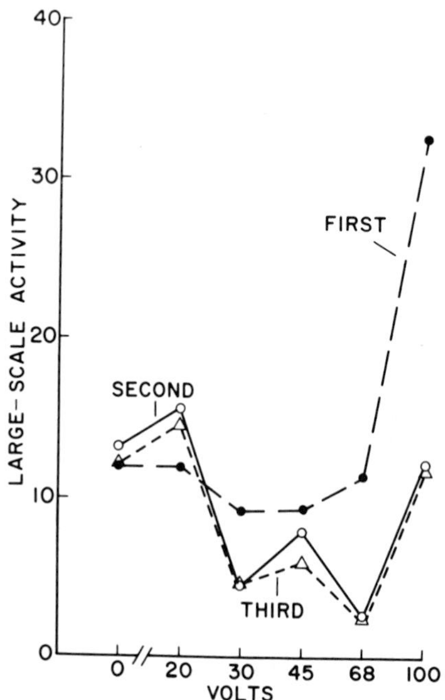

FIG. 11. The rat's large-scale activity in a runway as a function of grid-floor shock intensity. The data are plotted in successive 2-min blocks (From Masterson, 1981).

levels of shock. The reward for this learning may be the avoidance of abnormally large peaks in current density, as suggested in Section V-B. When a rat moves over the grids, its paws repeatedly make and break electrical contact. Either when a rat touches its paw to a "hot" grid or when it retracts its paw, a transition point occurs during which the paw is in minimal contact with the grid. At that point, a significant quantity of current may be forced through the minimal contact area, resulting in a painful transient peak of current density. It seems plausible that rats become immobile at low shock levels in order to avoid these peaks.

One prediction we can make from this hypothesis is that LSA suppression should be positively related to source impedance. This is because higher source impedances produce better current regulation, and better current regulation promotes larger peaks in current density when a paw makes or breaks grid contact (see Section V-B). Consequently, higher source impedances should lead to more LSA suppression than lower impedances.

The runway escape thresholds reported in Section IX-B provide a test of this last conclusion. These thresholds should be elevated by LSA suppression, since runway traversal is a large-scale response (Masterson 1981). If LSA suppression increases with source impedance, it follows that the runway escape threshold likewise should be an increasing function of source impedance: smallest for the 35-kΩ source, larger for the 150-kΩ source, yet larger for the 600-kΩ source, and largest of all for the constant current 500-V FVAC source (where R_{SOURCE} is several megohms at low shock levels). To check out this prediction, we must convert the escape thresholds in Table 1 to the same equally aversive scale for comparison purposes. Converting to equally aversive 500-V source current levels, the equivalent escape thresholds for the 35, 150, 600 kΩ sources and the 500-V source are 0.08, 0.10, 0.12, and 0.22 mA. Thus, the runway escape thresholds provide some evidence that the locomotor activity suppression effect increases as a function of source impedance, in accordance with the hypothesis that rats suppress their activity in order to minimize transient peaks in current density.

Here is an interesting puzzle: if the transient peaks in current density produced by locomotion at low shock levels increase as a function of source impedance, why are the 150 kΩ, 600 kΩ and 500-V sources all minimally variable at low levels (Section VII-D)? Shouldn't the larger peaks promoted by the 500-V source produce greater variability than the lesser peaks promoted by the lower impedance 150-kΩ and 600-kΩ sources? The solution to this puzzle is that the larger the transient peaks produced by locomotion, the more animals will learn to curtail their locomotion to avoid the peaks! Thus, the minimal variability of the 500-V source at low intensities may not be an intrinsic feature of that source, but rather a product of a learned adaptation of the animals.

In conclusion, the suppression by low intensity shock of the rat's locomotor activity places a practical power limit of around 0.3 mA (or equivalent) on intensities for use in active escape training. The conjecture that this activity suppression is due to the rat's avoiding movement—and hence the associated peaks in current density—is supported by an analysis of the runway escape threshold data in Table 1.

D. *Limits of Usable Intensities of Subcutaneous Shock*

Kelly and Glusman (1964) found the escape threshold for subcutaneous shock in a cat to be about 1.0 mA (a titration schedule was used—see Section X-C). Such a high value is consistent with Campbell and Moorcroft's (1970) observation that subcutaneous shock is less aversive to rats than footshock by a factor of about 10. For example, Campbell and Moorcroft found that a 3-mA subcutaneous shock was equal in aversiveness to a 0.2-mA grid-floor shock from the 500-V constant current FVAC source. Since 0.2 mA is among the lowest usable grid-floor shock levels for rats, it is likely that 3 mA is near the lower limit of usable subcutaneous shock.

Campbell and Moorcroft (1970) implanted $\frac{3}{8}$-in. solid-silver ring electrodes in the necks and hind-ends of rats. Pulsed shock (133 msec *on*, 67 msec *off*) was used because pilot work had indicated that pulsed shock produced less physical damage and disruption than continuous shock. However, even with this precaution, evidence of tissue damage and/or muscular tetanization occurred above 5 or 6 mA, corresponding to an equally aversive grid-floor shock intensity of around 0.6 mA. Thus, anyone using rats and similar electrodes would be wise not to exceed a shock intensity of 5 or 6 mA.

E. *Limits on Usable Intensities of Aquatic Shock*

Scobie and Herman (1972) have measured reaction and escape thresholds for goldfish. Parallel stainless steel plates presented the shock. Shock levels were reported in units of voltage gradient, the voltage impressed across the plates divided by the distance between the plates (Section II-C). The reaction (twitch or dorsal-fin extension) threshold to a single pulse of shock is around 0.2 V/cm. Using swimming over a barrier as the response and using pulsed shock, Scobie and Herman found the escape threshold to be around 0.65 V/cm.

To estimate the upper limit of shock for goldfish, Scobie and Herman noted the onset of debilitation in escape performance (swimming over a barrier) above 2.22 V/cm. Escape performance was a *decreasing* function of shock intensity above this value.

F. *Use of Aversion Thresholds to Measure Analgesia*

The sensitivity of the aversion threshold as measured by the forced-choice technique (Section X-C) makes it an ideal objective index of the analgesic potency of pain-suppressing drugs. For example, Boldovici and Cicala (1968) found increases in the aversion threshold caused by aspirin and also by meprobamate, and Houser and Paré (1972) found increasses in their rats' shock-aversion thresholds when they were injected with morphine. An important feature of the Houser and Paré study is the use of a repeated-measures design; aversion thresholds were obtained for each rat in each of the five drug-dose conditions.

G. *Partitioning the Usable Range of Grid-floor Shock into Just Aversive Differences*

How many discriminably different levels of aversiveness lie between the lower and upper limits of usable shock? How should one space successive shock intensities in experiments using more than two shock levels? Both questions can be answered by measuring *just aversive differences*. Two shock stimuli are called "just aversively different" if animals select the smaller over the larger 75% of the time in a forced-choice situation (see Section X-F). Two such shocks are said to be separated by one *just aversive difference* (JAD). Counting up the total number of JADs between the aversion threshold and the 5% tetanization threshold yields the total number of "just aversively different" shocks. Furthermore, JADs can be used to select several shock intensities for use in an experiment. A sensible strategy would be to space the intensities according to the animal's ability to distinguish between the amounts of aversiveness they cause. This can be done by selecting successive intensities that are the same number of JADs apart.

Figure 12 shows an accumulated JAD scale for rats and grid-floor shock from the constant current 500-V FVAC source.[3] Successive JADs can be determined by reading up the ordinate or by inspecting the successive JAD points lying on the solid curve. It will be noted that there are 26.2 JADs between the aversion threshold (0.041 mA) and the 5%-tetanization threshold (3.8 mA). Thus, the total number of usable "just aversively different" grid-floor shocks is about 26.

The JAD function is very nearly linear from the aversion threshold up to about 0.5 mA. Since the current scale is logarithmic, it follows that small-to-moderate currents equally spaced on a logarithmic scale will be separated by the same number of JADs, as recommended above. Above 0.5 mA, however, the curve bends over, indicating that currents with equal logarithmic spacing have progressively fewer JADs between them. For example, at the extreme end of the curve there are only four JADs separating 1 mA and the 3.8 mA 5%-tetanization threshold.

Accumulated JAD plots for other sources that produce minimally variable grid-shock in rats (Section VII-D) can be obtained by using the appropriate equal aversion function (Section VIII-B) to transform the abscissa. In Fig. 12, a scale of equally aversive 150-kΩ FIAC source

[3]The JAD scale was obtained as follows: A second-degree polynomial was fitted to the data in Figs. 1–12 of Campbell and Masterson, excluding the 0-kΩ and 35-kΩ points. The fitting procedure minimized the sum of the squared deviations of predicted Log JAD from the data. The resulting function was used to estimate successive JADs by the accumulation procedure recommended by Luce and Edwards (1958).

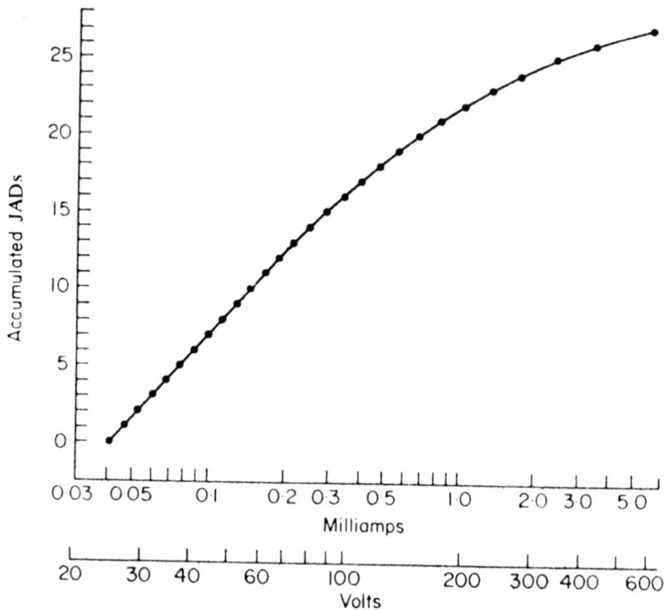

FIG. 12. Accumulated just aversive differences (JADs) for the constant current 500-V FVAC source and for the 150-kΩ FIAC source (rats and grid-floor shock). (From Masterson & Campbell, 1972, Fig. 10, p. 53.)

voltages is presented beneath the 500-V source current levels. Using this as the abscissa, the curve becomes an accumulated JAD scale for the 150-kΩ source.

The relationship between the JAD scale and current depicted in Fig. 12 can be summarized very accurately by a fourth-degree polynomial:

$$Y = A + BX + CX^2 + DX^3 + EX^4.$$

If X is the logarithm of current and Y is the JAD scale value, the polynomial coefficients are 21.86, 10.10, −5.049, 0.2919, and 0.7153 (in the order they appear in the equation). For the inverse relationship, where X is the JAD scale value and Y is the logarithm of current, the coefficients are −1.381, 0.04607, 0.001878, −0.0001475, and 0.000004470.[4]

[4]The procedure used to fit the polynomial equation minimizes the sum of squared deviations of predicted Y from the data in Fig. 12.

X. An Outline of Basic Techniques for the Measurement and Control of Electric Shock Motivation

The earlier sections of this chapter have made many references to Campbell and Masterson's techniques for measuring shock aversiveness as well as the variability of shock aversiveness. While the details of these techniques can be found in the B. A. Campbell and Masterson 1969 article, it would be helpful to have a concise outline of this methodology. This will aid the general reader seeking greater clarification of the methods upon which a large number of our conclusions are based. It will also aid the researcher who might wish to apply these techniques to new situations.

A. *Measuring the Subject's Resistance*

This step is essential for the case where shock is to be specified in terms of current (as with a constant current type of stimulator), and the subject's resistance is too variable to permit accurate calibration with the subject in the circuit (as is the case for grid-floor shock). Calibration must then be performed with a "dummy-subject" fixed resistor in place of a real subject. The appropriate value of a dummy resistor can be determined only on the basis of an earlier determination of the function relating the subject's time-averaged resistance to current level.

Fixed impedance sources avoid this calibration problem by specifying shock in terms of the setting of the source voltage V_{SOURCE}; in this case, however, a knowledge of the subject's resistance is useful in selecting a fixed R_{SOURCE} value. For the case of rats and grid-floor shock, we found that keeping R_{SOURCE} as large or larger than R_{SUBJECT} is a sufficient condition for minimal variability of aversiveness (Section VII-D). In the absence of concrete information, a similar condition might be applied to other animals with grid-floor shock. Certainly, R_{SOURCE} should not be much less than R_{SUBJECT}.

Techniques for measuring the average resistance of subjects exposed to grid shock are described by Campbell and Teghtsoonian (1958), who used them to determine the function linking R_{SUBJECT} to the intensity of the shock. Similarly, Messing and Campbell (1971) described the determination of a similar function for a rat with subdermal electrodes.

B. Description of the Spatial Preference Technique

In traditional psychophysics, subjects are required to choose which of two neutral stimuli (e.g., illumination levels) is the most (or least) intense. By analogy, Campbell and Masterson had rat subjects choose the least aversive of two noxious stimuli in a spatial preference situation.

The spatial preference technique was pioneered by Moss (1924) and refined by B. A. Campbell (1955). A subject is placed in a rectangular box, and the subject's position in the box is continuously monitored. The apparatus is programmed to deliver a particular noxious stimulus when the subject stands on one side of the box. A different noxious stimulus is delivered when the subject stands on the other side of the box. By shifting its location, the subject can determine which of the stimuli is delivered. The result is a "forced-choice" procedure for measuring the animal's preference between any pair of noxious stimuli, or between a single noxious stimulus versus the absence of noxious stimulation.

In nearly all the Campbell–Masterson experiments, each rat received a single session of standardized duration (actual duration values varied between experiments). The session was divided into several subintervals, and the amount of time spent on each side was recorded for each subinterval. This allowed the experimenter to detect temporal trends in the preference data and to throw out transient (preasymptotic) data from the beginning of the session. The method of recording the animal's position in the box used a tilting grid floor. Mounted on a central axis, the floor was allowed to tilt slightly—just enough to open and close a microswitch.

C. Measuring the Lower Limits of Usable Shock Intensities: Aversion Thresholds and Escape Thresholds

The aversion threshold is the smallest shock intensity that is "just barely aversive," and as such, defines the lower limit of usable shock levels.

B. A. Campbell (1957) defined the *aversion threshold* as the intensity of a noxious stimulus that animals avoid 75% of the time in the spatial preference situation. In the present context, animals are presented with a low intensity shock when they stand on one side of the preference box versus no shock if they stand on the other side. When the shock intensity is *well below* the threshold of aversiveness, the animals will show a 50%–50% preference between no shock and shock. When the shock intensity is *well above* the threshold of aversiveness, the subjects will show a strong or nearly 100%–0% preference for no shock over shock—that is, 100% avoidance of the shock. The aversion threshold is the intensity of shock that produces an *intermediate* preference for no shock over shock of 75%–25%—that is, 75% avoidance of the shock.

In practice, the aversion threshold is determined by measuring the percentage preference for no shock over shock for several low intensities and then *interpolating* the shock intensity value that produces a 75% preference value. To do the interpolation, begin by transforming the percentage preference scores in order to eliminate most of the curvature visible in a graphical plot of percent preferences versus shock intensity. The normal deviate transformation is a good candidate. A straight-line equation can be fitted to the transformed data by the method of least squares. The straight-line equation is then used to estimate the shock intensity corresponding to a 75% preference value.

The rat grid-floor shock aversion thresholds presented in Table 1 (Section IX-B) were obtained by testing a separate group of rats for each of the shock levels compared with no shock in the preference situation. It is also possible to use the same rats over again at each of the comparison shock levels (B. A. Campbell & Masterson, 1969, pp. 15–18). The latter method has the advantage that it requires far fewer animals. Houser and Paré (1972) have shown that the latter method can be repeated over successive days with the same rats. On each of 27 days, they measured the aversion thresholds of six rats. On some days, the rats were injected with varying doses of morphine. Interspersed between these days were placebo days on which the rats received saline injections. The reliability of this repeated measures technique is demonstrated by the consistency of the aversion thresholds measured on the placebo days.

We will define an *escape threshold* as the shock intensity that produces intermediate performance in a situation where animals are repeatedly required to perform some active response to escape from shock. When the intensity of a shock is *well below* this threshold, animals rarely will be motivated to escape from the shock. When the intensity of a shock is *well above* the escape threshold, animals will be motivated to escape from the shock on every trial. Thus, the escape threshold is the intensity of shock that motivates an *intermediate* escape response rate of 50%, that is, half the trials.

The aversion threshold, as measured by the described spatial preference technique, is apt to be significantly lower than an escape threshold. In addition to an escape contingency, the spatial preference situation contains a passive avoidance contingency: An animal can avoid the shock by remaining on the no-shock side of the preference box. This "staying" response requires no energy expenditure, and therefore would be expected to provide a more sensitive index of low levels of aversiveness than an active escape response.

Similar energy-expenditure considerations suggest that the value of an escape threshold will depend on the nature of the active escape response employed. Hence, it is inappropriate to speak of "*the* escape threshold." However, despite this ambiguity, escape thresholds provide a useful estimate of the lowest shock intensity that can be employed in various active escape-learning situations.

The *titration* technique introduced by B. Weiss and Laties (1958) provides a simple but elegant means for measuring escape thresholds. The technique is similar to one developed by Békésy (1947) for measuring auditory detection thresholds. The shock intensity delivered to the subject is periodically *increased* by a timer. Each escape response performed by the subject *decreases* the shock intensity. When the timer increases the shock to a level significantly above the escape threshold, the animal responds to decrease the shock to a level sufficiently below the escape threshold. As a result, the animal "tracks" its own escape threshold.

B. Weiss and Laties (1959, 1963) have explored the effects of various parameters of their "titration schedules" using bar-pressing as the escape response, and rats, monkeys, and humans as subjects. They found, for example, that all three types of subjects tolerate higher shock intensities with more rapid increments than with slower increments, probably because faster increments demand higher rates of escape responding—that is, higher energy expenditure.

A variation of the titration technique can be used with fixed-trial escape situations. On each trial, the animal is given a limited amount of time (e.g., several seconds) to make the escape response. The shock level used on the following trial is then decreased or increased depending on whether the animal escaped or failed to escape on the preceding trial. The runway escape thresholds for rats reported in Section IX-B were obtained in this manner.

D. Measuring the Upper Limits of Usable Shock Intensities: Tetanization Thresholds and Deterioration of Escape Performance

The practical upper limit for grid-floor shock is the intensity that just begins to produce symptoms of tetanization in a few subjects. The symptoms include immobilization and an inability to release the stainless steel grids. In practice, one can present a series of shock intensities to subjects and note the percentage of the animals that display symptoms of tetanization. By interpolation, one can then determine the intensity at which a small proportion of subjects (e.g., 5%) evidence tetany.

Another procedure for determining the highest-usable shock intensity is to determine the intensity at which performance begins to deteriorate in a simple escape situation. Presumably, such deterioration reflects undesirable adverse effects of the shock on the subject's muscular coordination. Scobie and Herman (1972) call this adverse reaction *debilitation,* and use it to pinpoint the maximum usable levels of water shock for goldfish. As is the case for escape thresholds, the point of onset of debilitation probably depends on the specific nature of the escape response.

E. *Translating between Shock Sources: Equal Aversion Functions*

Campbell and Masterson defined two shock stimuli as being *equal in aversiveness* when animals display a 50%–50% preference between them in the spatial preference situation.

In order to determine the level L_1, which is equally aversive to a level L_2 of a second source, one selects several comparison levels of the first source that are known to be roughly comparable to L_2 in aversiveness (these might be determined by a pilot experiment). Groups of animals are then forced to choose between these L_1 comparison levels versus L_2 in the spatial preference situation. The percentage preference for L_2 will be an increasing function of the L_1 comparison levels, starting at values well below 50% at the lowest level and rising to values well above 50% at the highest level. By fitting a smooth curve to these data, one can interpolate the 50% preference point, corresponding to the level L_1 of the first source that is equally aversive to the L_2 level of the second source. This curve-fitting procedure is the same as the one we described for interpolating the value of the aversion threshold (see Section X-C).

So far, we have determined the level L_1 of the first source that is equal in aversiveness to a level L_2 of the second source. The job now is to repeat this process for *several* levels of the second source that uniformly span the range of usable second-source intensities (Sections X-C and X-D). Then one graphs the equally aversive levels of one source against the levels of the other source. The final step is to fit a smooth curve to this graph. This curve is an *equal aversion function.*

An *equal aversion function* summarizes the description of equally aversive L_1–L_2 pairs by transforming levels L_2 of the second-shock source into equally aversive levels L_1 of the first shock source (or vice versa). As such, it permits the researcher to translate back and forth between equally aversive levels of the two sources.

F. *Measuring the Discriminability of Discomfort: Just Aversive Differences (JADS)*

The just aversive difference technique for measuring the variability of the aversiveness of shock stimuli relies on the assumption that variations in shock aversiveness interfere with the rats' ability to discriminate between the average amounts of aversiveness produced by different shock intensities. The logic behind this assumption is easily illustrated by making an analogy with the standard statistical *t*-test. The ability of the *t*-test to accurately "discriminate" between two average scores depends on the amount of variability in the raw scores. The greater the variability in the raw-score populations, the lower will be the probability for an accurate "discrimination." Similarly, when there is more momentary variation in shock aversiveness, the animal will be less likely to perceive correctly the average difference in aversiveness between two adjacent shock intensities.

For each intensity of a shock source, the corresponding *just aversive difference (JAD)* is the *change* in intensity that is just barely discriminable in terms of aversiveness. For example, consider a 0.40-mA intensity for the constant current 500-V FVAC source used with a grid floor to shock rats. What is the smallest *change* in current that is just barely discriminable in terms of aversiveness? In the spatial preference situation, rats were given forced choices between 0.40 mA and various neighboring current levels (B. A. Campbell & Masterson, 1969). When 0.40 mA and the neighboring current level are far apart, the discrimination of their aversiveness will be easy, and strong, or 100%–0%, preferences will occur for the lower intensity. When the currents are so close together that their average difference in aversiveness is completely masked by momentary variations (for example, due to changing grid positions), the preference will be equally divided, or 50%–50%. The just aversive difference is the separation of currents that produces an *intermediate* 75%–25% preference for the lower current. In this particular case, the separation turns out to be 0.06 mA. In other words, the rats showed a 75%–25% preference for 0.34 mA versus 0.40 mA, and also for 0.40 mA versus 0.46 mA. Therefore, for a 0.40 mA intensity, the corresponding JAD is 0.06 mA.

In practice, the 75%–25% points were determined by interpolation. The method is similar to that used to determine aversion thresholds (Section X-C). A graphical plot of preference for 0.40 mA as a function of the neighboring current level has an s-shaped curvature. However, normal deviate transformations of the percentage preferences were very nearly a linear function of the neighboring current levels. The current levels that would produce 25% and 75% preferences for 0.40 mA were interpolated from a least-squares fitted straight-line function. The JAD is computed by subtracting these interpolated current values and then dividing their differences by 2.

This procedure was repeated for several current levels of the 500-V ac source. The result was a graph with current intensity plotted on the horizontal axis and corresponding JADs plotted on the vertical axis (B. A. Campbell & Masterson, 1969, p. 31).

As mentioned earlier, the JAD provides an index of the momentary variations in aversiveness that can prevent subjects from discriminating differences in average aversiveness. The greater the JAD, the lower the discriminability and, by inference, the larger the variability.

To compare JADs (and hence variability of aversiveness) across different shock sources, it is necessary to convert their values to a common scale of aversiveness. Campbell and Masterson selected current intensity of the 500-V FVAC source as a standard scale and converted all their other sources to equally aversive current levels by means of the equal aversion functions in Section VIII-B. The JADs were transformed by finding the 500-V source current levels that are equally aversive to the interpolated 25% and 75% levels mentioned two paragraphs back. The differences between the resulting current levels was then divided by 2.

Campbell and Masterson (p. 32) summarized the transformed results in a graph with source intensity plotted in equivalent 500-V source current units along the horizontal axis, and JADs plotted in the same units on the vertical axis. JAD functions for the 150-kΩ, 600-kΩ, and 500-V ac sources overlap on this graph, indicating that they are equally variable. The plots for the 0-kΩ (constant voltage) and 35-kΩ FIAC sources and for a 500-V electronically regulated constant current dc source are above the others, indicating *greater* variability.

In addition to providing an empirical solution to the problem of discovering least variable (in aversiveness) shock sources, JAD functions provide one way of assessing subjective differences in aversiveness. Such an assessment helps the researcher select a reasonable spacing of several intensities in experiments where shock level is a parameter. This application was discussed in Section IX-G.

References

Ali, J. S., & Reiter, L. A self-contained, regulated, burst-firing constant-current ac shock generator. *Behavior Research Methods and Instrumentation,* 1977, **9,** 326–333.

Azrin, N. H. Some effects of two intermittent schedules of immediate and non-immediate punishment. *Journal of Psychology,* 1956, **42,** 3–21.

Azrin, N. H. A technique for delivering shock to pigeons. *Journal of the Experimental Analysis of Behavior,* 1959, **2,** 161–163.

Azrin, N. H., Hopwood, J., & Powell, J. A rat chamber and electrode procedure for avoidance conditioning. *Journal of the Experimental Analysis of Behavior,* 1967, **10,** 291–298.

Barfield, R. J., & Sachs, B. J. Sexual behavior: Stimulation by painful electrical shock to skin in male rats. *Science,* 1968, **161,** 392–395.

Békésy, G. V. A new audiometer. *Acta Oto-Laryngologica,* 1947, **35,** 411–422.

Bijou, S. W. The development of a conditioning methodology for studying experimental neurosis in the rat. *Journal of Comparative and Physiological Psychology,* 1942, **44,** 91–106.

Bitterman, M. E. Animal learning. In J. B. Sidowski (Ed.), *Experimental methods and instrumentation in psychology.* New York: McGraw-Hill, 1966.

Boldovici, J. A., & Cicala, G. A. Increased aversion thresholds in rats as a function of aspirin and meprobamate administration. *Psychological Record,* 1968, **18,** 389–394.

Bolles, R. C. Shock density and effective shock intensity: A comparison of different shock scramblers. *Journal of the Experimental Analysis of Behavior,* 1966, **9,** 553–556.

Bolles, R. C. Species-specific defense reactions and avoidance learning. *Psychological Review,* 1970, **71,** 32–48.

Bresler, D. E., & Bitterman, M. E. A shocking grid for pigeons. *Behavior Research Methods and Instrumentation,* 1974, **6,** 471–472.

Campbell, B. A. The fractional reduction in noxious stimulation required to produce "just noticeable" learning. *Journal of Comparative and Physiological Psychology,* 1955, **48,** 141–148.

Campbell, B. A. Auditory and aversion thresholds of rats for bands of noise. *Science,* 1957, **125,** 596–597.

Campbell, B. A., and Bloom, J. M. Relative Aversiveness of Noise and Shock, *Journal of Comparative and Physiological Psychology,* 1965, **60,** 440–442.

Campbell, B. A., & Masterson, F. A. Psychophysics of punishment. In B. A. Campbell & R. M. Church (Eds.), *Punishment and aversive behavior.* New York: Appleton, 1969.

Campbell, B. A., & Moorcroft, W. H. Relative aversiveness of subcutaneous shock and footshock in the rat. *Behavioral Research Methods and Instrumentation,* 1970, **2,** 222–224.

Campbell, B. A., & Teghtsoonian, R. Electrical and behavioral effects of different types of shock stimuli on the rat. *Journal of Comparative and Physiological Psychology,* 1958, **51,** 185–192.

Campbell, J. M., & Jerison, H. J. A modification of the Hoffman-Fleshler grid shock scrambler. *Journal of the Experimental Analysis of Behavior,* 1966, **9,** 689-690.

Church, R. M., LoLordo, V. M., Overmier, J. B., Solomon, R. L., & Turner, L. H. Cardiac responses to shock in curarized dogs: Effects of shock intensity and duration, warning signals and prior experience with shock. *Journal of Comparative and Physiological Psychology,* 1966, **62,** 1–7.

Coughlin, R. C., Jr. Inexpensive pubis electrodes for delivering shock to pigeons. *Journal of the Experimental Analysis of Behavior,* 1970, **13,** 368.

Davidon, R., & Boonin, N. A constant current stimulus-generator. *American Journal of Psychology,* 1956, **69,** 466–468.
de Toledo, L., & Black, A. H. A technique for recording heart rate in moving rats. *Journal of the Experimental Analysis of Behavior,* 1965, **8,** 181–182.
Dinsmoor, J. A. A new shock grid for rats. *Journal of the Experimental Analysis of Behavior,* 1958, **1,** 182.
Dunlap, K. Standardizing electric shocks for rats. *Journal of Comparative Psychology,* 1931, **12,** 133–135.
England, S. J. M. A constant power shock source and electronic grid scrambler with historical introduction. *Perceptual and Motor Skills,* 1964, **18,** 961–975.
Etscorn, F. A home tank aquatic shuttlebox. *Behavior Research Methods and Instrumentation,* 1974, **6,** 77.
Ferster, C. B., & Skinner, B. F. *Schedules of reinforcement.* New York: Appleton, 1957.
Findley, J. D., & Ames, L. L. A note on time out from avoidance with the chimpanzee. *Journal of the Experimental Analysis of Behavior,* 1965, **8,** 419–423.
Forbes, R. W., & Bernstein, A. L. The standardization of sixty cycle electrical shock for practical use in psychological experimentation. *Journal of General Psychology,* 1935, **12,** 436–442.
Gibson, R. H. Communication by electrical stimulation of the skin. *Space Research Coordination Center Report,* 1965, No. 21.
Granda, A., Matsumiya, Y., & Stirling, C. E. A method for producing avoidance behavior in the turtle. *Psychonomic Science,* 1965, **2,** 187–188.
Green, R. T. The absolute threshold of electric shock. *British Journal of Psychology,* 1962, **53,** 107–115.
Hake, D. F., & Azrin, N. H. An apparatus for delivering pain shock to monkeys. *Journal of the Experimental Analysis of Behavior,* 1963, **6,** 297–298.
Hall, R. D., Clayton, R. J., & Mark, R. G. A device for partial restraint of rats in operant conditioning studies. *Journal of the Experimental Analysis of Behavior,* 1966, **9,** 143–145.
Hill, H. E., Flanary, H. G., Karnetsky, C. H., & Wikler, A. Relationship of electrically induced pain to amperage and wattage of shock stimulus. *Journal of Clinical Investigation,* 1952, **31,** 464–472.
Hoffman, H. S. A flexible connector for delivering shock to pigeons. *Journal of the Experimental Analysis of Behavior,* 1960, **3,** 330.
Hoffman, H. S., & Fleshler, M. Aversive control with the pigeon. *Journal of the Experimental Analysis of Behavior,* 1959, **2,** 213–218.
Hoffman, H. S., & Fleshler, M. A relay sequencing device for scrambling grid shock. *Journal of the Experimental Analysis of Behavior,* 1962, **5,** 329–330.
Hoffman, H. S., & Ratner, A. M. A shock-delivering system for newly hatched precocial birds. *Journal of the Experimental Analysis of Behavior,* 1974, **22,** 575–576.
Horner, J. L., Longo, N., & Bitterman, M. E. A classical conditioning technique for small aquatic animals. *American Journal of Psychology,* 1960, **73,** 623–626.
Horner, J. L., Longo, N., & Bitterman, M. E. A shuttlebox for fish and a control circuit of general applicability. *American Journal of Psychology,* 1961, **74,** 114–120.
Houser, V. P., & Paré, W. P. A method for determining the aversion threshold in the rat using repeated measures: Tests with morphine sulfate. *Behavior Research Methods and Instrumentation,* 1972, **4,** 135–137.
Hurwitz, H. M. B., & Dillow, P. V. The effect of constant power shock on the acquisition of a discriminated avoidance response. *Psychonomic Science,* 1966, **5,** 111–112.
Kaplan, M., Jackson, B., & Sparer, R. Escape behavior under continuous reinforcement as a function of aversive light intensity. *Journal of the Experimental Analysis of Behavior,* 1965, **8,** 321–323.

Kelly, N. D., & Glusman, M. Aversive thresholds for subcutaneous electrical stimulation in the cat. *Psychonomic Science,* 1964, **1,** 207–208.

Kirby, R. H. Acquisition, extinction, and retention of an avoidance response in rats as a function of age. *Journal of Comparative and Physiological Psychology,* 1963, **56,** 158–162.

Lilly, J. C. The balanced pulse-pair waveform. In D. E. Sheer (Ed.), *Electrical stimulation of the brain.* Austin: University of Texas Press, 1961.

Lubow, R. E. An integrated response and reinforcement unit for classical and operant conditioning of large mammals. *Journal of the Experimental Analysis of Behavior,* 1964, **7,** 423–424.

Luce, R. D., & Edwards, W. The derivation of subjective scales from just noticeable differences. *Psychological Review,* 1958, **65,** 222–237.

Lydic, R., & Anson, J. A modified shock-delivery system for quail. *Journal of the Experimental Analysis of Behavior,* 1974, **22,** 441–443.

Markowitz, H., & Saslow, M. G. A reliable silent electronic shock scrambler. *Journal of the Experimental Analysis of Behavior,* 1964, **7,** 267–268.

Masterson, F. A. *Equal aversion functions as predictors of instrumental responding.* Doctoral dissertation, Princeton University, 1965.

Masterson, F. A. Escape from noise. *Psychological Reports,* 1969, **24,** 484–486.

Masterson, F. A. Is termination of a warning signal an effective reward for rats? *Journal of Comparative and Physiological Psychology,* 1970, **72,** 471–475.

Masterson, F. A. Suppression of the rat's locomotor activity at low intensities of electric footshock. *Behavioral Research Methods and Instrumentation,* 1981, in press.

Masterson, F. A., & Campbell, B. A. Techniques of electric shock motivation. In R. D. Myers (Ed.), *Methods in psychobiology* (Vol. 2). New York: Academic Press, 1972.

Masterson, F. A., Crawford, M., & Bartter, W. D. Brief escape from a dangerous place: The role of reinforcement in the rat's one-way avoidance acquisition. *Learning and Motivation,* 1978, **9,** 141–163.

Messing, R. B. Experiments in animal psychophysics. Doctoral dissertation, Princeton University, 1970.

Messing, R. B., & Campbell, B. A. Summation of pain produced in different anatomical regions. *Perception and Psychophysics,* 1971, **10,** 225–228.

Mickle, W. A. The problem of stimulation parameters. In D. E. Sheer (Ed.), *Electrical stimulation of the brain.* Austin: University of Texas Press, 1961.

Moss, F. A. Study of animal drives. *Journal of Experimental Psychology,* 1924, **7,** 165–185.

Muenzinger, K. F., & Walz, F. C. An examination of electrical-current-stabilizing devices for psychological experiments. *Journal of Genetic Psychology,* 1934, **10,** 477–482.

Overmier, J. B. Instrumental and cardiac indices of Pavlovian fear conditioning as a function of US duration. *Journal of Comparative and Physiological Psychology,* 1966, **62,** 15–20.

Overmier, J. B., & Seligman, M. E. P. Effects of inescapable shock upon subsequent escape and avoidance responding. *Journal of Comparative and Physiological Psychology,* 1967, **63,** 28–33.

Owen, J. E., & Kellermeier, A. P. A mercury switch grid scrambler for aversive conditioning. *Journal of the Experimental Analysis of Behavior,* 1966, **9,** 51–52.

Paré, W. P. Age, sex, and strain differences in the aversive threshold to grid shock in the rat. *Journal of Comparative and Physiological Psychology,* 1969, **69,** 214–218.

Parks, E. R., & Sterritt, G. M. Stimulator-operated grid scrambler for reliable delivery of shock to animals. *Journal of the Experimental Analysis of Behavior,* 1964, **7,** 261–262.

Plumer, S. I. *Effects of caudate stimulation on learning and performance*. Doctoral dissertation, University of Delaware, 1971.

Reus, J. F., Houser, V. P., & Paré, W. P. An electronic constant current shock generator for low current levels. *Physiology and Behavior*, 1971, **7**, 635–637.

Scobie, S. R., & Herman, B. H. Detection, reaction, escape and debilitation thresholds for electric shock in goldfish. *Learning and Motivation*, 1972, **3**, 442–456.

Skinner, B. F., & Campbell, S. L. An automatic shocking-grid apparatus for continuous use. *Journal of Comparative and Physiological Psychology*, 1947, **40**, 305–307.

Snapper, A. G. A relay-transistor sequential grid scrambler. *Journal of the Experimental Analysis of Behavior*, 1966, **9**, 173–175.

Solomon, R. L., & Wynne, L. C. Traumatic avoidance learning: Acquisition in normal dogs. *Psychological Monographs*, 1953, **67** (4, Whole No. 354).

Stewart, R. A., & Campbell, S. L. A constant current shock source for providing direct or alternating current output. *Behavior Research Methods and Instrumentation*, 1970, **2**, 224–226.

Torgerson, W. S. *Theory and methods of scaling*. New York: Wiley, 1958.

Trapold, M. A., & Fowler, H. Instrumental escape performance as a function of the intensity of noxious stimulation. *Journal of Experimental Psychology*, 1960, **60**, 323–326.

Walker, J. J., & Bitterman, M. E. An improved shocking surface for pigeons and rats. *Behavior Research Methods and Instrumentation*, 1968, **1**, 76–78.

Weiss, B., & Laties, V. G. Fractional escape and avoidance on a titration schedule. *Science*, 1958, **128**, 1575–1576.

Weiss, B., & Laties, V. G. Titration behavior on various fractional escape programs. *Journal of the Experimental Analysis of Behavior*, 1959, **2**, 227–248.

Weiss, B., & Laties, V. G. A foot electrode for monkeys. *Journal of the Experimental Analysis of Behavior*, 1962, **5**, 535–536.

Weiss, B., & Laties, V. G. Characteristics of aversive thresholds measured by a titration schedule. *Journal of the Experimental Analysis of Behavior*, 1963, **6**, 563–572.

Weiss, J. A tail electrode for unrestrained rats. *Journal of the Experimental Analysis of Behavior*, 1967, **10**, 85–86.

Wycoff, L. B., & Page, H. A. A grid for administering shock. *American Journal of Psychology*, 1954, **67**, 154.

Index

T